The Princeton Review.

W9-BZC-405

Cracking the
AP®
WORLD
HISTORY EXAM

2014 Edition

The Staff of The Princeton Review

PrincetonReview.com

Random House, Inc. New York

The Princeton Review
111 Speen Street, Suite 550
Framingham, MA 01701
E-mail: editorialsupport@review.com

ISBN 978-0-307-94626-3
ISSN: 1546-9077
eBook ISBN: 978-0-307-94627-0

Editor: Selena Coppock
Production Editor: Dustin Helmer
Production Coordinator: Keren Peysakh

Printed in the United States of America on partially recycled paper.

10   9   8   7   6   5   4   3   2   1

2014 Edition

Editorial

Robert Franek, Senior VP, Publisher
Mary Beth Garrick, Director of Production
Selena Coppock, Senior Editor
Calvin Cato, Editor
Kristen O'Toole, Editor
Meave Shelton, Editor
Alyssa Wolff, Editorial Assistant

Random House Publishing Team

Tom Russell, Publisher
Nicole Benhabib, Publishing Director
Ellen L. Reed, Production Manager
Alison Stoltzfus, Managing Editor

Acknowledgments

First to my wife, Sharon, for all her support. To Jerry Bentley and Howard Spodek, whose texts provided an initial framework. To Ellen Mendlow and Alex Freer, who helped a first-time author chart the rough waters. And last, to all my students, who keep me coming back to the classroom. —M.A.

I would like to thank my husband, Paul, and son, Jordan, for being patient and understanding and enduring innumerable pizza dinners while I worked on this book. I'd also like to thank Monty Armstrong, David Daniel, and the editors for all of their help and encouragement. Because this book covers an extremely broad discipline, they each gave me positive feedback and improved the portions of this book that I authored. —A.K

Special thanks to Daniel Poochigian for his work on this edition.

Contents

Part I
Using This
Book to Improve
Your AP Score

PREVIEW: YOUR KNOWLEDGE, YOUR EXPECTATIONS

Your route to a high score on the AP World History Exam depends a lot how you plan to use this book. Start thinking about your plan by responding to the following questions.

1. Rate your level of confidence about your knowledge of the content tested by the AP World History Exam:

    A. Very confident—I know it all
    B. I'm pretty confident, but there are topics for which I could use help
    C. Not confident—I need quite a bit of support
    D. I'm not sure

2. If you have a goal score in mind, circle your goal score for the AP World History Exam:

    5   4   3   2   1   I'm not sure yet

3. What do you expect to learn from this book? Circle all that apply to you.

    A. A general overview of the test and what to expect
    B. Strategies for how to approach the test
    C. The content tested by this exam
    D. I'm not sure yet

YOUR GUIDE TO USING THIS BOOK

This book is organized to provide as much—or as little—support as you need, so you can use this book in whatever way will be most helpful to improving your score on the AP World History Exam.

- The remainder of **Part One** will provide guidance on how to use this book and help you determine your strengths and weaknesses

- **Part Two** of this book will:
  - provide information about the structure, scoring, and content of the AP World History Exam
  - help you to make a study plan
  - point you towards additional resources

- **Part Three** of this book will explore various strategies:
  - how to attack multiple-choice questions
  - how to write effective essays
  - how to manage your time to maximize the number of points available to you

- **Part Four** of this book covers the content you need for the AP World History Exam.

- **Part Five** of this book contains practice tests.

You may choose the use some parts of this book over others, or you may work through the entire book. This will depend on your needs and how much time you have. Now let's look at how to make this determination.

HOW TO BEGIN

1. **Take a Test**

   Before you can decide how to use this book, you need to take a practice test. Doing so will give you insight into your strengths and weaknesses, and the test will also help you make an effective study plan. If you're feeling test-phobic, remind yourself that a practice test is a tool for diagnosing yourself—it's not how well you do that matters but how you use information gleaned from your performance to guide your preparation.

   So, before you read further, take Practice Test 1 starting at page 361 of this book. Be sure to do so in one sitting, following the instructions that appear before the test.

2. **Check Your Answers**

   Using the answer key on page 387, count how many multiple-choice questions you got right and how many you missed. Don't worry about the explanations for now, and don't worry about why you missed questions. We'll get to that soon.

3. **Reflect on the Test**

   After you take your first test, respond to the following questions:

   - How much time did you spend on the multiple-choice questions?

   - How much time did you spend on each essay?

   - How many multiple-choice questions did you miss?

   - Do you feel you had the knowledge to address the subject matter of the essays?

   - Do you feel you wrote well organized, thoughtful essays?

   - Circle the content areas that were most challenging for you and draw a line through the ones in which you felt confident or did well.

4. **Read Part Two of this Book and Complete the Self-Evaluation**

   As discussed in the Goals section above, Part Two will provide information on how the test is structured and scored. It will also set out areas of content that are tested.

As you read Part Two, re-evaluate your answers to the questions above. At the end of Part Two, you will revisit and refine the questions you answer above. You will then be able to make a study plan, based on your needs and time available, that will allow you to use this book most effectively.

5. **Engage with Parts Three and Four as Needed**

Notice the word *engage*. You'll get more out of this book if you use it intentionally than if you read it passively, hoping for an improved score through osmosis.

Strategy chapters will help you think about your approach to the question types on this exam. Part Three will open with a reminder to think about how you approach questions now and then close with a reflection section asking you to think about how or whether you will change your approach in the future.

Content chapters are designed to provide a review of the content tested on the AP World History Exam, including the level of detail you need to know and how the content is tested. You will have the opportunity to assess your mastery of the content of each chapter through test-appropriate questions and a reflection section.

6. **Take Test 2 and Assess Your Performance**

Once you feel you have developed the strategies you need and gained the knowledge you lacked, you should take Test 2, which starts at page 407 of this book. You should do so in one sitting, following the instructions at the beginning of the test.

When you are done, check your answers to the multiple-choice sections. See if a teacher will read your essays and provide feedback.

Once you have taken the test, reflect on the areas where you still need to work, and revisit the chapters in this book that address those deficiencies. Through this type of reflection and engagement, you will continue to improve.

7. **Keep Working**

As discussed in Part Two, coming up next, there are other resources available to you, including a wealth of information on AP Central. You can continue to explore areas that can stand to improve and engage in those areas right up to the day of the test.

Part II
About the
AP World
History Exam

THE STRUCTURE OF THE WORLD HISTORY EXAM

The AP World History Exam is divided into two sections: multiple choice and free-response essays. Section I of the test is comprised of 70 multiple-choice questions to be answered in 55 minutes. Section II of the test begins with a ten-minute reading period (time to review the documents you must use for the first essay question), followed by a two-hour period to write three essays.

HOW THE WORLD HISTORY EXAM IS SCORED

Once the multiple-choice section of your test has been scanned and your essays scored by readers, ETS (your local testing giant) applies a mysterious formula that converts your raw score numbers to a 120-point scale. Somehow they turn 70 possible multiple-choice points into 60 points, and 27 possible essay points into another 60 points.

But that's not all the magic they do. They then take your score (up to 120 points) and convert it to the standard AP 1 to 5 score that you see when you rip open the test results that come in the mail. Seems like a little bit of a letdown to do all this work for a 4, doesn't it? However, a 4 or a 5 is the score that will most likely get you what you want from the college or university you'll attend—college credit for World History. A 3 is considered passing and might get you college credit; then again, it might not. Therefore, your goal is to get at least a 3, preferably a 4 or 5. If you receive below a 3, it is highly unlikely that you will get college credit for your high school AP course, but you still get a grade for that class. A good grade in an AP class always looks good on your transcript.

The tricky part about the 1 to 5 scoring system is that it is designed to compare you to everyone else who took the AP World History Exam during a given year. But if the test that year was particularly tough, the top 25 percent or so of scorers will still score 4's and 5's. In other words, if all the scaled (0–120) scores are somewhat low, the top end will still earn high marks. Of course, the opposite is also true—if everyone does an excellent job, some people will end up with 2's and 1's.

What Do The Scores Mean?

Qualification	Score	% of Testers
Extremely well qualified	5	6.9%
Well qualified	4	15.7%
Qualified	3	30.5%
Possibly qualified	2	29.4%
No recommendation	1	17.4%

Student score distributions from the May 2012 College Board AP World History Exam.

OVERVIEW OF CONTENT TOPICS

The AP World History Exam divides all history into six major periods from about 10,000 years ago to the present. On the multiple-choice section of the test, the distribution of questions is as follows:

Period	Date Range	Percent of Questions
Period 1: Technological and Environmental Transformations	c. 8000 b.c.e. to c. 600 b.c.e.	5%
Period 2: Organization and Reorganization of Human Societies	c. 600 b.c.e. to c. 600 c.e.	15%
Period 3: Regional and Transregional Interactions	c. 600 c.e. to c. 1450	20%
Period 4: Global Interactions	c. 1450 to c. 1750	20%
Period 5: Industrialization and Global Integration	c. 1750 to c. 1900	20%
Period 6: Accelerating Global Change and Realignments	c. 1900 to the present	20%

Now, you may be wondering why the first period spans thousands of years while the last period spans a little more than 100 years. When more and more societies came into being and got more complex, world history also got more complex. Also, we have more historical accounts and documents to study from recent history than we do from ancient history, so we simply know more about what happened in the last 100 years. Even though there are 8000 years in the first period, 800 in the third period, and just over 100 in the last period, you can study each period for the same amount of time. The review of history included in this book divides world history into the periods covered on the exam in order to help guide your study.

By the Way
While the multiple-choice section of the test asks questions from each of the above periods, these questions do not appear in any particular order. In other words, when you take the multiple-choice part of the exam, you'll jump from the Roman Empire to the present back to the Middle Ages back to the present and so on. Some students find it a challenge to shift gears rapidly from hunter-gatherers to NAFTA to Galileo, so be sure to do a few trial runs on the practice tests in Part III of this book.

Free-Response Questions (a.k.a. the Essays)

In the free-response section of the exam, you are asked to write three essays, each in response to a question. The questions are:

The document-based question or DBQ: As the name implies, the DBQ is based on a collection of four to ten documents that you must use in order to answer the question. Luckily, you will have 10 minutes at the start of the essay portion of the test to read the given documents prior to writing your essay. That may not sound like a lot right now, but don't worry. Our chapter on the DBQ will tell you exactly what to do with those 10 minutes.

The continuity and change-over-time essay: Again, as the name implies, you need to answer a question about how something changed over a certain period of time and how it remained the same. These questions tend to deal with large global issues such as technology, trade, culture, migrations, or biological developments. Our chapter on change over time and comparative essays will help you get organized for this essay.

The comparative essay: The comparative essay typically asks you to compare how two societies responded to a major theme or event. Our chapter on change over time and comparative essays will help you get organized for this essay.

WHAT DO THEY WANT FROM ME?

What is the AP World History Exam really testing? In a nutshell: Can you make connections between different societies over different periods of time? In other words, for any given period of history, can you explain who was doing what? How did what they were doing affect the rest of the world? What changed about the society during this period of time? To show what you know about world history, keep this big-picture perspective in mind as you study and answer multiple-choice questions or construct essays. To help you do this, keep an eye out for certain recurring themes throughout the different time periods. Specifically, be on the lookout for the following:

- How did people interact with their environment? Why did they live where they did? How did they get there? What tools, technology, and resources were available to them? How was the landscape changed by humans?

- What new ideas, thoughts, and styles came into existence? How did these cultural developments influence people and technology (for example: new religious beliefs or Renaissance thought)?

- How did different societies get along—or not get along—within a time period? Who took over whom? How did leaders justify their power? Who revolted or was likely to revolt? And were they successful?

- How did economic systems develop and what did they depend on in terms of agriculture, trade, labor, industrialization, and the demands of consumers?

- Who had power and who did not within a given culture and why? What was the status of women? What racial and ethnic constructions were present?

For each time period covered in Part II of this book, you will find boxes that identify these major themes, plus a Big Picture overview and a Pulling It All Together summary for each period. The introduction to Part II will fill you in on how to use these tools as you study.

HOW AP EXAMS ARE USED

Different colleges use AP Exams in different ways, so it is important that you go to a particular college's web site to determine how it uses AP Exams. The three items below represent the main ways in which AP Exam scores can be used:

- **College Credit.** Some colleges will give you college credit if you score well on an AP Exam. These credits count towards your graduation requirements, meaning that you can take fewer courses while in college. Given the cost of college, this could be quite a benefit, indeed.

- **Satisfy Requirements.** Some colleges will allow you to "place out" of certain requirements if you do well on an AP Exam, even if they do not give you actual college credits. For example, you might not need to take an introductory-level course, or perhaps you might not need to take a class in a certain discipline at all.

- **Admissions Plus.** Even if your AP Exam will not result in college credit or even allow you to place out of certain courses, most colleges will respect your decision to push yourself by taking an AP Course or even an AP Exam outside of a course. A high score on an AP Exam shows mastery of more difficult content than is taught in many high school courses, and colleges may take that into account during the admissions process.

OTHER RESOURCES

There are many resources available to help you improve your score on the AP World History Exam, not the least of which are your teachers. If you are taking an AP class, you may be able to get extra attention from your teacher, such as obtaining feedback on your essays. If you are not in an AP course, reach out to a teacher who teaches American History, and ask if the teacher will review your essays or otherwise help you with content.

Another wonderful resource is AP Central, the official site of the AP Exams. The scope of the information at this site is quite broad and includes:

- Course Description, which includes details on what content is covered and sample questions
- Full-length practice test
- Essay prompts from previous years
- AP World History Exam Tips

The AP Central home page address is: http://apcentral.collegeboard.com/apc

The AP World History Exam Course home page address is: http://apcentral.collegeboard.com/apc/public/courses/teachers_corner/4484.html

Finally, The Princeton Review offers tutoring for the World History Exam. Our expert instructors can help you refine your strategic approach and add to your content knowledge. For more information, call 1-800-2REVIEW.

DESIGNING YOUR STUDY PLAN

As part of the Introduction, you identified some areas of potential improvement. Let's now delve further into your performance on Test 1, with the goal of developing a study plan appropriate to your needs and time commitment.

Read the answers and explanations associated with the multiple-choice questions (starting at page 387). After you have done so, respond to the following questions:

- Review the Overview of Content Topics at page 10–11 above and, next to each one, indicate your rank of the topic as follows: "1" means "I need a lot of work on this," "2" means "I need to beef up my knowledge," and "3" means "I know this topic well."

- How many days/weeks/months away is your AP World History Exam?

- What time of day is your best, most focused study time?

- How much time per day/week/month will you devote to preparing for your AP World History Exam?

- When will you do this preparation? (Be as specific as possible: Mondays & Wednesdays from 3 to 4 pm, for example)

- Based on the answers above, will you focus on strategy (Part Two) or content (Part Three) or both?

- What are your overall goals in using this book?

Part III
Test-Taking Strategies for the AP World History Exam

PREVIEW ACTIVITY

Review your responses to the first three questions on page 4 of the Preview section in Part I and then respond to the following questions:

- How many multiple-choice questions did you miss even though you knew the answer?

- On how many multiple-choice questions did you guess blindly?

- How many multiple-choice questions did you miss after eliminating some answers and guessing based on the remaining answers?

- Did you create an outline before you wrote each essay?

- Did you find any of the essays easier or harder than the others—and, if so, why?

HOW TO USE THE CHAPTERS IN THIS PART

For the following Strategy chapters, think about what you are doing now before you read the chapters. As you read and engage in the directed practice, be sure to appreciate the ways you can change your approach. At the end of Part Three, you will have the opportunity to reflect on how you will change your approach.

Chapter 1
How to Approach Multiple-Choice Questions

WELL, WHAT DO YOU KNOW?

As we mentioned in the introduction, to do well on the multiple-choice section of the AP World History Exam, you need to know two things: (1) world history (à la Advanced Placement), and (2) how to show that you know world history. One way to prove that you know world history is by correctly answering the number of multiple-choice questions necessary to score 3 or above.

Obvious, right? Then why is it that lots of students who know world history don't get a great score on the test? Could it be because there are 70 questions to answer in 55 minutes? Or is it because they know the history but don't know how to wade through the answer choices efficiently?

Students often don't perform to the best of their ability on the AP World History Exam because in addition to knowing the history, they need to know how to analyze the questions, get rid of the bad answer choices, and find the correct answer in a short period of time. That's what this chapter is all about.

Guessing on the AP Exams

As of May 2011, the AP exams no longer subtract one quarter of a point for incorrect answers—the infamous "guessing penalty." Instead, students are assessed only on the total number of correct questions. It is really important to remember that if you are running out of time, you need to fill in all the bubbles before the time for the multiple-choice section is up. Even if you don't plan to spend a lot of time on every question and even if you have no idea what the correct answer is, you need to fill something in. We don't recommend random guessing as an overall strategy, but taking smart guesses at the right time can substantially increase your raw score on the multiple-choice section of the test. Let's see when guessing can help you.

There are four answer choices for each multiple-choice question. If you were able to eliminate just one wrong answer for each question on the entire multiple-choice section, random odds say you would get one-fourth of the questions correct. That's about 17 questions. Even if you get rid of just one wrong answer from each question throughout the test, you begin to gain points. When you get to questions in which you can't eliminate any options, use what we call your letter of the day (LOTD). Selecting the same answer choice each time you guess will increase your odds of getting a few of those skipped questions right.

And Furthermore

Guessing also raises your score because it saves you time. Seventy questions in 55 minutes is a lot. In fact, it's about 45 seconds per question. How can you possibly answer that many questions in that short a period of time? Two ways: Guess and Go, or Don't.

Guess and Go

Consider the following thought processes of two AP World History test takers on this question:

1. Signed in 1215 c.e., England's Magna Carta was a document that

    (A) increased the wealth of the European nobility
    (B) established England as a monarchy under King Richard
    (C) guaranteed individual liberties to all men
    (D) contained articles that were the foundation for modern justice

Student One	Student Two
The Magna Carta—*I know it was that charter in England in the 1200s that made the king accountable for his actions, so the answer can't be (A) so cross it off. Who was that king? Was it John? I think so. That gets rid of (B). Now, is it more accurate to say that the original document guaranteed individual liberties to all men or that some of the articles became foundations for modern justice. Individual liberties for all men...hmmm...foundations for modern justice. Both sound possible. Was it liberties for all men? I thought so but maybe not or not all men or not at the time. Did the Magna Carta influence modern justice? I think so but in what way exactly? Could it be described as foundational to modern justice? Hmmm....*	*The* Magna Carta—*that charter in England in the 1200s that made the king accountable for his actions. Cross off (A). The king was...John...yeah, King John. That gets rid of (B). (C)...hmmm...did the Magna Carta guarantee individual liberties to all men? Maybe, not sure so leave it. (D)...did it contain articles that became foundations of modern justice? Could have. Guaranteed for all men or foundations of modern justice? I'm not sure, but I think (C) is too strong—guaranteed for all men. I'll guess (D).* *Next question. The printing press was invented by Gutenberg sometime near the Reformation. Cross off (A) and (C)...*

In the above scenario, Student One continues to deliberate between (C) and (D) while Student Two goes on to the next question. What's the difference? Student Two did all the work she could, considered the remaining options, then took a smart guess and moved on. Student One did all the work he could, then got stuck trying to make a decision between the two remaining options. As the test progresses, Student One will lag further and further behind Student Two, not because he knows less world history, but because he is less willing to take that guess and move on. To do well on the AP World History Exam, you need to do what you can but then be willing to take your best guess and move on to the next question.

Three Out of Every Four Choices Are Bad

Imagine that you are an AP World History Exam writer (you never know, it could happen). As you begin, you first formulate the question portion of the question (or the stem), then craft your correct answer. But your work does not stop there.

Once you are satisfied with the correct answer, you need to create three wrong answer choices. How would you come up with respectable wrong answer choices quickly? Probably by looking at closely related facts or words that remind you of the question, or by thinking of almost-true and partially true answers. In other words, you create distractor answers that appear to be likely options. Distractors are meant to trip up a test taker who doesn't know the history, doesn't know how to wade through multiple-choice answers, or is rushing to finish.

For example, let's say you have crafted a question about a similarity between Christianity and Islam.

2.   The spread of Islam and the spread of Christianity were similar in that members of both religions

(A)

(B)

(C)

(D)   actively strived to convert members of other belief systems

Now that you have your question and your correct answer, what wrong answers could be inserted that might attract a tester who is unsure of the correct response? You could insert something that is true about one religion but not necessarily of the other. For example, look at choices (A) and (B).

2. The spread of Islam and the spread of Christianity were similar in that members of both religions

(A) were required to make a journey to the Holy Land once in the course of their lifetimes

(B) believed that their main prophet (Jesus for Christians, Mohammad for Muslims) was the one true son of God

(C)

(D) actively strived to convert members of other belief systems

(A) is true of Islam but not Christianity, and (B) is true of Christianity but not Islam. What else could you fill in? Something that is true of both religions but does not answer the question. To do this, you must make sure that part of the answer choice (often the second half) makes that choice clearly wrong. For example, look at answer choice (C).

2. The spread of Islam and the spread of Christianity were similar in that members of both religions

(A) were required to make a journey to the Holy Land once in the course of their lifetimes

(B) believe that their main prophet (Jesus for Christians, Mohammad for Muslims) was the one true son of God

(C) ascribed to a monotheistic view in which the only way to salvation is through the rejection of all other beliefs, both sacred and secular

(D) actively strived to convert members of other belief systems

Notice how (C) begins with something that is true of both religions, but then incorrectly describes rejecting beliefs that are both sacred and secular. It also does not have to do with the spread of the religions. A tester who reads this question in a hurry might see:

Islam and…Christianity were similar…(C), ascribe to a monotheistic view. That's it.

You get the idea. Why are we making you create AP World History questions? So that you can avoid the mistakes you are expected to make on the exam. How often have you read the answer choices to a question, assuming each is a plausible answer but only one of them is right? When you do that, you spend a whole lot of time considering the options. For example:

> *(A), Were required to make a journey to the Holy Land once in the course of their lifetimes. Well, I know that Muslims have to. Did early Christians have to? I don't think so, but maybe. I guess it's possible. What about (B)? Major prophet…Jesus or Mohammad, son of God. Well, Jesus, yes. Mohammad was the main prophet…do Muslims consider him the son of God? I don't know for sure. I don't think so, but I guess it is possible too. Well, how about (C)? Ascribe to a monotheistic view…yes…salvation through the rejection of other beliefs? Hmmm…both sacred and secular. Hmmm…well, the first part is true. I'm not so sure about that second part, but maybe it was true. I don't know what the rule was about secular beliefs. Then again, the question is about the spread of religion, so it really doesn't answer the question. What about (D)? Actively strive to convert members. Well, yes, I think both of these religions did that. That's a possibility.*

Processing each answer choice as if it is a good possibility leads to considering far too many things that a critical eye would see as wrong right away. Instead, work through this question assuming each answer is wrong until proven right.

> *(A), Were required to make a journey to the Holy Land…Muslims yes, but I don't think Christians. Cross it off. (B), Jesus or Mohammad, one true son of God. True for Jesus, I don't think so for Mohammad. Cross it off. (C), Monotheistic, yes, reject other beliefs, not sure, skip it and come back. (D), Actively strive to convert members of other belief systems. Definitely.*

Notice how you can process answers much more quickly and efficiently when you are reading them with a critical eye? Different approaches may very well get you to the correct answer, but it will take a whole lot longer. You could also get caught up in a wrong answer, spending too much time trying to figure out why it might be right instead of remembering that it is probably wrong. On the other hand, reading with a critical eye allows you to cross off answers more aggressively, so by the time you get to (D), you feel pretty sure that it is the answer. And what if we had crossed off all the answer choices? No problem. Just start over and read a little more carefully. It is better to be a little too aggressive than to consider every answer choice a viable option.

Process of Elimination

Every time you read an AP World History Exam question, remember that three out of four answer choices you are reading are wrong. Use the Process of Elimination (POE) to get rid of what you know is wrong as you go through the choices. Then deal with any answer choices you have left. For most questions, you will be able to eliminate one to two answer choices relatively quickly. That leaves you with one to two answer choices to consider and take a better-than-blind guess among. We will talk more about POE throughout the rest of this chapter. Just remember to read answer choices as "wrong until proven right" and you'll be on your way to showing what you know on the multiple-choice part of this test.

If you can't eliminate any answers, it's best to skip the question altogether. Mark these skipped questions in some distinctive way so that you can come back to them later if you have time, and make sure you leave a space on your answer sheet. Always keep in mind that the multiple-choice section is difficult, if not impossible, for most students to finish—a score of 50 is good! Focus on accuracy as you work through this section.

HOW TO CRACK AP WORLD HISTORY MULTIPLE-CHOICE QUESTIONS

To do well on the multiple-choice section of the exam, you need to solve each question step by step. The best way to learn this process is to take a look at a sample AP World History Exam question.

3.   When the Europeans arrived in sub-Saharan Africa in the 1400s and 1500s, the African slave trade was

(A) just beginning
(B) well established and about 500 years old
(C) still under the control of Muslim traders
(D) not economically viable and did not interest the Europeans

Step 1: Read the Question and Put It in Your Own Words

First you must make sure that you understand what the question is asking. Read the sample question again. What is it really asking? If you are having trouble figuring it out, answer the questions *When?*, *Who?*, *What?* For example, in the above question about slave trade, you can answer in the following way:

> When? *1400–1599*
>
> Who? *Europeans and sub-Saharan Africa*
>
> What? *Slave trade*

Then, rephrase the question so that it is clear to you.

What was up with the African slave trade in the 1400–1500 period?

Step 2: Answer in Your Own Words

Once you've rewritten the question, take a moment to call up the relevant history that you know. If it is a topic you know well, it will be easy to come up with an answer. If you can't come up with a full answer, think of a few key points that you do know about the topic. Here's an example of what you might know about the slave trade from 1400–1500.

It already existed in both Africa and Europe, so it wasn't new.

If you can't answer the question completely, you can still use what you do know to get rid of wrong answer choices using the Process of Elimination.

Step 3: Process of Elimination

Even if you do not know exactly what was going on with the slave trade in the 1400s and 1500s, you can use the little you do know to eliminate wrong answer choices. Remember to read each answer choice with a critical eye, looking for what makes it wrong. Cross off the choices that you know are wrong; leave ones that you are uncertain about or you think are right.

Let's review what we know so far about the question. When? *1400–1599*. Who? *Europeans in Africa*. What? *Slave trade*. What do you know about slave trade in 1400–1599? It was not new. Armed with this information, take a look again at the answer choices.

(A) just beginning
(B) well established and about 500 years old
(C) still under the control of Muslim traders
(D) not economically viable and did not interest the Europeans

Take a look at answer choice (A). Was it just beginning? No. Cross off (A)—this cannot be the answer to the question. You may not be sure about (B) or (C), but what about (D)? Was slavery economically viable or interesting to Europeans? It must have been or it would not have become so extensive. Your common sense tells you that (D) cannot be the answer, so cross it off and move along. If you have no idea between (B) and (C), at least it's now a 50-50 shot, so what should you do? Guess and move on.

Step 4: Guess and Go

After using POE, you have a fifty-fifty shot of guessing the right answer on our sample question. Let's look at answer choice (C). The Europeans arrived on the west coast of sub-Saharan Africa while the Muslims were on the east coast. Remember the Indian Ocean trade and the Swahili culture? If that is the case, then (C) cannot be the answer. The answer must be (B): well established and about 500 years old.

Can you see how taking a moment to frame the question can help you find the right answer quickly and easily? Knowing just some of the information can be enough to get you to a smart guess. This does not mean that you should not learn as much of the history as possible. The more you know, the easier it will be to eliminate wrong answer choices and zero in on the correct answer. However, using the steps and POE will help you get to the right answer quickly by making the most of the information you know.

Step by Step by Step by Step

Let's walk through the Four Steps to solving an AP World History multiple-choice question again.

4. Matrilinearity was found in which of the following societies?

    (A) Rome
    (B) Sumer
    (C) Bantu
    (D) Byzantium

Step 1: Read the Question and Put It in Your Own Words

What does matrilinearity mean? Matri is like matriarch—has to do with females or females as leaders. Linear means in a line like lineage.

When? *Looks like early times*

Who? *Female rulers*

What? *Early rulers who were woman*

So in which society did the rulers come from the female line?

Step 2: Answer in Your Own Words

Not sure. Definitely not Rome, probably not Byzantium either. They had major male-dominance going on.

Step 3: Process of Elimination

I know that (A) and (D) are out, so I'll cross them off. (B) and (C) remain.

Step 4: Guess and Go

I don't know about any of these three societies, so I'll guess (C).

As it happens, you're right—the answer is (C): Bantu. Even if you didn't pick (C), if you eliminated as many as you could and then wasted no further time fretting over the unknowns before you picked one and moved on, then you did the right thing. Good job!

Your Turn

Now it's your turn. Use the Four Steps to solve the following multiple-choice question.

5. Which of the following is an example of Chinese influence in Japan during the sixth, seventh, and eighth centuries?

   (A) The expansion of European culture to the island of Japan

   (B) The adoption by Japan of the Chinese civil service exam for government employees

   (C) The Taika Reforms enacted after the death of Prince Shotoku

   (D) The conversion of most Japanese Shinto to Buddhism

Step 1: Read the Question and Put It in Your Own Words

Step 2: Answer in Your Own Words

Step 3: POE

Step 4: Guess and Go

Here's How to Crack It

First, note that the question is asking for an example of China's influence on Japan during the sixth, seventh, and eighth centuries (there is your When? and Who?). What do you know about Japan during this time period? China had just started to influence Japan. Lots of reforms took place, but Japan didn't adopt everything Chinese—for example, Confucianism. Knowing that, let's use POE.

(A) is about European culture. Had European culture touched Japan at this time? No, it had barely touched China let alone Japan, so cross off (A). (B) is out if you remember that Japan did not embrace Confucianism, and that Confucianism was a big part of Chinese government and the Chinese civil service exam. You may not remember anything about the Taika Reforms, but you might recall that while the Japanese embraced Buddhism, they did not give up Shinto but rather practiced both simultaneously. That eliminates (D). Your answer must be (C).

So Far, So Good EXCEPT...

Not all questions are asked in a straightforward manner on the AP World History Exam. For example:

6. All of the following are results of bubonic plague, which swept through China and Europe from the 1200s to the 1600s, EXCEPT

    (A) social unrest
    (B) tremendous population loss
    (C) a decrease in wages
    (D) less rigidity between social classes

Approach these questions using the same Four Steps. During Step 1, rephrase the question to make it clear what you have to do to find the right answer.

Step 1: Read the Question and Put It in Your Own Words

When? *1200–1699. Into the Age of Exploration, Renaissance, etc.*

Who? *China/Europe*

What? *Bubonic plague. Lots of people died, had an impact on everyone*

Four of the following things happened because of bubonic plague. Which one didn't?

Step 2: Answer in Your Own Words

I know a lot of people died and there were not enough people to work, and that everyone had to draw together to get things done, but I forget what else happened.

Step 3: POE

Remember that on EXCEPT or NOT questions, three of the answer choices are true while one is not true. Instead of trying to choose the answer, make a note next to each as to whether it is true or not. Then pick the "not."

(A) social unrest	not sure
(B) tremendous population loss	T
(C) a decrease in wages	not sure
(D) less rigidity between social classes	T

Step 4: Guess and Go

Because you are looking for the answer that is not true, cross out (B) and (D). Now consider (A) and (C). Could social unrest have been the result of thousands of people dying? Sounds plausible, so cross off (A). Consider that you can pick (C) confidently if you remember that the massive labor shortage actually raised the average wage for both farm laborers and skilled artisans.

By the way, the bubonic plague led to less rigidity between social classes because it decimated the population of all social classes, and therefore people needed to learn new skills (beyond their traditional classes) to make up for the loss of people in other social classes. This led to an overlap in social and economic classes.

When to Bail

Remember that you are on a fairly tight time schedule for this test. You need to make sure that you spend your time on questions that will pay off. If you read a question and have absolutely no idea what is being asked or know as soon as you read a question that you do not know the subject matter, mark it in some way, then move on. Better to skip a few along the way than to run out of time before you get to questions at the end that you know about. After you go through the section once, you can always return to any remaining questions.

Notice that Steps 1 and 2 can vary quite a bit based on the question. Also, the more you can frame the history in Step 2, the easier it will be to cross off wrong answer choices and zero in on the right answer. For example, instead of just saying that the What? in the last question was the bubonic plague, we took a minute to add what that meant at the time: lots of people died, had an impact on everyone. Taking a moment to think of this additional information helped get to the answer quickly and easily.

Practice Set 1

Step 1 and Step 2

Take a few moments to practice Steps 1 and 2. The better you are at interpreting questions and coming up with your own answers before you get to the answer choices, the easier it will be to POE and Guess and Go! Answers can be found on pages 40–43.

1. During the Cold War era, the United States and the Soviet Union were reluctant to become involved in direct military conflict mainly because of

Step 1: Read the Question and Put It in Your Own Words

Step 2: Answer in Your Own Words

2. In the sixteenth and seventeenth centuries, European mercantilism in Latin America led to

Step 1: Read the Question and Put It in Your Own Words

Step 2: Answer in Your Own Words

3. One way in which the Maya, the Songhai, and the Gupta cultures were similar is that they

Step 1: Read the Question and Put It in Your Own Words

Step 2: Answer in Your Own Words

4. The teachings of Confucius encouraged people to

Step 1: Read the Question and Put It in Your Own Words

Step 2: Answer in Your Own Words

Step 3 and Step 4

Here are the answer choices that go with the questions you just worked through. Now that you've framed the history, use that information to POE and Guess and Go. Be sure to check EVERY answer before picking one! Answers can be found on pages 40–43.

1. During the Cold War era, the United States and the Soviet Union were reluctant to become involved in direct military conflict mainly because of

    (A) pressure from many of the nonaligned nations
    (B) the role of the United Nations as peacekeeper
    (C) increased tensions in the Middle East
    (D) the potential for global nuclear destruction

2. In the sixteenth and seventeenth centuries, European mercantilism in Latin America led to

    (A) the exploitation of people and resources
    (B) the European Renaissance
    (C) the Protestant Reformation
    (D) the growth of democratic forms of government

3. One way in which the Maya, the Songhai, and the Gupta cultures were similar is that they

    (A) developed great civilizations without major influence from Western Europe
    (B) emerged as a result of nationalist movements of the twentieth century
    (C) thrived due to a prosperous trade economy with Portugal and other European nations
    (D) became dependent on slave trade in order to maintain enough laborers to tend to their profitable sugar cane crop

4. The teachings of Confucius encouraged people to

    (A) embrace a heliocentric view of the solar system
    (B) follow a code of moral conduct
    (C) accept the teachings of the Pax Romana
    (D) worship the one true God who watches over and cares for his people

CHECK YOUR ANSWERS ON PAGES 40–43 BEFORE MOVING ON!

Take a Picture

You will occasionally see a question that asks you to interpret an illustration such as a painting, poster, political cartoon, or map. Treat these questions as you would any other. Just follow the steps and don't read too much into the illustration. Try the following example:

The above poster was most likely used as

(A) British propaganda during the Boer War
(B) American propaganda during World War II
(C) British propaganda during World War I
(D) American propaganda during World War I

In the space on the next page, solve this question using the Four Steps. Study the poster for clues as to the When? Who? and What?

Step 1: Read the Question and Put It in Your Own Words

Step 2: Answer in Your Own Words

Step 3: POE

Step 4: Guess and Go

Here's How to Crack It

The question asked what the poster was used for. You probably guessed the What? to be propaganda. For the When? and Who?, look at the words at the top of the poster. Did you remember that Hun was the term used by the British in reference to the Germans? If you did, you could eliminate (B) and (D) for having nothing to do with the British. Even if you didn't recognize that term, look at the smaller type underneath—England? Belgium? Whatever else it might be, it's definitely not the American KKK and Reconstruction. Because the British were referencing the Germans, the answer must be (C) British propaganda during World War I. If you knew that the term Hun referred to the Germans in WWI, but did not remember who said it, you could have eliminated all but (C) and (D) and then taken a smart guess.

What He Said

Sometimes you will be given a quotation and asked to either interpret the quote or identify the person who said it. As always, use the steps to frame your answer and take a smart guess. Try the next one using the Four Steps.

"Which, O Bhikkhus, is this Middle Path the knowledge of which the Tathagata has gained, which leads to insight, which leads to wisdom, which conduces to calm, to knowledge, to the Sambodhi, to Nirvana?"

The person who would most likely be associated with this quote is a

(A) Muslim
(B) Christian
(C) Polytheist
(D) Buddhist

Here's How to Crack It

Many times the key to solving a quotation comes from only one or two words of the quotation. In this case, the word is Nirvana. Nirvana has to do with what religion? If you remember, great. If you cannot remember exactly which religion strives for Nirvana, you probably know that it is Eastern. Let's say you remember that it is one of the Indian religions. What answers can you eliminate? (B) and (C). From there, take a smart guess between Muslim and Buddhist. The answer is (D): Buddhist.

> **What About the Tough Stuff?**
> While POE is a great thing, some AP World History questions can be tough. You will often be able to get it down to two or three choices, but then you will really need to know your stuff to find the right answer. To be totally prepared for the exam, make sure you know the history in Part II of this book, and don't be afraid to do as much as you can before you Guess and Go.

Not So Bad, Huh?

That's pretty much all you need to know to score your best on the multiple-choice section of the exam. Oh yeah, that, and a bunch of history. Most of the rest of your work in this book will be about reviewing the history. Remember, however, what we said at the beginning of this book—knowing the history is really important, but knowing how to demonstrate that you know it is just as important. That's where your multiple-choice strategy comes in.

As you practice, remember to process everything using the Four Steps.

Step 1: Read the Question and Put It in Your Own Words

Step 2: Answer in Your Own Words

Step 3: Process of Elimination (POE)

Step 4: Guess and Go

If you know the history in Part IV of this book, use these steps, and have an essay strategy, you will be able to show what you know.

Practice Set 2

Now that you have the basics of cracking these types of questions let's practice.

Answers can be found on pages 43–45.

1. The primary purpose of the Dawes Plan was to

    (A) contain the spread of communism to newly formed nations in sub-Saharan Africa through direct economic support
    (B) ensure that Latin American nations maintained economic ties with the United States
    (C) allow Germany to rebuild its economy while also fulfilling its reparation responsibilities after World War I
    (D) temporarily occupy Japan as it transitioned from a monarchy to a democracy after World War II

2. The concept of bushido is most similar to

    (A) feudalism
    (B) chivalry
    (C) manorialism
    (D) meritocracy

3. The Han dynasty (200 B.C.E. to 200 C.E.) had a stable government for centuries, due in part to all of the following EXCEPT

    (A) the strong military force with which the government, under the leadership of Asoka, the Warrior Emperor, expelled the Hun invasion
    (B) the adoption and growth of the Confucian system of civil administration
    (C) the Mandate of Heaven, which inclined Emperors to rule fairly and justly
    (D) the creation and exportation of goods such as paper, silk, and gun powder along the Silk Road

4. Common to Latin American revolutions before 1915 was

    (A) the influence of European intellectual movements
    (B) the important role played by women in instituting change
    (C) the installation of representative democracies in nearly all new nations
    (D) the importance of foreign intervention in the success of revolutions

5. The Peace of Augsburg was an example of

    (A) gentlemen's agreement
    (B) mutual defense
    (C) enlightened absolutism
    (D) religious tolerance

6. Which of the following is an accurate list of the permanent members of the United Nations Security Council?

    (A) China, Japan, United States, Russia, Great Britain
    (B) China, Russia, United States, France, Great Britain
    (C) Russia, Japan, United States, Italy, Great Britain
    (D) Russia, China, United States, France, Italy

7. The Siege of Vienna was important because it

    (A) marked the beginning of the end of Ottoman military conquests in Europe
    (B) was the first attempt of the Ottoman Empire to advance into Western Europe
    (C) precipitated a Christian Crusade to retake Vienna from the Turks
    (D) was the first time a secret alliance between European nations was tested

8. All of the following are examples of attempts by early humans to gain control over nature EXCEPT

    (A) constructing sundials
    (B) plowing fields
    (C) domesticating animals
    (D) settling in river basins

9. The establishment of the Hanseatic League (1241 c.e.) was significant because it

   (A) set a precedent for large, European trading operations
   (B) organized to become the first joint-stock company
   (C) comprised nearly 50 port cities along the Mediterranean Sea
   (D) held exclusive rights to trade along the Silk Road

10. "Sing, O goddess, the anger of Achilles son of Peleus, that brought countless ills upon the Achaeans. Many a brave soul did it send hurrying down to Hades, and many a hero did it yield a prey to dogs and vultures, for so were the counsels of Jove fulfilled from the day on which the son of Atreus, king of men, and great Achilles, first fell out with one another."

   The above quote is from which of the following texts?

   (A) The Vedas
   (B) Homer's Iliad
   (C) Hobbes' Leviathan
   (D) The Code of Hammurabi

CHECK YOUR ANSWERS ON PAGES 43–45 BEFORE MOVING ON!

ANSWER KEY

Practice Set 1

Step 1 and Step 2

1.   Try to anticipate the answer on this one even before you look at the answer choices. Why would two superpowers not want to fight each other?

Step 1: Read the Question and Put It in Your Own Words

Why were the U.S. and the Soviet Union reluctant to get into direct military conflict during the Cold War?

Step 2: When? Who? What?

When? The Cold War era

Who?   The United States and the Soviet Union

What?   Reluctance to get involved militarily

Try to think of everything you know about "military conflict" during the time period of the Cold War. The Cold War was after World War II, right? How did World War II end in Japan? Remember the Cuban Missile Crisis? That was during the Cold War. What did that involve?

2.   Notice that this question tells you that European mercantilism occurred during the sixteenth and seventeenth centuries. A lot of times, questions give you information. Look at the questions themselves as clues.

Step 1: Read the Question and Put It in Your Own Words

When? The sixteenth and seventeenth centuries

Who?   Europeans doing, Latin Americans receiving

What?   Mercantilism

What did European mercantilism in Latin America lead to in the sixteenth and seventeenth centuries?

Step 2: Answer in Your Own Words

If you remember what mercantilism was, this question is a gift. If you don't remember mercantilism, think about everything you know about Europe's involvement in Latin America during the sixteenth and seventeenth centuries.

3.   Sometimes you'll get questions that seemingly don't give you very many clues in the question to work with.

Step 1: Read the Question and Put It in Your Own Words

When? The question doesn't say, but it certainly isn't contemporary (the verb were) and it doesn't refer to the same time period. When the test writers ask you to compare cultures, remember that those cultures may have existed during different time periods.

Who? The Maya, the Songhai, and the Gupta

What? Similarities. Any similarity. Just one. That's all you need.

How were the Maya, Songhai, and Gupta cultures similar?

Step 2: Answer in Your Own Words

It's hard to anticipate what the answer is going to be, but even if you don't remember the details of all three cultures, if you remember one or two, you should focus on the details that you remember so that you can pick an answer choice that is consistent with what you do know.

4. Sometimes questions rely on very specific knowledge of just one thing. In this case, it's just one person.

Step 1: Read the Question and Put It in Your Own Words

When? The question doesn't tell us, but we know it was during and possibly after the life of Confucius.

Who? Confucius

What? Teachings and encouragement

Confucius encouraged people to do what?

Step 2: Answer in Your Own Words

Even though this question seems like it doesn't give you very much information, it does if you remember some basics. If you recall that Confucius lived in China and lived a long time ago, that's enough to start focusing on the answer. All you have to do is think of everything you know about traditional China and you can start to zero in on an answer.

Step 3 and Step 4

Now evaluate the answer choices and use POE to get rid of bad answers.

1. **D** Focus on answer choices that make the most sense. You should certainly be attracted to answer choice (D), because even if you don't remember much about the Cold War, it just makes sense that global nuclear destruction would make two countries reluctant to fight. If you recall that the two superpowers had nuclear weapons and that WWII, which preceded the Cold War, ended with the United States dropping atomic bombs on Japan, answer choice (D) should definitely stick out. (A) doesn't make much sense, because nonaligned nations means that they didn't take sides in the Cold

War, which means that they probably didn't impact it very much. You might be attracted to (B), but if you recall that both the United States and the Soviet Union were members of the United Nations Security Council, making the organization somewhat useless in addressing Cold War concerns, so this answer choice doesn't make much sense. Finally, (C) definitely describes an event that was true during the Cold War era, but it wasn't the cause for the reluctance for direct military conflict. Direct military conflict in the Middle East was somewhat common, just not between the Soviet Union and United States (except, to a certain degree, in Afghanistan). Make sure you focus on the who in the question. Even if you aren't sure of why answer choices (A) through (C) are incorrect, it's hard to argue with answer choice (D). When you find an answer choice that has to be true, it probably is. Because only one answer choice can work, the other three can be eliminated.

2. **A**   Mercantilism was all about exploitation. The policy advocated the creation of colonies for the purpose of increasing exports from the mother country while not technically increasing imports to the mother country (mercantilist countries essentially stole resources from the colonies). If you remember anything at all about mercantilism, you gotta go with (A). Even if you don't remember anything about mercantilism, you still should go with (A) because you should know that Europe colonized Latin America.

   All of the other answer choices can be eliminated if you focus on the When?, Who?, and What? of the question. (B) can be eliminated because the European Renaissance had nothing to do with Latin America. (C) can be eliminated because the Protestant Reformation was an event that primarily affected Europe, not Latin America—and not because of Latin America, either. You can be even more comfortable crossing off (C) if you also remember that Latin America is extremely Catholic as opposed to Protestant. Finally, cross off (D); democracies didn't start developing until long after the sixteenth and seventeenth centuries. It wasn't until after the American and French Revolutions that democratic movements started to get rolling, and it wasn't until the twentieth century that democracies started taking root in Latin America.

3. **A**   Even if you just remember one of the three civilizations, you can get this question correct because (A) applies so clearly to any one of them. If you remember that the Maya, for example, existed for centuries before the first Europeans arrived in the New World, you're done. Even if you're not sure about the other three answer choices, (A) is definitely true. The same, of course, is true of the Songhai in Africa and the Gupta in India.

   The other answer choices make no sense even if you remember the When? and What? of just one of the cultures. All of the cultures existed long before the twentieth century, so get rid of (B). None of the cultures traded with Portugal. Think of the time periods here. The Gupta Empire existed in the fourth through sixth centuries c.e. Portugal had been part of the Roman Empire and wasn't even a country, but more of a region, and was being invaded by Visigoths during this time period. As for (D), you can eliminate it as soon as you see "sugar cane" as a profitable crop because it doesn't fit with any of the cultures.

4. **B**   If you remember anything about Confucius or traditional China, (B) is the obvious choice here; Confucius' code of conduct clearly dominated the culture of traditional China.

The other answers have no connection with Confucianism. (A) is out, because Ptolemy of Alexandria (second century C.E.) and Copernicus (sixteenth century C.E.) were the two figures most closely associated with the heliocentric model. (C) is about the Pax Romana, which describes the period of stability in the Roman Empire between the reigns of Augustus (27 B.C.E.–14 C.E.) and Marcus Aurelius (161–180 C.E.). As for (D), Confucianism is generally considered a system of ethics, not a religion in the strictest sense.

Practice Set 2

1. **C**   Germany could not repay its war debts to France and England (no surprise given the state of the economy), so France sent troops into the Ruhr Valley where German steel was manufactured. This further compromised Germany's ability to fulfill its obligations, and again brought Europe to the brink of war. Charles Dawes (an American banker) developed a more flexible repayment schedule for Germany based on economic growth. The Dawes Plan also gave low-interest loans to Germany to help jump-start key industries.

   This is a bit of a factoid (don't get it confused with the Dawes Act, which is something completely different!), but remember that anything you can think of that's related may help you cross out answers. If you remember that this had to do with America and Europe, you could go ahead and cross out at least (A), (B), and (D). If you know the Dawes Plan related to World War I, you have another good reason to get rid of (D), which describes something that happened after World War II.

2. **B**   Bushido is a term associated with the shogunate period in Japan. The aristocratic-warrior class of the samurai followed a strict code of honor known as bushido. It is most similar to chivalry, because both stressed discipline, respect, and bravery.

   Using POE, you can get rid of (A) and (C) because even though the code of bushido was practiced during Japanese feudalism, it isn't the same thing as feudalism or manorialism, both of which were also practiced in Europe. Feudalism and manorialism were social and political structures, ways of organizing society, not what would be described as "concepts." Also, guilds are organizations, not "concepts." While (D) is a concept, so that's good, it has nothing to do with bushido.

3. **A**   Asoka ruled the Mauryan empire in India during the third century B.C.E. The Han Dynasty, on the other hand, was in China. Its stability was due to all three reasons in the incorrect answer choices.

   Using POE, you can eliminate any answer choices that were true of the Han dynasty. (B) was definitely true of the Han dynasty (and through much of China's history). The adoption of Confucianism as the basis of state administration led to the creation of a highly skilled government bureaucracy, which of course led to stability. (C) is incorrect: According to the Mandate of Heaven, a king or emperor ruled only with the approval of Heaven, and would continue to prosper only if they ruled justly and wisely. The Mandate was a belief which arose during the earlier Zhou dynasty and was influential in the Han dynasty and beyond. And finally, choice (D) helped to expand and stabilize the economy of Han China, and the ensuing prosperity further promoted China's stability.

4. **A** The Enlightenment in Europe had a profound effect on educated people beyond Europe's shores, especially in Europe's colonies. The writings of intellectuals such as Locke, Rousseau, and Montesquieu impacted the American Revolution, French Revolution, and Latin American revolutions.

Even if you're not sure of the right answer, you can eliminate the wrong answer choices that don't make sense, or that are inconsistent with what you remember about history. Eliminate (B); Latin American society was highly patriarchal, as were most societies prior to 1915. That leaves you with (A), (C), and (D). (C) can be eliminated: Many Latin American nations became dictatorships. (D) can be eliminated because the revolutionaries were born in Latin America and succeeded with the support of popular uprisings, not foreign armies. That leaves you with (A), which makes a lot of sense. The Enlightenment inspired revolutions in general, such as the American Revolution and the French Revolution. It just makes sense, then, that it also impacted the Latin American independence movements of the nineteenth century, especially when you consider that San Martin and Bolivar were educated peninsulares, who were well-schooled in European affairs.

5. **D** During the mid-fifteenth century, Charles V had a difficult time preventing Protestantism from spreading through the Holy Roman Empire. In 1555, he and the prevailing German princes signed the Peace of Augsburg, which allowed each prince to choose the religion his subjects would follow.

Using POE, you can eliminate (C) because enlightened absolutism is an oxymoron—an internally contradictory idea. (A) would mean the Peace of Augsburg was an informal agreement, and (B) makes it sound like a military strategy—neither of these is true, as it was a formal agreement to end religious conflict.

6. **B** If you don't remember all the permanent members, use POE with the ones of which you are sure. The United States is in all the choices so that won't help. You probably know that Japan is not a permanent member because the council was established right after WWII and Japan was not high on anyone's list at that time. In fact, Japan was occupied by the United States and forced to demilitarize, so it certainly would not be on the security council. Eliminate (A) and (C). That leaves you with (B) and (D), Great Britain versus Italy. Again, because of when the council was formed, your best guess is (B), Great Britain. Remember, Great Britain still had an empire through the 1940s.

7. **B** In 1529, Ottoman Turks tried (unsuccessfully) to capture the Austrian city of Vienna. Beginning in the 1300s, the Turks began to make inroads into Europe, first in the Balkans, then by taking Constantinople (which then became Istanbul), then conquering parts of Romania and Hungary.

To use POE, try to remember that the Siege of Vienna occurred in the sixteenth century. That means that (C), the Crusades, is out because they began in 1096 and ended in 1302. (A) is also out because the Ottoman influence in Europe lasted into the twentieth century. (D) has to go because, first of all, it doesn't make sense because there's no way the test writers could know if and when all secret alliances were tested because some of them are "secret" and perhaps still unknown. (D) also doesn't work because the siege of Vienna had nothing to do with Austria's alliances (secret or otherwise)—the Ottomans wanted to make inroads into Western Europe for their own expansionist purposes, not because they were trying to test alliances in Europe.

8. **D**   Settling in a river basin exemplifies how nature often controlled where people needed to live in order to survive, not the other way around. This is especially true if you remember that civilizations continued to settle in river basins even though they were often devastated by unpredictable floods.

To use POE, first remember that three of the answer choices are examples of peoples' attempts to control nature and one is not—your answer is the one that is not an example of this. (B) and (C) are direct efforts to use or harness natural resources in order to grow or otherwise provide food. (A) is more subtle—while sundials did not give humans control over the elements of time, they did give humans the knowledge required to use patterns of time for their own purposes.

Tip: Notice how one answer is not like the others; comparing answers is a great way to see small, yet crucial, differences that can help you eliminate wrong answers. (A), (B), and (C) are all material things or techniques, while (D) denotes a different kind of activity.

9. **A**   The Hanseatic League was a major trading operation comprised dozens of northern European cities. The existence of the league helped pull Europe out of the relative isolation it experienced under feudalism during the Middle Ages by increasing contact among different parts of Europe, which then led to increased trade between Europe and other parts of the world. By establishing a monopoly on trade in northern Europe, the Hanseatic League helped contribute to a culture of expansionism and mercantilism, which of course dominated developments during the Age of Exploration.

Using POE, you can eliminate (B) because a "league" isn't a company but rather an association, and joint-stock companies didn't come onto the scene until after the Commercial Revolution in the sixteenth century (the Muscovy Company—founded in 1555—and the Dutch and British East India Companies—both chartered in the 1600s—were among the first). If you can remember the "where" of the Hanseatic League, that will help you quickly eliminate (C) and (D) because the league was in northern Europe and primarily served as a way of regulating trade among northern European ports.

10. **B**   This one might be tough if you're not familiar with the details of any of these texts, but you can still use clues from the passage. We know there's a reference to a goddess, and there are other characters that seem godlike ("hero" and "king of men"). We also know there's a group referred to as the Achaeans. The quote also has a poetic quality to it—"Sing, O goddess" and "Many a brave soul did it send" aren't exactly everyday ways of speaking.

Through POE, we can probably eliminate (D) because it doesn't sound like a legal code. You can get rid of (C) if you know that Hobbes was an English writer during the Enlightenment who wrote about things like the social contract and free will; this doesn't seem to fit. That leaves you with (A) and (B). The Vedas, if you recall, is a collection of the essential beliefs and mythologies of Hinduism. The Iliad is a poem of ancient Greek mythology. Poetic language fits both, and both traditions have gods, so it's a toss-up, unless you remember that Achilles (as in Achilles heel) is a Greek warrior. You may remember that Achaeans were Greeks (recall the Achaean League). Whenever you have quotations, look for clues that help you identify the culture. Then go with the author who is from that culture.

Chapter 2
How to
Approach
Essay Questions

HOW TO BE A WRITER...AN AP WORLD HISTORY ESSAY WRITER, THAT IS

Once you complete the multiple-choice part of the test, you'll get a short break while tests are collected and essay booklets are handed out. Then comes the essay portion of the exam. You'll be given a ten-minute reading period prior to the start of the essay-writing section, and then two hours to write three essays. While you are given approximate guidelines, you are not told how long to spend on each essay or when to move on to the next essay.

What's in a Name?

The three essays you'll need to write are the document-based question (or DBQ), the change-over-time essay, and the comparative essay. You can probably gather from the names what you need to do in each essay—the document-based question provides you with a set of documents on which to base your essay; the change-over-time essay asks you to analyze the changes and continuities that occurred within a certain period of time; and the comparative essay asks you to compare and contrast two episodes, cultures, religions, or other historical phenomenon from a given period.

Writing a thesis for an AP World History Exam essay is a little different from other theses you may have learned to write in English class. Luckily, there is a basic format you can use for all three AP World History essays. While there are some minor variations for each, the overall style you use can be the same. In the next two chapters, we will walk you through each essay type, giving you guidelines for exactly how to write each essay and show what you need to know. But before we go into the specifics, let's take a minute to look at the basic format you should use for all of your AP World History Exam essays.

What Are You Talking About?

The key to writing a good AP World History Exam essay is to tell the reader what you are going to talk about before you talk about it. The AP World History Exam refers to this as your thesis. In fact, writing a good thesis is worth 1 to 2 of 9 possible points on each essay, and it is the first thing that the essay grader will look for. The scoring rubric (the guidelines readers use to score your essays) requires readers to answer the following questions about each of your essays:

- Do you have a comprehensive, analytical, and explicit thesis?
- Is your thesis acceptable?

So What Does an Analytical Thesis Look Like?

Put simply, <u>an analytical thesis includes a clear description of why the central claim of your essay is correct</u>. These statements alone would not receive points for "adequacy."

- Buddhism's spread through China was very important to the development of Chinese culture.
- In the area of trade, North America and Latin America underwent significant change between 1750 and the present.

These vague, general, and weak statements add nothing to your essay, and leave the reader with a laundry list of questions that remain unanswered: What exactly does the term "Buddhism" denote here? What, exactly, "spread"? When did this occur? In what context? "Very important" how? What were Buddhism's specific effects? What specific aspects of culture did it touch on, and how do we know?

<u>Clear, explicit theses will use specific details to delimit the scope of the discussion.</u> The first thesis would be vastly improved by the addition of more details such as:

- As Buddhism began to spread from India through China in the first century c.e., the influence of its religious principles in a society troubled—at least among lower classes—by warfare and want is demonstrated by the Confucianists' negative reaction to it as well as the lasting political effects it left in its wake.

Why is this better than the first version? Yes, it has more words, but what do those extra words do? The reader now has more details regarding what spread, when this spread took place, what the context of that spread was, and what kind of support will be referenced in the rest of the essay. Most importantly, it answers the question, "Why was the spread of Buddhism important?" The reader now knows that Buddhism was important because it caused meaningful changes in different areas of Chinese society, which the essay should describe in more detail.

Remember also that a thesis isn't just one sentence; it can be a group of statements. Therefore, you can start with a more general sentence, but you have to then follow it up with additional sentences that provide all the necessary elements described above. Together, these statements must

- state your claim clearly
- define terms, context, and chronology of the events under discussion
- describe why your claim is true

Lastly, a clear, analytical thesis isn't there just for the reader's benefit. A strong analytical thesis serves as a map that you should follow as you write the remainder of the essay. If your thesis at first is too vague, it may be that you haven't thought through what you want to say yet, so take more time to organize your ideas. Once you craft a strong thesis, make sure that the rest of your essay supports the basic ideas your thesis introduces.

So What Is "Acceptable"?

To write a solid, acceptable thesis for each of your essays, remember to do three things: Give 'Em What They Want, Show 'Em Where You Got It, and Help 'Em Get There.

The two most common essay cues you will see are "analyze" and "compare and contrast." Sometimes you will see both in the same essay question.

To really analyze you must explain how and why something happens and what the impacts of that something were. For example, to return to the spread of Buddhism in China—analysis of this process would include explaining how it spread to China, why it was appealing to the Chinese, and finally, how it impacted Chinese society over both the short and long-term.

To "compare and contrast" deals with similarities and differences; however, it is not enough to point out what is similar or different: Buddhism existed in both India and China. It is far more important to explain what causes the similarities and differences—in essence, to analyze why: Because of Buddhism's appeal to the lower classes, it spread throughout India and China, however, acceptance differed because it was perceived as a threat to the Confucian order in China.

Give 'Em What They Want

Your essay reader is trained to look for certain specific criteria in your essay. To make sure that she finds what she's looking for (and to ensure that you get credit for including all that stuff), begin by using the question to develop a thesis that includes key phrases from the question AND sets up the structure of your argument. For example, a typical question is:

3. Compare and contrast the impact of nationalism in Europe versus the impact of nationalism in the European colonies throughout the nineteenth and twentieth centuries.

Do not just reword the question by using a simple introductory sentence such as: There were many similarities and differences between nationalism in Europe and its colonies.

This sentence is a waste of space that doesn't tell the reader anything. Instead, your first sentence should clearly indicate what is to come in the rest of the thesis and the body of the essay and why nationalism was important.

The opening sentence of your thesis might read something like this:

Nationalism was a driving force throughout much of the nineteenth and twentieth centuries, but it had a very different flavor in Europe than in most European colonies.

Notice the key phrases that were included in the sentence: Nationalism, Europe, European colonies, and nineteenth and twentieth centuries. Also note that the sentence is worded to imply contrast. Just to make sure that all aspects of the question are covered, the next sentence could read as follows:

> *While nationalism for both groups meant pride in and commitment to one's own "nation," nationalism in Europe—which often meant racism or desire for domination—became synonymous with national expansion and conquest of other peoples, while nationalism in the colonies meant self determination—freedom from European rule, and the nation's right to determine its own destiny.*

This sentence continues the contrast, but opens with a comparison, so as not to overlook the similarities in the responses of the two countries (something you must do to get a good score).

Try It

To make sure you include all the necessary elements in the opening sentence of your thesis, circle each key phrase as you process the question. Try it on the following example:

2. Choose TWO of the areas listed below and discuss the impact of the spread of Islam from its inception to 1450 on each area. Be sure to describe each area prior to the introduction of Islam as your starting point.

Sub-Saharan Africa	The Middle East
The Byzantine Empire	Spain (the Iberian
Western Europe	Peninsula)
China	India
	Northern Africa

Did you circle key words and phrases like spread of Islam, inception to 1450, impact on each area? Once you circle the key phrases and select your countries/areas, try writing your opening sentence below.

_____

_____

_____

Your opening sentence should read something like the following:

From its inception to the early 1400s and beyond, the spread of Islam had a major impact on both the Iberian Peninsula (Spain) and the Middle East.

Show 'Em Where You Got It

Because you are writing an essay about something from history, the essay must be based on historical fact as opposed to your opinion. Once you let your reader know what you are going to say, you need to support what you are going to say by adding evidence. You've already done half the work by circling the key phrases. Once you know what the key phrases are, make sure that you introduce some evidence for each one. For example, look again at the first two sentences of our nationalism thesis:

> *Nationalism was a driving force throughout much of the nineteenth and twentieth centuries, but it had a very different flavor in Europe than in most European colonies. While nationalism for both groups meant pride in and commitment to one's own "nation," nationalism in Europe—which often meant racism or desire for domination—became synonymous with national expansion and conquest of other peoples, while nationalism in the colonies meant self determination—freedom from European rule, and the nation's right to determine its own destiny.*

The second sentence in our thesis alludes to historical events—colonization and expansion was the result of European nationalism, while independence movements were the result of colonial nationalism. Because the thesis is just an intro to the body of the essay, you don't need to go into detail, but you do need to begin to pull in evidence at this stage of the game. The next sentence could go on to state more specifically some of the results of nationalism for each group.

Different but Equal

Each type of essay also requires something slightly different for its thesis. For example, most change-over-time questions ask that you detail the starting point for changes as well as the changes themselves. Therefore, you need to include a statement about the starting point and evidence to support your statement.

Provide information about starting points for change for the Islam example from above.

_____

_____

_____

_____

Depending on the countries or regions you chose, your essay should now read something like this:

> The spread of Islam had a major impact on both the Iberian Peninsula (Spain) and the Middle East from its inception to the early 1400s and beyond. Despite the relatively early split into two camps—the Shia and the Sunni—over a disagreement about who should succeed Mohammad as the leader of the faith, Islam spread rapidly throughout the Middle East, due in part to the fact that although Muslims were intent on converting those they conquered, they were also flexible and tolerant of different forms of religious expression. By the middle of the eighth century, Muslims held parts of southern Iberia and southern parts of Italy and were intent on moving further into Europe, which threatened the Christians who dominated most of the regions to the north.

If this were a document-based question, your evidence would be documents rather than historical information you know. The DBQ has some additional details you'll need to include, but you'll learn more about that in the next chapter.

Help 'Em Get There

The last sentence in your thesis can be as important as the first because it helps the reader get from your intro into the bulk of what you have to say. Make the transition to the body of the essay with a sentence that opens with something like, "To better understand these changes…" or "To better understand these documents…" For example:

> To better understand how nationalism led to the struggle for independence in many European colonies, one must first examine how nationalism, among other factors, led to the establishment of many of these colonies.

In the space below, try writing a transitional sentence for the essay on Islam:

_____

_____

_____

_____

_____

Your sentence could read something like the following:

> *To better understand the impact of Islam on both the Middle East and Spain during this period, one must first take a look at what these areas were like prior to the introduction of Islam.*

As you know, each type of essay requires a slightly different kind of thesis. The next two chapters will go through this in more detail. Keep this page marked for future reference. Here is a quick summary of the specs for each type of thesis you will write.

DBQ Thesis
- Open with something like, "After reviewing these documents, it is clear that..."
- Rephrase the question as an answer; include all key phrases.
- Address each part of the question with a statement and a document reference or an example (compare, contrast, and change over time as appropriate).
- Make the transition to the body of the essay by citing the additional document: "To better understand how these documents relate to each other, a document about *x* would be useful..."

Change-Over-Time Thesis
- Rephrase the question as an answer; include all key phrases.
- Address each part of the question with a statement and evidence.
- Make the transition to the body of the essay with a sentence like, "To better understand these changes..."

Comparative Thesis
- Restate the question as an answer; include all key phrases.
- Address each part of the question with a statement and evidence.
- Include both similarities and differences.
- Make the transition to the body of the essay with a sentence like, "To better understand the similarities and differences between these two societies..."

But What About the Rest?

Of course, the thesis is only the beginning of your essay, but getting the beginning right can really make writing the rest of the essay much easier. The next two chapters will walk you through the specifics of each type of essay. In addition, there are some basic rules of writing essays for standardized tests that will help you score your best. Here are the points to keep in mind while writing each AP World History Exam essay.

- Essays should be a minimum of 4 to 6 paragraphs: Opening (thesis), Body, Body, Body, Closing.
- Use transitional words and trigger words to highlight important points.

Good Transitional Words

Contrast or Change	Similarity or Continuity
but, however, although, though in contrast, alternatively	*since, moreover, similarity, as well as, still, likewise, therefore*

- Write neatly. An essay that cannot be read will not receive a good score.
- If you don't know how to spell a word, choose another. Readers are not supposed to grade your spelling, but poor spelling can cast a shadow on the rest of your essay.
- Watch your time. Spending too much time on the first essay could mean running out of time on the last essay. The next two chapters include timing guidelines for each essay.
- Think before you write. In fact, do more than think—make notes, jot ideas, create an outline. The more work you do before you write, the neater and more organized your essay will be. The next two chapters will give you details on exactly how much prep work to do for each essay.

Chapter 3
How to Approach Document-Based Questions (DBQ)

IT'S ALL IN THE DOCUMENTS

The first essay you'll see on the essay portion of the AP World History Exam is the document-based question (DBQ). As the name implies, this question is based on a bunch of documents (typically 4–10) that cover one topic, usually in or around a particular period of time. For example, your DBQ may require you to analyze a set of documents about trading practices before and during the Age of Exploration. The documents may include a map of trade routes, a letter from a merchant to his ruler at home, or some codified laws regarding particular trade agreements. Your job is to work through the documents to determine how they relate to each other, what changes can be seen over time, how the author's background may have influenced the contents of the document, and so on.

Before the start of the essay portion of the exam, you will be given ten minutes to read the documents for the DBQ. To do well on this essay, you need to know exactly what to do with those ten minutes. And to do that you need to know exactly what you are expected to write. Let's begin by looking at the directions and the scoring rubric for the DBQ.

What the Directions Say

Here is a sample of the directions for the DBQ.

> Directions: The following question is based on the accompanying Documents 1–9. The documents have been edited for the purpose of this exercise. Write your answer on the lined pages of the Section II free-response booklet.
>
> The question is designed to test your ability to work with and understand historical documents. Write an essay that:
>
> - Has a relevant thesis and supports that thesis with evidence from the documents.
> - Uses all of the documents.
> - Analyzes the documents by grouping them in as many appropriate ways as possible. Does not simply summarize the documents individually.
> - Takes into account both the sources of the documents and the author's point of view.
> - Identifies at least one type of additional document.

You may refer to historical information not mentioned in the documents.

What the Directions Mean

Here's what the directions are really asking you to do:

1. Create a relevant thesis and support that thesis with the documents. Did you answer the question that was asked? Make sure that your thesis directly addresses the question posed and accurately describes the contents of your essay. Be sure that the documents can be used to support your arguments—students often make the mistake of creating an interesting thesis only to find that the documents don't really support that thesis.

2. Analyze the documents. Your analysis must acknowledge the source of the documents and the author's point of view, which means that you must demonstrate that you understand who wrote each document and when it was written. You should also be able to explain the following:
   - What was the context (historical, political, or cultural environment) in which the document was authored? What else was going on around the author at the time this was written?
   - How does this author's perspective affect what he or she wrote and why? What is the author's position in society (gender, age, educational level, political or religious belief system)? How do these attributes inform what the author writes?
   - How does the content and tone of the document relate to that of the other documents? What does one document say that another doesn't? What accounts for these differences?
   - When was the document written? Who was the intended audience, and what was the author trying to express?

3. Group the documents in at least two different ways, but preferably in three different ways.

4. Identify and explain at least one, but preferably two or more, additional types of documents or points of view that are not represented in the documents and how they would add to your argument.
   - What types of documents offer information that is not already present?
   - What points of view are missing that would make your argument stronger? Consider groups typically not represented (women, working class, peasants).
   - Why is this additional document or point of view important?

So to write a decent DBQ essay, you need to write an essay that opens with a thesis, support that thesis with all of the documents, then analyze and group the documents together (more on this later), and include additional documents or points of view.

How the DBQ Is Scored

The DBQ and all the AP World History Exam essays are first read for a basic core of items fittingly called the *Basic Core*. In order to score at least a 7 (out of 9) on the DBQ, your essay must contain all of the following:

Basic Core Rubric for the Document-Based Question Essay

Item	Points
Has acceptable thesis	1
Understands the basic meaning of the documents (may misinterpret one)	1
Supports thesis with appropriate evidence from ALL documents (supports thesis with appropriate evidence from all but two documents)	2 (1)
Analyzes point of view in at least two, but preferably three, documents	1
Analyzes documents, groups them in at least 2, but preferably 3 ways	1
Identifies and explains the need for an additional document or point of view	1
SUBTOTAL	7

Note: Even though the official AP guidelines call for only one additional document, AP graders tell us that they are really looking for two such documents.

While knowing how essay graders score your essay is useful, this doesn't tell you much about how to actually *write* your essay. Below, we've provided a checklist of questions you should always refer to as you work, which is intended to make all of this information easier to understand.

Document-Based Question Essay

What to Do	Basic Core Requirements	Points
Write a good thesis	Is your thesis acceptable?	1
Interpret the evidence within the documents.	Do you understand the basic meanings of the documents used in this essay?	1

Support your thesis.	Have you supported the thesis with appropriate evidence from ALL of the documents?	2
Analyze the documents and identify author's point of view.	Have you analyzed the author's point of view in at least two, but preferably three, documents?	1
Group the documents in at least two different ways.	Have you analyzed the documents by grouping them in at least two, but preferably three, ways?	1
Identify and explain the need for other types of documents to clarify the issue.	Have you identified and explained the need for two types of additional documents AND explained why you need them?	1
SUBTOTAL		7

If you are now thinking, "Well, that's nice, but I want a 9," no problem. If the person who scores your essay can answer yes to *all* of the Basic Core items, he or she will then look for Expanded Core items in your essay. If your essay contains two or three of the Expanded Core items, you get an 8 on the DBQ. If it contains more than 3 of the Expanded Core items, and it is exceptionally well written, you get a 9 on your essay.

Expanded Core Rubric for the Document-Based Question Essay

Expanded Core Requirements	Points
Do you have a comprehensive, analytical, and explicit thesis?	
Have you used the documents well as evidence?	
Have you shown careful and insightful analysis of the documents?	
Have you analyzed point of view in most or all documents?	0–2
Have you analyzed the documents in additional ways—syntheses, comparisons, groupings?	
Have you brought in additional relevant historical evidence not found in the documents?	
Have you explained why additional document(s) are missing or needed?	
SUBTOTAL	2

How to Earn Expanded Core Points

Remember: Graders only look to the Expanded Core if you have already earned all 7 possible points of the Basic Core elements. To move beyond that takes some extra work on your part.

Notice how several of the items in the Expanded Core are simply more detailed versions of the Basic Core. To get an 8 or 9 on your essay, concentrate on doing a great job with at least two of the things that are in both the Basic Core and the Expanded Core. For example, in our interpretation of the directions, we tell you to group the documents in at least *two* different ways. The Basic Core only requires that you group the documents in one way, but the sixth rubric of the Expanded Core is about analyzing the documents in additional ways such as groupings. By always grouping your documents in *two or more* different ways, chances are you will earn this Expanded Core point.

To earn another Expanded Core point, focus on improving your thesis. To get an extra point from the Expanded Core, you need a thesis that is "comprehensive, analytical, and explicit." If you don't feel you have written a great thesis but know the topic well enough to add some additional historical evidence, add it. Just to be sure, choose another item that is in both core lists and make an extra effort on that item as well.

The point is that you do not need to write an essay that accomplishes all the Basic Core and all the Expanded Core items; instead, choose at least three Expanded Core items and be sure to include them in all the essays you write. That way, as long as you don't miss any Basic Core items, you should earn an 8 or 9.

THE DOCUMENTS

Of course, before you can write anything, you need to work your way through the given documents. Effectively *working* the documents (not just reading them) is almost as important as writing the DBQ essay. Let's spend a few minutes learning exactly how to process the documents so that you can put together that 7+ essay.

Give Me Ten Minutes and I'll Give You the World

Is ten minutes really enough time to get through the documents? That depends on how well you know the topic. Most testers need at least the full ten minutes to work through the documents and prepare to write the essay. But what if the proctor says "go" and you are not yet finished planning your essay? Keep working the documents. The actual writing of your essay will take less time if you are well prepared when you begin. Use the ten minutes you are given plus any additional time you need (up to ten more minutes) to plan your essay. Once you've gotten a handle on the documents and organized your thoughts, it will probably take you only about 20 to 30 minutes to actually write the essay.

Work Those Documents

When the reading period begins, open to Part A (the DBQ). You do not need to read the directions thoroughly—you will have them memorized before you get to the testing room. Circle the total number of documents you have to read (contained in the first sentence of the directions). Next, scan the directions quickly—they should be just like the ones you've used for practice, but make a quick scan just to be sure. You may not be instructed to use all of the documents, but you should anyway, just in case. Then get to the question.

Step 1: Process the Question

You cannot begin to think about the documents until you know what you are being asked to do. Read the question carefully. Underline the important stuff (such as time period, culture, location) and circle what you are supposed to analyze and the actions you need to take (e.g., compare and contrast, change over time, etc.). Also note what the additional document is supposed to do.

Look at the following example of a DBQ:

1. Using the documents, compare and contrast the attitudes toward women found in various cultures from about 1800 b.c.e. until the early 200s, c.e. Are there indications of change over time? What kinds of additional document(s) would be most helpful in furthering your analysis?

Based on the question, what do you know the documents are about?
Attitudes toward women in various cultures during various periods.

What are you being asked to do?
Compare and contrast the attitudes and look for any changes over time.

What could an additional document do?
Clarify how existing attitudes affected women's daily lives.

> ### But Where?
> For the essay portion of the test, you will receive a green booklet that has the essay questions in it plus space to plan your essays, and a sealed pink answer booklet. Use the spaces in the question booklet to do your prep work—outlining, summarizing documents, brainstorming. Don't be shy about what you write in the green booklet—the scorers won't see your notes. In fact, it is good to remember that you will only receive credit for what you wrote in the pink answer booklet. Even if your teachers in school sometimes give you credit for outlining, AP readers will not.

Step 2: Build a Framework

Once you've gotten a handle on the question, use it to create a framework for processing the documents you are about to read. For example, if a question asked you to compare and contrast two major religions, you would create a compare-and-contrast chart of the two religions in question. You can fill in the chart as you work through the documents. If the question asks you if there was any change over time, create a space in which you can easily note any changes you come across. In the example above, the question asks you to both compare and contrast attitudes of different cultures and to look for any change over time. Your framework for this question might look like this.

Similarities in attitudes toward women	Differences in attitudes toward women

Changes in attitudes toward women?

_____

_____

_____

_____

_____

These first two steps should take about two minutes. Then it's time to hit the documents.

Step 3: Work the Documents

Notice we didn't say "read the documents." Reading is too passive a word for what you need to do. As you read each document, summarize and analyze it in light of your framework (what you need to use it for). For example, look at the following document that goes with our example.

Document 1

Source: Christian Bible, Old Testament (Deuteronomy), primarily written in seventh century b.c.e. but based on ancient religious code.

When a man takes a wife and marries her, if then she finds no favor in his eyes because he has found some indecency in her, and he writes her a bill of divorce and puts it in her hand and sends her out of his house, and she departs out of his house, and if she goes and becomes another man's wife, and the latter husband dislikes her and writes her a bill of divorce and puts it in her hand and sends her out of his house, or if the latter husband dies, who took her to be his wife, then her former husband, who sent her away, may not take her again to be his wife, after she had been defiled; for that is an abomination before the Lord, and you shall not bring guilt upon the land which the Lord your God gives you for an inheritance.

First, circle the source, making note of the writer and time period or other relevant information. This document came from the Old Testament. What was the attitude toward women at that time? Clearly women were little more than possessions. A husband had the ability to hand his wife her walking papers pretty much at will and would only commit a sin against God if he took her back after her second husband dumped her.

Let's see how this compares to the second document.

Document 2

Source: The Code of Hammurabi, 1792–1750 b.c.e.

If a man's wife, who lives in his house, wishes to leave it, plunges into debt, tries to ruin her house, neglects her husband, and is judicially convicted: if her husband offers her release, she may go on her way, and he gives her nothing as a gift of release. If her husband does not wish to release her, and if he takes another wife, she shall remain as servant in her husband's house.

If a woman quarrels with her husband, and says: "You are not congenial to me," the reasons for her prejudice must be presented. If she is guiltless, and there is no fault on her part, but he leaves and neglects her, then no guilt attaches to this woman, she shall take her dowry and go back to her father's house.

This document came from the Code of Hammurabi, written from 1800–1700 B.C.E. What was the attitude toward women under the Code of Hammurabi? While women still seem to be considered possessions, they have a few more rights. For example, if she tells him he is a jerk and is proven right, she gets to go home with her dowry, guilt-free. Notice, too, the increased level of judiciary involvement. The decisions seem to be less at the whim of the husband.

Try working the next three documents.

Document 3

Source: Plutarch, excerpt from "Women's Life in Greece and Rome," Moralia, 242 c.e.

27.   When music is played in two parts, it is the bass part which carries the melody. So in a good and wise household, while every activity is carried on by husband and wife in agreement with each other, it will still be evident that it is the husband who leads and makes the final choice.

Document 4

Source: Ban Zhou, leading female Confucian and imperial historian under Emperor Han Hedi, from Lessons for Women, an instruction manual in feminine behavior, 100 c.e.

If a husband be unworthy, then he possesses nothing by which to control his wife. If a wife be unworthy, then she possesses nothing with which to serve her husband. If a husband does not control his wife, then the rules of conduct manifesting his authority are abandoned and broken. If a wife does not serve her husband, then the proper relationship between men and women and the natural order of things are neglected and destroyed. As a matter of fact the purpose of these two [the controlling of women by men, and the serving of men by women] is the same.

Document 5

Source: Excerpt from "The Laws of Manu," the Rig Vedas, 100 b.c.e.–200 c.e.

[In the Rig Vedas (collection of hymns to the Aryan gods) of Classical India, Manu is the father of humanity.]

74. A man who has business (abroad) may depart after securing a maintenance for his wife; for a wife, even though virtuous, may be corrupted if she be distressed by want of subsistence.

75. If (the husband) went on a journey after providing (for her), the wife shall subject herself to restraints in her daily life; but if he departed without providing (for her), she may subsist by blameless manual work.

76. If the husband went abroad for some sacred duty, (she) must wait for him eight years, if (he went) to (acquire) learning or fame six (years), if (he went) for pleasure three years.

77. For one year let a husband bear with a wife who hates him; but after (the lapse of) a year let him deprive her of her property and cease to cohabit with her.

78. She who shows disrespect to (a husband) who is addicted to (some evil) passion, is a drunkard, or diseased, shall be deserted for three months (and be) deprived of her ornaments and furniture.

What did you notice about these documents? Any differences or changes? Document 3, written in Greece and Rome in the third century, shows clearly the attitudes of that time and culture—husband and wife are partners, but the husband is in command. Document 4 is the only document so far that was written by a woman. Notice how in Document 4 the woman is still subservient, but the discussion is about the responsibilities of both men and women? Document 5, which was written about the same time as Document 4, has far more detailed laws regarding the conduct of husbands and wives. Again, women are clearly subservient, yet men are charged with definite responsibilities to their wives.

You get the idea. A typical DBQ would have a few more documents, but let's just use these five to walk through the rest of the steps.

Step 4: Frame Them and Group Them

Once you've worked the documents (or as you go along), fill in your framework from what you've read. For example, using the four documents we just read, try filling in the compare-and-contrast chart.

Your chart should look something like this:

Similarities in attitudes toward women	Differences in attitudes toward women
All Documents—women subservient to men *All Documents—women far fewer legal rights*	*Doc 1—women property, men free to do whatever* *Doc 3—women subservient but more on equal footing* *Doc 2 and 5—more laws regarding male conduct* *Doc 4 and 5—analysis of both male and female roles/responsibilities; husbands culpable for wives* *Doc 4—written by woman; tone different. "If husband unworthy."*

What are the changes that have occurred over time in our example so far? Women went from being mere possessions with men free to make decisions (like to divorce their wives) without any judicial involvement, to more laws governing male conduct and more rights for women (though meager). Although the question doesn't specifically mention it, we should also be aware of the influence of culture when it came to the treatment of women. Some differences that appear in these documents may be a result of not only a change in thought process over time but also a differing attitude of a particular culture (e.g., Document 3). If we were to read the rest of the documents that accompany this question, we would likely see even greater changes in the attitudes toward and treatment of women.

Putting Them Together

In addition to filling in your framework, you also want to begin grouping the documents in at least two different ways. For this example, you can group the documents by the ones that pertain to specific rules or laws governing a husband's conduct versus ones that simply discuss roles and responsibilities. If we were to read the remaining documents, we may find a few more that were written by women and look for the similar characteristics in those documents. You may also wish to group the documents to clearly delineate changes that occurred over time. Remember that grouping the documents at least two different, insightful ways can help you earn up to four Basic Core points and one Expanded Core point: one point for using all the documents; one point for supporting your thesis with the document groupings; two points for grouping them in at least two different, insightful ways (this can get you one Basic Core point and one Expanded Core point); and one point for demonstrating that you understand the meaning of the documents through your ability to group them in various ways.

Step 5: Analyze and Add

In order to get all the Basic Core points, you must analyze at least two documents for bias or point of view, and you must answer the additional document part of the question.

Point of View

Choose one document to analyze for point of view. To select the best document to analyze, pay close attention to who wrote the document and when it was written. Both can influence the author's point of view. Choose a document that clearly expresses a point of view and also one for which you can indicate an alternate interpretation of the information. For example, in our sample documents, Document 4 was written by Ban Zhou, the leading female Confucian during the Han age in China. Could the fact that she is a woman coupled with the fact that she was a Confucian have influenced what she chose to write? Absolutely. Look at her document again.

Document 4

Source: Ban Zhou, leading female Confucian and imperial historian under Emperor Han Hedi, from *Lessons for Women*, an instruction manual in feminine behavior, 100 C.E.

If a husband be unworthy, then he possesses nothing by which to control his wife. If a wife be unworthy, then she possesses nothing with which to serve her husband. If a husband does not control his wife, then the rules of conduct manifesting his authority are abandoned and broken. If a wife does not serve her husband, then the proper relationship between men and women and the natural order of things are neglected and destroyed. As a matter of fact the purpose of these two [the controlling of women by men, and the serving of men by women] is the same.

She tended to focus on worthiness and the interaction between husbands and wives. She even put their responsibilities on equal footing, something that we did not see in any of the other documents. She did not live in an age in which women questioned their subservient role. Therefore, instead of challenging the roles, she tried to find a way to make sense of the subjugation of women. The period in which she lived clearly influenced her point of view. These are the types of issues you want to bring into your analysis of point of view.

Point of View

Try to analyze for point of view in each document. Typically a number of the documents will read in a way that indicates strong or slightly skewed opinions. So pay attention to who wrote them and when they were written. From among our sample documents, which would you consider easy to analyze for point of view? How about Document 3? It pertains to Greek and Roman societies and was written in the third century. Take a look at it again.

Document 3

> Source: Plutarch, excerpt from "Women's Life in Greece and Rome," Moralia, 242 c.e.
>
> 27.   When music is played in two parts, it is the bass part which carries the melody. So in a good and wise household, while every activity is carried on by husband and wife in agreement with each other, it will still be evident that it is the husband who leads and makes the final choice.

It reads almost as advice from one to another about how a marriage should be. Interestingly, the attitude of the Greeks and Romans toward women seems positive, yet clearly considered their role as secondary in a marriage. Could that be perhaps a result of the time and culture? Absolutely. The person (presumably a man) who wrote this was likely giving loving, caring advice to a friend, yet he does not acknowledge what a more modern reader would likely think about the subjugation of the woman in the marital relationship. This form of bias was imbedded in the culture of that time. This is therefore a good document to use to exemplify how context and culture can clearly influence a person's perspective.

Now find at least two, but preferably three, more documents and analyze them for point of view.

Additional Document

So as not to forget this step, make a note of it now, and then plan to include it as part of your opening thesis.

In our example, the additional document part of the question asked the following:

What kinds of additional document(s) would be most helpful in furthering your analysis?

In order to assess how the attitudes of a culture affected women's daily lives during a certain period, what type of document or documents would be helpful? What about either more documents written by women that reflected their thoughts or daily experiences, or a document that chronicled the daily responsibilities of women in the given period? Should they be everyday-type documents, like shopping lists, or letters to a family members? Should they more formal, like instructions on how to do something? *Be sure to explain why you feel these documents will add to your analysis;* just describing a document will not earn you the point.

Step 6: Organize the Documents

So far you've processed the question, built a framework, worked the documents to fill in that framework, grouped and regrouped the documents, analyzed the documents for point of view, and determined the type of additional document you need and why. (Whew! You must be exhausted!) Now it's time to organize your documents so that you know which ones you are using as support, which ones you are analyzing and exactly how you plan to group them. This last step will act as the outline for your essay.

Use the following chart to organize your essay.

Thesis	You will open your essay with a thesis. In your thesis, reference the strongest supporting documents. As part of your outline, decide which documents represent the core of your thesis and include them in your opening paragraph. Also, jot down a few brief notes about your thesis before moving on. (Be sure to make your notes on scratch paper—not in the essay booklet.)
Support	List the documents that you plan to use to support your thesis. Include all the documents you mention in your thesis (in the first paragraph). Also feel free to include any other document that will lend additional support.
Group One	First, group the documents in the most obvious way. For example, if you are asked to compare and contrast a set of documents, break the documents into two groups so that each group contains documents with similar features but the two groups clearly contrast each other.
Group Two	Regroup the documents in a way that shows some sort of insight into how the documents relate to each other. For example, if you first created groups by putting together documents with obvious similarities, regroup them in a way that shows something different or less obvious about the documents. If the question asks about change over time, regroup the documents to show how things changed over some period.
Point of View	List the documents you have chosen to analyze for point of view. Plan to discuss them after one or both of your groupings. Decide how you can compare and contrast them with your point of view document and/or with your thesis.

	Number of Documents	Use this as a checklist to be sure you include all of the documents in your essay. List the number of documents you've been given, then go through each category and check off the document number as you come to it. If you finish your check and realize that you omitted one (or more) documents, go back to that document to determine where you can use it (support, analyze, or group).
	Additional Documents	Once you've grouped your documents, consider what other kind or kinds of documents would add something interesting to the analysis of the question posed. Be sure to include reasons why a particular extra document would be useful.

Use our sample documents to fill in the organizational chart below.

DBQ Essay Organizational Chart

	Document Number(s)	Comments
Thesis		
Support		
Group 1		
Group 2		
Group 3		
POV 1		
POV 2		
Number		
Additional Documents		

How did you do? Your chart should look something like the following:

DBQ Essay Organizational Chart

	Document Number(s)	Comments
Thesis	*Doc 1—possessions, no laws* *Doc 2—more laws* *Doc 5—still more laws and responsibilities*	*Attitudes toward women from 1800 b.c.e. up to approx. 200 c.e. definitely changed but not a lot. Early times, women as property, men could do whatever. Later, laws governing conduct of husbands that were slightly more fair to wives…*
Support	*Documents 1, 2, and 5.* *Document 3 softer yet holds women in same position* *Document 4 to show changes and difference in perspective*	
Group 1	*1 & 3 versus 2 & 5*	*Shows no law versus more laws and judicial involvement. Could include others.*
Group 2	*4 (and others) versus* *1, 2, 3, & 5 (and others)*	*Written from the female perspective versus from the male perspective.*
Group 3	*1, 2, 3, 4, and 5 versus others*	*All define women only in terms of the role of wife. Other docs may not.*
POV 1	*Doc 3*	*Written by man giving advice to a friend.*
POV 2	*Doc 4*	*Written by a Confucian woman.*
Number	*1, 2, 3, 4, 5, __, __*	*Check off each as it is used in your outline so that you know that you have used them all.*
Additional Documents		*One that portrays a woman who lived during one of the periods mentioned (in the provided docs) showing her defining herself as a citizen or individual rather than just as a wife.* *Possibly one that shows a woman questioning her position in society, wanting more.*

Remember that you will have more documents to use, which will make your essay groupings more diverse. The way you group the documents should support your thesis and show changes or contrast as well.

> ### How Long Is Ten Minutes?
> Right now this process may seem as if it will take two hours as opposed to ten minutes. You need to practice doing it a few times to get a feel for how much time to spend on what. You may find that you can fill in your framework as you analyze the documents, or identify the documents' point of view as you go. The more you practice, the more efficient you will become. Remember, however, that analyzing the documents is as important as writing the essay. If you need to use the first five to ten minutes of your writing time to finish your analysis or outline, it will be time well spent.

DBQ THESIS

To create an effective thesis, you must first make sure that you are answering the question asked. As we talked about in the intro to AP essays beginning on page 48 (if you didn't read it before, now's a good time), there are some basic rules of good AP essay theses.

Give 'Em What They Want—Answer the question by restating key phrases from the question. Don't simply rewrite what you were given; rather, write your response as an answer, but be sure to include the important phrases that were in the question.

Show 'Em Where You Got It—AP World History Exam essays are all about the evidence. Use your framework to support your assertions right from the beginning. Remember that evidence in your thesis is merely introductory—save the details for the body of the essay.

Help 'Em Get There—Make a clear transition from your thesis to the body of your essay by using a phrase like, "To better understand the differences between these two societies…" or "To better understand the changes that occurred…" One way to earn your Basic Core point for additional documents is to suggest, describe, and justify the inclusion of the additional document as part of this last sentence. That way, you won't forget to include it and it makes for a good transition.

For our example, your thesis would flow something like the following:

> *From a review of the five documents presented, it is clear that the role of women in various cultures from 1800 b.c.e. into the 200s was primarily one of servitude or worse in comparison to our contemporary ideas about the rights of women. However, there is also evidence that over time, women were seen less as subject only to the rule of law laid down by an individual (usually a husband) and more as people whose (albeit limited) rights were overseen by the rule of law. In earlier eras, women were seen more as property than as people, and that only men reserved the right to divorce with no lingering responsibility to care for their wives. However, some societies began to hold men more accountable for their treatment of women, a trend which eventually came to other societies as well, though at different times. With this added protection of the law, women are not only more protected, but are also held more accountable for their own conduct.*

When you write your thesis paragraph, imagine that a reader will only read your essay if they are convinced to do so by your first paragraph (no pressure). Then, use your framework to write the body of your essay. Your framework can act as both your outline and your checklist—once you've written the bulk of your essay, quickly scan through to make sure you didn't leave anything out. Finally, close with a recap of your points and get on to the next essay.

Before going on, try writing your own thesis and the rest of this DBQ essay on a separate piece of paper. When you have finished, take a moment to "grade" it using the DBQ rubric, or ask a classmate or parent to evaluate it using the rubric.

HOW LONG SHOULD THIS GO ON?

The AP folks suggest 50 minutes for the DBQ—10 minutes of prereading time and 40 minutes of actual writing time. Remember that the 10 minutes of prereading time is a set thing—you cannot begin writing during that period, and you wouldn't want to anyway. Once the proctor says you can start writing, you may begin writing if you are ready, or simply continue with the six steps if you have not yet finished them. But how long is too long? We recommend you spend no more than 10 additional minutes working through the documents and planning your essay. In other words, you need to begin writing by 10 minutes into the essay-writing part of the test. As we mentioned earlier, you can write a great DBQ essay in 20 to 30 minutes, but you don't want to cut into writing time for the other two essays.

AP essay graders tell us that spending too much time on the DBQ is an obvious problem for many students, who often end up earning only 1 or even 0 points on the other two questions. Blowing off the last two questions will seriously endanger your score! Remember: *all three questions count the same*, so be sure to leave yourself adequate time to get to the other two questions.

PUT IT ALL TOGETHER

Now it's your turn to try out the DBQ process. Below is another sample DBQ. Remember to use all the steps and not to shortchange the prework on the documents. The more comfortable you are with the documents, the easier it will be for you to write this essay. If you wish, you can keep track of your time. **Do not time yourself.** Rather, note your start time, then note how long it took you to analyze the documents. When you are finished with the essay, note the time you finished. This will give you a rough idea of how much time you would like to have for the essay and how much time you need to shave off in practice (remember, the DBQ can take up to 50 minutes—10 minutes for prereading and 40 minutes of the 120 minutes you have for writing).

When you have finished, ask a classmate to score your essay using the scoring rubric at the beginning of this chapter.

Directions: The following question is based on the accompanying Documents 1–6. (The documents have been edited for the purpose of this exercise.) Write your answer on notebook paper.

This question is designed to test your ability to work with and understand historical documents. Write an essay that:

- Has a relevant thesis and supports that thesis with evidence from the documents.
- Uses all of the documents.
- Analyzes the documents by grouping them in as many ways as possible. Does not simply summarize the documents individually.
- Takes into account both the sources of the documents and the authors' points of view.
- Explains the need for at least one additional type of document.

You may refer to relevant historical information not mentioned in the documents.

1. Given the documents below, compare and contrast the preambles of several modern constitutions. What other additional document(s) would help give a fuller picture of how the constitutions of these countries compare to the constitutions of other countries?

Document 1

Source: Preamble to Constitution of Japan, 1946.

We, the Japanese people, acting through our duly elected representatives in the National Diet, determined that we shall secure for ourselves and our posterity the fruits of peaceful cooperation with all nations and the blessings of liberty throughout this land, and resolved that never again shall we be visited with the horrors of war through the action of government, do proclaim that sovereign power resides with the people and do firmly establish this Constitution. Government is a sacred trust of the people, the authority for which is derived from the people, the powers of which are exercised by the representatives of the people, and the benefits of which are enjoyed by the people. This is a universal principle of mankind upon which this Constitution is founded. We reject and revoke all constitutions, laws, ordinances, and rescripts in conflict herewith. We, the Japanese people, desire peace for all time and are deeply conscious of the high ideals controlling human relationship and we have determined to preserve our security and existence, trusting in the justice and faith of the peace-loving peoples of the world. We desire to occupy an honored place in an international society striving for the preservation of peace, and the banishment of tyranny and slavery, oppression and intolerance for all time from the earth. We recognize that all peoples of the world have the right to live in peace, free from fear and want. We believe that no nation is responsible to itself alone, but that laws of political morality are universal; and that obedience to such laws is incumbent upon all nations who would sustain their own sovereignty and justify their sovereign relationship with other nations. We, the Japanese people, pledge our national honor to accomplish these high ideals and purposes with all our resources.

Document 2

Source: Preamble to the Constitution of India, 1949.

We, the people of India, having solemnly resolved to constitute India into a sovereign socialist secular democratic republic and to secure to all its citizens:

JUSTICE, social, economic and political;

LIBERTY of thought, expression, belief, faith and worship;

EQUALITY of status and of opportunity; and to promote among them all FRATERNITY assuring the dignity of the individual and the unity and integrity of the Nation;

In our constituent assembly this twenty-sixth day of November, 1949, do hereby adopt, enact and give to ourselves this constitution.

Document 3

Source: Preamble to the Constitution of the Republic of (West) Germany, 1949.

Conscious of their responsibility before God and men, animated by the purpose to serve world peace as an equal part in a unified Europe, the German People have adopted, by virtue of their constituent power, this Constitution.

The Germans in the States [Länder] of Baden-Wurttemberg, Bavaria, Berlin, Brandenburg, Bremen, Hamburg, Hesse, Lower Saxony, Mecklenburg-Western Pomerania, North Rhine-Westphalia, Rhineland-Palatinate, Saarland, Saxony, Saxony-Anhalt, Schleswig-Holstein and Thuringia have achieved the unity and freedom of Germany in free self-determination. This Constitution is thus valid for the entire German People.

Document 4

Source: Preamble to the Constitution of France, 1958.

The French people hereby solemnly proclaim their dedication to the Rights of Man and the principle of national sovereignty as defined by the Declaration of 1789, reaffirmed and complemented by the Preamble to the 1946 Constitution.

By virtue of these principles and that of the free determination of peoples, the Republic offers to the Overseas Territories that express the will to adhere to them new institutions based on the common ideal of liberty, equality, and fraternity and conceived with a view to their democratic evolution.

Document 5

Source: Preamble to the Constitution of the People's Republic of Vietnam, 1992.

In the course of their millennia-old history, the Vietnamese people, working diligently, creatively, and fighting courageously to build their country and defend it, have forged a tradition of unity, humanity, uprightness, perseverance and indomitableness for their nation and have created Vietnamese civilization and culture.

Document 6

Source: Preamble to the Constitution of the Democratic Republic of the Congo, 1992.

Unity, Work, Progress, Justice, Dignity, Liberty, Peace, Prosperity, and Love for the Fatherland have been since independence, notably under mono-partyism, hypothesized or retarded by totalitarianism, the confusion of authorities, nepotism, ethnocentrism, regionalism, social inequalities, and violations of fundamental rights and liberties. Intolerance and political violence have strongly grieved the country, maintained and accrued the hate and divisions between the different communities that constitute the Congolese Nation.

Chapter 4
How to
Approach
Free-Response
Questions

CHANGE-OVER-TIME AND COMPARATIVE ESSAYS

The other two AP World History Exam essays bear some resemblance to the DBQ and require similar strategies to achieve good scores: a solid thesis, evidence to support all assertions, etc. However, for each of these essays, you must provide the evidence from the resources in your brain on this subject—there are no documents to work from. This can either be a good thing or a bad thing, depending on how well you know the topic. Luckily, most change-over-time questions and comparative questions give you some amount of choice. While you won't be able to pick the topic or period, you will often be asked to choose one or two countries, religions, or cultures, from a set that is provided to you.

The good thing about doing the DBQ first is that your mind is already geared toward supporting your statements with evidence, something you must do to get a good score on these essays. If it is helpful to you, think of the bits of info you know about a topic as your "mini-documents" when organizing your essay. As with the DBQ, you will create a framework in which to place the evidence you will use (i.e., your "documents" or bits of info from your brain). Once you've completed your framework, writing your change-over-time or comparative essay is a lot like writing your DBQ.

Always Have to Be Different

There are some differences, of course, as the name of each question implies. The rest of this chapter will detail the two remaining essay types, provide you with strategies and guidelines for each and, of course, give you some practice. And, if you are feeling a little anxious about getting an essay topic for which you don't know the history, relax. Part II of this book not only reviews the salient points of each period covered on the exam, but also points out important changes and comparisons within each period.

But Before We Get Started...
First, just a reminder about the thesis: As you write your thesis, keep in mind the basic rules of good AP essay theses (if this sounds like Greek to you, make sure you reread Chapter 2, "How To Approach the Essay Questions").

- Give 'Em What They Want
- Show 'Em Where You Got It
- Help 'Em Get There

CHANGE-OVER-TIME (AND CONTINUITY) ESSAY

Change over time is a major theme of historical study. An important aspect of understanding world history is recognizing these changes and understanding what caused them. The concept of change is tested in the multiple-choice questions, but also is the focus of its own essay. However, this essay also expects you to be able to discuss continuities that accompany these changes. Let's take a look at the directions and scoring rubric for this type of essay and prepare an approach.

What the Directions Say

The following is a sample of the directions for the change-over-time essay:

> Directions: You are to answer the following question. You should spend 5 minutes organizing or outlining your essay. Write an essay that:
>
> - Has a relevant thesis and supports that thesis with appropriate historical evidence.
> - Addresses all parts of the question.
> - Uses historical context to show change over time and/or continuities.

Yeah, we see that and/or in the last line, too, but AP essay graders tell us that this is misleading. You MUST include continuities as well as changes over time in this essay to maximize your scoring potential!

What the Directions Mean

Here's what you are supposed to do.

1. Write a thesis that points out the change over time. Support your thesis with historical evidence.
2. Answer all parts of the question.
3. Show the change over time using relevant history.

   Contrast how things turned out with how things were originally, and weigh what changed against what remained the same.

4. Analyze the process of change and/or continuity over time. Explain how and why it happens.

So, to write a decent change-over-time essay you are going to write an essay with a thesis that identifies a change over time for each country or period required, support that thesis by referencing relevant history and contrast that change with a starting point or with something that did not change.

What It Was, What It Is—Not!

It is not enough to simply talk about how it was and then talk about how it is. For example, an essay that says, "Prior to 1948 the Jewish people had no homeland. In 1948, Israel was established" does not delineate the causes or events that led up to the establishment of the nation. To write a successful change-over-time essay, you need to talk about how things were prior to the change, and then make it clear why things changed. "In the early twentieth century, few people saw the need for the establishment of an independent Jewish state. However, once the world saw the massive genocide of Jews that took place during World War II, support for the establishment of Israel began to grow." You MUST cover the historical development!

What If I Don't Know the Subject?

While the change-over-time essay may be a little less daunting than the DBQ, you run the risk of encountering a topic with which you are not that familiar. Luckily, most change-over-time questions give you choices, such as "Select two countries and discuss…" The issues on the change-over-time essay tend to be global ones such as technology, trade, demographic change, or culture, so make sure you are ready to discuss these topics. Part II of this book will highlight important historical changes so you can start filing stuff away in your brain. Learn the content and the changes and you should be well prepared for this essay.

Like the DBQ, the change-over-time essay is scored first for a Basic Core of items. If your essay has all the Basic Core items (i.e., earns all 7 of the Basic Core points), it is then considered for Expanded Core items.

Basic Core Rubric for the Change-Over-Time Essay

Basic Core	Point(s) Possible
Is your thesis acceptable? (Did it address the global issues and the correct time period(s)?)	1
Have you addressed all parts of the question, even if you have not done so completely or in a balanced fashion?	2
Have you addressed most parts of the question? For example, you may not have addressed continuity.	(1)
Have you substantiated the thesis with appropriate historical evidence?	2
Have you done so partially?	(1)
Have you made effective use of historical context to show the change over time?	1
Have you analyzed the process of change over time and/or continuity?	1
SUBTOTAL	7

Notice that you can receive partial credit—1 point instead of 2 points—for some of the items. The other two points come from Expanded Core items. Once again, let's connect the Basic Core items to what you are supposed to write.

Change-Over-Time Essay

What to Do	Basic Core Requirements	Point(s) Possible
Write a thesis that addresses the global issues in the question and covers the correct time period(s).	Is your thesis acceptable?	1
Address all parts of the question. (Both change and continuity)	Have you addressed all parts of the question, even if you have not done so completely or in a balanced fashion? Have you addressed most parts of the question? For example, you may not have addressed continuity.	2 (1)
Support your thesis with appropriate historical evidence.	Have you substantiated the thesis with appropriate historical evidence? Have you done so partially?	2 (1)
Show the change over time using relevant history. Include the characteristics of historical periods to explain the context of change.	Have you made effective use of historical context to show the change over time?	1
Analyze the process of change and continuity. Describe what changed and how it changed, not just what the results of change were.	Have you analyzed the process of change over time and/or continuity?	1

How do you get a 9 on the change-over-time essay? If you earn all 7 Basic Core points, the person scoring your essay will then look for Expanded Core items in your essay. The more Expanded Core items you add, the more likely you will receive an 8 or 9 on your essay.

Expanded Core Rubric for the Change-Over-Time Essay

Expanded Core Requirements	Points
Do you have a comprehensive, analytical, and explicit thesis? Have you analyzed all parts of the issue (e.g., time, continuity and change, causes and effects, and a global scope)? Have you given ample historical evidence to prove your thesis? Have you provided connections to ideas, events, and other issues in some imaginative way?	0–2
SUBTOTAL	2

Once again, some of the items in the Expanded Core are a more detailed version of the Basic Core items. To get an 8 or 9 on your essay, concentrate on doing a great job with at least three of the elements that are in both the Basic Core and the Expanded Core.

Putting Pen to Paper

Before you begin, you need to plan your essay. Because you don't have to analyze documents, you won't need as much planning time. Use the following steps to organize your essay.

Step 1: Process the Question

Once again, before you can write the essay, you need to be sure you are clear on exactly what you are expected to do. Notice that the Basic Core places a heavy emphasis on answering all parts of the question. To make sure you don't miss any part of the question, circle each key phrase as you process the question. Take a look at the following example:

2. Choose ONE of the following political units (countries, empires, etc.) and discuss how technological developments from 1450 to 1750 changed its global influence. Be sure to describe its position of power and influence in the beginning of the period as your starting point.

    England   Russia
    Portugal   Ottoman Empire
    Spain   China
    Germany   France

What key phrases did you circle? Your list should include one of the above countries plus the phrases technological developments from 1450 to 1750, global influence, and position of power and influence in the beginning of the period as your starting point. What are you being asked to do? Choose one of the countries or empires listed, and discuss its role as a global player in the early 1400s or so (before some technological impact). Then walk through the technology or technologies that had an impact on the country, and describe the impact—what changes occurred as a result.

Step 2: Build a Framework

Once you have pulled apart the question, build a framework. The purpose of this framework is not only to provide you with an outline for your essay, but also to ensure that you don't miss any part of the question.

To build your change-over-time framework, begin by choosing the number of countries as instructed. The above example asks you to choose one country. Once you have made your choices, create a chart like the one on the following page.

	Country 1
Baseline: What was its role in the world in 1400s/pre-technology?	
Impact: What technologies had an impact on it? Why and in what way?	
Change: What changes occurred to its role in the world as a result of the technology?	
Continuity: What remained the same despite technological innovations?	

If you had been asked to select two countries, you would create a chart that had a column for each country.

Step 3: Build Your Essay

After you've created your framework, fill it in to build your essay. Be sure to fill in not only the information about each segment, but also the evidence (bits of info stored in your brain) to support each answer. For example, if you chose to discuss the impact of navigational technology on Portugal and what remained the same despite that technology, you might fill in your chart like this:

	Portugal
Baseline: What was its role in the world in 1400s/pre-technology?	
Impact: What technologies had an impact on it? Why and in what way?	*Navigational tools allowed for long sea journeys. For example, magnetic compass & astrolabe.* *These tools allowed Portugal to navigate and explore first the Indian Ocean and later the Atlantic.*
Change: What changes occurred to its role in the world as a result of the technology?	
Continuity: What remained the same despite technological innovations?	*Portugal, a small country, was over-shadowed by its aggressive neighbor Spain, which also ventured far and wide but had more resources. Nautical technology didn't help in land wars, or to protect borders.*

Completing your framework with both what changed and supporting evidence will help you create most of your essay. Here is the chart again. Choose the country or empire you would like to write about for this question and complete the chart below.

	Country:
Baseline: What was its role in the world in 1400s/pre-technology?	
Impact: What technologies had an impact on it? Why and in what way?	
Change: What changes occurred to its role in the world as a result of the technology?	*diminished influence and power*
Continuity: What stayed the same despite technological innovations?	

Step 4: Write It

Once you've filled in your framework, it's time to start writing. As with the DBQ, your thesis is critical and must be supported by facts. First, Give 'Em What They Want—answer the question by including key phrases from the question. Next, Show 'Em Where You Got It by supporting each of your assertions with some introductory evidence (save the details for the body of the essay). Finally, Help 'Em Get There by transitioning the readers from the thesis to the body of the essay with a phrase like, "To better understand the changes that occurred during this time…" Here's an example of how your thesis for this essay might read.

> *Technological advances in the period from 1450 to 1750 had a major influence on Portugal's position in the global sphere. The development of nautical technologies rapidly made Portugal a world leader in exploration because the country was strategically placed near the coast of Africa, had long-standing trade relations with Muslim nations, and was home to Prince Henry the Navigator (son of Portugal's John I), who sponsored and helped train Portugal's explorers in the most up-to-date navigation technologies and techniques. The development of lanteen sails, which allowed ships to travel in any direction regardless of the wind direction, and three-masted caravels, which were larger ships that were not only capable of holding huge sails but also had lots of storage space to hold provisions for long journeys, suddenly made travel across the oceans feasible. In addition, the inventions of the astrolabe and magnetic compass, both of which were used to help sailors find their way, significantly increased the ability of these ships to reach*

their final destinations. The results were huge. Portugal suddenly became a global power. It established colonies in the New World and increased trade with Asia over sea routes. As a result, Portugal spread its language, religion, and culture to other parts of the world, changing the cultural landscape so profoundly that we still live with the consequences. To better understand the changes in Portugal's global position that took as a result of these technological developments, one must first understand Portugal's role in the global sphere prior to the Age of Exploration.

As you continue your essay, make sure that you address each portion of the question and that you support your claims with evidence. A good model to follow: after your introductory paragraph, each paragraph should address one change or continuity with specific evidence. In this case, a straightforward narrative of Portugal's history won't be enough to answer the question successfully. AP essay readers tell us that they often have to really search for what the changes and continuities are—and they often don't find them. Be sure to spell it out for the grader, the sooner they find your examples, the sooner they give you points.

Before going on, try writing your own thesis for the above example, then continue on into at least the first two paragraphs, one that discusses a change, and one that explains continuity. Use the following space for your work:

_____

_____

_____

_____

_____

_____

_____

_____

_____

_____

_____

_____

_____

_____

_____

_____

_____

_____

_____

It's a Matter of Time

For both the change-over-time essay and the comparative essay, the AP folks suggest 40 minutes—5 minutes of planning and 35 minutes of writing. We recommend from 5 to 8 minutes of planning, again because a well-planned essay is easier and faster to write. You do need to be careful here, however. If you run out of time on your last essay and fail to include some core stuff, that can definitely hurt your essay score.

Use the practice essays at the end of this chapter plus the practice tests in Part III to determine how long you ideally would have to write each essay, then shave off time through practice. Truthfully, a well-planned change-over-time or comparative essay can be written in 20 minutes, leaving you a few minutes to go back and reread what you wrote.

COMPARATIVE ESSAY

Two down, one to go. By the time you get to the comparative essay, you will have been testing for more than two hours and writing for more than an hour. Because you will want your mind to be on autopilot at this point in the test, you need to make sure you are totally comfortable with this final type of essay.

AP essay readers tell us that, even though this essay is perhaps the easiest, it is also the one that students often score the lowest on. This may be the result of fatigue, but may also be the result of poor time management. Don't let this happen to you! Leave yourself time to do your best on this essay, and try to focus; this is your last task!

Making comparisons is a huge part of understanding world history. It comes up in the multiple-choice questions as well as the DBQ and change-over-time essays. To help you out with this aspect of the test, Part II of this book highlights some of the more critical subjects for comparison throughout the six periods of world history.

I'd Rather Compare than Change
By the way, you do not need to write AP World History Exam essays in the order in which they appear. You are given two hours to write the three essays (plus the initial ten-minute reading period for the DBQ documents). You can write the essays in any order you want. You can also spend as much time on one essay as you want; however, the more time you devote to one essay means proportionately less time for the other two. We strongly recommend you do the DBQ first because you will have processed the documents during the prereading period. However, if you read the change-over-time essay and feel uncomfortable with the topic, or if you just prefer to write comparative essays, feel free to do the comparative essay before the change-over-time essay.

The comparative essay typically involves how two societies responded to a major theme or event. (Remember that comparing means finding similarities and dissimilarities!) Remember how we mentioned at the beginning of the book to be on the lookout for certain big-picture ideas or themes as you review your history? This is where that information will be most helpful. The major themes tested on the AP World History Exam comparative essay include the following:

- How different societies responded to events, to each other, or to other societies
- How different societies changed—or didn't—in response to an event
- How different societies developed
- How different societies responded to new technologies or new ideas

The directions and scoring rubrics for the comparative essay are very similar to those for the change-over-time essay. Therefore, the steps to writing the comparative essay will also be similar to the change-over-time essay.

Here are the directions.

Directions: You are to answer the following question. You should spend 5 minutes organizing or outlining your essay. Write an essay that:

- Has a relevant thesis and supports that thesis with appropriate historical evidence
- Addresses all parts of the question
- Makes direct, relevant comparisons

What the Directions Mean
Here's what you are supposed to do.

1. Write a thesis that makes your major points of comparison.

   Support your thesis with historical evidence.

2. Answer all parts of the question.

3. Make at least two direct, relevant comparisons of the given societies.

   Include both similarities and differences. (You lose a core point if you don't.)

4. Analyze relevant reasons for those similarities and/or differences. Explain why these societies are similar or different.

To write a good comparative essay, you will need to write an essay with a thesis, support that thesis by referencing relevant history (sound familiar so far?), and compare and contrast as the question indicates, making sure you include not only similarities but also differences.

Basic Core Rubric for the Comparative Essay

Basic Core	Point(s) Possible
Is your thesis acceptable? (Do you compare the issues or themes specified?)	1
Have you addressed all parts of the question, even if you have not done so completely or in a balanced fashion?	2
Have you addressed most parts of the question? (For example, do you address similarities but not differences?)	(1)
Have you substantiated the thesis with appropriate historical evidence?	2
Have you done so partially?	(1)

Have you shown at least one or two relevant, direct comparisons between or among the societies?		1
Have you identified at least one reason for a similarity or difference identified in a direct comparison?		1
SUBTOTAL		7

Again the Basic Core for the comparative essay is worth 7 points (you can get partial credit for some items). The other 2 points come from Expanded Core items. Once again let's connect the Basic Core items to what you are supposed to write.

Comparative Essay

What To Do	Basic Core Points for Doing It	Point(s) Possible
Write a thesis that clearly states your claim. Why do you believe this claim is true?	Is your thesis acceptable? Do you compare the issues or themes specified?	1
Address all parts of the question.	Have you addressed all parts of the question, even if you have not done so completely or in a balanced fashion?	2
	Have you addressed most parts of the question? For example, do you address similarities but not differences?	(1)
Support your thesis with appropriate historical evidence.	Have you substantiated the thesis with appropriate historical evidence?	2
	Have you done so partially?	(1)
Make at least two direct, relevant comparisons.	Have you shown at least one or two relevant, direct comparisons between or among the societies?	1
Include a similarity or difference in your comparison(s).	Have you shown at least one reason for a similarity or difference identified in direct comparison?	1
SUBTOTAL		7

To get an 8 or 9 on the comparative essay, you need to focus on expanding three areas of your essay that are covered in both the Basic Core and the Expanded Core. Here is the Expanded Core for the comparative essay.

Expanded Core Rubric for the Comparative Essay

Expanded Core	Point(s) Possible
Do you have a comprehensive, analytical, and explicit thesis? Have you analyzed all relevant parts of the issue (e.g., chronology, themes, connections, interactions, continuity and change, cause and effect?) Have you given ample historical evidence to prove your thesis? Have you related your comparisons to a larger global context? Have you made direct comparisons (and/or contrasts) between and among societies? Have you consistently analyzed the causes of the similarities and/or differences? Have you addressed all parts (similarities and differences, both regions) of the question evenly?	0–2
TOTAL	2

Writing Your Comparative Essay

Use the same steps to plan the comparative essay as you used to plan the change-over-time essay. Take about five minutes to plan your essay before you begin writing.

Step 1: Process the Question

Circle the key phrases in the following example:

3. Western incursion was a common theme in the years from 1750–1914. Different societies responded to the outside forces in a variety of ways. Compare and contrast the responses between TWO of the following societies. Be sure to address the reaction of the native populations.

    China
    India
    Latin America
    Africa

Does your circled list include Western incursion, from 1750–1914, compare and contrast the responses, and reaction of the native population? Remember also to circle the two societies on the list that you want to focus on! What are you being asked to do? Compare and contrast the reactions of two societies to the invasion of Western culture and ideology. To do this, you will need to note what each society was like before Western influences were felt and how each reacted to the imposed changes.

Step 2: Build a Framework

Build a framework similar to the one you used for the change-over-time essay.

	Society 1	Society 2
Element of Western incursion and each society's response:		
Similarities:		
Differences:		

Step 3: Build Your Essay

After you've created your framework, fill it in to build the essay. Be sure to enter both the information about each segment and the evidence to support each answer.

Using the above example, select two societies and complete the chart below.

Element of Western incursion and each society's response:		
Similarities:		
Differences:		

Step 4: Write It

Once you've filled in your framework, it's time to start writing. As you write your thesis, remember to Give 'Em What They Want, Show 'Em Where You Got It, and Help 'Em Get There. Write an analytical thesis for the sample question in the space provided. Be sure to include both the focus of your essay and WHY you believe your claim is true.

_____

_____

_____

_____

_____

_____

_____

_____

_____

_____

How did you do? Did you Give 'Em What They Want? Do your opening sentences read something like the following?

> *Western imperialism in both China and Latin America brought about different responses, in part because the nature of the imperialism was very different in each place. While both regions experienced aggressive European influences, in Latin America the size of the native population had already been dramatically reduced by genocide and disease and was then replaced by European immigrants and African slaves. In other words, Europe established colonies and replaced existing cultures with their own. In China, on the other hand, the native population was subjected to European spheres of influence—far more economic than cultural—but the underlying culture remained largely intact. The Europeans established their spheres of influence "on top of" existing Chinese culture, as opposed to "instead of." This difference between the underlying nature of imperialism in Latin America and China had a profound influence in the way each region eventually responded to Western imperialism.*

Going on…

> *In Latin America the successful independence movements were initiated by the descendents of European colonists, and, in the case of Haiti, a freed slave. Therefore, the independence movements were similar to the American Revolution in that they were motivated more by who would control the region (Europe or locals) rather than which culture would dominate. Even after Latin American countries won their independence, the original native population remained subservient to the descendents of Europeans. Spanish and Portuguese remained the official languages. Catholicism remained the dominant religion.*

> *In China, the reaction against European spheres of influence was far more cultural in nature. The native Chinese were trying to remove European influence, not just European control…*

Take some time now to finish writing your essay on a separate sheet of paper. Once you have written your own, ask a classmate or teacher to critique your work.

PUTTING IT ALL TOGETHER

Now that you know how to write each of these essays, it's time to practice. Here are a few more essays for you to practice your AP essay writing skills. If you can, team up with another student in your AP class and take turns grading each other's essays using the scoring rubric.

Example 1

Directions: You are to answer the following question. You should spend 5 minutes organizing or outlining your essay. Write an essay that:

- Has a relevant thesis and supports that thesis with appropriate historical evidence.
- Addresses all parts of the question.
- Uses historical context to show change over time and/or continuities.

2. Analyze the political, social, and economic impact of ONE of the following belief systems on China from about 500 b.c.e. to about 1000 c.e.. In your analysis, be sure to discuss the reasons for continuities as well as changes.

> Confucianism
> Legalism
> Daoism
> Buddhism

Example 2

Directions: You are to answer the following question. You should spend 5 minutes organizing or outlining your essay. Write an essay that:

- Has a relevant thesis and supports that thesis with appropriate historical evidence.
- Addresses all parts of the question.
- Makes direct, relevant comparisons.

3. Compare and contrast the impact of exploration and colonization on Africa and the Americas.

Chapter 5
Using Time
Effectively
to Maximize
Points

Very few students stop to think about how to improve their test-taking skills. Most assume that if they study hard, they will test well, and if they do not study, they will do poorly. Most students continue to believe this even after experience teaches them otherwise. Have you ever studied really hard for an exam, then blown it on test day? Have you ever aced an exam for which you thought you weren't well prepared? Most students have had one, if not both, of these experiences. The lesson should be clear: Factors other than your level of preparation influence your final test score. This chapter will provide you with some insights that will help you perform better on the AP World History Exam and on other exams as well.

PACING AND TIMING

A big part of scoring well on an exam is working at a consistent pace. The worst mistake made by inexperienced or unsavvy test takers is that they come to a question that stumps them, and, rather than just skip it, they panic and stall. Time stands still when you're working on a question you cannot answer, and it is not unusual for students to waste five minutes on a single question (especially a question involving a graph or the word *except*) because they are too stubborn to cut their losses. It is important to be aware of how much time you have spent on a given question and on the section you are working. There are several ways to improving your pacing and timing for the test:

- Know your average pace. While you prepare for your test, try to gauge how long you take on 5, 10, or 20 questions. Knowing how long you spend on average per question will help you identify how many questions you can answer effectively and how best to pace yourself for the test.

- Have a watch or clock nearby. You are permitted to have a watch or clock nearby to help you keep track of time. It is important to remember however that constantly checking the clock is in itself a waste of time and can be distracting. Devise a plan. Try checking the clock after every 15 or 30 questions to see if you are keeping the correct pace or whether you need to speed up, this will ensure that your cognizant of the time but will not permit you to fall into the trap of dwelling on it.

- Know when to move on. Since all questions are scored equally, investing appreciable amounts of time on a single question is inefficient and can potentially deprive you of the chance to answer easier questions later on. If you are able to eliminate answer choices do so, but don't worry about picking a random answer and moving on if you cannot find the correct answer. Remember, tests are like marathons; you do best when you work through them at a steady pace. You can always come back to a question you don't know. When you do, very often you will find that your previous mental block is gone, and you will wonder why the question perplexed you the first time around (as you

• Consistent Pace

gleefully move on to the next question). Even if you still don't know the answer, you will not have wasted valuable time you could have spent on easier questions.

- <u>Be selective.</u> You don't have to do any of the questions in a given section in order. If you are stumped by an essay or multiple-choice question, skip it or choose a different one. In the section below, you will see that you may not have to answer every question correctly to achieve your desired score. Select the questions or essays that you can answer and work on them first. This will make you more efficient and give you the greatest chance of getting the most questions correct.

- Use process of elimination on multiple-choice questions. Many times, one or more answer choices can be eliminated. Every answer choice that can be eliminated increases the odds that you will answer the question correctly. The section on multiple-choice questions will go through strategies to find these incorrect answer choices and increase your odds of getting the question correct.

Remember, when all the questions on a test are of equal value, no one question is that important, your overall goal for pacing is to get the most questions correct. Finally, you should set a realistic goal for your final score. In the next section, we will break down how to achieve your desired score and ways of pacing yourself to do so.

GETTING THE SCORE YOU WANT

Depending on the score you need, it may be in your best interest not to try to work through every question. Check with the schools to which you are applying.

Beginning with the May 2011 exam, AP exams in all subjects no longer include a "guessing penalty" of a quarter of a point for every incorrect answer. Instead, students are assessed only on the total number of correct answers. A lot of AP materials, even those you receive in your AP class, may not include this information. It is really important to remember that if you are running out of time, you should fill in all the bubbles before the time for the multiple-choice section is up. Even if you don't plan to spend a lot of time on every question and even if you have no idea what the correct answer is, you need to fill something in.

TEST ANXIETY

Everybody experiences anxiety before and during an exam. To a certain extent, test anxiety can be helpful. Some people find that they perform more quickly and efficiently under stress. If you have ever pulled an all-nighter to write a paper and ended up doing good work, you know the feeling.

However, too much stress is definitely a bad thing. Hyperventilating during the test, for example, almost always leads to a lower score. If you find that you stress out during exams, here are a few preemptive actions you can take.

- Take a reality check. Evaluate your situation before the test begins. If you have studied hard, remind yourself that you are well prepared. Remember that many others taking the test are not as well prepared, and (in your classes, at least) you are being graded against them, so you have an advantage. If you didn't study, accept the fact that you will probably not ace the test. Make sure you get to every question you know something about. Don't stress out or fixate on how much you don't know. Your job is to score as high as you can by maximizing the benefits of what you do know. In either scenario, it is best to think of a test as if it were a game. How can you get the most points in the time allotted to you? Always answer questions you can answer easily and quickly before you answer those that will take more time.

- Try to relax. Slow, deep breathing works for almost everyone. Close your eyes, take a few, slow, deep breaths, and concentrate on nothing but your inhalation and exhalation for a few seconds. This is a basic form of meditation, and it should help you to clear your mind of stress and, as a result, concentrate better on the test. If you have ever taken yoga classes, you probably know some other good relaxation techniques. Use them when you can (obviously, anything that requires leaving your seat and, say, assuming a handstand position won't be allowed by any but the most free-spirited proctors).

- Eliminate as many surprises as you can. Make sure you know where the test will be given, when it starts, what type of questions are going to be asked, and how long the test will take. You don't want to be worrying about any of these things on test day or, even worse, after the test has already begun.

The best way to avoid stress is to study both the test material and the test itself. Congratulations! By buying or reading this book, you are taking a major step toward a stress-free AP World History Exam.

Part IV
Content Review for the AP World History Exam

HOW TO USE THIS BOOK TO TAKE ON THE WORLD

Now that you know the kinds of questions to expect on the AP World History Exam, you're ready to take on the world!—or at least the review of AP World History. Part IV of this book is designed to maximize your AP World History review. Here's how it is organized:

- Six Periods, Five Chapters. The AP World History Exam divides world history into six distinct time periods, as we discussed in Chapter 1. However, we've decided to combine Periods 1 and 2, which cover the years 8000 B.C.E.–600 B.C.E. and 600 B.C.E.–600 C.E. respectively, into one chapter—Ancient Stuff (8000 b.c.e.–600 C.E.)—for ease of reviewing. Together these periods make up about 20% of the questions that will appear on the AP World History Exam. The other four chapters are Really Old Stuff (600–1450), Old Stuff (1450–1750), Not So Old Stuff (1750–1914), and Recent Stuff (1914–present).

- Get the Big Picture. Each chapter begins with a "Stay Focused on the Big Picture" section so that you will—you guessed it—stay focused on the big picture while you review. To do well on this test, you're going to need to demonstrate that you not only have specific knowledge of people and events (what the multiple-choice questions are all about), but also be able to connect them together and know how to think about concepts with a wide-angle lens (that's what the essays are all about).

- Make Those Connections. Each chapter reviews the salient points of that period; the Compare Them, Contrast Them, Note the Change, and Focus On boxes help you make connections between different societies (that's the whole point of this test, remember?).

- Pull It All Together. Each chapter ends with a "Pulling It All Together" section to once again help you focus on the major points of the period.

KNOW WHERE YOU ARE IN THE WORLD

The AP exam—particularly in the essays—frequently refers to cultural regions of the world. So it is important to know where you are! The map shows you the most commonly defined regions. Be aware that they don't always match up with physical boundaries. For example, parts of North Africa may be included when we're talking about the Middle East, and sub-Saharan Africa and Southeast Asia may be considered part of the Islamic world.

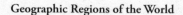

Geographic Regions of the World

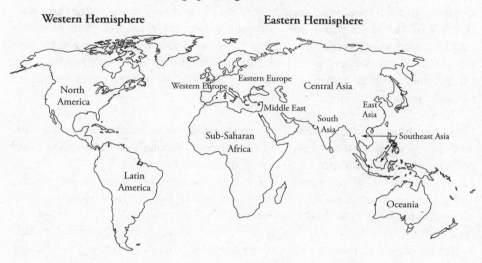

HOW TO GET THE MOST OUT OF YOUR REVIEW

Here's what we suggest. Read through each chapter once. You'll probably remember most of the people, places, events, and concepts from your AP class. The chapters will help you review and pull together the major points. This part won't be as detailed as the book from your AP class, or else this book would be as thick as your textbook, which would be kind of pointless. As you read through each chapter, consult your textbook if you've forgotten something entirely. After you finish going through a chapter once, spend some time in your AP textbook (or another world history source) going over the stuff you either didn't know or didn't remember. Then go back to the chapter to do mini-reviews of certain areas and to focus on the big-picture concepts and connections taking place in that period.

No, After You

It does not matter in which order you choose to review the material. If you love the Renaissance and hate the Middle Ages, review Old Stuff first and Really Old Stuff later. If you know that your knowledge of the Foundations era is lacking but you are pretty confident in what you know about recent history, dive into Ancient Stuff first. This review is meant to be dynamic—we expect that you will return to it repeatedly as you prepare for your exam.

In addition, as we mentioned in the introduction to this book, you may wish to flip back and forth between your history review and your testing strategies practice. We would advise you to work through at least the multiple-choice section of Part I before you get to the test, but it is really up to you. If you want to get a jump start on your history review and save the techniques for later, go ahead. On the other hand, you may wish to mix them up and see how our strategies are helping you gain points.

No matter how you decide to organize your review, we do suggest that you continue to practice your test strategies and essay writing throughout the course of your preparation. As we said before, knowing this history is not enough—you need to be able to show what you know on test day. Once you review a chapter, practice writing an essay based on one of the comparisons or significant changes that took place within the period. Make up multiple-choice questions for a classmate and quiz each other. Once you've done your first pass through the history, take a full-length diagnostic test so that you can get a feel for what the real thing will be like. The bottom line is: Do not leave all your test strategy practice to the last minute. Instead, use that practice to enhance your history review and zero in on the key concepts of each period.

'Nuff said. Let the review begin…

Chapter 6
Ancient Stuff: Around 8000 B.C.E. to Around 600 C.E.

I. CHAPTER OVERVIEW

There's a lot of stuff in this chapter—nine thousand years' worth. So before you begin, read through the outline below so you'll know where to find what you're looking for when you return to this chapter for a mini-review. (Remember, the key to doing well is to go through the chapter once, delve into the areas you are clueless or semi-clueless about, then return here for a mini-review.)

I. Chapter Overview

   You're reading it!

II. Stay Focused on the Big Picture

   Organize the zillions of facts from the 9,000 years covered in this chapter into some big-picture concepts.

III. History Review through 600 C.E.

This is the bulk of the chapter, where we plow through the major civilizations, people, and events. Again, we suggest that if you're totally clueless on a section, review the corresponding section in your textbook. Here's a list of the major sections.

 A. Nomads: Follow the Food
 B. Settling Down: The Neolithic Revolution
 C. The Big, Early Civilizations: Rivers Deliver
 D. Early Mesoamerica and Andean South America: For Every Rule There's an Exception
 E. The Classical Civilizations: Mesoamerica
 F. The Classical Civilizations: India and China
 G. The Classical Civilizations: Mediterranean
 H. The Late Classical Period: Empires Collapse and People on the Move

IV. Major Belief Systems through 600 C.E.

Although we'll make reference to the major belief systems within the history review, we've provided this separate section so that they're all grouped together in one place and you can refer to them easily. Major belief systems had a huge impact on the development of civilizations, so they're important to review in detail. Also keep in mind that you'll need to know the background of the major belief systems as you review the material in later chapters.

V. Technology and Innovations through 600 C.E.

   Farming tools, metallurgy, and ability to manipulate the environment move humans from nomadic hunters and gatherers to builders of civilizations and empires

VI.   Changes and Continuities in the Role of Women

Women lose power as humans start to settle down. A comparative look at trends in different regions of the world.

VII.   Pulling It All Together

A quick review of the review that focuses on themes and trends

VIII.   Timeline of Major Developments 8000 B.C.E. to 600 C.E., organized by time and place

II. STAY FOCUSED ON THE BIG PICTURE

As you review the details of the ancient civilizations in this chapter, stay focused on some big-picture concepts, including the following:

1.   What are civilizations all about? Think about what makes a civilization a civilization in the first place. As you read through this chapter, we'll give you some ideas. Focus on things like the existence and development of cities, formal institutions (including political, economic, and religious), different social levels and occupations, the use of technology (we're not talking the Internet here, but basic and hugely important things such as wheels and weapons), the arts, and methods of communication and transportation.

2.   How does change occur within a society? When change occurs, think about what caused it. Sometimes a society changed because it was exposed to a different way of doing things when it interacted with another culture (an effect that is sometimes called cultural diffusion). Other times a society changed because its members invented something new, or realized how to use something in a new way. Always pay attention to why things changed in a particular society or civilization.

3.   How are people impacted by, and how do they impact, geography and climate? Focus on the interaction between people and nature. We'll draw your attention to this issue constantly in this chapter. Geography and climate help to explain where people live and build cities, why people suddenly move from one place to another, and how early civilizations chose to defend themselves against attack. They also greatly influenced which civilizations interacted with, or were isolated from, other civilizations. But people also use technology to impact their surroundings. Civilizations change the landscape by diverting water, moving natural resources, and building transportation networks. Nature impacts people; people impact nature. It's a great, big complicated cycle…that's why the AP people love to talk about it so much.

III. HISTORY REVIEW THROUGH 600 C.E.

Historians, including the AP course, use periods of time to organize history. Be aware that not everything will fit neatly into a predetermined period, but we'll try to group events.

The first period we will look at is defined by the fact that everything that happened in these 10,000 years sets the stage or provides the foundation for what happens later. This period is marked by some major changes: Figuring out farming and what happens when there actually is enough to eat, developing technologies and ideas to support cities (and to take over other civilizations), the rise of most major world religions, and finally, the collapse of the classical empires. Not bad for one chapter, huh?

A. Nomads: Follow the Food

Imagine early people. Really early people. They hadn't yet built cities. They didn't know how to farm. Their sole focus in life was to satisfy their most basic needs: shelter and food. Because they didn't have any advanced tools and hadn't yet developed anything as sophisticated as farming, the best way for them to get shelter was to find it, and the best way to get food was to follow it.

You won't be asked a lot of questions about nomadic societies. However, you do need to understand why the development of more stable civilizations (which you will be asked a lot of questions about) was so significant, and the best way to do that is to learn what came before them. As you review world history before the Neolithic Revolution, focus on only the major developments. During this time period, those include the development of spoken language, the ability to control and use fire, and the ability to make simple tools out of stone.

Foraging Societies: Hunt and Gather

Foraging societies (hunter-gatherer clans) were composed of small groups of people who traveled from point to point as the climate and availability of plants and animals dictated. Because they depended on nature for sustenance, they were also at the mercy of nature. Climate changes, disease, famine, and natural disasters could endanger or eliminate entire communities. Even when times were good, foraging societies were limited by the capacity of their surroundings, and by their inability to store food long-term. Members of these societies did not build permanent shelters and had only a few personal belongings. Think about how much you can carry in your backpack: That will give you an idea how many possessions they had.

Pastoral Societies: Taming the Animals

Pastoral societies were characterized by the domestication of animals. These societies were often found in mountainous regions and in areas with insufficient rainfall to support other forms of settlement. Many of these societies used small-scale agriculture to supplement the main food supply of animal products (usually milk or eggs, which were much easier to produce and store than meat). The extended family was a major institution. Women had very few rights; however, these societies were more egalitarian than those that came later. Stratification and social status, which were limited in foraging societies, were based on the size of one's herd in pastoral societies. But as in foraging societies, people in pastoral societies had few personal possessions. Even though they had domesticated animals (as opposed to having to hunt for animals), they didn't settle down in towns because they had to continually search for new grazing areas and water for the herds.

As pastoral societies increasingly domesticated more and more animals, they also began to experiment with securing a more dependable food supply through the cultivation of plants. This was a revolutionary development that led to…

B. Settling Down: The Neolithic Revolution

Agricultural Societies: This Is My Land

In a span of several thousand years from approximately 8000 B.C.E. to 3000 B.C.E., groups of people moved from nomadic lifestyles to agricultural lifestyles and town and city life. This transition period is often called the **Neolithic** ("New Stone") **Revolution** or the **Agricultural Revolution**. Keep in mind that we still aren't talking about full-blown civilizations. People still lived in relatively small, independent groups or communities. To be sure, the towns and cities that they built were bigger than anything else that came before them, but civilizations on a grand scale didn't get rolling until around 3000 B.C.E., give or take a few centuries, depending on the region of the world.

Here's how it worked: When people figured out how to cultivate plants, they could stay in the same place, as long as there was good soil and a stable source of water. Because they also knew how to domesticate animals and use simple tools, they could rely on a relatively varied and constant supply of food, and this encouraged them to stay in the same place for longer periods of time.

Staying in the same place changed things dramatically, because people in a community stayed within close proximity of each other, which added to their sense of unity and helped them build and sustain cultural traditions. What's more, unlike nomadic societies, agricultural communities were not just collections of people, but people tied to a particular piece of land. In other words, they began to think of property in terms of ownership.

Contrast Them: Nomadic versus Agricultural Societies

The difference between nomadic and agricultural societies is about more than just moving around versus staying put. It also involves emotional and psychological issues. Think about it this way: When you and everybody else is on the move a lot, the land more or less belongs to everybody. But when people stay in the same place for generations, they begin to think of the particular piece of land that they live on as home—*their* home. If someone else comes along and drinks from their river or builds a house on *their* hill, they might begin to think of the newcomers as intruders or invaders, not as neighbors. Once nomads started interacting with sedentary societies through trade or conflicts, things started to get complicated.

Important Consequence of Agriculture: A Food Surplus

Imagine two people who only grow enough food for themselves. They both have to farm all day every day. There's little time left to do anything else. Now imagine that one person farms enough food for two people. The second person can do something else, say, make tools or dig an irrigation ditch or study to become a philosopher or religious leader. Now imagine that one person can farm enough food for five people, or ten people, or a hundred people. Now the other ninety-nine people can build towns, organize armies, develop a system of writing, create art, experiment, and discover new technologies. In other words, individual labor becomes specialized. Each person can get really good at doing a particular task because he or she no longer has to worry about where the next meal is coming from.

As agricultural societies became more complex, organized economies, governmental structures, and religious organizations began to emerge to keep things as predictable and orderly as possible. Suddenly, there was society, or the beginnings of what we'd call a civilization.

With the invention of irrigation techniques, lands that previously couldn't be farmed could be used for additional surpluses. This would lead to more growth and complexity, which would lead to more agricultural advancements, which would lead to more growth and complexity, and so on.

Focus On: What Contributes to the Development of a Civilization? As described above, specialization of labor is key. If everyone has to farm to have enough food, a great civilization won't develop. If a certain number of farmers can provide a surplus of food, then other people in the community are free to build, invent, and create tools, art, and institutions.

Impact of Agriculture on the Environment

There's no question that the Agricultural Revolution had an impact on the environment. Farming villages began to dramatically change the lay of the land by diverting water, clearing land for farming, and creating farmland where none previously existed. As villages grew into more permanent towns and cities, roads were built to link them, further altering the landscape. Stones were unearthed and cut to build increasingly large buildings and monuments. All of this activity led to a world in which land and resources were continually being reconfigured to fit the needs of growing, geographically stable populations.

What's more, the impact on the animal kingdom was equally momentous. With the development of large-scale agriculture, animals began to be used not only as a source of food and clothing, but also as a direct source of agricultural labor. For example, oxen were used to pull plows on ever-expanding farmland. This enabled farmers to increase the size of their fields dramatically because they no longer had to turn the soil by hand.

Technology: Metal Workers Deserve Medals

If there had been a stock market for new technologies in the Neolithic Era, it would have attracted many investors. During this period, hard stones such as granite were sharpened and formed into farming tools such as hoes and plows. Pottery was made to use for cooking. Weaving was invented to shape baskets and nets; more complex and comfortable clothing was designed. Eventually, wheels were invented for use on carts, and sails for use on boats. The list goes on and on.

But perhaps one of the most significant advances of the Neolithic Era was the knowledge of how to use metals. This greatly advanced the development of not only tools, but also weapons. When people figured out how to combine copper with tin to create an even harder metal, bronze, the building of civilizations was well on its way. This development was so significant that some people call the latter part of the Neolithic Era the Bronze Age. Bronze was superseded by the discovery of iron, but more on that later.

C. The Big, Early Civilizations: The Rivers Deliver

Most of the world's early great civilizations were located in river valleys. Think about it. Rivers provided a regular supply of water, which is, of course, necessary for survival. Also important is that the lowlands around rivers tend to be covered with soil that is loaded with nutrients, which are deposited when the river recedes after floods to nourish the soil. The river itself may be home to animals and plants could also provide food for people. Rivers were also a vital means of transportation.

When we talk about civilizations, we're talking about large areas of land with large populations and distinct, organized cultures, as opposed to the smaller farming communities that characterized earlier time periods. Pay attention to the social, political, and economic developments of the civilizations in this section: These developments are what made them civilizations in the first place.

A piece of advice: Do not assume that all civilizations were headed by a central authority. Many early civilizations, in fact, were composed of loosely connected city-states, which were made up of an urban center and the agricultural land around it under its control. These city-states were sometimes combined into one because they shared common cultural characteristics; but they were also independent of each other in many ways and often competed with each other. This is true in modern times as well, of course. When we speak of Western civilization, for example, we mean a whole host of countries that have similar characteristics and cultures but that are distinct from one another and, often, compete with one another.

Major early civilizations developed and became dominant starting at around 3000 to 2000 B.C.E. They were located in Mesopotamia, Egypt, India, and China.

Mesopotamia: Lots of Water, Lots of History

Mesopotamia literally means "land between the rivers"; the rivers were the Tigris and the Euphrates. A series of ancient civilizations—most notably Sumer, Babylon, and Persia—thrived along their banks. Mesopotamia is part of a larger area of relatively arable land known as the Fertile Crescent, which extends westward from Mesopotamia toward the Mediterranean.

Unfortunately, the flooding of the Tigris and Euphrates Rivers was very unpredictable, so some early settlements were frequently washed away. But soon people learned to build canals and dikes, and began to build their towns farther uphill, enabling large city-states to emerge. By 3000 B.C.E., Ur, Erech, and Kish were the major city-states of the first major civilization of Sumer.

Sumer: The First Major Mesopotamian Civilization

Sumerian civilization rose in the southern part of Mesopotamia. In addition to successful agriculture and river management, the Sumerians developed a form of writing known as **cuneiform**. Scribes used this form of writing to set down laws, treaties, and important social and religious customs; soon the use of cuneiform spread over the trade routes to many other parts of the region. Trade was also enhanced by the introduction of the wheel, a major development that greatly reduced the time it took to transport both goods and people between two points.

Sumerians also developed a twelve-month calendar and a math system based on units of sixty (as in sixty seconds and three-hundred-sixty degrees). They used geometry, as well, to survey the land and to develop architectural enhancements such as arches and columns.

Sumerians were **polytheistic**, meaning that they worshipped more than one god. The interesting thing about Sumerian polytheism was that each city-state had its own god that was worshipped only by its people. In addition, there were a bunch of gods that all the city-states worshipped collectively. Sumerians built temples, called **ziggurats**, which were terraced pyramids, to appease their gods. They believed that when disaster struck—such as a particularly devastating flood—it was because the gods were angry.

Disaster often struck; no temple could stop the relentless flow of invasions of Sumeria. And by around 1700 B.C.E., the civilization had been completely overthrown; however, its conquerors adopted many Sumerian traditions and technologies.

From Sumer to Babylon to Nineveh to Babylon

As the Sumerian city-states declined, the city of Akkad, which was north of Sumer, rose to dominate the region. The Akkadians major contribution was they developed the first known code of laws, which they wrote in cuneiform, which they learned from the Sumerians. But by 1700 B.C.E., Akkad was overrun by a new powerhouse in Mesopotamia, **Babylon**. King Hammurabi of Babylon expanded on this idea of a code of laws by developing an extensive code that dealt with every part of daily life. **The Code of Hammurabi**, as it has come to be called, is often credited as a significant step toward our modern legal codes. It distinguished between major and minor offenses (a big deal at the time) and it established a sense of justice and fairness by applying the laws to nearly everyone (the beginnings of "rule of law").

But Babylon quickly fell due to the invasions of the Kassites and then the **Hittites**. By 1500 B.C.E., the Hittites dominated the region, especially because they learned how to use iron in their weapons. Because iron is a lot stronger than bronze, the Hittites quickly became a military superpower.

As you've no doubt figured out by now, news spread fast even in the ancient civilizations. As soon as one civilization figured out a new way to do something, the information was passed via the trade routes to other groups, who would quickly adopt and adapt the new technology to suit their cultures. In this way, within a hundred years, the **Assyrians** had learned to use iron, the very technology the Hittites had used to defeat them. This enabled them to establish a capital at Nineveh and, eventually build an empire that swept across the entire Fertile Crescent. Highly disciplined but cruel, the Assyrian army was hated by those it conquered. As a result, there were frequent uprisings against the Assyrian authorities, who, in response, sent large groups of people into exile. This action too played a part in enhancing cultural diffusion across the entire region and beyond.

In spite of their power, within a few hundred years, the Assyrians were defeated by the Medes and the Chaldeans. The Chaldean king, **Nebuchadnezzar**, rebuilt Babylon as a showplace of architecture and culture. He extended his empire throughout the Fertile Crescent, as the Assyrians had done before him. But like all the civilizations before it, the new Babylon was doomed to fall. A new civilization, the **Persian Empire**, developed into a major world force.

Focus On: Continuity through Change

You probably won't be asked a lot of specific questions about the long list of civilizations that emerged, one after the other, in Mesopotamia in the centuries between the Sumerian and Persian Empires. However, the Code of Hammurabi and the growing use of iron are both pretty big developments. That said, we've given you a quick review because it is essential that you understand, and can demonstrate, that as civilizations were conquered, their cultural heritage, religions, laws, customs, and technologies were rarely lost. Commonly, conquering civilizations adopted and adapted the customs and technologies of those they defeated. The series of civilizations that grew, and then fell, in Mesopotamia demonstrates this point well.

Ancient Egypt: Stay Awhile Along the Nile

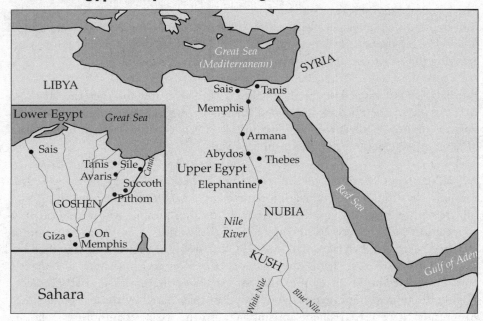

The Egyptian Empire (1450 B.C.E.)

The ancient **Egyptian** civilization developed along the Nile River, where the soil was rich and the agricultural opportunities were plentiful. The Nile cuts through an otherwise arid landscape, so the people clustered along the riverbanks, where, in addition to farms, they constructed towns and cities. Though we often think of ancient Egypt in terms of massive construction projects, such as the pyramids, most Egyptians lived in smaller towns. Unlike the Tigris and Euphrates Rivers, the Nile floods at a predictable time of the year and in relatively predictable stages. This made it possible for the ancient Egyptians to follow a very stable agricultural cycle and compile substantial food surpluses.

Three Kingdoms in One Civilization

You might remember from your studies that, as various dynasties rose to and fell from power, ancient Egypt was reorganized into different kingdoms. You don't need to remember all the details about the many kingdoms, but you should know that there were three major ones—Old, Middle, and New—and that it was during the New Kingdom that the ancient Egyptian civilization reached its height. By 1400 B.C.E., it stretched from the upper Nile River valley (at least 800 miles upstream from Memphis) through the eastern Mediterranean regions of Palestine and parts of Asia Minor (present-day Turkey).

Egyptian Achievements

Even before the Old Kingdom, the entire river valley was united under **King Menes**, who built his capital at Memphis and led efforts to manage the floodwaters and build drainage and irrigation systems. As a result of the unification, the civilization became wealthy and powerful. Rulers, known as **pharaohs**, directed the construction of obelisks and the pyramids, enormous tombs for their after-life. In addition, the Egyptians used a writing system to communicate. Known as **hieroglyphics**, this system consisted of a series of pictures (hieroglyphs) that represented letters and words. The Egyptians were also very interested in astronomy, which led to their creation of a fairly reliable calendar.

Over time, the civilization became dependent on trade because its people needed a constant supply of timber and stone for their many ambitious building projects, and because their culture valued luxuries such as gold and spices. Besides giving them access to the goods they wanted and needed, trading had an enormous impact on the Egyptians because it brought them into contact with other civilizations.

You Can Take It with You

Like most Mesopotamian societies, the Egyptians were polytheistic. The most significant aspect of their religious beliefs was the focus on life after death—the afterlife. Many societies shared this belief, but the Egyptians were convinced they could take earthly belongings with them to the afterlife, where they would be happy and well-fed and would continue doing many of the same things they did while in their earthly lives. They also believed that they would be able to use their bodies in the afterlife, and this led to the invention of mummification, a process of preserving dead bodies (although this was only available to the elite members of Egyptian society). The pharaohs, as you know, built huge pyramids to house their mummified bodies and earthly treasures.

Egyptian Women, Hear Them Roar

The first female ruler known in history was **Queen Hatshepsut**, who ruled for 22 years during the New Kingdom. She is credited with greatly expanding Egyptian trade expeditions. The relatively high status of women extended beyond royalty with most Egyptian women enjoying more rights and opportunities to express individuality than their counterparts in Mesopotamia. During the New Kingdom in particular, women could buy and sell property, inherit property, and choose to will their property how they pleased. Women also had the right to dissolve their marriages.

That said, women were still expected to be subservient to men and were valued most when they bore children. Young girls were also not educated nearly as well as young boys.

Egyptian Social Structure: Another Pyramid

The tombs of the pharaohs weren't the only pyramids in Egypt. Egyptian social structure was in the form of a pyramid as well.

At the top of the pyramid was the pharaoh, of course, and below him were the priests. Below the priests were nobles, followed by merchants and skilled artisans, which included physicians; at the bottom of the pyramid was the largest group: peasants. The peasants worked the land and generated most of the wealth for the kingdom. Specifically, the pharaoh owned all the land in the kingdom, so the goods produced on the land were considered his property. Typically, the peasants were expected to give over half of what they produced to the kingdom. Also at the bottom level of the pyramid were the slaves, who were mostly either prisoners of war captured during the Egyptian conquest of surrounding regions, or the descendents of those prisoners. It cannot be denied that most slaves lived a hard life, but in many cases they were not much worse off than many of the free peasants. Slaves worked on the land or on irrigation or building projects alongside the peasants, and on occasion were appointed to trusted positions within the government or within the palaces.

Ancient Egypt in Decline

By 1100 B.C.E. and for the next thousand years, ancient Egypt fell into decline, and both the Assyrian Empire and the Persian Empire conquered parts of this once-great civilization. Later, the Greeks occupied Egypt, and eventually the Romans completely absorbed Egypt into their empire. More on the Greeks and Romans later.

Indus Valley Civilization: Indus Industry Ruled

Like Mesopotamia and Egypt, the **Indus Valley** civilization was built along the banks of a river system. But because of the huge mountains north and west of the Indus River, contact with outside civilizations was more limited there than in Mesopotamia, which was under continual threat by invaders. That is not to say that the Indus Valley was entirely cut off. The **Khyber Pass** through the Hindu Kush Mountains provided a connection to the outside world and was used by merchants on trade excursions. Later, as you might guess, it also gave invading forces a way into the land.

Compare Them: The Decline of Egypt and Mesopotamian Civilizations
Be sure to take note of the fact that whenever a civilization became powerful and prosperous, it attracted a lot of attention and envy from its neighbors, who wanted a piece of the action. Typically, this was the breeding ground for invasions. By the time it came under attack, the wealthy civilization was often so big it couldn't adequately protect all its borders, so over a period of time it began to weaken. This was true of the empires that arose in Mesopotamia and in ancient Egypt. As you continue to read, you'll learn that it was true of the Greeks and Romans as well.

From at least 2500 to around 1500 B.C.E., the ancient Indus Valley civilization stretched for more than 900 miles along the Indus River in what today is northwestern India. Its two major cities, **Harappa** and **Mohenjo-Daro**, were each home to perhaps more than 100,000 people—enormous cities by ancient standards. There is strong evidence that the cities were master-planned, uniformly constructed, and had sophisticated wastewater systems. This indicates that the Indus people had a strong central government, probably led by a priest-king. Like the major religions of Egypt and Sumer, those in the Indus Valley were polytheistic.

Like the architecture of its cities, Indus Valley industry was top-notch. In addition to using technologies such as potter's wheels, the Indus Valley farmers grew cotton, and its artisans made cloth. This became an extremely important trade item among merchants traveling through the Khyber Pass to Mesopotamia.

Sometime around 1900 B.C.E., the cities of the Indus Valley were abandoned, for reasons that remain unknown today. All that is known is that, by 1500 B.C.E., the civilization crumbled with the arrival of the Aryans.

The Arrival of the Aryans

The Aryans were nomadic tribes from north of the Caucasus Mountains (near the Black and Caspian Seas). Using horses and advanced weaponry, they easily defeated the populations in the Indus Valley. Each of the Aryan tribes migrated to India independently; over a period of time, they began to settle in the Indus Valley, where they would give up their nomadic lifestyles.

The important thing to remember about the Aryan conquest of the Indus Valley is the establishment of their religious beliefs on the Indian subcontinent, in particular their belief in reincarnation. The Aryans, yet another polytheistic people, recorded their beliefs and traditions in the Vedas and the Upanishads. Over centuries, these early Aryan beliefs evolved to form the basis for what later became **Hinduism**, which is discussed in detail in Section IV of this chapter.

The Aryan social structure also had a major impact on later developments in India. Combined with Hinduism, it formed the basis of what later became the caste system. Initially, the Aryan social structure divided its people into three classes, in this order from top to bottom: warriors, priests, and peasants. Later, a class of landowners and merchants would be added above the peasant class; and the priest class (known as **Brahmans**) would be moved above the warrior class because they were considered closer to the gods.

In the early days of this system, movement between classes was allowed. But as the system became more complex and ingrained in society, it became more rigid. Eventually, subcastes were added to the four main castes, and social mobility among the castes was prohibited. Because members of different castes could not marry, children were born into the same castes as their parents, and stayed there.

Early China: Shang on the Hwang

Shang China rose in the Hwang Ho River Valley (also known as the Yellow River Valley), and like other river-basin communities, used its stable agricultural surplus to build a trade-centered civilization. At its height, Shang controlled large parts of northern China and was militarily quite powerful. Thousands of its workers built walls around the towns and cities along the river; its warriors used chariots to defeat their enemies. The Shang dynasty controlled the Yellow River Valley from around 1600 to around 1100 B.C.E.

However, Shang China had limited contact with the rest of the world, though it did trade with Mesopotamia (a very long journey!). The Shang were so isolated, in fact, that they believed themselves to be at the center of the world, which explains why they called their civilization "All Under Heaven." This belief contributed to the Shang's ethnocentric attitude, which means they considered themselves superior to all others.

The Shang certainly had reasons to be proud. Not only were they accomplished bronze workers, but they also used horse-drawn chariots, developed the spoked wheel, and became experts in the production of pottery and silk. What's more, they devised a decimal system and a highly accurate calendar.

Focus on the Family

The extended family was an important institution in many ancient civilizations across the globe, but nowhere was it more important than in Shang China. There, multiple generations of the same family lived in the same household in a **patriarchal** structure (led by the eldest male). Shang religion held that gods controlled all aspects of peoples' lives; people also believed they could call on the spirits of their dead ancestors to act as their advocates with the gods. This gave the extended family even greater significance.

Enter the Zhou

Around 1100 B.C.E., the Shang were ousted by Wu Wang, who established the **Zhou Dynasty** (also spelled Chou Dynasty), which maintained many of the traditions and customs developed under the Shang Dynasty (sound familiar?). The Zhou ruled China for nearly 900 years, longer than any other dynasty. Think of how long the United States has existed as an independent country, then multiply it by four. Now you have an idea how long the Zhou dynasty existed.

The Zhou Dynasty believed in what was called the **Mandate of Heaven**, meaning that heaven would grant the Zhou power only as long as its rulers governed justly and wisely. Put another way, the Zhou Dynasty would remain in power only as long as it had the blessing of heaven.

The Zhou developed a feudal system in China, similar to that of Europe during the Middle Ages (which we'll talk about more in the next chapter). The king was the ruler of the entire empire, but because it was too big for one person to manage, nobles were given power over smaller regions within the empire. This worked out well for a couple hundred years. The king gave each noble protection as long as the noble remained loyal to him. But as time passed, a number of the nobles built up a lot of wealth and power within the regions under their control and eventually split off into independent kingdoms. Some of the most complex kingdoms developed **bureaucracies** within their governments, which was a way of organizing government tasks by department, or **bureau**, so that different parts of the government could specialize and stabilize. A bureaucratic form of government remained popular in China for thousands of years. Eventually, though, fighting and warfare among the feudal kingdoms brought an end to the Zhou Dynasty in 256 B.C.E.

West Africa: Bantu Migrations and the "Stateless Society"

Beginning around 1500 B.C.E., farmers in the Niger and Benue River valleys in West Africa began migrating south and east, bringing with them their languages (from the **Bantu** family of languages) and their knowledge of agriculture and metallurgy. These migrations, usually referred to as the **Bantu migrations**, continued over the course of the next 2,000 years. Bantu speakers gradually moved into areas formerly occupied by nomads. Some of the nomads simply moved on, and some of them adopted the more sedentary culture of the Bantu.

It is generally believed that the migration was spurred by climactic changes, which made the area now known as the Sahara Desert too dry to live in. People moved south out of the Sahara into the Bantu's homeland, which in turn caused them to move to the forests of Central Africa, then eventually beyond the forests to the east and south.

However, not all Bantu-speakers moved away. Further north in the upper Niger River valley can be found the remains of Jenne-Jeno, believed to be the first city in sub-Saharan Africa. Beginning as a small fishing settlement around 250 B.C.E. and reaching urban size in 400 C.E., **Jenne-Jeno** is unusual because although it reached urban density, its architecture suggests that it was not a hierarchically organized society. Instead, archeologists believe that it was a unique form of urbanism comprising a collection of individual communities. It just goes to show, once again, that not all human societies have followed the same path toward sophistication, and that urbanization doesn't necessarily mean centralization.

Focus On: Migrations

Why do people migrate? People migrate for the same reason animals do: to find food and a hospitable environment in which to live. Nomadic peoples by definition are migratory, moving from place to place with the seasons to follow food sources. Agricultural peoples also migrated, following the seasons and therefore agricultural cycles. To maintain a stable home, people also migrated to avoid natural disasters or climatic changes that permanently change the environment, making it too hot and dry (the Sahara Desert's expansion), too cold (Ice Ages), or too wet (flooding cycles of major rivers such as the Yellow River in China).

Migration isn't always solely the result of random environmental change. Overpopulation of a particular area can exhaust the food supply, forcing people to move elsewhere, often displacing a smaller or weaker population in the process. Massive migrations of people from Ireland during the famines of the mid-nineteenth century were caused by a mix of politics, destructive farming methods, and an unpleasant fungus that wiped out the populace's main source of food. The Jewish diaspora, the slave trade, and the waves of immigrants coming from Europe to the Americas in the late nineteenth and early twentieth centuries are examples of more modern-day migrations caused by people rather than nature.

D. Early Mesoamerica and Andean South America: For Every Rule There's an Exception

In the Americas, two early civilizations existed: the **Olmec**, in what we know today as Mexico, from 1500 to 400 B.C.E., and the **Chavin** in the Andes from 900 to 200 B.C.E.

The Olmec were an urban society supported by surpluses of corn, beans, and squash. Like most early societies, they mastered irrigation techniques and constructed large-scale buildings; they were polytheistic, and developed a system of writing and a calendar.

The Chavin were another urban civilization, and their people were also polytheistic. But, while mostly agricultural, they also had access to the coast, and therefore supplemented their diet with seafood. The Chavin developed ways to use metals in tools and weapons. Interestingly, the Chavin used llamas as their beasts of burden.

If much of this sounds familiar to you, it's because the Olmec and the Chavin developed similarly to other early civilizations discussed previously. So why bring them up separately? Two reasons. First, they demonstrate that the same patterns of development occurred in an entirely different part of the globe, a part that had no contact with the other civilizations discussed in this chapter. This suggests that developments within civilizations can occur independently—not necessarily as a result of exposure to other civilizations.

Second, neither the Olmec nor the Chavin civilization developed in a river valley. True, the Olmec and Chavin had access to water from streams and small rivers, but no major river system served as the generator of agricultural production or as the hub of culture and transportation. Their existence, therefore, disproves the hypothesis that river valleys are essential for the emergence of early civilizations. That's not to say, however, that rivers aren't extremely important—after all, the civilizations in the river valleys were among the most powerful and wealthy in all history.

Contrast Them: Olmec and Chavin Civilizations and Other Early Civilizations
Although you probably won't have to remember the details of the Olmec and Chavin civilizations, you should definitely remember this: They are unique in that they didn't develop in river valleys, as did all the other major early civilizations.

E. The Classical Civilizations: Mesoamerica

Although the Maya are often grouped with later Mesoamerican empires, the Aztec and the Inca, they were actually contemporary with Rome, Han, and Gupta and develop some of the same characteristics of these early empires.

Mayan Civilization: In Search of More Slaves

From about 300 B.C.E. to about 800 C.E., Mayan civilization dominated present-day southern Mexico and parts of Central America. The Mayan civilization was similar to many other civilizations at that time in that it was a collection of city-states; however, all the city-states were ruled by the same king. Interestingly, like the Egyptians, the Maya were pyramid-builders, and also wrote using hieroglyphics. The golden age of the Mayan Civilization was from about 500 to about 850 C.E. During that time, the Maya produced many great works of scholarship and developed a complex calendar system, but we know the most about its architecture and city planning because many remains have been discovered. No question, the Maya built tremendous cities—Tikal, the most important Mayan political center, may have been populated by as many as 100,000 people.

The Maya divided their cosmos into three parts: the heavens above, the humans in the middle, and the underworld below. The Maya believed that the gods created humans out of maize (one of the main Mayan dietary staples) and water. They also believed that the gods maintained agricultural cycles in exchange for honors, sacrifices, and bloodletting rituals.

Mayan warfare was somewhat unique in that it was imbued with a tremendous amount of religious significance. Days of religious ritual would precede a battle, and the King and nobility would actively participate in combat. One unique characteristic of Mayan warfare was that it was generally conducted not to gain territory, but to acquire slaves, who were used in large-scale building projects and in agricultural production. The Maya had no large animals, as horses and oxen would not arrive until much later with the Europeans, so humans were their primary source of labor.

Similar to most agricultural societies, the majority of the people were peasants or slaves. Kings, priests, and hereditary nobility were at the top of the social pyramid. Merchants also enjoyed a high status.

The Maya used advanced agricultural techniques, such as the ridged field system, to make the most of the rainfall and swamp conditions of the region. Cotton and maize were widely cultivated; the Maya are known for their elaborate cotton textiles. Many well-preserved ruins of this civilization remain today, including the tiered temple at Chichen Itza, which is similar in design to the Egyptian pyramids and Mesopotamian ziggurats, and several ball courts, which were used for a ritual sport throughout ancient Mesoamerica. Significantly, the Mayan calendar, based on a number system that included zero, was among the most accurate for its time. The Mayan calendar runs only through 2012, giving rise to all sorts of wild end-of-the-world predictions, but if you're reading this book in 2013, it probably means the calendar only stopped because the Mayans got tired of counting days. Since you're reading this book now, it's safe to say that the calendar only stopped because the Mayans got tired of counting days.

F. The Classical Civilizations: India and China

Your AP World History Exam will likely focus on four empires in India and China that existed from around 300 B.C.E. to around 550 C.E. These four empires are the Maurya and Gupta in India, and the Qin and Han in China. Keep in mind that to fully understand these four empires, you will also need to review some of the major belief systems discussed in Section IV of this chapter.

1. The Mauryan Empire in India (321 to approximately 180 B.C.E.)

Around 330 B.C.E., Alexander the Great conquered the Persian Empire and continued into India (more on this in a few pages). During this time, the Aryan culture and belief systems continued to spread throughout India. Then, around 321 B.C.E., a new empire arose in India, one that would come to be the largest in that country to date. Spanning from the Indus River Valley eastward through the Ganges River Valley and southward through the Deccan Plateau, the **Mauryan Empire** was founded by **Chandragupta Maurya**, who unified the smaller Aryan kingdoms into a civilization. But it would be his grandson, **Ashoka Maurya**, who would take the empire to its greatest heights.

A major reason that the Mauryan Empire became so powerful and wealthy was trade. Indian merchants traded silk, cotton, and elephants (among hundreds of other items) to Mesopotamia and the eastern Roman Empire. Another reason was its powerful military. Interestingly, it was its military strength that eventually caused a dramatic change in the empire. Stricken with disgust and filled with remorse for a very violent and bloody victory his forces claimed over the Kalinga in southeast India, Ashoka converted to **Buddhism**. For the rest of his reign, Ashoka preached nonviolence and moderation. (As you'll learn in Section IV of this chapter, during the previous century, Buddhism had recently taken root in this otherwise Hindu region.)

Ashoka is also known for his **Rock and Pillar Edicts**, which were carved on—you guessed it—rocks and pillars throughout the empire. These edicts reminded Mauryans to live generous and righteous lives. Following Ashoka's conversion and commitment to Buddhism, the religion spread beyond India into many parts of Southeast Asia.

2. The Gupta Dynasty in India (320–550 C.E.)

After Ashoka's death in 232 B.C.E., the Mauryan Empire began to decline rapidly, primarily due to economic problems and pressure from attacks in the northeast. But between 375 and 415 C.E., it experienced a revival under Chandra Gupta II, known as **Chandra Gupta the Great**. The **Gupta Empire** was more decentralized and smaller than its predecessor, but it is often referred to as a golden age because it enjoyed relative peace and saw significant advances in the arts and sciences. For example, Gupta mathematicians developed the concepts of pi and of zero. They also devised a decimal system that used the numerals 1 through 9 (which were diffused to the Arabs and became known as **Arabic numerals**).

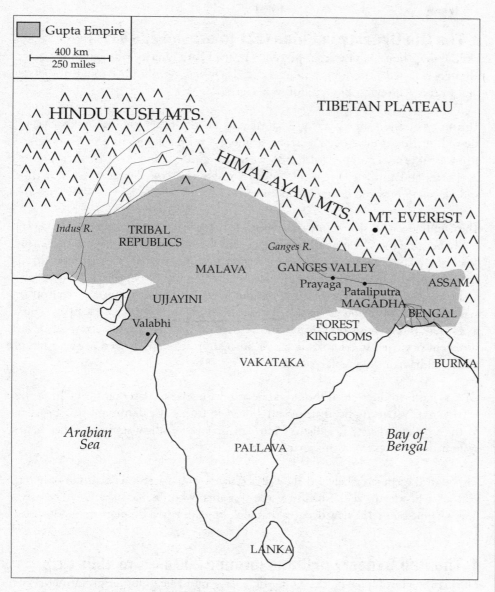

The Gupta Empire (Fourth–Fifth Century C.E.)

By the time of the Gupta Dynasty, Hinduism had again become the dominant religion in India. Hinduism reinforced the caste system, meaning that Indian social structures were very rigid. Though the empire as a whole was enjoying an era of peace, prosperity, and artistic endeavors, women were increasingly losing their rights. Totally under the control of men, Indian women lost the right to own or inherit property, and could not participate in sacred rituals or study religion. And stemming from an increasingly urban society that placed a growing importance on the inheritance of property, child marriage (involving girls as young as six or seven) also became the norm during this era. The Gupta Dynasty collapsed under pressure from the White Huns in 550 C.E.

3. The Qin Dynasty in China (221 to around 209 B.C.E.)

Unlike the Zhou Dynasty that preceded it, the **Qin Dynasty** was extremely short. Though it lasted little longer than a decade, it was significant enough to earn a spot in this AP review book 2,200 years later.

The story of the Qin Dynasty is similar to all the other civilizations we've reviewed, in that it developed a strong economy based on agriculture; it organized a powerful army equipped with iron weapons; and it conquered the surrounding territories and unified the region under a single emperor. Same story, new time and place. So how did it earn its spot here?

The Qin Dynasty is the empire that connected separate fortification walls that eventually became the **Great Wall of China**. That fact is more than just an interesting piece of trivia; it tells us that the empire was incredibly well organized, centralized, and territorial. Qin Shihuangdi, also known as **Qin Shi Huang**, was the dynasty's first emperor, and he recentralized various feudal kingdoms that had split apart at the end of the Zhou Dynasty; standardized all the laws, currencies, weights, measures, and systems of writing; and refused to tolerate any dissent whatsoever. If dissent occurred in a book, he had it burned; if dissent occurred in the mind of a scholar, he had the scholar killed.

Given that introduction, it should come as no surprise to you that Qin China was patriarchal. What might surprise you, however, is that the dominant belief system of the Qin rulers was Legalism. (You can review Legalism and the other belief systems in Section IV of this chapter.)

Although the emperor believed the Qin Dynasty would last forever, it fell only one year after his death, at the hands of the peasants, who resented the Qin Dynasty's heavy-handedness. The new dynasty that took its place lasted for more than 400 years.

4. The Han Dynasty in China (around 200 B.C.E. to 460s C.E.)

During the **Han Dynasty**, the **Xiongnu**, a large nomadic group from northern Asia who may have been Huns, invaded territories extending from China to Eastern Europe. But the Huns were much more successful in Europe than they were in China, largely due to the skills of **Wu Ti**, often called the Warrior Emperor, who greatly enlarged the Han Empire to central Asia. Trade thrived along the Silk Road to the Mediterranean; more significantly, along this same route, Buddhism spread. As usual, the trade routes carried far more than luxury items; they carried culture.

One of the most significant developments that took place during the Han Dynasty was the civil service system based on the teachings of Confucius. The Han believed that those involved in government should be highly educated and excellent communicators. To ensure strong candidates, the Han developed a civil service examination, a very difficult test lasting for several days. Though, ostensibly, the exam was open to everyone, generally only the wealthy could afford to prepare for it. The consequence was a government bureaucracy that was highly skilled and that contributed to stability in the system of government for centuries.

Also during this time, the Chinese invented paper, highly accurate sundials, and calendars, as well as making important strides in navigation, such as the invention of the rudder and of the compass. And, like all the other major civilizations, they continued to broaden their use of metals.

G. The Classical Civilizations: Mediterranean

From approximately 2000 B.C.E. to around 500 C.E., two Mediterranean civilizations, Greece and Rome, dominated the region. Countless books have been written on these two empires. There is no doubt that your AP textbook dedicated a considerable chunk to the details of these two powerhouse civilizations. Why all the fuss? Simply put, Western civilization as we know it today essentially began with these two empires. The Sumerians, the Babylonians, the Egyptians, the Hebrews, and the Phoenicians laid the groundwork, but the Greeks and the Romans left the most pervasive and obvious influence behind. Perhaps their most important contribution is the concept of representative government, but the Greeks and Romans, and the Persians also made lasting contributions to art, architecture, literature, science, and philosophy.

1. Persian Immersion

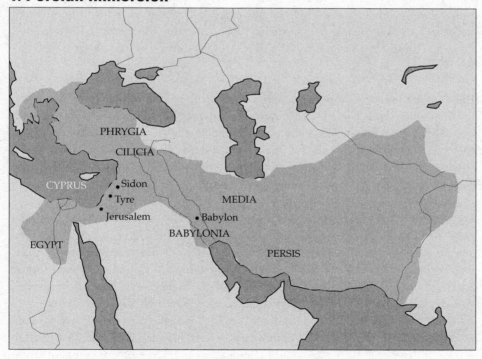

The Height of the Persian Empire (c. 500 B.C.E.)

The Persians established a big empire—a really big empire—that, by 500 B.C.E., stretched from beyond the Nile River Valley in Egypt around the eastern Mediterranean through present-day Turkey and parts of Greece, and then eastward through present-day Afghanistan. Huge! They did this by conquering all those earlier ancient civilizations in Mesopotamia you just read about, the Babylonians, the Lydians, the Phoenicians, and the Egyptians. On account of the vast expanse of their empire, they delegated local administration of their provinces, or **Satrapies**, to important people in the provinces. As long as the governor, or **satrap**, paid his taxes and contributed soldiers to the Great King whenever they were requested, the satrapy was allowed a wide range of self government, which was vital to keeping such a far flung empire of so many different cultures together.

To improve transportation and communication across the vast empire, the Persians built a series of long roads. The longest was the **Great Royal Road**, which stretched some 1,600 miles from the Persian Gulf to the Aegean Sea.

We'll talk more about the Persian Empire later, because they butted heads with the other major world empires.

Lydians, Phoenicians, and Hebrews, Oh My!

Within and near the Persian Empire, many smaller societies existed and kept their own identities. Among these were the Lydians, Phoenicians, and Hebrews.

The **Lydians** are important because they came up with the concept of using coined money to conduct trade rather than using the barter system, in which goods are exchanged for other goods. This, of course, led to a monetary system of consistent prices and allowed people to save money for future use. The idea of coined money, like everything else, spread over the trade routes and soon just about everybody was doing it.

The **Phoenicians** are important, first, because they established powerful naval city-states all along the Mediterranean (you'll read more about this later), and, second, because they developed a simple alphabet that used only 22 letters as opposed to the much more complex cuneiform system. The Greeks later adopted the Phoenician alphabet, and from there it spread and changed, and eventually led to the system of letters you are reading on this page.

The **Hebrews** are significant because of their religious beliefs called Judaism. The Hebrews were the first Jews. In contrast to previous civilizations in the Fertile Crescent and beyond, the Hebrews were monotheistic, meaning they believed in one god. By around 1000 b.c.e., the Hebrews had established Israel in Palestine on the eastern shores of the Mediterranean Sea. Although they were frequently invaded by neighboring empires (e.g., Nebuchadnezzar enslaved them), they managed to maintain their identity, in large part because they believed they were God's chosen people. Under the Persians, the Hebrews were freed from captivity and continued to develop a distinct culture that would later lead to the development of major world religions. Much more about Judaism can be found later in this chapter.

2. Greece

Ancient Greece was located on a peninsula between the waters of the Aegean and Mediterranean Seas. Because the land in Greece is mostly mountainous, there wasn't much possibility for agricultural development on the scale of the ancient river valley civilizations. But Greece did have natural harbors and mild weather, and its coastal position aided trade and cultural diffusion by boat, which is precisely how the Greeks conducted most of their commercial activity. The Greeks could easily sail to Palestine, Egypt, and Carthage, exchanging wine and olive products for grain. Eventually, they replaced the barter system with a money system (remember where this developed? Hint: Lydia, oh Lydia), and soon Athens became a wealthy city at the center of all this commercial activity.

Greece's limited geographical area also contributed to its dominance. Land was tight, so Greece was always looking to establish colonies abroad to ease overcrowding and gain raw materials. This meant that the Greeks had to have a powerful military. It also meant that they had to develop sophisticated methods of communication, transportation, and governance.

Social Structure and Citizenship: It Takes a Polis...

Like the other early civilizations, Greece wasn't a country then in the way that it is now. Instead, it was a collection of city-states, very much like those of early Mesopotamian civilizations in Sumer or Babylon. Each city-state, known as a **polis**, shared a common culture and identity. Although each polis was part of a broader civilization and shared a common language and many similar traditions, each was independent from, and often in conflict with, the others.

The two main city-states were **Athens** and **Sparta**. Athens was the political, commercial, and cultural center of Greek civilization. Sparta was an agricultural and highly militaristic region. Most citizens in Sparta lived a very austere, highly disciplined existence (which explains where modern-day terms such as "Spartan existence" come from). All the boys, and even some of the girls, received military training, which stressed equality but not individuality.

Each polis was composed of three groups.

- Citizens, composed of adult males, often engaged in business or commerce
- Free people with no political rights
- Noncitizens (slaves, who accounted for nearly one-third of the people in Athens, and who had no rights)

Among the citizens, civic decisions were made openly, after engaging in debates. All citizens were expected to participate. This practice led to Athens being regarded as the first democracy. But it's important to point out that only adult males could participate, so it was not a democracy in the modern sense of the word. (Interestingly, it was in Sparta, not Athens, where women held a higher status and were granted greater equality than women of other city-states.)

It's also important to point out that democracy in Athens did not develop immediately. As Athens grew more and more powerful, the government changed from a monarchy to an aristocracy, and finally to a democracy. (Note: You may be asked about Draco and Solon. Just know that they were aristocrats who worked to create the democracy in Athens and to ensure fair, equal, and open participation.)

Ironically, it was slavery that enabled the Greeks to develop their democracy. It was by slave labor that Greek citizens found themselves with free time to meet and vote and to create great works of art and philosophy. Slaves, obtained by various means, were the private property of their owners. They worked as laborers, domestic servants, and cultivators. Educated or skilled slaves became craftsmen and business managers. Some owners helped slaves set up small businesses and then kept part of the profits; and in a few cases, slaves who earned and saved enough money could eventually buy their freedom.

Greek Mythology: Many Gods

The Greeks were polytheistic. The myths surrounding their gods, like those of Zeus and Aphrodite, are richly detailed and still hold our interest to this day. As you know by now, most early civilizations were polytheistic (the Hebrews being a notable exception), but Greek polytheism was unique in one major respect: The Greek gods were believed to possess human failings—they got angry, got drunk, took sides, and had petty arguments. Greek mythology remains part of Western heritage and language. Every time we refer to a task as "Herculean" or read our horoscopes, we're tipping our hats to the ancient Greeks.

War with Persia: Greece Holds On

Prior to the development of the democracy in Athens, Greece was involved in a series of wars that threatened its existence. The **Persian Wars** (499–449 B.C.E.) united all the Greek city-states against their mutual enemy, Persia. (Recall that the Persian Empire was the largest empire in the eastern Mediterranean and Mesopotamia to date.) Much of Athens was destroyed in these wars, but Greece held on and the wars ended in a stalemate. Two huge victories by the Greeks, one at Marathon and the other at Salamis, allowed the Greeks to maintain control of the Aegean Sea. With Persia held back, Greece was free to enter into an era of peace and prosperity, which is often called the **Golden Age of Pericles**.

The Golden Age of Pericles: Athens Wows the World

The Golden Age of Pericles (480–404 B.C.E.) saw Athens become a cultural powerhouse under the leadership of **Pericles**. Pericles established democracy for all adult males. It was also under Pericles that Athens was rebuilt after its destruction by the Persians (the Parthenon was built during this reconstruction). And it was under Pericles that Athens established the **Delian League** with the other city-states, an alliance against aggression from its common enemies. Philosophy and the arts flourished, and continued to do so for the next two centuries.

In philosophy, we find the names many would regard as the most famous of all the ancient Greeks: **Socrates, Plato**, and **Aristotle**. They believed that truth could be discerned through rational thought and deliberate and careful observation, and that virtue and the quest for goodness would lead to internal peace and happiness. Some of their observations proved false in time, especially with regard to the functioning of the universe on a cosmic scale, or microcosmic scale, but it was the process they established, rather than the actual conclusions they drew, that were so revolutionary. Although our modern understanding of the world differs in many ways from theirs, these three men are still revered today as the fathers of rational thinking.

During the Golden Age, Greek drama was dominated by the comedies and tragedies of Aeschylus and Euripides; the sculptures of Phidias adorned the streets; and Greek architecture earned its place in history with its distinctive Doric, Ionic, and Corinthian columns. Math and science thrived under the capable instruction of Archimedes, Hippocrates, Euclid, and Pythagoras (you probably remember the Pythagorean theorem from geometry—guess which famous Greek that came from).

Of course, cultural achievement existed in Greece prior to the Golden Age. **Homer**, for example, wrote the epic poems the *Illiad* and the *Odyssey* a few centuries earlier; they are widely regarded as Western civilization's first two masterworks of literature. But make no mistake about it, during the Golden Age, the arts and sciences became firmly cemented into the Western consciousness. The accomplishments of this period served as the inspiration for the European Renaissance and the Enlightenment nearly two millennia later—which is why we're making such a big deal out of them here.

Trouble Ahead for Athens

Although Athens dominated the Delian League with its powerful navy, other Greek city-states in the Aegean allied themselves with Sparta's great army to form the Peloponnesian League. Athens and Sparta, as leaders of their respective alliances, became increasingly fearful and envious of each other's power. After years of increasing tensions, a trade dispute involving the city of Corinth pushed Athens and Sparta into the **Peloponnesian War** (431–404 B.C.E.). Athens attempted a defensive strategy, hiding behind its great walls while allowing the Spartan army to ravage its farmlands. This worked well for the Athenians for a time until two tragedies occurred. First, a great plague afflicted the city, killing vast numbers of the population including Pericles. Then, Athen's navy suffered a devastating defeat at Syracuse on the island of Sicily. Athens was never the same again.

Although they could have, Sparta didn't destroy Athens out of respect for the defeated city's former role in the Persian War. Sparta failed to dominate the region for long; despite its victory, it was so weakened by the war that it became vulnerable to outside aggression. The **Macedonians**, under the rule of Philip III of Macedon, who reigned from 359 to 336 B.C.E., invaded Athens from the north and conquered the entire region. Fortunately, Philip respected Greek culture and, rather than destroy it, encouraged it to flourish.

Alexander Adds Greatness

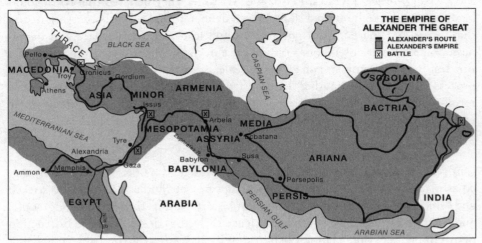

The Height of Alexander the Great's Empire, Fourth Century B.C.E.

The Macedonians didn't stop with Greece. Philip's son, **Alexander the Great**, who was taught by Aristotle, widely expanded Macedonian dominance. Under Alexander, they conquered the mighty Persian Empire and moved eastward to the shores of the Indus River in what today is India, eventually creating the largest empire of the time. However, the strain of such conquests took its toll on the usually vigorous Alexander and he died at the age of 33 in Babylon as he and his army were returning to Macedonia. Before his corpse got cold, however, his generals quickly fought over the spoils of his empire, dividing it amongst themselves.

Along with its size, the Macedonian Empire is notable for the fact that it adopted Greek customs and then spread them to much of the known world. Consequently, much of the world became connected under a uniform law and common trade practices. Therefore, **Hellenism**—the culture, ideals, and pattern of life of Classical Greece—didn't perish as a result of the victories over Athens and Sparta; instead, it came to be influential far beyond its original borders.

In the immediate aftermath of the expansion of Hellenism, the economies of Athens and Corinth revived through trade. Of the three Hellenistic empires, the Ptolemaic Empire became the wealthiest. Alexandria, its capital, was built at the mouth of the Nile. Wisely, Ptolemaic Dynasty in Egypt rulers did not interfere in Egyptian society, and, eventually, Ptolemaic Egypt also became a cultural center, home of the Alexandria Museum and Alexandria Library, the latter of which contained the most scrolls of any location in the empire, perhaps the whole world.

When Alexander the Great died at age 33, his empire started to crumble. Because the Macedonians were focused on the East and on Egypt, the door was open in the West for a new power to rise to the world stage. That power was the Romans.

3. Rome (509 B.C.E.–476 C.E.)

Geographically, Rome was relatively well-situated. The Alps to the north provided protection from an invasion by land (although, ultimately, not enough). The sea surrounding the Italian peninsula limited the possibility of a naval attack unless a large armada floated across the sea. Yet, although somewhat isolated, Rome was also at a crossroad. It had easy access to northern Africa, Palestine, Greece, and the Iberian Peninsula (modern-day Spain and Portugal), which meant easy access to the rest of the world.

Roman Mythology: More Gods

Like the Greeks, the Romans were polytheistic. (Every time you see a cupid on a Valentine's Day card, you see the impact of Roman mythology on our world today.) Many of their gods were of Greek origin, though appropriately renamed to suit their culture and language.

Social Structure in Rome: Organized and Patriarchal

The social and political structure in the Roman Republic consisted of **patricians** (land-owning noblemen), **plebeians** (all other free men), and slaves. Does this sound familiar? It should. It's very similar to the social structure of ancient Greece. Roman government was organized as a representative republic. The main governing body was made up of two distinct groups: the Senate, which comprised patrician families, and the Assembly, which was initially made up of patricians, but later was opened to plebeians. Two consuls were annually elected by the Assembly. The consuls had veto power over decisions made by the Assembly.

This structure was much more stable than the direct democracies of the Greek polis, in which every male citizen was expected to participate on a regular basis. In a republic, the people have representatives, so they don't have to vote on every issue. This is similar to the constitutional democracy we have in the United States. Everyone in this country votes for representatives, so it's correct to call our system a democracy; however, our representatives in Congress vote on all the major issues, so our system of government is also very much a republic. Indeed, the structure of our government was modeled on the system used in the Roman Republic. Instead of two consuls, though, we have one, known as the president.

Early on, Rome developed civil laws to protect individual rights (in some ways similar to our Bill of Rights). The laws of Rome were codified (remember that the idea of a code was Hammurabi's, in Babylon) and became known as the **Twelve Tables of Rome** (the concept of "innocent until proven guilty" originated here). Later, these laws were extended to an international code that Rome applied to its conquered territories.

The social structure of the Roman family centered on the *pater familias*—eldest male in the family—though women did have considerable influence within their families, with some supervising a family business or family estate. Roman women could own property, as well, but they were, nevertheless, considered inferior to men, just as in Greek society. And, as in Greece, slavery was an important element of the social structure of Rome—at one point, slaves comprised one-third of the population, most of whom came from conquered territories. Although life was difficult for all slaves, generally, those living and working in the cities had better conditions than their country counterparts, and some had the possibility of freedom.

Roman Military Domination: All Directions, All the Time

As Rome expanded, Carthage, a city-state in North Africa with powerful ambitions of its own, became its first enemy. It didn't take long for this conflict to escalate into full-fledged wars, which came to be called the **Punic Wars**. These lasted on and off from 264 through 146 B.C.E.

The First Punic War (264–241 B.C.E.) was fought to gain control of the island of Sicily; Rome won this one. The Second Punic War (218–201 B.C.E.) began with an attack by Hannibal, a Carthaginian general considered one of the greatest military geniuses of all time. In an amazing feat, **Hannibal** led his army all the way to northern Italy, crossed the Alps (on elephants no less!), and surprised the Romans, who were expecting an attack from the south. Hannibal's army destroyed many towns and villages to the north of Rome and were on the verge of destroying Rome. But a Roman army had landed in North Africa, forcing Hannibal to return to Carthage to defend his city. Carthage eventually agreed to sue for peace, and this made Rome the undisputed power in the western Mediterranean. Fifty years later, the Third Punic War (149–146 B.C.E.) was instigated by Rome. Rome invaded Carthage and burned it to the ground. With Carthage out of the picture, Rome continued its expansion throughout the Mediterranean.

Part of that expansion was to obtain Greece by defeating the Macedonians. The Romans also fought the Gauls to the north and the Spaniards to the west. Warfare aided the spread of Roman culture (which, you'll recall, was linked to Greek culture) throughout much of western Europe and the Mediterranean. To maintain their vast empire, the Romans built an extensive road network and aqueducts, and greatly enlarged their navy.

Collapse of the Republic and the Rise of Imperialism

Following the Punic Wars, and even as Roman influence grew, the situation in and around Rome was becoming unsettled. Several events caused this restlessness. First, large landowners had begun using more slaves from the conquered territories. This displaced many small farmers, who moved into the cities, causing overcrowding among the plebeians and not enough jobs to support them. Second, the Roman currency was devalued, causing a high rate of inflation. This meant that the plebeians did not have enough money to buy the things they previously could afford. Third, political leaders began fighting amongst themselves. The result was that the power of the Senate weakened, ultimately to be transferred to three men, who came to be known as the **first triumvirate**: Pompey, Crassus, and Julius Caesar.

Caesar was given power over southern Gaul (France) and other parts of Europe. He chose not to conquer Germany, which would later prove significant. (Germany developed a different culture and would ultimately serve as a training ground for groups intent on conquering Rome.) Civil war between the Senate and Caesar's followers resulted in pushing Pompey and Crassus out of the picture, after which Caesar became "emperor for life." But his life didn't last long. His angry senators assassinated him in 44 B.C.E.

After the death of Julius Caesar, a **second triumvirate**, composed of Octavius, Marc Antony, and Lepidus, came to power. Things didn't improve the second time around. Power again shifted to one person, **Octavius**, who rose to power, assumed the name Augustus Caesar, and became emperor. The days of the Roman Republic were over once and for all. Rome was now an empire led by a single emperor.

Pax Romana: Peace and Prosperity

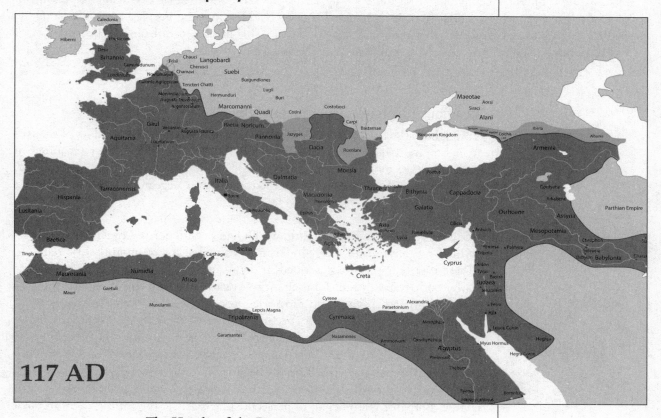

The Height of the Roman Empire

Under Augustus, Rome became the capital of the Western world. Augustus established the rule of law, a common coinage, civil service, and secure travel for merchants. With all these elements in place throughout the empire, stability returned to its people, and for 200 years, they enjoyed a period of peace and prosperity known as the *Pax Romana* (Roman Peace). Interestingly, however, though many of the laws were uniform throughout the empire during this period, a number of traditional customs of the people in the conquered territories survived. This, of course, meant that the distinct groups within the empire, such as the Hebrews or the Egyptians, maintained their individual cultural identities.

Under imperial power, the Roman Empire expanded to its largest geographical proportions through additional military conquests. But more important in the history of the Roman empire was the growth of the arts and sciences during this time. For centuries, Greece had been the arts center of the Western world. With the Roman peace, however, the arts in Rome flourished, especially literature (notably, Ovid's *Metamorphoses* and Virgil's *Aeneid*) and architecture (marked by the building of the Pantheon, Colosseum, and Forum). Science also reached new heights. Ptolemy looked to the heavens and greatly influenced achievements in astronomy, while Roman engineers went to work on roads and aqueducts.

Compare Them: *Pax Romana* with the Golden Ages of Greece, Gupta,and Others
In case you haven't noticed a pattern, we'll point it out for you. When a major empire greatly expands its territory, it becomes the center of artistic and scientific energy. This is because it has a tremendous amount of wealth flowing into its capital from its conquered regions, and because the people have the freedom and confidence to pursue goals other than military protection. This happened in Rome, Athens, Gupta India, Han China, and the other civilizations we've discussed so far.

Religious Diversity: New Chiefs of Beliefs

Throughout the days of the Roman Republic and during the early days of the Roman Empire, **paganism** was the state religion. Roman citizens were required to make sacrifices to traditional Roman gods. But shortly after the reign of Augustus, a new religion developed in the Mediterranean and Aegean regions. That religion was **Christianity**.

Christianity grew out of Judaism, which had been practiced by Hebrews in Palestine for thousands of years. Judaism was the first major monotheistic religion. (These two religions are described in detail in Section IV of this chapter.) Initially, both Judaism and Christianity were tolerated by the Romans. The Romans allowed the conquered territories to practice their own faiths as long as doing so didn't interfere with the functioning of the empire. Eventually, however, Jewish resistance to Roman control led to the suppression of Judaism. And as the apostles of Jesus and missionaries extended the influence of Christianity throughout the empire, the Romans began to see the new religion and its leaders as threats to both paganism and their power. To make it clear who was in charge, Emperor Nero began to persecute Christians, even killing them in open spectacles at the Colosseum. These acts of violence failed to stop the spread of Christianity. Only when Emperor **Constantine** himself issued the **Edict of Milan** in 313 c.e. did the persecution end. And by 391 c.e., Christianity became the official religion of the Roman Empire. Since then, it continues to be one of the world's most influential religions.

H. Late Classical Period: Empires Collapse, and People on the Move

During the late Classical Period (200–600 C.E.), all the greatest civilizations that the world had known collapsed. This included the fall of Han China, the Gupta Empire in India, the western part of the Roman Empire in the Mediterranean, and the mysterious decline of the Maya.

1. Collapse of the Maya

Nobody's sure exactly what happened to the Maya. Some say it was disease or drought or the declining health of the large peasant population. Others say it was internal unrest and warfare. Chances are, like other collapses, an expanding population gradually exhausted their environment and could not respond to the needs of their population. But whatever the reasons, the Maya started to desert their cities in the ninth century C.E. and the great civilization fizzled out.

2. Collapse of Han China

The Han dynasty was interrupted by the reign of **Wang Mang** (9–23 C.E.), who established the Xin dynasty after seizing the throne from the ruling Liu family, successfully using the belief in the Mandate of Heaven to undermine them. Wang Mang had been a respected government official before he took power, but soon made some disastrous missteps that weakened the empire and his control over it. Attempted reforms of land ownership and the currency were unsuccessful and caused chaos in the local economy among both the rich and poor. Waging war on the edges of the empire led to conscription of a resentful population and heavy taxation of landowners, which forced them to pay farmers less money for more work. Persistent famines, devastating floods along the Yellow River, and increasing commodity prices added to the resentment and fueled peasant uprisings which Wang Mang's enemies used to their advantage. The Xin Dynasty came to an end in 23 C.E. with the death of Wang Mang in battle.

The Han Dynasty was restored a couple of years later, but full recovery proved impossible and, in 220 C.E., the government collapsed. For the next 400 years, China was divided into several regional kingdoms.

3. Collapse of the Gupta Empire

The Gupta Empire fell for one simple reason: It was invaded by the Huns—not Attila's forces, which invaded Europe, but another group, the White Huns. The Gupta were able to hold off the Huns for the first half of the fifth century, but they did so at a tremendous cost, which weakened the state. By the end of the fifth century, there were Hun kingdoms in western and northern India. Though the underlying culture of India (including Hinduism and the caste system) survived the invasion, the empire did not.

4. Collapse of the Western Portion of the Roman Empire

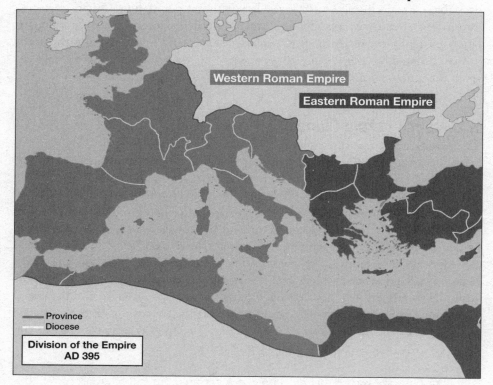

The Division of the Roman Empire

One historical event that has been endlessly debated over time is the fall of the Roman Empire. Some of these theories are reasonable, others much less so. Many try to assign a single cause to this momentous occurrence, but the situation was much more complicated.

In short, however, it can be said that it was internal decay, in combination with external pressure (Attila's Huns, among others groups), that brought about the fall of the Roman Empire. The sheer size of the empire and the huge expense of maintaining it, coupled by a succession of weak—or just plain bad—leaders, and a series of epidemics, are all factors that caused the empire to collapse.

In 284 C.E., **Diocletian** had become emperor. He attempted to deal with the increasing problems by dividing the empire into two regions run by co-emperors. He also brought the armies back under imperial control, and attempted to deal with the economic problems by strengthening the imperial currency, forcing a budget on the government, and capping prices to deal with inflation. Despite Diocletian's innovations and administrative talents, civil war erupted upon his retirement in 305 C.E.

After rising to power in 306 C.E. as a co-emperor, **Constantine** defeated his rivals and assumed sole control over the empire in 322 C.E. He ordered the building of **Constantinople** at the site of the Greek city of Byzantium, and in 340 C.E., this city became the capital of a united empire. Constantine, too, was an able emperor, but the problems of shrinking income and increased external pressures proved insurmountable. After his death, the empire was again divided into two pieces, east and west. The eastern half thrived from its center at Constantinople; the western half, centered in Rome, continued its spiral downward.

Rome faced external pressure from invaders on all of its frontiers especially from the middle of the third century on. One such invader was the powerful and well-organized Sassanid Persian empire who took over in Iran in 224 C.E. The Sassanids practiced the Iranian faith of **Zoroastrianism** and used that to consolidate their power. They enjoyed a powerful military which was able to defeat the Romans in many engagements, though the two empires managed to fight each other to a standstill by the year 627. In addition to the Persians, Germanic barbarians happened to attack the Roman empire at the same time, especially when the Romans were embroiled in costly civil wars or wars against the Persians. In defense, Roman authorities put Germanic peoples such as the Visigoths (who had adopted Roman law and Christianity) on the borders. But in the early fifth century, Attila and his Huns began to press on the Germanic tribes; in response, they began to press on the Roman Empire. Because the Germanic tribes had no other place to retreat from the Huns, they crossed the border into Roman territory. The Visigoths sacked Rome in 410 C.E., and by 476 C.E., the Roman emperor had been deposed. The fall of the western half of the Roman Empire was complete. The eastern half would survive, but not as the Roman Empire. It was later renamed the Byzantine Empire.

Contrast Them: The Fall of Han China, the Gupta Empire, and Rome

Two major causes of decline threaten any empire: internal (such as economic depression, natural catastrophes, and social unrest) and external (for example, invading armies). Unlike China, for example, which would later see a return to greatness, Rome would never again be at the center of such a great empire. The momentum had clearly changed to favor the invading German tribes and the powerful Byzantium Empire in the East

Western Rome 476 C.E.	Gupta 550 C.E.	Han China 220 C.E.
Tax revolts by upper class and church exempt from taxes	Not enough taxes for military defense	Officials exempt from taxes; difficult to collect from peasant population
Decrease in trade upon which economy depended		Population increases lead to less land per family
25 of 26 emperors died violently in one 50 year span		Corruption of court officials
Division of empire weakened the west half	Land divisions increased power of provincial officials	Unable to control large estate owners
Unable to defend against migratory invasions of Goths and Huns	Unable to defend against invasions by the White Huns	Constant conflict with the nomadic Xiong-nu who invaded after collapse

5. Cultural Diffusion 200–600 C.E.

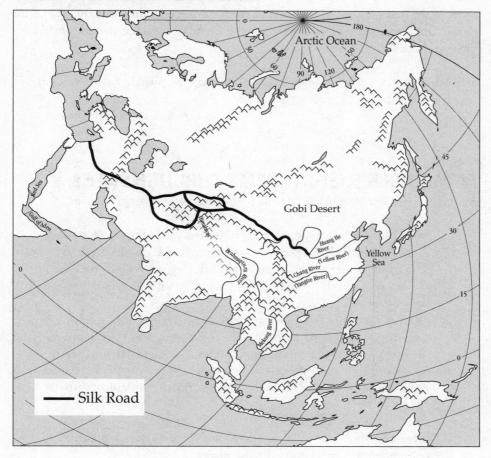

The Silk Road

Around the same time that major empires were collapsing, the known world was becoming an increasingly smaller place. Trade routes were flourishing, bringing cultures, religions, and invading tribes into constant contact with each other. Major trade routes over land, like the Silk Road from China to the Roman Empire, took months to traverse. Pastoral communities along the way provided protection, shelter, and supplies for the merchants, in exchange for payment. This meant that merchants not only interacted with people at their destination but also on the journey.

Unfortunately, disease traveled the same trade routes (and with invading armies). To give just a couple of examples, the Mongols carried the Black Death to China; Rome and China suffered from measles and smallpox epidemics, which quickly spread through the empires.

And, as we mentioned earlier, religion also followed the roads of the merchants. Buddhism spread through East and Southeast Asia by way of trade routes. Christianity spread rapidly in the Mediterranean via both land and sea. Even the invading Germanic tribes were converted. By 600 C.E., Christianity had taken root as far away as Britain.

By now, you're also well aware that it was not just merchants and missionaries that were on the move. As entire groups expanded their territories, they also put down roots in the new lands. The Anglos and the Saxons moved into Britain. The Huns moved into India. Only China and parts of East Asia seemed spared massive influxes of outsiders.

The world was clearly changing. The stage was set for entirely new developments, which is what the next chapter is all about.

IV. MAJOR BELIEF SYSTEMS THROUGH 600 C.E.

As you review the major belief systems below, keep a few things in mind.

1. Most of these belief systems have impacted world history from their inception through the present era. That said, the discussion here focuses on the impact of these systems during the ancient era. We'll talk more about the impact of these religions on later world events in subsequent chapters.
2. Most of the major religions have had schisms (divisions), resulting in a variety of subgroups and sects. The test writers will focus more on the overall religion than on particular sects (though there are a few exceptions that we'll get to in future chapters, such as the Protestant Reformation within Christianity and the rise of fundamentalism in Islam).
3. Don't focus only on the theological or philosophical basis of each belief system, but also on the impact they had on social, political, cultural, and even military developments.
4. Pay attention to where each belief system started and where it spread. As merchants and warriors moved, so did their religious beliefs. By looking at where religions branched out or came into conflict with one another, you'll get a good understanding of which cultures frequently interacted with each other.

For your convenience, here's a quick listing of the belief systems covered in this section.

A. Polytheism
B. Confucianism
C. Daoism
D. Legalism
E. Hinduism
F. Buddhism
G. Zoroastrianism
H. Judaism
I. Christianity

Note that Islam is not included here. Why? Because Islam didn't come onto the scene until after 600 C.E. We'll talk a lot about Islam in the next chapter.

A. Polytheism

Cultures that Practiced It

The vast majority of ancient civilizations were polytheistic. Through 600 C.E., the religions of all of the Mesopotamian and Mediterranean empires were polytheistic, except for the Hebrews and the Christians. In the east, Aryan religions, Hinduism, and traditional Chinese systems were polytheistic. Some Buddhist sects were polytheistic, as were some Daoist sects.

Nuts and Bolts

Polytheists believe in multiple gods who impact daily life on earth to varying degrees, sometimes for good, and sometimes not. For example, prior to the rise of Christianity, the ancient Greeks and Romans worshipped numerous gods who had very human qualities and who sometimes battled each other. In ancient Egypt, the gods were often considered benevolent and kind, while in ancient Sumer, the gods were to be feared, and hence had to be appeased on a regular basis.

Broader Impact

Polytheism had a major impact on the development of civilization: It was absolutely at the center of art and architecture in most of the civilizations we have discussed so far. Many of the grand works of these civilizations were dedicated to the gods, or made to appease them. More significantly, because the practice of polytheism in most early civilizations was very complicated and filled with rituals, it led to the rise of a priestly class, whose members controlled most of the communication between the people and their gods. Thus, these civilizations became dependent on an elevated group of people who controlled their collective destinies, and rigid social structures with priests near the top quickly developed. Finally, because some polytheistic civilizations had separate gods for each city-state, as well as collective gods for the civilization as a whole, such as the systems practiced in Sumer and ancient Greece, the rise and fall of various city-states was seen as a drama played out not only on earth, but also in the heavens. This added validity to a city-state's claim for predominance when it celebrated military success.

B. Confucianism

Cultures that Practiced It

Confucianism was developed specifically for the Chinese culture, and was widely practiced throughout China from around 400 B.C.E. onward.

Nuts and Bolts

The son of an aristocratic family from northern China, Confucius spent most of his life trying to gain a high position in government. But he was very strong-willed, and often his thinking was at odds with state policy. As a result, he never achieved his goal. Instead, he served as an educator and political advisor, and in this role he had a tremendous influence on China. He attracted many followers, some of whom helped share his teachings, and others who collected his thoughts and sayings in the Analects, which would come to have a profound influence on Chinese thinking, both politically and culturally.

The most important distinction to make about Confucianism is that it is a political and social philosophy—not a religion. Though fundamentally moral and ethical in character, it is also thoroughly practical, dealing almost solely with the question of how to restore political and social order. Confucianism does not deal with large philosophical issues or with religious issues, such as salvation or an afterlife.

Confucianism focuses on five fundamental relationships: ruler and subject, parent and child, husband and wife, older brother and younger brother, and friend and friend. When each person in these relationships lives up to his or her obligations of those relationships, society is orderly and predictable.

Confucianism concentrates on the formation of junzi, individuals considered superior because they are educated, conscientious, and able to put aside personal ambition for the good of the state.

There are also several values that Confucianism stresses:

>   *Ren*—a sense of humanity, kindness, and benevolence
>
>   *Li*—a sense of propriety, courtesy, respect, and deference to elders
>
>   *Xiao*—filial piety, which means a respect for family obligation, including to the extended family

Confucius believed that individuals who possessed these traits would be not only good administrators but also influential in the larger society because they would lead by example. He also was convinced that to restore political and social order, morally strong individuals were required to exercise enlightened leadership. This is why Confucius did not support a particular political system, but rather favored good people running whatever system was in place. Under Confucianism, women in China were considered of secondary status, although children were taught to honor their mothers as well as their fathers.

Broader Impact

Because Confucianism was an ethical, social, and political belief system, as opposed to a religion, it was compatible with other religions. In other words, a person could, for example, practice both Buddhism and Confucianism simultaneously.

This flexibility enabled Confucianism to flourish. Government leaders, too, embraced it, because it was intended to create an orderly society. Its widespread acceptance eventually led to a distinctive Chinese culture in which communities became extremely tight-knit; members had duties and responsibilities to many others in the community from birth to death.

Confucianism did not, however, have a similar impact on the rest of the world, because it evolved only within the context of the Chinese culture.

C. Daoism

Cultures that Practiced It
Some Chinese practiced Daoism, from around 500 B.C.E. onward.

Nuts and Bolts
The *Dao* (also spelled *Tao*) is defined as the way of nature, the way of the cosmos. Founded by Lao-tzu, a legendary Chinese philosopher, this belief system is based on an elusive concept regarding an eternal principle governing all the workings of the world. The *Dao* is passive and yielding; it accomplishes everything yet does nothing. One image used to demonstrate this is of a pot on the potter's wheel: The opening in the pot is nothing, yet the pot would not be a pot without it. Daoists sometimes also use the image of water, soft and yielding, yet capable of wearing away stone. From this comes the idea that humans should tailor their behavior to the passive and yielding nature of the *Dao*. Thus, ambition and activism only bring chaos to the world. Within Daoism is the doctrine of wuwei, disengagement from worldly affairs, a simple life in harmony with nature. Daoism isn't completely passive, however. Daoist priests often used magic that was intended to influence the spirits.

Broader Impact
Daoists advocated the formation of small, self-sufficient communities and served as a counter-balance to Confucian activism. And as an advocate of harmony with nature, Daoism promoted scientific discoveries. Daoists became great astronomers, chemists, and botanists.

Daoism's impact, though, is greater than its philosophy. It's notable because it co-existed with Confucianism, Buddhism, and Legalism in China. One of the things to remember about Daoism, therefore, is that it added to the complexity of China, which in turn added to the uniqueness of China and other Eastern civilizations as separate and distinct from the Western world.

> **Contrast Them: Daoism and Confucianism**
> Though Daoism and Confucianism shared a core belief in the Dao, or "the Way," they diverged in how each understood how the Dao manifested itself in the world. While Confucianism is concerned with creating an orderly society, Daoism is concerned with helping people live in harmony with nature and find internal peace. Confucianism encourages active relationships and a very active government as a fundamentally good force in the world; Daoism encourages a simple, passive existence, and little government interference with this pursuit. Despite these differences, many Chinese found them compatible, hence practiced both simultaneously. They used Confucianism to guide them in their relationships and Daoism to guide them in their private meditations.

D. Legalism

Cultures that Practiced It

The Chinese, specifically during the Qin Dynasty, are the most notable practitioners of Legalism.

Nuts and Bolts

Legalism developed at around the same time as Confucianism and Daoism. It maintained that peace and order were achievable only through a centralized, tightly governed state. Simply put, Legalists didn't trust human nature and, therefore, advocated the need for tough laws. They believed that people would be made to obey through harsh punishment, strong central government, and unquestioned authority. They focused only on things that were practical or that sustained the society. Not surprisingly, then, Legalists believed that two of the most worthy professions were farming and the military.

Broader Impact

By adopting Legalism, the Qin Dynasty was able to accomplish the unification of China swiftly, and the completion of massive projects like the building of the Great Wall. But because Legalism also caused widespread resentment among the common people, who suffered under it, Legalism inadvertently led to wider acceptance of Confucianism and Daoism.

> **Contrast Them: Legalism and Confucianism**
> Although both Legalism and Confucianism are social belief systems, not religions, and both are intended to lead to an orderly society, their approaches are directly opposed. Confucianism relies on the fundamental goodness of human beings, whereas Legalism presupposes that people are fundamentally evil. Therefore, Confucianism casts everything in terms of corresponding responsibilities, whereas Legalism casts everything in terms of strict laws and harsh punishment. The Han successfully blended the best of both philosophies to organize their dynasty.

E. Hinduism

Cultures that Practiced It

The various cultures of the Indian subcontinent practiced Hinduism.

Nuts and Bolts

Hinduism began in India with the Aryan invaders. Review the history of India in Section III of this chapter if you need to.

Hindus believe in one supreme force called Brahma, the creator, who is in all things. Hindu gods are manifestations of Brahma—notably Vishnu, the preserver, and Shiva, the destroyer. The life goal of Hindus is to merge with Brahma. But because that task is considered impossible to accomplish in one lifetime, Hindus also believe that who you are in this life was determined by who you were in a past life; and how you conduct yourself in your assigned role in this life will determine the role (caste) you are born into in a future life. If you behave well and follow the dharma (the rules and obligations of the caste you're born into), you'll keep moving up the ladder toward unification with Brahma. If not, you'll drop down the ladder. This cycle of life, death, and rebirth continues until you achieve moksha, the highest state of being, one of perfect internal peace and release of the soul.

There is no central sacred text in Hinduism, though the Vedas and the Upanishads, sources of prayers, verses, and descriptions of the origins of the universe, guide Hindus.

Broader Impact

Hinduism is a religion as well as a social system—the caste system. In the caste system, you are born into your caste, and if you are dissatisfied with it, it's an indication you are not following the dharma; therefore, you will have an even worse lot in the next life. This explains why most faithful Hindus quietly accepted their station in life. Though they knew social mobility within one lifetime was out of the question, they were confident that they would accomplish it at death if they lived according to the tenets of Hinduism.

Hinduism's close identification with the caste system and the Indian social structure and customs have prevented its acceptance in other parts of the world. In recent years, modern Hindus are beginning to rebel against the strictures of the caste system. But Hinduism as a whole remains a powerful force—even regarding its adherents' relationship to the animal kingdom, because Hindus believe they can be reincarnated as animals.

Hinduism later spawned another religion—Buddhism.

F. Buddhism

Cultures that Practiced It

Eastern civilizations, most notably in India, China, and Southeast Asia, as well as Japan, practiced Buddhism.

Nuts and Bolts

Buddhism was founded by a young Hindu prince named Siddhartha Gautama, who was born and lived in Nepal from 563 through 483 B.C.E. He rejected his wealth to search for the meaning of human suffering. After meditating under a sacred bodhi tree, he became the Buddha, or Enlightened One.

There is no supreme being in Buddhism. Rather, Buddhists follow the **Four Noble Truths**.

- All life is suffering.
- Suffering is caused by desire.
- One can be freed of this desire.
- One is freed of desire by following what's called the Eightfold Path.

The Eightfold Path is made up of right views, right aspirations, right speech, right conduct, right livelihood, right endeavor, right mindfulness, and right meditation. Following this path enables you to move toward nirvana, the state of perfect peace and harmony. The goal in one's life is to reach nirvana, which may or may not take several lifetimes, meaning that Buddhists also believe in reincarnation. Buddhism holds that anyone can achieve nirvana; it is not dependent on an underlying social structure, such as the caste system.

After the death of Buddha in 483 B.C.E., Buddhism split into two large movements, **Theravada**, also known as **Hinayana**, Buddhism and **Mahayana** Buddhism.

Theravada (Hinayana) Buddhism emphasizes meditation, simplicity, and an interpretation of nirvana as the renunciation of human consciousness and of the self. In Theravada Buddhism, Buddha himself is not considered a god, and other gods and goddesses have very little significance. (Theravada means "the Way of the Elders"; Hinayana means "the Lesser Vehicle.")

Mahayana Buddhism ("The Greater Vehicle") is a more complicated form of Buddhism, involving greater ritual than Buddha specified. Mahayana Buddhism appealed to people who believed that the original teachings of Buddha did not offer enough spiritual comfort; therefore, they began to hypothesize that other forms of salvation were possible. In Mahayana Buddhism, the Buddha himself became a godlike deity. Moreover, other deities appear, including bodhisattvas, those who have achieved nirvana but choose to remain on Earth. Mahayana Buddhists also relied more on priests and scriptures. Detractors of this form of Buddhism view these additions as being too similar to the Hinduism that Buddha disapproved of.

You probably won't have to know the details of the two Buddhist movements, but you should know that they exist.

Broader Impact

Because it did rejected social hierarchies of castes, Buddhism appealed strongly to members of lower rank. And because Buddhism isn't attached to an underlying social structure, it can apply to almost anyone, anywhere. As a consequence, it spread rapidly to other cultures throughout Asia.

When Ashoka, the Mauryan Emperor who became appalled by one too many bloody battles, was moved to convert to Buddhism, the religion really took off as a major force in Asia. Eventually, however, in India, Buddhism was reabsorbed into Hinduism, which remained the dominant belief system there. In China, Japan, and Southeast Asia, Buddhism continued to thrive. And as it spread via the trade routes, the cultures of Asia intertwined.

G. Zoroastrianism

Cultures that Practiced It

Iranians, especially under the Sassanid Empire, Central Asians, and some Indians practiced Zoroastrianism.

Nuts and Bolts

Zoroastrianism was created sometime in the second millenium B.C.E. in Central Asia and is typically attributed to the prophet Zoroaster. Zoroastrianism is a dualistic faith, which means that they believe in two gods representing good and evil. Ahura Mazda, the main god of good and truth, tries to lead his followers into overcoming the forces of evil and chaos, and humanity must play a role in ensuring that order survives. Thus, the individual actions of a person through his or her life determines the spiritual salvation of that soul, for Ahura Mazda will triumph over chaos at some point in the future. When chaos has been removed from the Universe, humans will transcend depending on their behaviors in their lifetimes. Its most important text is the Avesta, of which mostly fragmentary bits survive. We rely on quotations from later sources to make up for those that are lost to us.

Broader Impact

Zoroastrianism was an important religion to Iranian peoples, though its importance grew immensely when the Sassanid Persian dynasty was founded. As the state religion of the Sassanid Empire, it engendered the Sassanid state wherever the Persians weren't ruling and led to crackdowns on Zoroastrians within the Roman Empire, since the Romans feared that practitioners could attempt to betray the empire to the Persians. However, its dualistic tendencies clearly influenced Christian thinking considerably, prior to Christianity becoming the state religion of the

Roman Empire, and led to another point of contact between cultures, this time in the realm of religion. Crazy how that works, huh!

H. Judaism

Cultures that Practiced It
The Hebrews practiced Judaism.

Nuts and Bolts
Judaism holds that God selected a group of people, the Hebrews, and made himself known to them. If they followed his laws, worshipped him, and were faithful, he would preserve them for all time. This group became the Jews, and Judaism became the first of the great monotheistic faiths.

Judaism is not centered on many of the concepts typically associated with a religion, although a belief in an afterlife, a set of traditions and doctrines, philosophy, and personal salvation are part of its makeup. At the center of Judaism is the awareness of a unique relationship with God.

Jews believe that they were created by God and live in a world created by a personal, sovereign God who created the world for humans to live in and enjoy and exercise free will. The destiny of the world is paradise, reached by human beings with divine help. The task of human beings is to honor and serve God by following the Laws of Moses, as contained in the Torah (the Jewish Bible, made up of the first five books of the Old Testament), to promote the ethics of the prophets, and maintain the identity of the people. Judaism, therefore, is both a religious practice and a societal custom.

Broader Impact
Judaism was the first of the major monotheistic faiths; as such, it spawned the other two major monotheistic religions, Christianity and Islam.

I. Christianity

Cultures that Practiced It

Originally a splinter group of Jews practiced the religion, but it quickly expanded into the non-Jewish community and throughout the Roman Empire.

Nuts and Bolts

Christianity came into existence with Jesus of Nazareth, a charismatic Jewish teacher who claimed to be the Son of God, the Messiah, for whom Jews had long awaited. Many people were attracted to his teachings of devotion to God and love for human beings. The Roman and Jewish leaders were not among them, so in approximately 30 C.E., Jesus was crucified. His followers believed that he rose from the dead and ascended into heaven, and Christianity was born.

Christianity is based on both the Old and New Testaments of the Bible. Christians believe that Jesus Christ is the Son of God and that forgiveness of sins, and ultimately everlasting life, is achievable only through belief in the divinity, death, and resurrection of Christ. The Christian view is that the world was made by a personal and sovereign God (like Judaism), but that the world has fallen from harmony with God's will. As the Son of God, Christ was the link between God and human beings. Human beings are expected to seek to know God, to worship him, and to practice love and service to him and to other human beings. Many early Christians also believed that it was their duty to share this message with the unconverted (as do many Christian sects today).

Broader Impact

In the early days, Christianity was spread by the disciples of Jesus and by Paul of Tarsus. Paul originally was an extreme anti-Christian who was converted by a vision of Christ and became a principal figure in propagating the new religion. With its emphasis on compassion, grace through faith, and the promise of eternal life regardless of personal circumstances, Christianity appealed widely to the lower classes and women. By the third century C.E., Christianity had become the most influential religion in the Mediterranean basin. Following a period of persecution, it became legal within, and then the official religion of, the Roman Empire; it continued to branch northward and westward into regions beyond the boundaries of the Roman Empire. In coming centuries, this marriage of Christianity and empire would profoundly affect developments in a large segment of the world. More on that in future chapters.

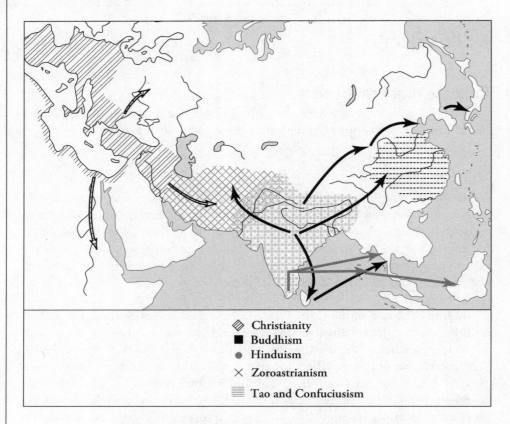

Map of World Religions circa 600 C.E.

By 600 C.E., interaction through trade, warfare, and migration had spread Christianity, Hinduism, and Buddhism far beyond their areas of origin. Christianity became the dominant force in what was left of the Roman Empire, while the Silk Road and Indian Ocean trade routes brought Buddhism and Hinduism into east and Southeast Asia.

V. TECHNOLOGY AND INNOVATIONS THROUGH 600 C.E.

Farming tools, metallurgy, and the ability to manipulate the environment cause humans to transition from nomadic hunters and gatherers to builders of civilizations and empires in this 10,000 year period. In order to farm successfully, people need tools, a way to transport what they've grown, and a place to store their surplus. Thus, the most important technologies developed by early civilizations included farming tools: ploughs, hoes, rakes, the wheel (and therefore the cart), and finally, pottery in which to store surplus for the off-season. While effective tools can be made out of bone and stone, they last longer and work more efficiently if they're made of metal. Copper was the first metal used, and other metallurgical techniques developed from there.

Once a society had enough goods, it needed a way to defend itself, and the knowledge that had helped make farming technology was used to create weapons and defense systems. It is not surprising that the first empires developed at the same time as iron technology and wheeled chariots, around 1500 B.C.E.! A major development in warfare, the stirrup, developed among the nomadic societies of the Eurasian steppe and spread to Chinese as early as the third century B.C.E. The stirrup arrived late in Europe because the mountainous geography of the Mediterranean world limited the use of chariots and horses there. Additionally, the horses were initially too small to carry heavily armored soldiers. Because of this, the armies of Rome and Greece were mostly made up of foot soldiers armed with spears and bows and arrows.

Ultimately, new technologies develop because they benefit society in some way. The earliest public works projects focused on irrigation—often simple dikes and canals to capture flood water and precious fertile silt. As cities grew, populations needed steady water supplies and a fairly reliable plumbing and sewage system. The large cities of the Indus River Valley (around 2500 B.C.E), had elaborate public and private sewers, and similar systems were built much later in the Roman Empire. The most visible technological achievements are massive architectural monuments built by all civilizations—pyramids, ziggurats, walls, temples, aqueducts, coliseums, theaters, and stadiums, and roads. These structures were used to assert the authority of leaders, facilitate the functioning of the state, and to keep the populace healthy, employed, and entertained.

A stable supply of food allowed people to develop specialized skills and crafts beyond the basic needs of their neighbors. Although a lot of the trade in early societies tended to be smaller luxury items—silk, cotton and wool, semi-precious gems, and jewelry; heavier goods including olive oil and spices were also traded.

To accomplish and keep track of all of the above, early societies developed means of communication and record keeping. Relatively accurate calendars were developed in all civilizations, but only the Maya had a 365-day solar calendar. Both the Maya and the Gupta separately invented the concept of zero. This was an especially inventive time for the Chinese; in addition to the building of Great Wall and the massive terra cotta army of the Qin, the Daoist scholars of the Han Dynasty developed windmills and wheelbarrows, worked on some early forms of gunpowder, figured out how to distill alcohol, and produced paper from a variety of accessible materials including tree bark.

VI. CHANGES AND CONTINUITIES IN THE ROLE OF WOMEN

An unfortunate fact of sedentary societies is that women lose power as people settle down, and women's roles in high-status food production became more limited. But women maintained power within the private sphere—by managing their households and taking responsibility for children's education, wives and mothers were often the unrecognized power behind the throne.

Although all of the early civilizations were decidedly patriarchal, women's freedoms differed depending on social status and class. Upper-class or elite women were more restricted in their public appearances, while lower-class women, peasants, and female slaves continued to work outside the home. Public veiling of upper-class women appears as early as the Babylonian Empire and is widespread by Greek and Roman times.

Cultural and religious values also impacted the status of women. In both Buddhism and Christianity, women were considered equals in their ability to achieve salvation or nirvana. In both religions, women could choose to remove themselves from traditional roles to become nuns and live separate from society in convents. Hinduism and Confucianism were much more structured and restricted. A Hindu woman could not read the sacred Vedas or participate in the prayers, and could not reach moksha in her lifetime. Daoism in China promoted a balance of male and female, but as Confucianism came to dominate, men were clearly considered superior to women. Under Confucian rule, some education was open to a large percentage of the female population, as it was believed they needed to be taught "proper" behavior and virtues.

Women's Status in Ancient Societies		
Rome/Greece	**India**	**China**
strict and patriarchal social divisions	strict patriarchal caste system	strict Confucian social order and guidelines for virtuous behavior
little land ownership	women were not allowed to inherit property	only sons inherit property
high literacy among upper class	forbidden to read sacred texts	upper classes educated in arts and literature and all educated in virtues
Spartan women were citizens	nope	nope
women could own businesses (especially widows)	needed large dowry and no remarriage for widows	arranged marriages though widows were permitted to remarry
women could be priestesses or later nuns	women could not achieve moksha	Buddhist convents and Daoism balances male and female

VII. PULLING IT ALL TOGETHER

There are many ways to think about the big-picture themes that have emerged in this chapter, but we'll stay focused on the three presented in Section II of this chapter.

1. Civilizations

By now, you should have a good understanding of the types of developments common to most civilizations; for example, agriculture, written language, and the use of metals all contributed to the growth of early civilizations. You should also be able to explain how civilizations grow when people are less concerned with where their next meal is coming from, and how they spread their influence (primarily through trade routes and conquest). And you should be able to describe what happens when civilizations become so dominant that they have no rivals (a period of peace and prosperity, or a golden age, emerges, making it possible to devote time and money to the arts and sciences). Finally, you should be able explain why those dominant civilizations begin to fall apart (they get too big, their own people get restless, foreign threats gain confidence and power).

By taking note of the patterns woven throughout the expansion and contraction of civilizations, you'll be well prepared to tackle the essays.

2. Sources of Change

Regarding change occurring in civilizations through cultural diffusion, keep in mind that the two main methods are through trade and conquest. Expansion of major belief systems also plays a major role, but don't forget belief systems followed the trade routes and the military movements, too.

You should be able to discuss some examples of changes brought about by invention and innovation. Two important ones are the use of the wheel and the use of iron.

Notice that some civilizations were more innovative while others more adaptive, but most cultures do both simultaneously. Whatever they invent, they spread to others; whatever they borrow, they adapt for their own purposes. That said, certain civilizations adapted an incredible amount from others—the Romans and the Macedonians, for example, from the Greeks.

3. Humans versus Nature

You should be able to name many ways in which civilizations have changed their surroundings to suit their own purposes. The digging of canals and irrigation ditches, stone-cutting, plowing, and metal-working are just a few examples. And don't forget the more subtle examples, such as the development of calendars and sundials, which were very significant in the human quest to predict and control nature for its own purposes. To be sure, humans can't change the repetitive patterns that underlie the yearly calendar, but by understanding those patterns and keeping track of them, humans can predict and use them for their own purposes.

Notice that as civilizations developed, they were less subject to natural events causing their demise, but more subject to other civilizations doing so. Notice also that as major belief systems developed, civilizations became less interested in appeasing the gods to protect them from the great unknowns, and more interested in internal peace, oneness with a great human force, or salvation. This corresponds to humans' ability to figure out nature. Thus, their focus of concern shifted from the need for bodily protection to the desire for internal peace.

As you continue to review the major world events in the upcoming chapters, always keep in mind that if you can compare, contrast, and figure out how things are changing, you will be able to write very thoughtful essays.

Important Terms

Agriculture
Agrarian
Bands/Clans
Barbarian
Bureaucracy
Civilization
City-states
Classical
Domestication
Economy
Egalitarian
Emperor
Empire
Feudalism
Foraging
Hierarchy
Hierarchical
Hunter-Gatherer
Irrigation
Monarchy
Monotheism
Neolithic
Nomadic
Pastoral
Paleolithic
Philosophy
Polytheism
River Valley
Sedentary
Settlement
Subsistence
Surplus
Sustenance
Theocracy
Traditional
Urbanization
Vassals

People, Places, and Events

Alexander the Great
Analects of Confucius
Bronze Age
Byzantium
Calendar
Code of Hammurabi
Cuneiform
Democracy
Eightfold Path
Four Noble Truths
Gothic Migrations
Great Wall
Han Dynasty
Hellenism
The Huns
Indian Ocean Trade
Iron Age
Jewish Diaspora
Legalism (China)
Pax Romana
Pyramids
Roman Republic
Roman Senate
Shang Civilization (China)
Shi Huang Di (Qin China)
Siddhartha Gautama
Silk Road Trade
The Torah
The Vedas of Hinduism
Xiongnu
Ziggurats

VIII. TIMELINE OF MAJOR DEVELOPMENTS 8000 B.C.E.–600 C.E.

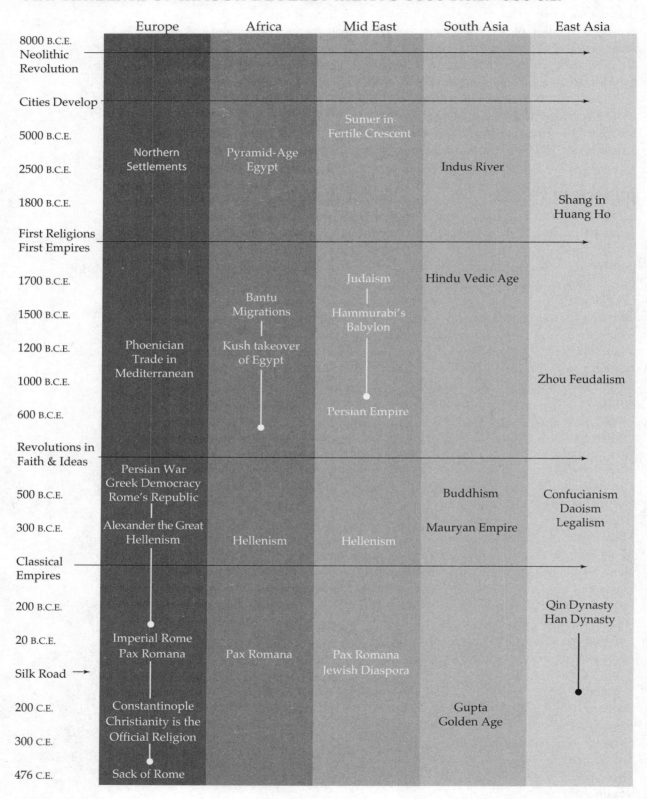

	Europe	Africa	Mid East	South Asia	East Asia
8000 B.C.E. Neolithic Revolution					
Cities Develop					
5000 B.C.E.	Northern Settlements	Pyramid-Age Egypt	Sumer in Fertile Crescent		
2500 B.C.E.				Indus River	
1800 B.C.E.					Shang in Huang Ho
First Religions First Empires					
1700 B.C.E.		Bantu Migrations	Judaism	Hindu Vedic Age	
1500 B.C.E.			Hammurabi's Babylon		
1200 B.C.E.	Phoenician Trade in Mediterranean	Kush takeover of Egypt			
1000 B.C.E.					Zhou Feudalism
600 B.C.E.			Persian Empire		
Revolutions in Faith & Ideas					
	Persian War Greek Democracy Rome's Republic				
500 B.C.E.				Buddhism	Confucianism Daoism Legalism
300 B.C.E.	Alexander the Great Hellenism	Hellenism	Hellenism	Mauryan Empire	
Classical Empires					
200 B.C.E.					Qin Dynasty Han Dynasty
20 B.C.E.	Imperial Rome Pax Romana	Pax Romana	Pax Romana Jewish Diaspora		
Silk Road →					
200 C.E.	Constantinople Christianity is the Official Religion			Gupta Golden Age	
300 C.E.					
476 C.E.	Sack of Rome				

REFLECT ACTIVITY

Respond to the following questions:

- For which content topics discussed in this Chapter do you feel you have achieved sufficient mastery to answer multiple choice questions correctly?

- For which content topics discussed in this Chapter do you feel you have achieved sufficient mastery to discuss effectively in an essay?

- For which content topics discussed in this Chapter do you feel you need more work before you can answer multiple choice questions correctly?

- For which content topics discussed in this Chapter do you feel you need more work before you can discuss effectively in an essay?

- What parts of this Chapter are you going to re-review?

- Will you seek further help outside of this book (such as a teacher, tutor, or AP Central), on any of the content in this Chapter—and, if so, on what content?

Chapter 7
Really Old Stuff: Around 600 C.E. to Around 1450

I. CHAPTER OVERVIEW

This chapter picks up where the last one left off—kind of. You'll notice that a few things discussed in this chapter actually occurred before 600 C.E. We included them because they fit in better with the topics covered here.

Remember: Read through this chapter once, then go back and focus on the things that you're not entirely clear about. Here's the chapter outline.

I. Chapter Overview

    You're reading it.

II. Stay Focused on the Big Picture

    Organize the many events that occurred during the 800 or 900 years covered in this chapter into some big-picture concepts.

III. Review of History Within Civilizations from 600 C.E.–1450.

    This is the largest section of the chapter. In it, we'll delve into developments in each region or major civilization. If you're totally clueless on any part of this section, consider also reviewing the corresponding topic in your textbook. After all, we're talking about 850 years of history, and this section is intended as a review, not as a primary source. Here's how we've organized the information.

    A. The Rise of Islam

    B. Developments in Europe and the Byzantine Empire

    C. Developments in Asia

    D. The Rise and Fall of the Mongols

    E. Developments in Africa

    F. Developments in the Americas

IV. Review of Interactions Among Cultures from 600 C.E.–1450

    To do well on the AP World History Exam, you need to understand more than just the events that occurred within each region or civilization. You need to understand how they interacted with and affected each other. This gets very complicated, so we've given the topic its own section. Make sure you review the material in Section III first. Once you have a firm understanding of the developments within each region of the world, this section will make a lot more sense. Here's how we've organized it:

II. STAY FOCUSED ON THE BIG PICTURE

As you review the details of the civilizations in this chapter, stay focused on the big-picture concepts and ask yourself some questions, including the following:

1. Do cultural areas, as opposed to states or empires, better represent history? Cultural areas are those that share a common culture, and don't necessarily respect geographical limitations. States, like city-states and nation-states (countries), and empires, have political boundaries, even if those boundaries aren't entirely agreed upon.

2. How does change occur within societies? As you review all the information in this chapter, you'll notice a lot of talk about trading, migrations, and invasions. Pay attention to why people move around so much in the first place, and the impact of these moves. And, don't forget, sometimes change occurs within a society because of internal developments, not because of external influences. Pay attention to that too.

3. How similar were the economic and trading practices that developed across cultures? Pay attention to monetary systems, trade routes, and trade practices. How did they link up?

4. How does the environment impact human decision making? Pay attention to the way states respond to environmental changes. Do they move or send out raiding parties? Are they able to respond quickly and successfully to environmental changes?

III. REVIEW OF HISTORY WITHIN CIVILIZATIONS 600 c.e.–1450

This period is defined by what rises out of the collapse of the Classical civilizations and by the interactions—both positive and negative—that develop between these new states. This period is one of tremendous growth in long-distance trade: the caravans of the various Silk Routes, the multi-ethnic Indian Ocean sailors, the trips across the Sahara to West Africa, and continued trade in the Mediterranean all occur from 600 to 1450 c.e. These 850 years were also defined by a long period of decentralization in Western Europe, and expansion on the trading empires of the Middle East and China. Remember interaction!

A. The Rise of Islam

In the seventh century, a new faith took hold in the Middle East. This faith, called Islam, was monotheistic, like Judaism and Christianity. The followers of Islam, called **Muslims**, believe that Allah (God) transmitted his words to the faithful through **Mohammad**, whose followers began to record those words in what came to be called the **Qu'ran** (recitation; also spelled Koran). Muslims believe that salvation is won through submission to the will of God, and that this can be accomplished by following the **Five Pillars of Islam**. These five pillars include

- confession of faith
- prayer five times per day
- charity to the needy
- fasting during the month-long Ramadan
- pilgrimage to Mecca at least once during one's lifetime

Islam is also guided by the concept of jihad, which means "to struggle." This refers to both the struggle to be a better Muslim and the struggle against non-believers.

Islam shares a common history with Judaism and Christianity. It accepts Abraham, Moses, and Jesus as prophets (although it does not accept Jesus as the son of God), and holds that Mohammad was the last great prophet. Like Christians, Muslims believe that all people are equal before God and that everyone should be converted to the faith. Early on, Islam split into two groups: Shia and Sunni. The split occurred over a disagreement about who should succeed Mohammad as the leader of the faith.

Allah Be Praised: Islam Takes Hold

Growing up in the city of **Mecca** in the Arabian desert (present-day Saudi Arabia), Mohammad was exposed to many different beliefs, in part because Mecca lay on the trade routes between the Mediterranean and the Indian Ocean. He was exposed to both Judaism and Christianity as a child, as well as the many polytheistic faiths that had traditionally influenced the region. Once he began preaching the monotheistic religion of Islam, which, as stated above, shares a foundation with Judaism and Christianity, he came into conflict with the leaders of Mecca, who had both a religious and economic interest in maintaining the status quo. In other words, the leadership in Mecca wanted to maintain the polytheistic shrines that attracted pilgrimages and brought wealth to the community. Persecuted, and threatened with death, Mohammad and his followers fled to **Medina** in 622 c.e. in what is known as the **hijra** (which also marks year 1 on the Muslim calendar). Mohammad and his followers found support in Medina and, in 630, he returned to Mecca and destroyed the pagan shrines—except for the Ka'ba, which became the focal point of Muslim pilgrimage.

From there, Islam spread throughout the Arabian Peninsula and beyond. The tenets of Islam came to be officially practiced in Muslim culture, similar to the way the tenets of Christianity were practiced in the Roman and Byzantine Empires. Lands where Islam was practiced were known as "Dar al Islam," or House of Islam. As Islam spread rapidly through the Middle East and Africa and toward Europe, Christian leaders became increasingly alarmed. More on that later.

The Empire Grows as the Religion Splits

When Mohammad died unexpectedly in 632, **Abu Bakr**, one of his first followers in Mecca, became caliph, the head of state, military commander, chief judge, and religious leader. You can think of the caliph as a sort of emperor and religious leader wrapped up in one person. He ruled an empire, but he also made pronouncements on religious doctrine. In other words, the Islamic empire was what's known as a **theocracy**, a government ruled by immediate divine guidance or by officials who are regarded as being divinely guided. But because it was ruled by a caliph, the theocratic Islamic Empire was referred to as a **caliphate**. Islam would eventually branch out beyond the boundaries of the Islamic Empire, and therefore exist independently as a religion, but in these early years, the growth of Islam was inextricably linked to the growth of this empire.

As time went on, the caliphs began to behave more like hereditary rulers, like those in a monarchy, except that there was no clear line of succession. The lack of clear succession caused a great deal of trouble down the road. The first four caliphs were Abu Bakr, Umar, Uthman, and Ali. The last of the four, Ali, was assassinated and was succeeded by his son, Hasan. But under pressure from a prominent family in Mecca, Hasan relinquished his title, making way for the establishment of the **Umayyad Dynasty**. This dynasty would enlarge the Islamic Empire dramatically, but it would also intensify conflict with the Byzantine and Persian Empires for almost a century.

During the Umayyad Dynasty, the capital was moved to Damascus, Syria, although Mecca remained the spiritual center. Also during the Umayyad reign, Arabic became the official language of the government; gold and silver coins became the standard monetary unit; and conquered subjects were "encouraged" to convert to Islam in order to establish a common faith throughout the empire. Those who chose not to convert were forced to pay a tax.

As noted above, the Islamic Empire grew enormously under the Umayyads, expanding as far as northern Africa and into Spain, where they ruled the southern Iberian peninsula from the city of Córdoba. Numerous times during the early eighth century, the Umayyads attacked the Byzantine capital of Constantinople, but failed to capture the city. That didn't stop them from going elsewhere, and in 732 C.E., the Islamic Empire began to make a move on Europe, by way of the Iberian Peninsula (Spain). At the time, Muslims held parts of southern Iberia and southern parts of Italy, while Christians dominated all the regions to the north. **Charles Martel** (686–741 C.E.), a Frankish leader, stopped the Muslim advance in its tracks as it tried to advance toward Paris, and so the Islamic Empire never flourished in Europe beyond parts of Spain and southern Italy. (More on the Franks and their activities a little later in the chapter.)

Despite the success of the Umayyad Dynasty (the **Dome of the Rock** was built on Temple Mount in Jerusalem during this time, and Córdoba was one of the richest and most sophisticated cities in Europe), problems with succession started to emerge. Eventually, the Muslims split into two camps, Shiite and Sunni. **Shiite (Shia) Islam** holds that Mohammad's son-in-law, Ali, was the rightful heir to the empire, based on Mohammad's comments to Ali. **Sunnis**, in contrast, though they hold Ali in high esteem, do not believe that he and his hereditary line are the chosen successors; rather, they contend that the leaders of the empire should be drawn from a broad base of the people. This split in Islam remains to this day.

As the Shia began to assert themselves more dramatically, the Umayyad Dynasty went into decline, and ultimate demise. In a battle for control of the empire against the forces of Abu al-Abbas (a descendent of Mohammad's uncle who was supported by the descendents of Ali, the Shia, and the Mawali—non-Arab Muslims), the Umayyad Empire was defeated (punctuated by the slaughter of some members of the family). It was replaced by the Abbasid Dynasty around 750 in all areas except Spain.

The Abbasid Dynasty: Another Golden Age to Remember

The **Abbasid Dynasty** reigned from 750 to 1258, that is, until the Islamic Empire was defeated by the Mongols (more on them later). Throughout this time, like all major empires, the Abbasids had many ups and downs, but they oversaw a golden age, from the early- to mid-ninth century, during which the arts and sciences flourished. The Abbasids built a magnificent capital at **Baghdad**, which became one of the great cultural centers of the world.

Like most of the other ancient civilizations we've discussed so far, the Islamic Empire was built around trade. The merchants introduced the unique idea of credit to the empire's trade mechanisms to free them of the burden—and the danger—of carrying coins. Necessarily, they also developed a system of itemized receipts and bills, innovations that were later used in Europe and elsewhere.

In addition to the importance of trade, manufacturing played an important role in the expansion of the Islamic Empire. Steel, for example, was produced for use in swords. Islamic advancements were also seen in the medical and mathematics fields. **Mohammad al-Razi**, for example, published a massive medical encyclopedia, which was unlike anything compiled before it. And Islamic mathematicians expanded the knowledge they had learned from India; their contributions are especially noteworthy in algebra.

An Abbasid army had the good fortune to defeat a T'ang Chinese army (more on them in a few pages) during the Battle of the Talus River in 751 c.e. This fight for control of Silk Road trading posts in central Asia is relatively unimportant (the Muslims won) except for the fact that the Chinese POWs were carrying paper money. Once the Abbasids figured out how to make paper, they could continue one of their most important activities, building libraries and universities and stocking them with scholarship from all over the known world. The location of the Muslims at the cross-roads of Europe and Asia allowed them to monopolize trade routes. The cosmopolitan cities of the Islamic caliphs thrived on trade, international scholars, and expansion, both military and cultural.

So despite the hostility between the European and Islamic worlds, the Islamic Empire is credited with playing a significant role in preserving Western culture. (Recall that the Byzantines did this too.) In contrast to European civilizations during the Middle Ages, which were highly decentralized and dismissive of their ancient past (more on that later in this chapter), the Arabs kept the Western heritage of the region alive. For example, when the Muslims encountered the classic writings of ancient Athens and Rome, including those of Plato and Aristotle, they translated them into Arabic. Later, when Muslims and Christians battled for control of the **Levant** (present-day Israel, Jordan, Syria, Lebanon and points north and south) during the European Crusades, Europe found its own history among the other treasures preserved in Arabic libraries and museums. This again demonstrates how the interaction between two peoples (even when violent) can lead to trade and cultural exchange.

The Muslims, similar to the Romans, were often tolerant of the local customs of the areas they conquered—although Christians and Jews were often persecuted in the Levant. That's not to say that the Islamic Empire didn't make every effort to convert the people it conquered (remember the tax we mentioned)? The point is, though it was a theocracy, its more flexible approach contributed to its rapid growth. The **Sufis**, Islamic mystics, were its most effective missionaries. They stressed a personal relationship with Allah, in contrast to other religions that emphasize a particular form of ritual. As you might guess, this made Islam highly adaptable to many different circumstances. By allowing, and even encouraging, followers to practice their own ways to revere Allah, and by tolerating others who placed Allah in the framework of other beliefs, the Sufis succeeded in converting large numbers of people to Islam.

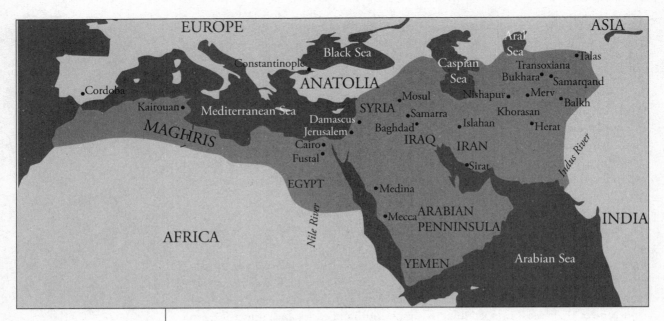

Map of the Abbasid Caliphate

Women and Islam: For Better, for Worse

In Arabia, women traditionally did not have property rights or inheritance rights; rather, women were essentially viewed as property themselves—of men. If a man divorced a woman, for example, he would keep her dowry (the money and property from her father that she brought with her into the marriage). This widespread—really, institutionalized—low status for women eventually led to a culture in which baby girls were seen as less valuable than baby boys. Tragically this often translated into female infanticide, the killing of an unwanted baby girl. (This gender bias was, by the way, common in many patriarchal societies.)

The Qu'ran, the sacred book of Islam, established between 651 and 652, changed much of this. Although women remained subservient to men and under their direction and control, they began to be treated with more dignity, had some legal rights, and were considered equal before Allah. If a man divorced his wife, he would have to return her dowry to her. More important, infanticide was strictly forbidden. Women gained considerable influence within the home—and in early Islamic society, women sometimes had influence outside it. Khadija, Mohammad's first wife, had been a successful businesswoman, for example.

Islamic society was still a man's world, however. Men were permitted to have as many as four wives, as long as they were able to support them and treated them equally. Women, on the other hand, had to be faithful to one man—in part because in this society land was passed through the males, and the identity of a boy's father couldn't be questionable. And, legally, women were treated unequally; a woman's testimony in court, for example, was given only half the weight of a man's. Restrictions for women even included what they wore: They had to be veiled in public—although this custom began in Mesopotamia and Persia, Islamic society adopted and adapted it.

Over time, Islamic society became more structured and more patriarchal. A woman's primary duty was singular: to be loyal to and care for her husband and family. Within that structure, however, women were highly protected, and in some ways more respected, under the Qu'ran than they previously had been.

Decline of the Islamic Caliphates: Internal Rivalries and Mongol Invasions

The Islamic empire regularly endured internal struggles and civil war, often arising from differences between the Sunni and Shia sects, and from ethnic differences between diverse groups in the rapidly expanding Muslim world. Numerous rival factions and powers developed, and although none of these threatened Islam, they did destabilize the central authority at Baghdad and cut tax revenues. The final blows came when Turkish warrior slaves revolted and established a new capital at Samarra in central Iraq, while other groups carved out pieces of the empire. There was a new Shia dynasty in northern Iran and constant threats from the Seljuk Turks, a nomadic Sunni group. And like the Romans before them, weakened by internal problems, the Abbasids also had external foes: the Persians, Europeans, and Byzantine.

It would be their most distant enemy, however, the Mongols, who would defeat them. During the crusades, in 1258, the **Mongols** overran the Islamic Empire and destroyed Baghdad, thereby signaling the end of the Abbasid Dynasty. Its people would flee to Egypt, where they remained intact but powerless. Eventually, the **Ottoman Turks** would reunite Egypt, Syria, and Arabia in a new Islamic state, which would last until 1918.

B. Developments in Europe and the Byzantine Empire

Developments in Europe and points east became quite complicated during the **Middle Ages**, which is the period after the fall of Rome and before the Renaissance. As you might recall from the last chapter, the Roman Empire, and eventually Christianity, was divided into two factions that split, reconnected, then split again. Ultimately, the eastern Roman Empire, centered in Constantinople, became the highly centralized government known as the Byzantine Empire; whereas, in the west, the empire collapsed entirely, although the religion retained a strong foothold. The important point to remember about all this is that even though both segments of the empire followed Christianity, they practiced different forms of the religion; moreover, their populations competed for supremacy.

Note the Change: As the Empire Turns

They meet. They flirt for a long time, then marry and settle in Rome. Things get tough, so they take a short break from each other, but get back together in Constantinople where they build a new house. After a time they separate from each other geographically, but remain married by religion. Eventually, they get a divorce and follow their own religious paths. Will they ever be able to rekindle the romance?

The history of the Roman Empire reads a lot like a bad soap opera. Recall from Chapter 6 that the Roman Empire united the entire Mediterranean for centuries. But it became too unwieldy to govern as a whole, so in 286 c.e., the empire was split into an eastern half and a western half, in what were hoped to be more manageable administrative regions. Then, in 313, Christianity was accepted in the empire; and in 330, when Constantine converted to Christianity, he reunited the empire at Constantinople. It was still the Roman Empire, it just wasn't centered in Rome. The empire split again in 395, while the Western half of the empire was sliced and diced by incoming barbarian tribes and disintegrated as a political unit in 476, at which time the eastern half became known as the Byzantine Empire. Almost 400 years later, in 800, the Pope decided to crown a new Western Roman Emperor in order to show that the Western half was not under the control of the Eastern Empire. The Western half would get a name change around 900 to become the Holy Roman Empire, centered in Germany. The Byzantines continued on as before in the east. So again there were two empires, but still one religion. That, however, was to change as well some two hundred years later when, in 1054, Christianity began to be practiced as two entirely separate religions: Roman Catholicism and Christian Orthodoxy.

As you review the events in this region, the important points to remember are

- the Byzantine Empire was a lot more centralized and organized than the Western empire
- both practiced Christianity, though not in the same way

The Byzantine Empire: The Brief Details

The **Byzantine Empire** was distinct from the Roman Empire. It used the Greek language; its architecture had distinctive domes; its culture in general had more in common with Eastern cultures like those of Persia; and its brand of Christianity became an entirely separate branch known as **Orthodox Christianity**.

Compared with what was going on at the height of the Roman Empire, much of Europe at the time was fragmented into small feudal kingdoms with limited power and fewer cultural and intellectual advancements. The Byzantine Empire, like the Islamic Empire to the south, was significantly different. The Byzantine emperors ruled by absolute authority, especially over the economy, whose industries, such as silk production (a trade learned from China), they monopolized. The Byzantines also used coined money, the value of which remained remarkably stable, making it a very desirable currency for business.

Under **Justinian**, who reigned from 527 to 565, the former glory and unity of the Roman Empire was somewhat restored in Constantinople. The region flourished in trade and the arts. Christian Constantinople and Islamic Baghdad rivaled each other for cultural supremacy. The Justinian period is perhaps most remembered for three things: (1) the **Justinian Code**, a codification of Roman law that kept ancient Roman legal principles alive (in the West these went unused for a time), and (2) the flowering of the arts and sciences, evident in the construction of major buildings and churches, most notably **Hagia Sophia**, an enormous cathedral that still stands today (but now as a mosque). The Byzantines are also remembered and admired for their mastery of the mosaic art form they used to decorate churches. Finally, and most importantly, Justinian is known for his ambitious plan to reconquer the lost provinces of the Western half of the Roman Empire. His plans went smoothly when his armies reconquered Africa from the Vandals, but intense siege warfare against the Ostrogoths in Italy that lasted 20 years halted Justinian's plans for further conquests. By the end of his reign, his empire was indeed larger, but at the cost of destroying what remained of Roman infrastructure in Italy, as well as bankrupting his coffers and exhausting the sources of his soldiers.

In contrast to the Roman Catholic emperors of the West, who regarded the Pope as the leader of the See of Rome, the Byzantine emperors nominated their own Patriarchs of the See of Constantinople. For centuries the two churches managed to tolerate each other while they butted heads for primacy over the whole of the Christian flock, but in time the differences, both political and religious, became too great. They disagreed over the sacrament of communion, whether priests should be allowed to marry, and the use of local languages in church. They even were at odds regarding the nature of God, specifically God as a trinity, and they disagreed over the placement of icons during worship. In 1054 C.E., unable to reconcile their differences, the Pope excommunicated the patriarch of Constantinople, who did the same to the Pope. From this point forward, the Church of Constantinople (otherwise known as Eastern Orthodoxy) influenced the East and Roman Catholicism influenced the West. Keep this schism in mind as you review the Crusades, Christian Europe's war with the Islamic world; the Byzantine is right in the middle!

Contrast Them: Religion and State in Roman Catholicism and Christian Orthodoxy

Remember that we said the secular empire was more centralized in the east (Byzantine Empire) than in the west (Roman Empire) during the Middle Ages? Interestingly, the reverse was true in terms of their religions. Christianity as practiced by Roman Catholics was very centralized with power stemming from Rome and services held in the Roman (Latin) form. In the east, Orthodox Christianity was more localized. Russian churches, for example, conducted services in their own language. In this sense local customs merged with Christian practices in the Orthodox Church.

A great deal of the evolution of these religions in these two empires centered on control. For stability, either the heads of the church or the heads of the state needed to be in control. During the Middle Ages, the West centralized power in the church, thereby decentralizing political power. Essentially that meant the existing political leadership was blessed by the church, hence often under the control of the church as well, at least in the early centuries of the Middle Ages. In the East, the situation was the exact opposite: Political emperors were in control of both politics and the church, and church practices were localized, but not political authority. The point to remember here is that in the early centuries of the Middle Ages, the East was more of a secular empire with an official church religion; the West was more of a religious empire with subservient political units.

Impact of Orthodoxy on Russia: Feast in the East

In the ninth century, the Slavic peoples of southeastern Europe and Russia were converted to Christianity by **St. Cyril**, an Orthodox Christian, who used the Greek alphabet to create a Slavic alphabet that to this day is used in parts of the region. Most of these areas were not part of the Byzantine Empire itself, but were influenced by it. When **Vladimir**, a Russian prince from Kiev, abandoned the traditional pagan religion and converted to Christianity, he also considered Islam, Judaism, and Roman Catholicism. Rumor has it that he chose Christian Orthodoxy because it had no restrictions about when or what he could and could not eat.

The dominance of Christian Orthodoxy in this region is significant because while western Europe followed one cultural path, eastern Europe followed another, and this had a tremendous impact on the development of Russia. The Russian Orthodox Church was aligned with Byzantine but not Roman traditions. So, when the Roman church reformed later (discussed in Chapter 6), the Russian and Greek churches did not. As a result of this, and the Mongol invasion (coming up soon), Russia became culturally different from the other great powers of Europe, which grew out of the Roman Catholic tradition.

Meanwhile Out West: The Franks versus the Muslims

The best place to begin a discussion of political developments in western Europe in the Middle Ages is with the Franks. After the classical Roman Empire fell apart, due in part to invasions from Germanic tribes, these tribes settled throughout western Europe. Most of the tribes converted to Christianity relatively quickly, though politically they continued to run their own shows. That meant they came into regular conflict with each other, and they formed alliances and expanded, sometimes enough to be considered kingdoms. The most significant of these early kingdoms was the Franks.

The **Franks** were a Germanic tribe that united under the leadership of **King Clovis** in the late fifth century. He built a rather large empire that stretched from present-day Germany through Belgium and into France. He converted to Roman Catholicism and established his capital in Paris. After he died, his empire was divided among his sons, after which it declined in influence.

Nevertheless, the empire did help the various peoples of western Europe solidify under a common culture, which made it easier for them to unify against Muslim invasions, which in the eighth century took over parts of Spain and Italy. **Charles Martel** (remember we mentioned him at the beginning of the chapter?) led the revolt against the advancing Muslim armies and in 732 defeated them at the **Battle of Tours**, not far from Paris. Again, interaction through conflict.

Martel then used his position as a political and military leader under the declining Frankish **Merovingian Dynasty** to put his sons forth as successors, thus founding the **Carolingian Dynasty** ("Carolus" is Latin for Charles). Martel had worked during his tenure to reunite the region under his control, and when his son **Pepin the Short** (there were several Pepins in Frankish history) ascended to the throne in 752 C.E., he chose to have his succession certified by the pope, a significant step that sent the clear signal that an empire's legitimacy rested on the Roman Catholic Church's approval.

Charlemagne: The Empire Strikes Back

Legend:
- Frankish Territory in 481
- Conquests of Clovis 481–511
- Conquests 531–614
- Conquests 714–768
- Conquests of Charlemagne 768–814
- Dependent territories
- *Avars* Peoples tributary to Charlemagne
- Kingdom of Siagrius in 486
- Visigothic kingdom of Toulouse in 507
- Boundaries of the empire in 814

Central Europe around the Thirteenth Century

In the centuries following the breakup of the Roman Empire, no true empire existed in western Europe. The Franks had built a large kingdom, but it could hardly be considered an empire by historical standards. It would be Pepin's son, Charles (747–814 c.e.), who would revitalize the concept of the empire in western Europe. Like his father, Charles was crowned by the pope in 800 and became known as **Charlemagne** ("Charles the Great").

The empire Charlemagne built would come to be called the **Holy Roman Empire** upon the coronation of Otto the Great in 962. It's important to point out that this empire had little in common with the original Roman Empire, other than the fact that power was once again centralized and Rome began to think of itself again as a world center. The size of the Holy Roman Empire, in comparison to its namesake, was relatively small. It included northern Italy, Germany, Belgium, and France. Nevertheless, it marked the beginning of western European ambition in terms of empire-building, especially among those in the church.

Under Charlemagne, a strong focus was placed on the arts and education, but not surprisingly with a much more religious bent—much of this effort centered in the monasteries under the direction of the church. And though Charlemagne was very powerful, his rule was not absolute. Society was structured around Feudalism (more on feudalism shortly). Thus Charlemagne had overall control of the empire, but the local lords held power over the local territories, answering to Charlemagne only on an as-needed basis. And because Charlemagne did not levy taxes, he failed to build a strong and united empire. After his death, and the death of his son Louis, the empire was divided among his three grandsons according to the **Treaty of Verdun** in 843.

The Vikings: Raiders from the Norse

During this time, western Europe continued to be attacked by powerful invaders, notably the Vikings from Scandinavia and the **Magyars** from Hungary. Although the **Vikings** were not the only raiders, they were perhaps the most successful. Beginning around 800, they used their highly maneuverable, multi-oared boats to raid well beyond their borders—on the open seas, up and down the North Atlantic coast, and along the inland rivers.

The Vikings got a bad reputation for raiding the Roman Catholic monasteries, but don't blame the Vikings. Island life means limited resources, and raiding was a normal consequence of the pressures on a growing society. The monasteries held much wealth and food, so they were natural targets. But raiding was just one aspect of Norse economy. The Vikings were also merchants and fishermen and developed some of the earliest commercial fisheries in northern Europe. These activities, along with the raids, led to settlements as diverse as Newfoundland, Canada around 1000 C.E., inland Russia, and northern France. The Vikings even got as far south as Constantinople, raiding it at least three times. In France, the Vikings were known as Normans (or north-men), the most famous of whom is William, who conquered Anglo-Saxon England in 1066. (Vikings, in the form of the Normans, had an enormous influence on England, particularly on the English language.)

Remarkably, however, in spite of their various victories, the Vikings, too, were converted to Christianity. This continued in a pattern of invading tribes assimilating to a common civilization in western Europe because of religion, not political power. Roman Catholicism became institutionalized at every level of life. By the middle of the Middle Ages, the Catholic Church had become the most powerful institution in western Europe and one of the most powerful institutions in the world.

European Feudalism: Land Divided

Feudalism, the name of the European social, economic, and political system of the Middle Ages, had a strict hierarchy. At the top was a king, who had power over an entire territory called his kingdom. Beneath him were the **nobles**, who in exchange for military service and loyalty to the king were granted power over sections of the kingdom. The nobles, in turn, divided their lands into smaller sections under the control of lesser lords called **vassals**. The vassals could also split their lands into smaller pieces and give custody of them to subordinate vassals, who could divide their lands into even smaller pieces in the custody of even more subordinate vassals, and so on. Below the vassals were **peasants**, who worked the land. For this system to work, everyone had to fulfill obligations to others at different levels in the hierarchy: to serve in the military, produce food, or serve those who were at a higher level. If, say, you were a lesser-lord, you were obliged to your lord, and you were obliged to your vassals as well.

The estates that were granted to the vassals were called **fiefs**, and these later became known as **manors**. The lord and the peasants lived on the manor. The peasants worked the land on behalf of the lord, and in exchange the lord gave the peasants protection and a place to live. Many of the manors were remarkably self-sufficient. Everything that was needed to live was produced on them. Food was harvested, clothing and shoes were made, and so on. Advances made in the science of agriculture during this time helped the manors to succeed. One such advance, called the **three-field system**, centered on the rotation of three fields: one for the fall harvest, one for the spring harvest, and one not-seeded fallow harvest (the latter allowing the land to replenish its nutrients). In this way, manors were able to accumulate food surpluses and build on the success. Lords directed what was called the "Great Clearing," the clearing of huge areas of forest for the creation of more farmland.

Compare Them: Ancient Civilizations and Those of the Middle Ages

You have no doubt noticed that European civilizations during the Middle Ages evolved in much the same way as the Mediterranean, Indus, and Shang civilizations a couple of thousand years earlier, and for the same reason: Agricultural surpluses enabled the early civilizations to build cities, which then made it possible to form complicated institutions and promote the arts and sciences.

In western Europe after the fall of the Roman Empire, the practice of feudalism caused life to be centered on small, self-sustaining communities that didn't initially generate much of a surplus. But as they subsequently built up storehouses of food and supplies, and as people came into greater contact with each other, they were freed to pursue other endeavors (at the discretion of their overseer, of course). As a result, we begin to see the emergence of craftspeople, individuals skilled in highly specialized ways. Towns and cities, too, began to grow, and, eventually, the Middle Ages came to an end.

The lord, as noted, owed his allegiance to the king, but only had direct contact with him when the king called upon the lord to provide a service. Otherwise, the lord was in charge of his own manor—his own life. And though the various fiefs were, in theory, self-sustaining, and the lords all beholden to the same ruler, conflicts erupted between feudal lords on a regular basis (this is where the term feud comes from). The etiquette of these disputes and rules of engagement was highly refined and flowed from the **code of chivalry**, an honor system that strongly condemned betrayal and promoted mutual respect. Most of the lords (and knights, who were also considered part of the nobility) followed the code of chivalry.

The feudal system, like most of the civilizations we've discussed so far, was male-dominated. Land equaled power, and only males could inherit land, so women were pretty much powerless. Specifically, when a lord died under the feudal system his land and title passed down via **primogeniture**, to his eldest son. Even noblewomen had few rights—though they were socially elevated (and have come to be romanticized in literature). They could inherit a fief, but they could not rule it. And their education was limited to only domestic skills. As usual in most early societies, noblewomen were admired and valued primarily for their "feminine" traits—their beauty or compassion—but were regarded essentially as property to be protected or displayed.

Peasants (called **serfs**) in the feudal social system, whether male or female, had few rights. As manorial life evolved, an increasing number of peasants became tied to the land quite literally: They couldn't leave the manor without permission from their lord. Peasants were not quite slaves, but not free either. Ironically, however, it was this "imprisonment" on the land that led to the serfs becoming highly skilled workers. In short, they learned how to do whatever it took to make the manor on which they worked self-sufficient.

Contrast Them: Feudal Europe and the Islamic Empire

Remember the Abbasid Dynasty? It flowered in the Islamic world at the same time that feudalism was taking root in western Europe. Islamic merchants were trading with the world while European lords were governing their manors. Baghdad became a center of learning and art in the Islamic Empire, whereas small, secluded monasteries became centers of learning in the early Holy Roman Empire. In summary, it can be said that in the early Middle Ages, educated Europeans became very provincial, while educated Arabs became more worldly.

As many of the serfs became skilled in trades other than farming, and Europe slowly but surely started trading with the rest of the world, some of these skilled crafts people began to earn extra income. Over time, this chipped away at the rigid social stratification of the manor system. When banking began in Europe, towns and cities started to gain momentum. The result was the emergence of a "middle class," made up of urban craftsmen and merchants. Their success lured more people into towns, in the hopes of making more money or learning new skills. By the eleventh century, western Europe was re-engaging with the world.

Height of the Middle Ages: Trading and Crusading

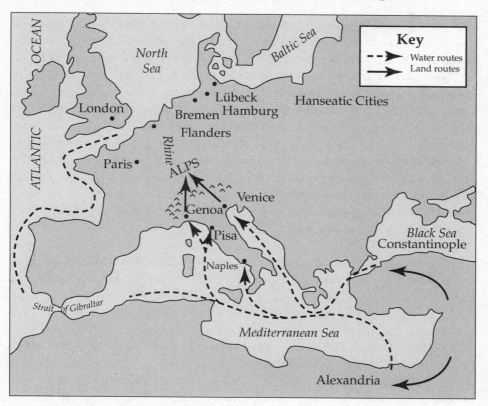

Trade Routes of the Hanseatic League (Thirteenth to Fifteenth Centuries)

Given the new importance of trade, towns with wealthy merchants arose near the once all-powerful manors. Towns were chartered on lands controlled by feudal lords (the charters gave the townspeople certain rights); and within the towns, the middle-class merchants, or **burghers**, became politically powerful. Like their manorial predecessors, the towns had a great deal of independence within the empire but were intrinsically more interdependent than the self-sufficient manors of the feudal system. Eventually, towns formed alliances, not unlike a city-state structure. One of the most significant alliances, the **Hanseatic League**, had an economic basis; established in 1358, it controlled trade throughout much of northern Europe. One effect of the interdependence of the towns was to initiate a drive toward nationhood; another was to increase social mobility and flexibility among the classes.

Among the greatest artistic achievements of the Middle Ages was its architecture, specifically its cathedrals. In the early Middle Ages, churches were built in the bulky Romanesque style; later architectural advancements led to what came to be called the Gothic style. Gothic cathedrals were designed to draw worshippers closer to God. To achieve this, architects of the day used "flying buttresses," which gave support for tall windows and vaulted ceilings. Over time, the cathedral became more than a place of worship; it became an art form and an arena for art. The church sponsored artists to adorn the inside of cathedrals with paintings and sculpture. Music, too, such as Gregorian chants, became an intrinsic part of ceremonies.

European contact with the Muslim world during the **Crusades** (military campaigns undertaken by European Christians of the eleventh through the fourteenth centuries to take over the Holy Land and convert Muslims and other non-Christians to Christianity) and over the trade routes helped spur new thought and broadened the perspective of these previously insular people (more on the Crusades in Section IV of this chapter). In time, people began to question organized religion (citing "reason"), which of course the church found threatening. This process of reasoning gave rise to **heresies**, religious practices or beliefs that do not conform to the traditional church doctrine. Sometimes what became defined as heresies were simply older beliefs that did not adapt to more mainstream changes in religious thought. In what may seem an irony today, many heretics wanted a return to the simpler ways of early Christianity; they rejected how worldly and wealthy the church had become.

Another important effect of people thinking more openly was the founding of universities, where men (not women) could study philosophy, law, and medicine, and learn from the advances made in Muslim cultures. In science, the ideas of Aristotle, Ptolemy, and other Greeks were brought to Europe through contacts with Islamic and Byzantine Empires (again, via trading and crusading). This progression, called **scholasticism**, also sometimes came into conflict with the church because it relied on reason rather than faith as its basis.

Doubts about the supremacy of religious dogma continued to emerge until the beginning of the thirteenth century when **Pope Innocent III** issued strict decrees on church doctrine. Under Innocent III, heretics and Jews were frequently persecuted, and a fourth, ultimately unsuccessful crusade was attempted. During this crusade, which seemed motivated by greed, the Crusaders conquered—and sacked—the already Christian Constantinople, and declared a Latin Empire. (This empire was short-lived, lasting only some fifty years, and ended when the Byzantines overthrew the Latins in 1261). A few years later, Pope Gregory IX set into motion the now-notorious **Inquisition**, a formalized interrogation and persecution process of heretics. Punishment for so-called nonbelievers ranged from excommunication and exile to torture and execution. Due to the pervasiveness of the church and its ultimate power at this time, it is sometimes referred to as the **Universal Church** or the **Church Militant**.

Late in the thirteenth century, **Thomas Aquinas** (1225–1274 C.E.), a famous Christian realist of this period, made significant inroads in altering Christian thought. He wrote *Summa Theologica*, which outlined his view that faith and reason are not in conflict, but that both are gifts from God and each can be used to enhance the other. His writings had a major impact on Christian thought, although the church remained a strict guardian of its own interpretations.

Focus On: The Bubonic Plague

Referred to as the Black Death, this epidemic originated in China where it killed an estimated 35 million people. It spread rapidly through Europe in the mid-fourteenth century. Its transmission was facilitated by new forms of commerce and trade, including Mongol control of the central Asian Silk Routes, that increased the interaction between Europe and Asia. First occurring in the 1330s, the epidemic spread westward with traders and merchants, and arrived in Italian port cities as early as 1347. Crowded conditions in Europe's cities and the lack of adequate sanitation and medical knowledge all contributed to its rapid spread. Within 50 years, a third of Europe's population was dead, traditional feudal hierarchies were obsolete, religious hatred intensified, and people lost faith in the power of the church. The dramatic changes brought by the epidemic sped up social and economic movements that were already impacting Europe. These included a shift toward a commercial economy, more individual freedoms, and development of new industries.

The Emergence of Nation-States: Power Solidifies

Keep in mind that during the Middle Ages, western Europe wasn't organized into countries (nation-states); rather it was broken up into feudal kingdoms. But by the close of the Middle Ages, western Europe began to organize along cultural and linguistic lines. People who spoke French aligned themselves with France. Those who spoke English united under the banner of England. We'll be talking a lot more about this in the next chapter, but for now, just keep this general concept in mind.

The various parts of Europe took different paths to achieve statehood during the thirteenth century. In Germany, for example, the reigning family died out without a suitable successor to the emperorship, so the region entered a period known as an **interregnum** (a time between kings). Germany and Italy became decentralized in a group of strong, independent townships and kingdoms, similar to city-states. In this environment, merchants and tradespeople became more powerful. In northern Germany, for example, the Hanseatic League (the influential association of merchants mentioned earlier) led the region's progress in international trade and commerce.

England, in contrast, unified much more quickly. Since the time of **William the Conqueror**, England had followed a tradition of a strong monarchy. But during the rule of King John, powerful English nobles rebelled and forced him to sign the **Magna Carta** (1215 c.e.). This document reinstated the feudal rights of the nobles, but also extended the rule of law to other people in the country, namely the growing burgher class. This laid the foundation for the Parliament. Initially, an assembly was established made up of nobles who were responsible for representing the views of different parts of England on law-making and taxation issues. After a trial period, the Parliament was established. Later, it was divided into two branches: the House of Lords (nobles and clergy) and the House of Commons (knights and wealthy burghers). The House of Lords presided over legal issues and advised the king; the House of Commons was concerned with issues of trade and taxation. The result was that England established its identity pretty early on.

The formation of France was bound up with England. In 987, **King Hugh Capet** ruled only a small area around Paris; for the next couple of hundred years, subsequent French kings expanded the territory. But beginning in the twelfth century, England began to claim large parts of present-day France. The English occupation of the French-speaking territories led to revolts and, eventually, to French statehood (the goal being to unite France under its own leadership). This effort would be spearheaded by an unlikely candidate.

As a teenager, **Joan of Arc**, a farm girl, claimed to have heard voices that told her to liberate France from the hands of the English, who had by the early fifteenth century claimed the entire French territory. Remarkably, this uneducated youngster somehow managed to convince French authorities that she had been divinely inspired to lead men into battle, and they supplied her with military backing. With her army, she forced the British to retreat from Orleans, but was later captured by the French, tried by the English, and burned at the stake by the French. Nevertheless, she had a significant impact on the **Hundred Years' War** (1337–1453) between England and France, which eventually resulted in England's withdrawal from France.

After the Hundred Years' War, royal power in France became more centralized. Under a series of monarchs known as **Bourbons**, France was unified and became a major power on the European continent.

At around the same time, Spain was united by **Queen Isabella**, the ruler of Castille (present-day central Spain). Power in the Spanish-speaking region of Europe had been divided for two reasons: first, Castille was one of three independent Spanish kingdoms, and therefore no single ruler controlled the region, and second, the peasants were split along religious lines (mostly Christian and Muslim), due to the lasting influences of the Muslim conquest of the Iberian Peninsula during the Middle Ages. To overcome these obstacles, Isabella married **Ferdinand**, heir to the Spanish Kingdom of Aragon, in 1469, thus uniting most of Spain in a single monarchy. Rather than compete with the church for authority, Isabella and Ferdinand, both Christians, enlisted the Catholic Church as a strong ally. Spanish statehood thrived under the new monarchy and the alignment with the Catholic Church effectively ended religious toleration in the region. The result was that non-Christians (predominantly Muslim and Jewish people) were forced to convert to Christianity or leave the country. This marked the beginning of the **Spanish Inquisition**. The consequences for non-Christian Spaniards were tragic; the consequences for the Spanish monarchy were huge. Newly unified and energized, Spain embarked on an imperial quest that lead to tremendous wealth and glory, eventually resulting in the spread of the Spanish language, Spanish customs, and Christianity to much of the New World (as you will see in the next chapter).

What About Russia?

Recall that eastern Europe and Russia at this time were very different from the West. The Eastern Orthodox Christians of this area spent much time and effort defending themselves from the colonization of various western invaders. It wasn't until 1242 that Russia succumbed to the **Tatars** (a group of Mongols from the east) under Genghis Khan. The Tatars ruled a large chunk of Russia for two centuries, leading to a cultural rift that further split eastern and western Europe.

By the fourteenth century the Mongol power started to decline and the Russian princes of Muscovy grew in power. By the late 1400s, Ivan III expanded Muscovy territory (the area surrounding Moscow) into much of modern-day Russia and declared himself **czar**, the Russian word for emperor or Caesar. As the center of the Eastern Orthodox Church, Moscow was declared the Third Rome, after the real Rome and Constantinople. By the mid-1500s, **Ivan the Terrible** (or the House of Rurik) had centralized power over the entire Russian sphere, ruling ruthlessly and using the secret police against his own nobles. The next chapter will go into more of the details about Russia. By this time, nationalism in Russia was well underway.

> ### Focus On: Urbanization
>
> If trade is the way you make your living, chances are you are spending lots of time in cities. Traders and merchants needed a place to meet and conduct business and this period saw the growth of urban culture throughout the world, mostly as a result of trade contacts and networks. Along with trade, cities showcased the wealth and power of the rulers who both controlled and benefited from the trade. Urban centers usually developed along trade routes or in locations necessary for strategic defense.
>
> In the early years, the most populous cities were in the Muslim world and China—cities that were part of the network of Silk Routes: Baghdad, Merv, and Chang'an. Prior to 1400, Constantinople was the only European city of any size and it was really considered part of the Eastern world. Along with their economic role, these cities became political and cultural centers for the new trade empires. After 1400, European cities begin to grow with Paris and the Italian city-states emerging as new trading powers.

C. Developments in Asia

1. China and Nearby Regions

The three powerful Chinese dynasties during this period, T'ang (618–907 C.E.), Song (960–1279 C.E.), and Ming (1368–1644 C.E.), developed Golden Ages with unique characteristics. T'ang and Song are grouped together (although they are very different) while the Ming came to power after a brief period of domination by Mongol invaders. You should understand from the outset that when we speak of China, we're actually talking about its influence throughout much of east and southeast Asia. We'll talk more specifically about Korea, Vietnam, and Cambodia in a minute. For now, you just need to understand that China had an enormous impact on cultural and political developments in those civilizations.

A Quick Review of the Rise and Fall and Rise and Fall and Rise

The **T'ang Dynasty** ruled China beginning in 618 C.E. Under **Emperor Xuan-zong**, the T'ang expanded Chinese territory into parts of Manchuria, Mongolia, Tibet, and Korea. By 907, however, the empire had become so large that local warlords gained more and more power, and the T'ang dynasty collapsed. In 960, after a brief era of restlessness, China was reunified under the **Song Dynasty** and Emperor Taizu. Despite a long period of peace and prosperity, the Song eventually fell to the Jurchen and then the Mongols until finally in 1279, the Mongols established the **Yuan Dynasty** in its place. That dynasty lasted less than a century. The Mongols were driven from China, and in 1368 the **Ming Dynasty** restored traditional Chinese rule to the empire.

From the seventh to the thirteenth centuries, the T'ang and then the Song Dynasties in China were accomplished in virtually every category of human endeavor—art, architecture, science, philosophy, porcelain-making, silk-weaving, construction of transportation systems, and more. Yet, it is probably poetry that made the T'ang Dynasty truly unique. Today, T'ang poetry tells us about daily life in China during that time. The Song built on the T'ang Dynasty's talent for poetry with more practical applications of words, in the form of encyclopedias and histories. Under the Song Dynasty, China developed printing processes, which facilitated the spread of its literary accomplishments throughout Asia, and later influenced the development of literature in Korea and Japan.

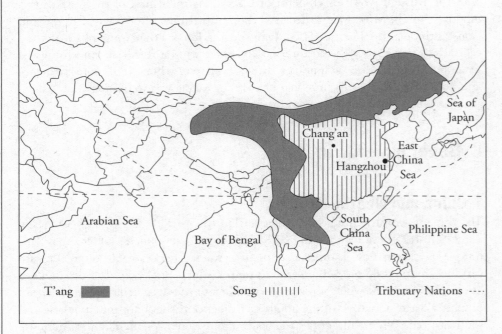

Extent of the T'ang (618–907 C.E.) and Song (960–1279 C.E.) Dynasties

At the height of both the T'ang and Song Dynasties, China was relatively stable. One of the many reasons for the stability was the bureaucratic system that was based on merit through the use of the civil service examinations (remember which dynasty created it? The Han Dynasty—see previous chapter for review). The T'ang and Song rulers continued to modify the civil service examination, but kept it focused on Confucian principles, which created a large core of educated, talented, and loyal government workers. The T'ang and Song also built an extensive transportation and communication network, including canals. They developed new business practices, including the introduction of paper money and letters of credit (hmmm…where have we seen these before?). All of this, of course, led to increased trade and cultural diffusion.

Because the power of the dynasties was based on trade and expansion, each developed an urban base to pursue their economic and political strategies. T'ang power was based on military garrisons along the central Asian trade routes and their capital at Chang'an (today Xi'an), the eastern terminus of the Silk Road and the largest city in the world at this time. This cosmopolitan city hosted a multinational and multireligious population. It was also the center of the T'ang **tribute system**, through which independent countries including Vietnam, Korea, Tibet, and various central Asian tribes, acknowledged the supremacy of the Chinese emperor and sent ambassadors to the city with gifts. Indirect rule of these vassal states spread Chinese influence far and wide and brought religion, among other things, into China. A similar tribute system would be repeated during the early years of the Ming Dynasty.

Focus On: Civil Service in China

The bureaucracy contributed to China's stability in huge ways because it generally stayed in effect even as dynasties changed. Regardless of who was in charge, the leaders generally depended on the bureaucracy to carry out the functions of government. And remember, since appointment to a civil service position was earned by a strong performance on the civil service examination, the civil service was a meritocracy (earned) as opposed to an aristocracy (inherited). So when power changed from ruling family to ruling family, it didn't impact the earned positions in the civil service.

Think about it in terms of the U.S. bureaucracy. No matter who gets elected president, most of the bureaucracy remains the same. Most CIA agents, Department of Agriculture employees, and IRS agents are going to keep their jobs regardless of who is president. Some of the higher-up positions get newly appointed leaders when a U.S. administration changes, but the underlying functions of the government remain remarkably stable.

Even when the Mongols ruled in China, the underlying bureaucracy remained. The Mongols brought in foreign government administrators, but the lower-level support and service jobs were kept by locals. Thus the system returned and stayed intact.

The Song Dynasty, under pressure from northern nomads, withdrew to the south and established a capital city at Hangzhou, the southern end of the Grand Canal. Here they concentrated on developing an industrial society, building on many of the ideas of the previous dynasty. An early form of **moveable type** resulted in an increase in literacy and bureaucrats among the lower classes. Printed books also spread agricultural and technological knowledge, leading to an increase in productivity and population growth. By the 1100s, the Song were an urban population with some of the largest cities in the world. Their wealth was based in part on their powerful navy and their participation in international trade throughout southeast Asia.

During the Song Dynasty, new technologies were applied to the military. Gunpowder started to be used in primitive weapons. The magnetic compass, watertight bulkheads, and sternpost rudders made the Chinese junks, as their ships were called, the best of their time. The junks were also used as merchant ships, of course.

Between 800 and 1100, iron production increased tenfold to about 120,000 tons per year, rivaling the British production of iron centuries later (in the 1700s). Song technology also included the production of steel, using water-wheel-driven bellows to produce the needed temperatures.

The introduction of Champa rice from Vietnam, a fast-ripening rice, linked with new agricultural techniques, increased food supplies. This led to a rapid population rise from 600 to 1200 C.E. China's population more than doubled, increasing from 45 million to 115 million. The urban centers expanded greatly.

Chinese Women: One Bound to Lead, Most Just Bound

One of the more incredible events during the T'ang Dynasty was the rise of **Wu Zhao**, who became the first (and to date, only) Empress of China at the death of her husband, Emperor Gaozong. An able ruler, she was both ruthless toward her adversaries and compassionate toward peasants. The vast majority of women in China, however, never gained that kind of power. Highly patriarchal, Chinese men considered women inferior, and like European men of the Middle Ages, they considered a woman's beauty and femininity as virtues worth protecting. During the Song Dynasty, adherence to a new Confucianism justified the subordination of women, and **foot binding** became a widespread practice. A woman's feet would be bound shortly after birth in an effort to keep them small—if kept bound for a long enough time, they wouldn't grow even as the rest of the body did. Large feet were considered masculine and ugly. This practice, which lasted for centuries among elite families, was not only painful, but also often deforming and sometimes crippling.

Religion in China: Diverse Beliefs

Following the fall of the Han Dynasty, there were a number of different religious influences in China, such as Nestorians, Manicheans, Zoroastrians, and Islam. But the religion that had the greatest impact by far was Buddhism, especially in two of its forms: Mahayana and Chan. Mahayana Buddhism appealed to many because of its emphasis on a peaceful and quiet existence, a life apart from worldly values. With its emphasis on meditation and appreciation of beauty, Chan (or Zen) Buddhism, won converts in the educated classes, who generally followed the tenets of Confucianism.

Both the Confucians and the Daoists reacted strongly to the spread of Buddhism. Many Confucians saw Buddhism as a drain on both the treasury and the labor pool, especially because Buddhism dismissed the pursuit of material accumulation. The Daoists saw Buddhism as a rival religion that was winning over many of its adherents. In the mid-800s under Emperor Wuzong, a wave of persecutions destroyed thousands of monasteries and reduced the influence of Buddhism in China.

Neo-Confucianism in China

As China turned away from other worldly ideas of the Buddhists during the late T'ang and early Song, new ideas about Confucian philosophy developed. Where older Confucianism had focused on practical politics and morality, the neo-Confucianists borrowed Buddhist ideas about the soul and the individual. This new tradition became the guiding doctrine of the Song Dynasty and the basis for civil service. At its core was a systematic approach to both the heavens and the role of individual. Filial piety, the maintenance of proper roles, and loyalty to one's superiors were again emphasized.

2. Japan

Because Japan consists of four main islands off the coast of mainland Asia, it was relatively isolated for thousands of years. Ideas, religions, and material goods traveled between Japan and the rest of Asia, especially China, but the rate of exchange was relatively limited. Only in recent centuries has Japan allowed Western influences.

Little is known of early cultures in Japan prior to 400 C.E., except that they were influenced by Korea and China. The first important ruling family was the **Yamato** clan, whose international connections helped them emerge as leaders in the fifth century. One of the unique things about Japan is that the Yamamoto clan was both the first and the only dynasty to rule it. The current emperor is a descendent of this same clan.

Early on, the **Shinto** religion took hold in Japan. Under Shinto, which means "the way of the gods," the Japanese worshiped the kami, which refers to nature and all of the forces of nature, both the seen and unseen. The goal under Shinto is to become part of the kami by following certain rituals and customs. The religion also encourages obedience and proper behavior. The Yamamoto clan claimed that the emperor was a direct descendant of the sun goddess, one of the main forces in the Shinto religion. This claim helped the Yamamoto stay in power—if you believe the emperor is divine, you're probably going to want to keep him around.

Can't Get Enough of China? Go to Japan.

In the sixth century, the influence of China in Japan increased dramatically. In 522, Buddhist missionaries went to Japan and brought with them Chinese culture. In no time, Chinese things were all the rage. Buddhism spread quickly, but interestingly, it didn't replace Shinto. Instead, most Japanese adopted Buddhism while also hanging on to their Shinto beliefs. In other words, they followed both religions simultaneously.

By the early seventh century, Chinese influence increased yet again. **Prince Shotoku** borrowed bureaucratic and legal reforms, which were modeled on the successes of the T'ang Dynasty in China. These reforms were enacted after his death as the **Taika Reforms** (645 C.E.). In the eighth century, when the Japanese built their new capital, they modeled it on the T'ang capital. At the risk of giving the impression that Japan became a "Little China," you should keep in mind one thing: the Japanese largely rejected Confucianism, as well as the idea of the civil service examination. Why? Both of these systems held the educated in high esteem. In Japan, education wasn't nearly as important as birth. The noble classes were hereditary, not earned.

Contrast Them: China and Japan

Even though China influenced Japan enormously, it didn't penetrate Japanese identity. Birth was more important than outside influence or education. The aristocracy remained strong. Despite the widespread influence of Confucianism and Chan (now Zen) Buddhism, Japanese continued to observe the rites of their indigenous religion, Shinto. Even at the height of T'ang influence, it can be said that Japan drew inspiration from China, but maintained its own distinctive traditions.

Here Come the Fujiwara: At Home in Heian

In 794, the capital was moved to Heian, and a new era of Japanese consciousness began. The Chinese influence abated, while the power of aristocratic families increased. One of the most powerful families, the **Fujiwara**, intermarried over several generations with the emperor's family and soon ran the affairs of the country. The emperor remained as a figurehead, but the real power had shifted to members of the Fujiwara family.

Under the Fujiwara, Japanese society experienced something like a golden age, especially in terms of literature. Japanese noblewomen were particularly prolific, especially when compared to women of other cultures. But by the twelfth century, power in Japan spread among a larger and larger pool of noble families, and soon they were fighting with each other for control over their small territories. In other words, Japan had devolved into a feudal system not unlike the one in Europe.

Feudal Japan

The interesting thing about feudalism in Japan is that it developed at around the same time as feudalism in western Europe, but it developed independently.

In 1192, Yoritomo Minamoto was given the title of chief general, or **shogun**, by the emperor. As with the Fujiwara family, the emperor was the figurehead but he didn't hold the real power. The real power was in the hands of the shogun.

Below the shogun in the pecking order were the **daimyo**, owners of large tracts of land, or the counterparts of the lords of medieval Europe. The daimyo were powerful samurai, which were like knights. They were part warrior, part nobility. They, in turn, divided up their lands to lesser samurai (vassals), who in turn split their land up again. Peasants and artisans worked the fields and shops to support the samurai class. Just as in European feudalism, the hierarchy was bound together in a land-for-loyalty exchange.

The samurai followed a strict code of conduct known as the **Code of Bushido**, which was very similar to the code of chivalry in Europe. The code stressed loyalty, courage, and honor; so much so that if a samurai failed to meet his obligations under the code, he was expected to commit suicide.

Interestingly, unlike under European feudalism, women in Japan were not held in high esteem. Remember that in Europe, noblewomen were given few rights, but they were adored, at least to the extent that they were beautiful and possessed feminine traits. In contrast, Japanese women lost any freedom they had during the Fujiwara period and were forced to live harsher, more demeaning lives.

> Compare and Contrast Them: European and Japanese Feudalism
> They were similar in terms of political structure, social structure, and honor code. They were different in terms of treatment of women and legal arrangement. In Europe, the feudal contract was just that, a contract. It was an arrangement of obligations enforced in law. In Japan, on the other hand, the feudal arrangement was based solely on group identity and loyalty. In both cases, the feudal arrangement was based on culture, and so the feudal system stayed around for a very long time.

3. Vietnam and Korea

Because China's dynastic leaders were intent on expanding by means of trade and force, Chinese armies had been in Korea and Vietnam as early as the Han Dynasty. But it was the large-scale military campaigns of the T'ang that resulted in cultural exchange in both regions.

Korea had its own independent and powerful dynasty, but in order to maintain the appearance of cordial relations with their powerful Chinese neighbors, the Koreans became a vassal-state of the T'ang. The gift-giving and exchanges resulted in Korean schools and the imperial court being organized like those of the Chinese, although the power of the royal houses and nobility in Korea prevented the development of a true bureaucracy based on merit. The tribute relationship was also responsible for the spread of both Confucianism and Chan Buddhism to Korea.

The Viet people of Southeast Asia were much less willing to accept even the appearance of a tribute relationship with their northern neighbors, and actively resisted the T'ang armies. Although a tribute relationship was eventually established, Confucian education was accepted, and an active trade relationship existed between the two entities, the Vietnamese maintained local traditions and continued to actively revolt against T'ang authorities. After the fall of the T'ang, the Vietnamese would maintain their independence in the face of later Chinese expansion.

4. India

As you should remember from the last chapter, India was the birthplace of two major religions: Hinduism and Buddhism. In the tenth century, another major religion made its way to the Indus valley: Islam.

The Sultan Ate at the Deli? Yes, the Delhi Sultanate

After defeating the disorganized Hindus, the Islamic invaders set up shop in Delhi under their leader, the sultan. Hence, this kingdom is referred to as the **Delhi**

Sultanate. For over three hundred years beginning in about 1206, Islam spread throughout much of northern India. While many Hindus held on to their religious beliefs under this theoretically tolerant regime, individual sultans were highly offended by Hinduism's polytheistic ways and did their best to convert them. Like non-Muslims under the Umayyads in Arabia, non-Muslims under the sultans in India had to pay a tax. But more than that, the sultans were capable of religiously motivated destruction. Hindu temples were sometimes destroyed, and occasionally violence erupted in communities.

Contrast Them: Hinduism and Islam

Islam on top of Hinduism was a strange concoction. Hinduism is polytheistic while Islam is monotheistic. Islam holds that all people are equal under God, while Hinduism upholds the caste system. To Islamic people, cows are food; to Hindus, cows are sacred. Hinduism sees itself as universal and exclusive; Islam sees itself as tolerant of other beliefs and even mixed with other beliefs. These two religions have always been a strange mix and have often clashed. If you don't remember how bad things got between the two groups in India, you'll review the consequences later in this book.

Despite the differences between the Islamic and Hindu cultures, an amazing amount of progress occurred in India under the sultans. Colleges were founded. Irrigation systems were vastly improved. Mosques were built, often with the help of Hindu architects and artists. And many Hindus in northern India converted. Sometimes the conversions were genuine; other times, they just made life easier. In any case, a considerable number of Hindus in northern India converted to Islam while the vast majority of Hindus in southern India held on to their traditions.

D. The Rise and Fall of the Mongols

The Mongols, the epitome of a nomadic culture, existed as a society for a long time before they became a force on the broader world scene. The Mongols were superb horsemen and archers and probably could have been a world power early on in the development of major civilizations. However, rivalries between tribes and clans kept them from unifying, so for centuries they fought with each other and remained fairly isolated from the rest of the world.

In the early 1200s, all that changed. Using his tremendous military and organizational skills, **Genghis Khan** (also spelled Chingiss Khan) unified the Mongol tribes and set them on a path of expansion that would lead to the largest empire the world had ever seen.

Genghis Khan unified several nomadic tribes of Mongolia and led the Mongol invasion of China in 1234, which was the beginning of the enormous Mongolian conquests. The **Mongol Empire** eventually spanned from the Pacific Ocean to eastern Europe. Following the death of Ghenghis Khan, his followers splintered off into different groups they called hordes. The members of these hordes elected a new Great Khan after Ghenghis and his successor, but by the election of Kublai Khan these hordes, or Khanates, were largely independent of any sort of central leadership from the homeland in Mongolia proper. The **Golden Horde** conquered the region of modern-day Russia. In China, **Kublai Khan** ruled. Mongols destroyed cities and were ruthless warriors, but once their domain was established, the empire was relatively peaceful, sometimes called the Pax Mongolica. The continuous empire allowed for the exchange of goods, ideas, and culture from one distant region to another. Mongols, who were illiterate, nomadic people prior to their conquests and education reforms brought about by Genghis Khan, eventually became assimilated into the cultures of the people they defeated.

Warning! You Are Now Entering a Golden-Age-Free Zone

One of the most striking things about the Mongols is that their empire was one of territory, infrastructure, and conquest, but not one of "culture." Because the Mongol Empire was so enormous and conquered so many different kinds of civilizations, it did not attempt to force a unified religion or way of life on its people. That being said, although the Mongols did not make many advances in the arts and sciences themselves, their superior infrastructure allowed for the exchange and spread of ideas. Genghis Khan also established the first pony express and postal system and gave tax breaks to teachers and clerics within his empire. In other ways, however, the Mongol Empire had a profoundly negative impact on conquered cultures, stifling cultural growth rather than contributing to it by having been so brutal in their initial raids.

> ### Contrast Them: The Mongol Empire and All Other Major Civilizations
> We've seen the golden age of Gupta. The golden age of Shang. The golden ages of Greece, Rome, and Islam. The Mongol Empire was larger than any of the empires that produced those golden ages. Yet rather than imposing their own cultural developments on the areas it conquered, it generally accepted or ignored those of the people they conquered. Unlike the sultans who took over India, the Mongols allowed their subjects to practice their own religions without interference. It should be pointed out that because the Mongol empire was so expansive, it tied much of the world together and served as a conduit across which ideas and culture spread from the Pacific to the Mediterranean and vice versa. It's just that it wasn't the Mongols' own culture.

Timur Wasn't Timid

In addition to invading Russia, Persia, Central Asia, and China, the Mongols also found time on their itinerary for a layover in India. They swept in under their leader, the untamed Timur Lang, who destroyed just about everything in sight and massacred thousands, and then just as quickly swept out. The sultanate was destroyed, but after **Timur Lang** (sometimes referred to as **Tamerlane**) returned to his capital in Samarkand, the Mongols pulled out as well. Just a few years later, the sultanate was restored. Islam continued to grow in India for the next few centuries under the Mogul Empire, even as many Hindus hung on to their beliefs. Look for more on this later.

How the Mongols Did It: No Rest Until Conquest

Imagine that you live in a village that lies in the path of an advancing Mongol horde. You've heard the stories. If you put up a fight, they'll pummel you. If you retreat to your house, they'll burn it. If you organize a resistance in your place of worship or civic building, they'll level it. You've also heard that if you just give in, they might spare your city, but they also might not. They're not really interested in changing your culture. So your only real choice, if you want to stay alive, is to give in. If you do, you may or may not be able to keep your life and your culture, but if you don't, you'll suffer a certainly grotesque death. What would you do?

In the 1200s and 1300s, a lot of people gave in. And those that didn't met their death. The Mongols weren't called ruthless warriors for nothing. They knew how to fight. But they were more than fierce fighters. They were also highly organized and highly mobile. Unlike the much-feared Roman army, which in its heyday could cover about 25 miles per day, the Mongol horsemen could cover about 90. Their bows, designed to be launched from horseback, had a range of up to 300 yards, way more than anybody else's. Their armies were divided into units, which were further separated into light and heavy cavalries and scouting units. They were extremely motivated—Genghis Khan punished traitors swiftly and rewarded the courageous generously. They were stealthy—they had an extensive network of spies that scouted their enemies before battle. Finally, their goals were made unmistakably clear—the consequences of putting up a fight against the Mongols meant certain destruction of the entire village, so most learned not to resist.

In short, they were really, really good at what they did: conquering.

The Mongol Impact

As mentioned earlier, the Mongols were great diffusers of culture. Some Mongols were assimilated by those they conquered. In Persia, for example, most Mongols became Muslim. Elsewhere, Mongols either couldn't absorb those they conquered or intentionally didn't. In China, for example, Kublai Khan, the grandson of Genghis, dismissed the Confucian scholars, forbade marriage between Mongols and Chinese, and wouldn't allow the Chinese to learn the Mongol language. Because the Chinese weren't allowed to **Mongolize**, they didn't. They kept their own identity, and when they finally kicked the Mongols out in 1368, the Chinese were able to establish the Ming Dynasty under traditional Chinese practices, which they had never lost.

There were, however, two major consequences of Mongol rule. The first is that Russia, which was conquered by the Golden Horde and treated as a vassal state, didn't unify or culturally develop as quickly as its European neighbors to the west. The second, and globally more important impact was that world trade, cultural diffusion, and awareness grew. Think about it: The Mongol empire touched Europe and very nearly touched Japan. It stretched southward to Persia and India making possible not only trade but also the transmission of the Black Plague in the fourteenth century. This one empire touched nearly all the major civilizations of the day. So, strange as it sounds, the often brutal Mongols, in their own way, brought the world together. By 1450, as the Mongol Empire was well into its decline, the world would never again be disconnected.

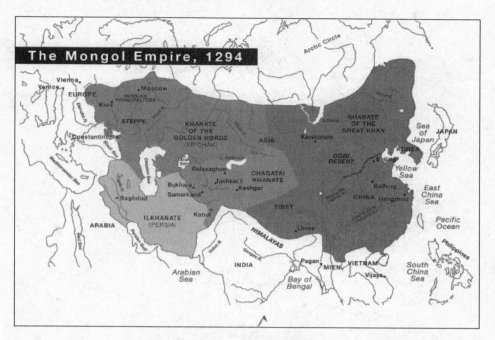

Map of the Mongol Khanates

E. Developments in Africa

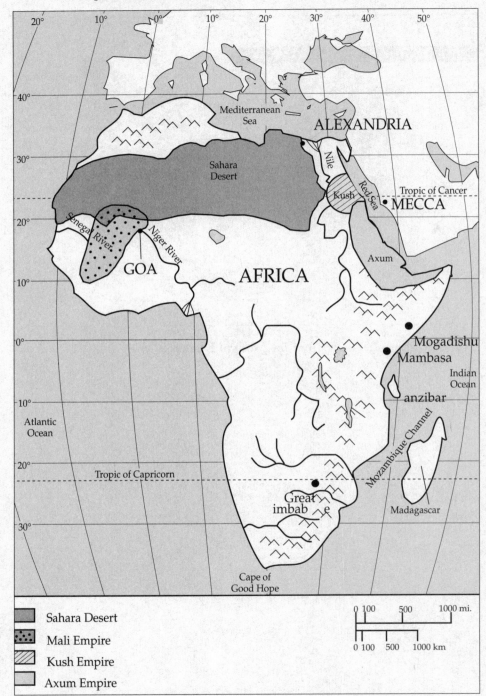

African Empires and Trade Cities

The most significant early civilizations in Africa for AP purposes were Egypt and Carthage, both of which were discussed in the previous chapter. Both of these civilizations were located in North Africa along the Mediterranean, north of the

Sahara Desert. But there were other civilizations in Africa too. Some of them existed long before 600 C.E., but we've included them in this section (rather than in the previous chapter) so that you can study them as a group.

Interaction Kush, Axum, and the Swahili Coast

The Kush and Axum civilizations developed to the south of Egypt in the upper reaches of the Nile River. **Kush** developed at about the same time as ancient Egypt, and at one point around 750 B.C.E. actually conquered it. Less than a hundred years later, however, Kush retreated southward back to its capital at Meroe, where it became a center for ironworks and trade.

After the Kush decline around 200 C.E., another empire, **Axum**, rose to greatness to the south (in modern-day Ethiopia). Although Axum never conquered any other civilization, it traded with them frequently, especially ivory and gold. In the fourth century, Axum converted to Christianity, and in the seventh century, many converted to Islam. These conversions illustrate that the people of Axum were in constant contact with the empires of the Mediterranean world. And that contact has had a long-standing impact. Ethiopia's large Christian community in present times is a direct result of the Axum conversion.

Remember that this entire period is dominated by interactions. In addition to interaction with the Mediterranean world through the Red Sea, the eastern coast of Africa was linked to India and Southeast Asia through the shipping lanes of the Indian Ocean trade. The east coast of Africa was populated by Bantu-speaking peoples who settled into lives of farmers, merchants, and fishermen. This area is known as the Swahili Coast, from the Arabic word for "coasters" or traders, and indeed the Swahili language is a mix of the original Bantu language supplemented by Arabic. Trade with the Muslims began in the early tenth century as Swahili traders brought gold, slaves, ivory, and other exotic products to the coast.

The incredible wealth generated by this trade resulted in the growth of powerful kingdoms and trading cities along the coast in advantageous locations. Like wealthy trading cities throughout the world, they became cultural and political centers. By the fifteenth century, what had previously been mud and wooden outposts had become impressive coral and stone mosques, public buildings, and fortified cities with trade goods from all over the world.

To facilitate political and economic relationships, the ruling elites and merchant classes of the eastern African kingdoms converted to Islam, but maintained many of their own cultural traditions. Eventually, Islam spread throughout most of East Africa.

The Other Side of the Sand: Ghana, Mali, and Songhai

Kush and Axum were in eastern Africa, along the Nile River and near the Red Sea. Therefore, they had easy access to other cultures. The cultures of Ghana, Mali, and Songhai, however, were in west Africa, south of the Sahara.

Need More Review?
Are a ton of different names swirling around in your brain? To help with memorization, pick up a box of our flashcards: Essential AP World History.

When the Muslim Empire spread across North Africa in the seventh and eighth centuries, these African kingdoms began trading with the larger Mediterranean economy. Islamic traders penetrated the unforgiving Sahara desert and reached the fertile wealthy interior of Africa, called sub-Saharan (beneath the Sahara), while African traders pushed northward toward Carthage and Tripoli. Previously, the desert had acted as one gigantic "don't-want-to-deal-with-it" barrier, so people typically didn't. Increasingly, however, caravans of traders were willing to do what they had to do to get to the riches on the other side of the sand. At first, the west Africans were in search of salt, which they had little of but which existed in the Sahara. When they encountered the Islamic traders along the salt road, they started trading for a lot more than just salt. The consequence was an explosion of trade.

Why were the Islamic traders so interested in trading with west African kingdoms? Because in Ghana (about 800–1000 C.E.) and Mali (about 1200–1450 C.E.), there was tons, and we mean tons, of gold. A little sand in your eyes was probably worth some gold in your hand. So the Islamic traders kept coming.

The constant trade brought more than just Islamic goods to Ghana and Mali; it brought Islam. For Ghana the result was devastating. The empire was subjected to a Holy War led by an Islamic group intent on converting (or else killing) them. While Ghana was able to defeat the Islamic forces, their empire fell into decline. By the time the Mali came to power, the region had converted to Islam anyway, this time in a more peaceful transition.

One of the greatest Mali rulers, **Mansa Musa**, built a capital at Timbuktu and expanded the kingdom well beyond the bounds of Ghana. In 1324, Musa made a pilgrimage to Mecca (remember the Five Pillars of Islam?) complete with an entourage of hundreds of gold-carrying servants and camels. The journey was so extravagant and so long and so impressive to everyone who saw it, that Musa became an overnight international sensation. Had the entertainment industry been fully established during that time, you can bet that Access Hollywood and US Weekly would have been all over the Musa moment.

But the largest empire in west Africa was formed in the mid-fifteenth century, when Songhai ruler Sonni Ali conquered the entire region and established the Songhai Empire. The Songhai Empire lasted until around 1600 C.E., and during its reign, Timbuktu became a major cultural center, complete with a university that drew scholars from around the Islamic world.

The Arts in Africa

Oral literature was an important part of life in most African communities. History and stories were passed from one generation to the next, not through written texts, but through storytelling. But the storytelling wasn't just grandpa sitting next to the fire. It was a production akin to a dramatic performance. The stories were told the same way for so many generations that people knew the lines. Everyone was able to participate in the storytelling by reciting responses at the appropriate times. Think about what it's like to watch Star Wars with a room full of people—parents, grandparents, kids—who've already seen it; that will give you a good sense of what oral literature meant to those cultures.

Early sub-Saharan African cultures are also known for their sculptures, particularly out of pottery and bronze. The **Benin** culture (near present-day Nigeria) mastered a bronze sculpting technique. They made clay molds around a wax carving, melted the wax, filled the mold with melted bronze, and, after breaking the clay mold, revealed some of the most beautiful early bronze work created by any civilization.

F. Developments in the Americas

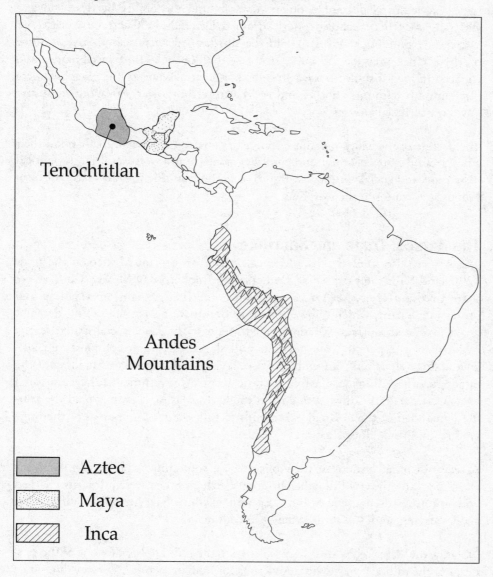

The American Civilizations

There were three great civilizations in what is now Central America and South America that developed before the arrival of the Europeans. One of the civilizations, the Maya, actually began around the time of the major classical civilizations and were discussed in the previous chapter. The other two civilizations, the Incas and Aztecs, were conquered by the Europeans after 1450. They will be discussed again in the next chapter. That said, we are including all three of them in this chapter so that you can review the cultural characteristics of these three civilizations in one place. We'll talk about their conquests in the next chapter.

Mayan Decline: Where Did They Go?

As a review, the Maya were organized in city-states ruled by a single king. Their largely agricultural peasant population was bound to nobility by ties of loyalty and religion. They occupied poorly drained lowlands in Central America and adapted by building terraces to trap the silt drained by numerous rivers. Some of these cities grew to be quite sizable—10,000 to 40,000 inhabitants, and engaged in long-distance trade as far north as central Mexico. But the cities were often at odds with one another and in Mayan territory, war was about capturing slaves or sacrificial victims.

The decline of the Maya remains a source of debate. They began to abandon their cities around 800 C.E. Environmental degradation and overuse of land, political dissension and social unrest, natural disaster, and outside invaders have all been proposed as causes of their decline.

The Aztecs: Trade and Sacrifice

The Aztecs, also known as the Mexica, arrived in central Mexico in the mid-1200s and built their capital at **Tenochtitlan** (modern-day Mexico City). More than anything else, the Aztecs are known for their expansionist policy and professional army, which allowed them to dominate nearby states and demand heavy taxes and captives. Warriors were the elite in the Aztec social structure (the majority of the people were peasants and slaves). Through conquest and alliances, the Aztecs built an empire of some 12 million people. But despite the huge size, they didn't use a bureaucratic form of government. The conquered areas were generally allowed to govern themselves, as long as they paid the tribute demanded of them. Roads were built to link the far-flung areas of the huge empire, and trade flourished.

Aztec women had a subordinate public role but could inherit property. Like women in most all other traditional civilizations, Aztec women were primarily charged with running the household, but they were also involved in skilled crafts, especially weaving, and—to some extent—in commerce.

Notably, the Aztec religious system was tied to the military because one of the purposes of the military was to obtain victims for human sacrifice. Tens of thousands of men and women were killed annually; many would be sacrificed simultaneously for an important religious occasion, such as the dedication of a new temple.

The Incas: My Land Is Your Land

The Inca Empire, set in the Andes Mountains in Peru, was also expansionist in nature. At its zenith, it is thought to have controlled more than 2,000 miles of South American coastline. The Incas controlled this territory using a professional army, an established bureaucracy, a unified language, and a complex system of roads and tunnels.

Like the Maya (and the Aztecs), the Incas had no large animals, so the prime source of labor was human. A large proportion of the population was peasants, who worked the land or on construction projects. They were expected to give a proportion of their harvest to support the ruling classes and to provide famine relief. These surpluses eventually became large enough to support large cities. The capital at Cuzco may have had as many as 300,000 people in the late 1400s.

Incan women were expected to help work the fields, weave cloth, and care for the household. They could pass property on to their daughters and even played a role in religion. The Incas were polytheistic, but the sun god was the most important and was at the center of the state religion. Like the Aztecs, the Incas practiced human sacrifice, but in much smaller numbers, usually choosing instead to sacrifice material goods or animals. Incan religion also had a very strong moral quality, emphasizing rewards for good behavior and punishments for bad. Like the Egyptians, Incan rulers were mummified after death and became intermediaries between the gods and the people.

For the Incas, the concept of private property didn't exist. Rather, the ruler was viewed as having descended from the sun and therefore owning everything on Earth. The military was very important because each new ruler needed to ensure his place in eternity by securing new land, and that meant conquest. There was a state bureaucracy, manned by the nobility, which controlled the empire by traveling on a complex system of roads.

The Inca were excellent builders, stone cutters, and miners. Their skills are evident from the ruins of the **Temple of the Sun** in Cuzco and the temples of **Machu Picchu**. They never developed a system of writing. However, they were able to record census data and keep an accounting of harvests on *quipu*, a set of knotted strings.

IV. REVIEW OF INTERACTIONS AMONG CULTURES 600 C.E.–1450

The purpose of this section is to help you pull together the history from this time period and view it from a global perspective. The examples below are by no means an exhaustive list of the ways that civilizations or groups of people interacted from 600 to 1450 C.E. To the contrary, they are examples that serve as a starting point in your studies. We strongly suggest that you add examples to the ones below as you work your way through this review and your materials from your class.

A. Trade Networks and Cultural Diffusion

Trade has always been a big deal historically speaking. Getting stuff and buying stuff is a huge incentive behind interactions. If you have everything you need and want, you can live in isolation. If you don't, and somebody else down the road has what you want, you've got two choices: take it or trade for it. If you're not into the whole conquest thing, then trading is probably your best option.

From 600 to 1450, trade exploded onto the world scene—so much so that the world after 1450 is inseparable from global interaction. Let's quickly review the global trade routes that you read about in this chapter.

- The Mediterranean Trade between western Europe, the Byzantine Empire, and the Islamic Empire
- The Hanseatic League (more details below)
- The Silk Road (used heavily again from about 1200 C.E. until about 1600 C.E.—see next page)
- The land routes of the Mongols
- Trade between China and Japan
- Trade between India and Persia
- The Trans-Saharan trade routes between west Africa and the Islamic Empire

Remember, too, that trade was not only aided by better boats and better roads, but also by monetary systems, lines of credit, and accounting methods that helped business boom. Record keeping and money management is key. If you're able to keep records or borrow money, you are by definition establishing a business relationship that extends into the future. Once you start thinking about a regular business-trade relationship extending into the future, you can get people to invest in that future, and pretty soon the wheels of international business are going 'round and 'round.

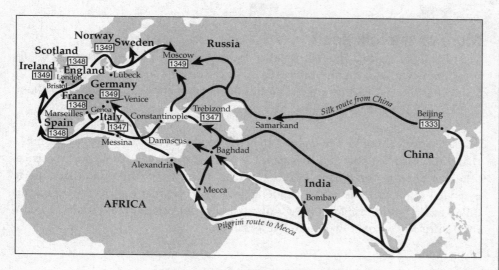

Spread of the Black Death (1333–1349 C.E.)

The trade routes are important, of course, not just because of their impact on business, but also because of their role in cultural diffusion. It is over the trade routes that religions and languages spread. It is over the trade routes that literature and art and ideas spread. And, unfortunately, it is over the trade routes that disease and plague sometimes spread. The **Bubonic Plague** (also called the Black Death) started in Asia in the fourteenth century and was carried by merchants along the trade routes all the way to Europe, where it destroyed entire communities and killed as many as one out of every three people in western Europe. The plague quickened the decline of feudal society because many manors weren't able to function.

In addition to the trade routes mentioned above, there's one that we haven't mentioned yet—the Indian Ocean Trade. It's important, so we'll go into it in some detail.

Indian Ocean Trade

Throughout the period covered in this chapter, the Persians and the Arabs dominated the Indian Ocean Trade. Their trade routes connected ports in western India to ports in the Persian Gulf, which in turn were connected to ports in eastern Africa.

Unlike boats that were used on the Mediterranean Sea, boats that sailed the Indian Ocean were, necessarily, more resilient to the large waves common in those waters. The traders learned to understand the monsoon seasons and direction of the winds, and scheduled their voyages accordingly. Despite these difficulties, the Indian Ocean trade routes were relatively safe, especially when compared to those on the Mediterranean, where constant warfare was a problem.

Since sailors often married the local women at the ends of their trade routes, cultures started to intermix rapidly. Many sailors took foreign wives home and created bilingual and bicultural families.

More on the Silk Road

You already know that the Silk Road connected China to the Mediterranean cultures even way back in the early days of the Roman Empire. You also need to know that the Silk Road was used heavily again from about 1200 C.E. until about 1600 C.E., during the reign of the Mongols.

The important thing to know about the Silk Road is that it carried so much more than silk. It carried porcelain and paper. It carried military technologies. It carried religions, such as Buddhism, Islam, and Christianity. It carried food. Because it extended so far and was used for so long, it's safe to say that East met West on the Silk Road. It's impossible to have a discussion about international trade and cultural diffusion without mentioning it by name.

More on the Hanseatic League

As you already know, the Hanseatic League was a collection of city-states in the Baltic and North Sea regions of Europe that banded together in 1241 to establish common trade practices, fight off pirates and foreign governments, and essentially establish a trade monopoly from the region to much of the rest of the world. It worked for a few hundred years. More than 100 cities joined the league. The result was enormous for two reasons. First, it resulted in a substantial middle class in northern Europe, a development that would drive changes in that region in later centuries (more on that in the next chapter). Second, it set a precedent for large, European trading operations that profoundly affected the Dutch and the English, which would also deeply affect the world in later centuries.

Was There a Global Trade Network?

If you think about it, after about 1200 C.E. or so, the world was very interconnected. Europe was trading with the Islamic world and Russia. The Islamic world was trading with Africa, India, and China. India was trading with China and eastern Africa. China was trading with Japan and southeast Europe. If you link up all the trade routes, goods could make their way from England to Persia to India to Japan. They could also travel to points north and south, from Muscovy to Mali.

The global network wasn't entirely controlled by one entity or laid out by one trading organization. It was more like a web of interconnected but highly independent parts. It required lots of managers at each site. It required people to be linked up through third and even fourth parties. No one person was managing it, and yet almost all major civilizations (except those in the Americas) were a part of it. In short, it was like the Internet, only in geographic space instead of cyberspace.

B. Expansion of Religion and Empire: Culture Clash

One of the most significant influences on cultural interaction and diffusion has been the expansion of empires and the intentional diffusion of religion. Keep in mind that when we say intentional diffusion of religion, we mean methods like missionary work or religious warfare. This is opposed to the natural spread of religious ideas that occurs when people come into contact with each other, like over the trade routes.

Here's a quick listing of some of the examples discussed in this chapter.

- The Mongol expansion into Russia, Persia, India, and China
- The Germanic tribes into southern Europe and England
- The Vikings' expansion from Scandinavia into England and western Europe
- The Magyars' push from eastern Europe into western Europe
- The Islamic Empire's push into Spain, India, and Africa
- The Crusades
- Buddhist missionaries to Japan
- Orthodox Christian missionaries into eastern Europe

When you think about it, the bulk of this chapter is about two things: the expansion of religion and empires leading to cultural contact, or the relative isolationism that resulted under the feudal systems in Europe and Japan. Another way to encapsulate this period: a time fueled by conquest and religious expansion. We've talked a lot about the efforts of expansionists that succeeded. We need to give you some more details about the efforts of some expansionists that didn't succeed, namely, the crusaders.

The Playground Isn't Big Enough for Two Bullies: Crusaders and Jihad

You'll recall that in the Middle Ages, the Islamic Empire expanded, and the Moors conquered much of Spain. The Christians felt threatened by the expansion of the Muslims, especially as Islam became entrenched in areas that the Christians identified with historically. So, in 1096 C.E. Pope Urban initiated the **First Crusade** in response to the success of the Seljuk Turks, who took control of the Holy Land (present-day Israel and Palestine). The Pope wanted Jerusalem, the most important city in Christianity, to be in the hands of Christians. He was also hoping that the efforts would help reunite the Roman Catholic Church with the Eastern Orthodox Church in Constantinople, which had split apart 50 years before the start of the crusades. The crusaders immediately set out to conquer the Holy Land, and initially captured several cities, including Antioch and, most important, Jerusalem. However, both cities quickly fell back into the hands of the Arabs.

Through the year 1204 C.E., a total of four crusades failed to produce results, and the Eastern Orthodox Church and the Roman Catholic Church separated even further (five more crusades followed, but were not successful in achieving major goals). As mentioned earlier, in the Fourth Crusade the Catholic Church sacked

Constantinople and established a short-lived Latin Empire there (most of the crusaders either died or returned to Europe). The impact on the Holy Land was violence and uncertainty. Most of the region remained in the hands of the Muslim Arabs, and the whole mess led to centuries of mistrust and intolerance between Christians and Muslims.

As you think about global interaction through conquest, there's much to point out about the Crusades. First, the Crusades were not only motivated by religious beliefs and purposes. There were economic and political incentives as well. No doubt there were some who fought for religious reasons, especially in the early crusades, but the lure of empire and wealth was certainly a major factor for many.

Second, even to the extent that it was a religious effort, the Crusades illustrate that religion, when combined with conquest and feelings of superiority, can be a very bloody enterprise. The death, rape, pillaging, and slavery perpetrated in the name of religion was startling. The same, of course, was true of Islamic conquests in India, Persia, and Africa. Because the religiously devout are sometimes willing to be martyred for their beliefs, intentional religious expansionism can be just as devastating and powerful as a politically driven military invasion.

Third, and perhaps most importantly for the AP, the Crusades prove that even the efforts of conquest and expansion that fail to reach their goals still have a major impact on world history: They lead to interaction between cultures that might not otherwise interact. The Crusades put Europe back into the sphere of the Eastern Mediterranean for centuries. That interaction fueled trade and an exchange of ideas. It also led to western Europe's rediscovery of its ancient past, which was being preserved by the Byzantine and Islamic Empires. That rediscovery fueled huge changes in Europe, which we'll talk about in the next chapter.

C. Other Reasons People Were on the Move

Interaction among and within civilizations occurred during this period in history for many reasons other than trade or conquest. As populations grew, people needed more room to spread out. This not only led to huge movements of people, like the Germanic tribes into southern Europe, but also to more crowded conditions on the manor or in small towns. The result was the burgeoning of ever-larger cities; once the cities became larger, more opportunities were created there, which pulled more and more people in from the countryside.

Some cities grew not just because of a general population increase, but because they were intentionally established as centers of civilization. Think about the empires in this chapter. The eastern Roman Empire, which of course became the Byzantine Empire, was specifically headquartered at Constantinople, which was specifically built as a center to draw people. In fact, capitals were moved all the time to create an aura of a rising empire. The Islamic Empire moved to Baghdad under the Abbasid Dynasty. The Fujiwara moved the capital of Japan to Heian. The Mongols built a city at Samarkand, as did the Malians at Timbuktu, and the Maya at Tikal. The list goes on and on. Every time an empire built a new city to flaunt itself, it drew thousands of people. This is true especially to the degree that these civilizations built universities, which by their nature drew people from around the empire. That meant people who weren't living in the same city in the past were now living together. The result? More cultural diffusion.

Pilgrimages were a third reason that people during this time period were constantly on the move. Rome and Constantinople certainly attracted thousands to their grand cathedrals, but the Islamic duty to travel to Mecca was no doubt the most significant destination of religious pilgrimages. Imagine the thousands upon thousands who traveled from the vast reaches of the Islamic world. Imagine the amount of cultural diffusion that occurred as a result. Just think of Mansa Musa and you'll be convinced.

V. TECHNOLOGY AND INNOVATIONS 600 c.e.–1450

Once again, it is interaction that leads to innovation. This period is marked by expanding trade, expanding empires and expanding interactions. All lead to increased wealth, frequent cultural borrowing, and the development of new ideas. Many of these new innovations came from the eastern societies–China and India, filtered through the Islamic world. By 1450, most of these new ideas had made their way back to Europe, following the Crusaders, merchants, and missionaries.

Islamic World	China
paper mills (from China)	gunpowder cannons
universities	moveable type
astrolabe and sextant	paper currency
algebra (from Greece)	porcelain
chess (from India)	terrace farming
modern soap formula	water-powered mills
guns and cannons (from China)	cotton sails
mechanical pendulum clock	water clock
distilled alcohol	magnetic compass
surgical instruments (syringe etc.)	state-run factories

In addition to ideas that began to move around the world, trade networks moved agricultural products. Some of these would result in great environmental changes, influence trade networks, and motivate exploration and conquest.

VI. CHANGES AND CONTINUITIES IN THE ROLE OF WOMEN

The spread of Islam, the openness of Christianity and Buddhism, the development of new empires based on wealth and acquisition of property, and the revitalization of neo-Confucianism impacted the status of women around the world. Continuing from the previous time period, restrictions on women's freedoms depended on which caste or class they belonged to. At the upper-most levels, a woman could overcome the status of her gender and assume leadership roles if there was no male heir or if the male heir was very young. But generally, as societies became more urban and wealthy, women, especially those of the elite or upper classes had their freedoms further restricted even as their status in society rose. This can be seen in the increased veiling of women in the Islamic world, the custom of foot-binding in neo-Confucian China, and the young age of marriage in South Asia.

Trade and the arrival of new religions did not significantly change the role of women in African societies—as pastoral nomads many of the African societies were relatively egalitarian. Even when sedentary lifestyles developed, women had a great deal of freedom and societies were often matrilineal and matriarchal. Women commanded a bride-price rather than having to give a dowry, and were considered a valuable source of wealth. "Mother of the King" was a political office in many African societies and women participated in specific religious rituals controlled solely by women. Although both Islam and Christianity found converts in Africa, women were less eager to convert than men and the practice of veiling was met with mixed reactions.

Changes in the status and role of women included access to more education as societies continued to prosper and interact. This is true of the Confucian cultures of China and Japan, where women were highly literate and expected to understand proper virtue and their role in the household. But overall, even when educated and wealthy, most women had far less power than their male counterparts and were subject to any number of cultural and legal restrictions.

Women's Status in Ancient Societies			
Europe	**Islam**	**India**	**China**
strict and patriarchal social divisions	equality in religion, but separate in mosque	strict patriarchal caste system	strict Confucian social order and guidelines for virtuous behavior
could inherit land and take oaths of vassalage, but property belonged to husband	received half inheritance of male children	child marriages	access to dowries and owned businesses
could bring a court case, but not participate in decision	testimony had less weight than male	practice of sati for widows	widow to remain with son; no property if remarried
division of labor; women in textiles		family textile labor	silk weaving as female occupation
Christian monogamy	concubines and seclusion in harems	marriage limited to caste members	concubines and seclusion in harems
education limited to upper class males	literate society	education limited	literate society, but state education limited to men
did not recognize illegitimate children	all children are seen as legitimate		
veiling of upper class	veiling in public	purdah: veiling or seclusion	foot-binding

VII. PULLING IT ALL TOGETHER

In the previous section, we hope that you were able to pull a lot of the history from this time period together in some meaningful ways, especially as it relates to cultural interaction.

There's no question that the spread and growth of religion had enormous consequences during this time period. That should be clear to you. There's also no question that the issue of centralization verses noncentralization seems to have an impact on a civilization. Look at what it meant for Europe, or for Japan, or China, or India. But beyond the issues of interaction, centralization, and the growth of religion, there's also something else you should be thinking about: how to organize the world in your head.

In modern times, we have clear boundaries between countries. But in addition to using those political boundaries, we talk of cultural regions all the time. We'll say things like "the West" or "the East." That's fine, but where's the dividing line? Is modern-day Russia part of the East or the West? What about Saudi Arabia? What about Japan?

In addition, we'll split even our own country into manageable pieces that don't have specific, exact geographic boundaries. We'll say "the South" and what we're referring to is a culture more than a place. Is Florida part of "the South?" Northern Florida probably is, but the rest of Florida has a very different feel.

We bring all this up because this kind of stuff is a big deal for the AP test writers. Sometimes it's easier to think about and write about history in terms of cultural areas, rather than political boundaries. "The Muslim World," for example, would mean not just countries that are predominately Muslim, but communities or individuals within non-Muslim countries who participate in the culture of Islam. Or think about the "Jewish community." In the time period covered by this chapter, Jews were scattered throughout Europe, Africa, and Asia. There was no Jewish state, only a Jewish culture. Yet, the Jewish culture maintained its identity.

In terms of the era that you've just reviewed, you might want to think of the world in terms of major cultural divisions. Religions help. You can think of developments in the Christian sphere, the Islamic sphere, the Hindu sphere, and the Buddhist sphere. But then don't forget that some of these spheres overlap, and some of them coexist with other religions or belief systems (Confucianism and Buddhism, for example). You can also think of developments in terms of expanding empires and feudal systems. Or even more generally, think of the world in terms of cultures that interacted and those that didn't.

However you choose to think about the world in terms of cultural areas or structural similarities, the important thing is that you try to analyze the history. Doing so will force you to make comparisons and contrasts among the cultures. And doing that will get your brain cranking in the way the AP exam will expect you to demonstrate. The more you think about how these cultures can be organized, the more familiar you'll be with world history.

Important Terms

Aristrocracy
Bureaucrats/Bureaucracy
Caliph/Caliphate
Chivalry
City-State
Civil Service
Credit
Cultural Diffusion
Decentralized
Dowry
Eastern Orthodox
Fiefs
Garrisons
Gothic
Hajj
Heresy
Heretic
Hijab (veil)
Illegitimate
Infrastructure
Interaction
Inquisition
Interrogation
Islam
Literate
Matriarch
Matrilineal
Medieval
Meritocracy
Middle Ages
Migration
Monetary System
Mosque
Muslim
Nation-State
Orthodox
Patriarch
Patriarchal
Persecution
Pilgrims
Pilgrimage
Primogeniture
Roman Catholic
Schism
Secluded

Serfs
Submissive
Subordinate
Theocracy
Trans-Continental
Tribute Systems
Urbanization
Vassals

People, Places, and Events

Byzantium
Baghdad, Iraq
Black Death
Bubonic Plague
Chang'an (Xi'an, China)
Constantinople (Istanbul, Turkey)
Crusades (1095–1291)
Empress Wu (T'ang China)
Feudalism (Japan and Europe)
Foot-Binding
Franks including Charlemagne
Ghengis Khan
Hanseatic League
Hundred Years War (1337–1453)
Indian Ocean Trade
Code of Justinian
Magna Carta (1215)
Mansa Musa
Neo-Confucianism
Sacking of Constantinople
St. Cyril and Cyrillic Alphabet
Schism in Christianity (1054)
Schism in Islam (650s)
Shintoism
Silk Road
Timbuktu
Tenochtitlan
William the Conqueror

VIII. TIMELINE OF MAJOR DEVELOPMENTS 600 C.E.–1450

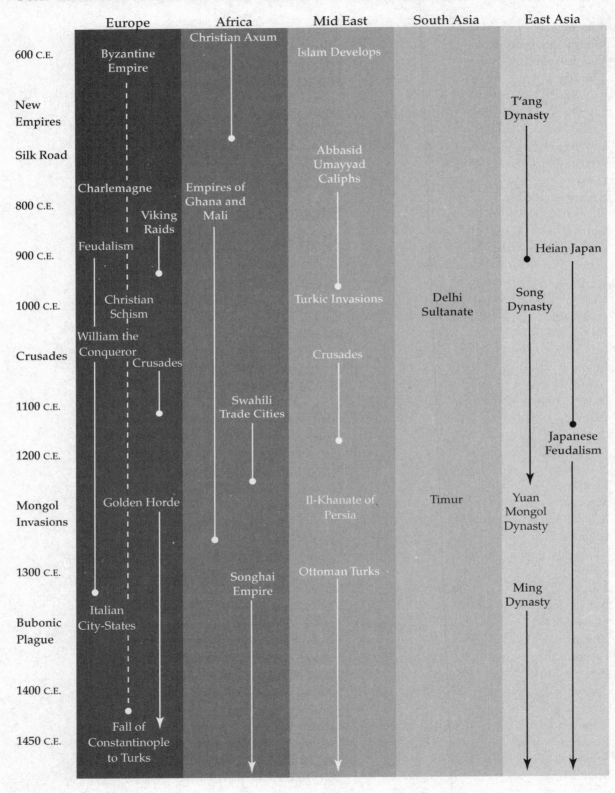

	Europe	Africa	Mid East	South Asia	East Asia
600 C.E.	Byzantine Empire	Christian Axum	Islam Develops		
New Empires					T'ang Dynasty
Silk Road			Abbasid Umayyad Caliphs		
800 C.E.	Charlemagne	Empires of Ghana and Mali			
		Viking Raids			
900 C.E.	Feudalism				Heian Japan
1000 C.E.	Christian Schism		Turkic Invasions	Delhi Sultanate	Song Dynasty
Crusades	William the Conqueror		Crusades		
	Crusades				
1100 C.E.		Swahili Trade Cities			
1200 C.E.					Japanese Feudalism
Mongol Invasions	Golden Horde		Il-Khanate of Persia	Timur	Yuan Mongol Dynasty
1300 C.E.		Songhai Empire	Ottoman Turks		Ming Dynasty
Bubonic Plague	Italian City-States				
1400 C.E.					
1450 C.E.	Fall of Constantinople to Turks				

REFLECT ACTIVITY

Respond to the following questions:

- For which content topics discussed in this Chapter do you feel you have achieved sufficient mastery to answer multiple choice questions correctly?

- For which content topics discussed in this Chapter do you feel you have achieved sufficient mastery to discuss effectively in an essay?

- For which content topics discussed in this Chapter do you feel you need more work before you can answer multiple choice questions correctly?

- For which content topics discussed in this Chapter do you feel you need more work before you can discuss effectively in an essay?

- What parts of this Chapter are you going to re-review?

- Will you seek further help outside of this book (such as a teacher, tutor, or AP Central), on any of the content in this Chapter—and, if so, on what content?

Chapter 8
Old Stuff: Approximately 1450 to Around 1750

I. CHAPTER OVERVIEW

By 1450 C.E., global interaction really got cranking. That's why this chapter only covers about 300 years, whereas the previous chapter covered nearly 800 years, and the first chapter covered an astonishing 8,000 years. Since the time period covered in this chapter is narrower, the amount of detail provided is greater. The rise of Europe as a major player on the world scene was very important during this time period, and because the AP focuses so much on the interaction among cultures, most of the regions of the world in this chapter are discussed in terms of their relation to Europe.

As with previous chapters, we suggest that you read through this chapter once, and then go back and focus on the things that you're not entirely clear about. To help you do that, here's the chapter outline.

I.   Chapter Overview

      You're reading it now.

II.   Stay Focused on the Big Picture

      Organize the huge social, political, and economic changes that occurred during this time period into some big-picture concepts.

III.   Major European Developments 1450 to 1750

This section focuses on developments that influenced all of Europe, as opposed to more localized developments that affected particular countries or empires. Of course, the developments discussed in this section had an impact beyond the borders of Europe, which is why they're so important to the study of world history. We've organized the major developments into two main groups.

      A.   Revolutions in European Thought and Expression

      B.   European Exploration and Expansion: Empires of the Wind

IV.   Developments in Specific Countries and Empires 1450 to 1750

After you've studied the major social, religious, economic, and political developments that swept through Europe and beyond, you should be able to put developments in individual countries and empires in the proper context. In addition to reviewing developments that occurred within the individual European powers, we'll help you review the unique civilizations that existed elsewhere on the globe, particularly the Ottoman Empire, India, China, and Japan. In the next chapter, we'll review the impact of European expansionism on Africa and Asia in the nineteenth century. Here's how we've organized this section.

A.   The European Rivals

      1. Spain and Portugal
      2. England
      3. France
      4. German Areas (The Holy Roman Empire, Sort Of)

B.   Russia Out of Isolation

C.   Islamic Gunpowder Empires: Ottoman, Safavid, and Mughal

D.   Africa

E.   Isolated Asia

V.   Technology and Innovations 1450–1750

Europe gets guns, builds big ships, and explores the world

VI.   Changes and Continuities in the Role of Women

Concubines, queens, and business women

VII.   Pulling It All Together

Refocus on the big-picture concepts now that you've reviewed the details.

VIII.   Timeline of Major Developments 1450–1750

Major developments organized by time and place

II. STAY FOCUSED ON THE BIG PICTURE

As you review the details of the developments in this chapter, stay focused on some big-picture concepts. As you read, keep in mind the following questions:

1.   Why did Europe become a dominant power during this time period? Was it because European nations vied for world dominance while other civilizations didn't, or because of technological superiority? Was it for some other reason? Why did some of the European nation-states develop vast empires while others did not? There are lots of legitimate answers to these questions, and the content of this chapter will help you think about some of them.

2.   What were some of the differences among the ways in which non-European cultures interacted with Europe? What influences contributed to these differences? What were the consequences? You'll notice that Euro-

pean powers penetrated different parts of the globe to different degrees. Pay attention to why this was true—it will not only tell you a lot about Europe, but also about those individual non-European cultures as well.

3. How did the global economy change during this time period? What was the impact on the world's civilizations? As you read, notice how economic considerations drove much of the world's interactions. Pay attention to how the larger global economy impacted the various regions of the globe.

4. What were the impacts of global interaction on the environment? Conversely, what were the impacts of the environment on human societies? What ideas, diseases, plants, and animals traveled the globe along with human settlement? The need for new resources brought massive changes, but at the same time, the environment acted on human societies, sometimes with disastrous consequences. Pay attention to the effects of the 500 year period of global cooling that began around 1500 and resulted in shortages of crops, famines, and susceptibility to diseases.

III. MAJOR EUROPEAN DEVELOPMENTS 1450–1750

During the three centuries covered in this chapter, profound changes occurred on the European continent. These changes affected life on all levels: the way people viewed themselves (their past, their present, and their future potential), the way governments viewed their authority, the way religion intersected with politics and individuality, and the way Europeans thought about and interacted with the rest of the world.

By the end of these 300 years, the European countries will have used their new technologies, new ideas of governing, and new forms economic organization to become the dominant world powers. Much of their success was based on competition and rivalry as they raced to secure faster trade routes, new colonial possessions, and attempted to gain control of key resources. And much of their success came at the expense of the land-based empires of Asia and the declining empires in the Americas.

So while the previous chapter was all about interactions, this one covers the period of European maritime empire-building that resulted from those initial interactions across Asia and the Indian Ocean As you review the enormous developments in Parts A and B below, think about how they were linked together and impacted each other.

A. Revolutions in European Thought and Expression

By the 1300s, much of Europe had been Christian for a thousand years. The feudal system had dominated the political and social structures for five hundred years, and the ancient classical civilizations of Greece and Rome had been almost entirely forgotten.

Life in the Middle Ages was dominated by local issues, concern for salvation, territorial disputes, the Black Death, a lack of education outside monasteries, and small-scale trade. As you read in the last chapter, near the end of the Middle Ages, countries began to unify under centralized rule. The Crusades exposed Christians to the advanced Islamic civilizations, increased trade fueled contact with other parts of the world, and universities became great centers of learning. This increased contact with foreign powers, and scholasticism exposed Europeans not only to developments in the rest of the world but also to history. Recall that the Byzantine and Islamic Empires had preserved much of the heritage of ancient Greece and Rome, even as they built unique civilizations of their own and made huge contributions to ancient texts, especially in the areas of mathematics and science. As Europe expanded its worldview and interacted more frequently with these two empires, it rediscovered its own past.

The combination of a rediscovered past and a productive present led to major changes in the way Europeans viewed the world and themselves. These new perspectives led to four massive cultural movements: the Renaissance, the Protestant Reformation, the Scientific Revolution, and the Enlightenment. These revolutions in expression and thought changed the world. In a span of just a few hundred years, Europe went from being a backward, isolated, self-involved outpost on the perimeter of the major civilizations to the east to the dominant civilization in the world.

We'll talk about the details of European global exploration and expansion later in this chapter. In the meantime, you should understand that this exploration and expansion were partly causing—and partly caused by—the major developments in thought and expression that are listed below.

1. The Renaissance: Classical Civilization Part II

After the Black Death abated and the population of Europe once again began to swell, the demand for goods and services began to increase rapidly. Individuals moved to the cities. A middle class made up of bankers, merchants, and traders emerged due to increased global trade. In short, Europe experienced an influx of money to go along with its newfound sense of history. It shouldn't be too surprising that a sizeable chunk of this money was spent on recapturing and studying the past.

Humanism: A Bit More Focus on the Here and Now

In medieval Europe, thoughts of salvation and the afterlife so dominated personal priorities that life on Earth was, for many, something to be suffered through on the way to heaven rather than lived through as a pursuit of its own. As Europeans rediscovered ancient texts, they were struck with the degree that humanity—personal accomplishment and personal happiness—formed the central core of so much of the literature and philosophy of the ancient writers. The emphasis began to shift from fulfillment in the afterlife to participating in the here-and-now.

This is not to say that Europeans suddenly became hedonistic, focused only on worldly pleasures. To the contrary, the Catholic Church and a focus on the afterlife remained dominant. However, Europeans were fascinated with the ancient

Greek and Roman concepts of beauty and citizenship, and as a consequence they began to shift their focus to life on Earth and to celebrating human achievements in the scholarly, artistic, and political realms. This focus on human endeavors became known as **humanism**. Its impact was far-reaching because a focus on present-day life leads to a focus on individuals, and a focus on individuality inevitably leads to a reduction in the authority of institutions.

THE ITALIAN STATE SYSTEM DURING THE RENAISSANCE

The Arts Stage a Comeback

The Renaissance literally means "rebirth," and this was nowhere more apparent than in the arts. In Italy, where powerful families in city-states such as Florence, Venice, and Milan became rich on trade, art was financed on a scale not seen since the classical civilizations of Greece and Rome. The **Medici** family in Florence, for example, not only ruled the great city and beyond (several family members not coincidentally became popes!), but turned it into a showcase of architecture and beauty by acting as patron for some of the greatest artists of the time, including **Michelangelo** and **Brunelleschi**.

Unlike medieval paintings, which depicted humans as flat, stiff, and out of proportion with their surroundings, paintings of the Renaissance demonstrated the application of humanistic ideals learned from the ancients. Painters and sculptors such as **Leonardo da Vinci** and **Donatello** depicted the human figure as realistically as possible. Careful use of light and shadow made figures appear full and real. Many artists were so committed to this realism that they viewed and participated in autopsies to fully understand the structure of the human body.

Artists also employed a technique known as linear perspective, developed by Tommaso Masaccio and Fillipo Brunelleschi, in which nearby objects were drawn bigger while far objects were drawn smaller; the lines of perspective merged into a distant focal point, giving the painting a three-dimensional quality. This use of perspective was a huge development toward realism.

The Catholic Church noticed the developments in artistic techniques, and soon the greatest artists were hard at work adorning the great palaces and cathedrals of Italy. For four years, 1508 to 1512 C.E., Michelangelo painted the now-famous ceiling of the Sistine Chapel while lying on his back on scaffolding. Meanwhile, Renaissance architects borrowed heavily from the Greek and Roman traditions to build huge domes on cathedrals in Florence and Rome.

The artistic movement that engulfed the Italian city-states also spread northward and westward through much of western Europe, although it was generally more subdued and often more religious there than it was on the Italian peninsula. Still, even in northern Europe, especially in artistic centers such as Flanders, the influences of the resurgent Western heritage could be felt. For example, the Dutch **Van Eyck** brothers and the German painter **Albrecht Dürer** adopted the naturalism of the Italian painters and gained fame as portraitists. While highly realistic in style, most northern paintings were religiously motivated, and therefore even secular paintings or portraits were filled with religiously symbolic objects and color choices that resonated with the Christian faithful.

Still, while the northern painters and sculptors were quite talented, they were outnumbered and in many cases outdone by their Italian counterparts. The bigger contribution of the northern Renaissance came not from the visual arts, but from literature.

> **Contrast Them: Art in the Middle Ages and the Renaissance**
> Medieval art was almost entirely religious; Renaissance art was religious and secular, combining both Christian and humanist elements. Medieval art existed mostly in cathedrals; Renaissance art was commissioned by both religious and secular leaders, and adorned public plazas and homes. Medieval art was flat and stiff; Renaissance art was realistic, softer, and more human. In short, Medieval art didn't try to be worldly; Renaissance art tried very much to be of this world.

Western Writers Finally Get Readers

Although printing was developed in China centuries earlier (remember which dynasty? The Song), moveable type wasn't invented in Europe until the mid-1400s, when **Johannes Gutenberg** invented the printing press. Prior to Gutenberg's invention, the creation of books was such a long and laborious task that few were made. Those that were made were usually printed in Latin, the language of scholars and the Roman Catholic Church. As a result, the typical person didn't read.

With the invention of the **printing press**, all that changed. Books became easy to produce and thus were far more affordable. The growing middle class fueled demand for books on a variety of subjects that were written in their own **vernacular**, or native language, such as German or French. The book industry flourished, as did related industries such as papermaking, a craft that was learned from the Arabs (who learned it from the Chinese—gotta love those trade routes!). More books led to more literate and educated people. The newly literate people desired more books, which continued to make them more educated, which again increased their desire for books, and so on.

Many of the first books and pamphlets that were published were practical or political in nature. In 1517 c.e., **Machiavelli**, for example, published *The Prince*, a how-to book for monarchs who wanted to maintain their power. The work had a profound impact because it suggested that monarchy should be distinct from the church and that a leader should act purely in self-interest of the state rather than on the basis of vague moral tenets (since then, the term *Machiavellian* often has a negative connotation, implying a ruler who is ruthlessly selfish, scheming, and manipulative). But the printed word extended well beyond the courts of nobles. It changed life for the developing middle class because reading became a casual endeavor. Books were printed for no purpose other than entertainment or diversion, and this led to literature that increasingly focused on the daily lives of regular people, and humanized traditional institutions such as the military or the nobility.

Literature blossomed in the Renaissance of northern Europe, especially in the Low Countries (today known as the Netherlands, Luxembourg, and Belgium) and in England. In the early sixteenth century, **Erasmus**, one of the most well-known learned men of the time, counseled kings and popes. He wrote *In Praise of Folly*, which satirized what he thought were the most foolish political moves to date. At around the same time, **Sir Thomas More** of England wrote *Utopia*, which described an ideal society, in which everyone shared the wealth, and everyone's needs were met. More and Erasmus were Christian humanists, meaning that they expressed moral guidelines in the Christian tradition, which they believed people should follow as they pursued their personal goals. The Renaissance also produced **William Shakespeare**, arguably the most famous European writer from this time. Shakespeare's works reflected the period well because they not only exemplified humanism in its extreme—focusing on character strengths and flaws, comedy and tragedy—but also illustrated the era's obsession with the politics and mythology of classical civilization. His play *Julius Caesar* and his poem *Venus and Adonis* are among his many works that explored the Classical world.

2. The Protestant Reformation: Streamlining Salvation

You might recall from the previous chapter that during the Middle Ages (600–1450), the Roman Catholic Church was an extremely powerful force in Europe. While political power was diffused under the feudal system, and while the various European princes and political powers frequently clashed with the pope, emperors and princes knew that their power increased if the church blessed their reign. As a consequence, the pope wielded considerable political power.

The church was the one institution that the people of western Europe had in common. It was a unifying force, an institution believed to be sanctioned by God. With such widely accepted credentials, the church held itself out as not only the undisputed authority on all things otherworldly, but also the ultimate endorsement on all things worldly. With one foot on Earth and the other in heaven, the pope—and with him the hierarchy of the Catholic Church—acted as the intermediary between man and God. Nearly everyone in Europe understood this clearly: To get to heaven, you had to proceed by way of the Catholic Church.

The church understood the power it had over the faithful. When it needed to finance its immense building projects plus pay for the huge number of Renaissance artists it kept in its employ, it began to sell **indulgences**. An indulgence was a piece of paper that the faithful could purchase to reduce time in purgatory (the place Roman Catholics believed they would go after death). There, they would expiate (look it up!) their sins and then be allowed to enter heaven. Because purgatory was not a happy place to go, people greatly valued the concept of reducing their time there. Selling indulgences was not only a means of generating income but also a way for the church to maintain power over the masses.

During this time, land-owning nobles grew increasingly resentful of the church, which had amassed an enormous amount of power and wealth and exploited a huge number of resources at the expense of the nobles. This resentment and mistrust fueled anti-church sentiments. The selling of indulgences propelled the frustration into the ranks of the peasant class and helped set the stage for confrontation. The selling of indulgences also confirmed to many the corrupt nature of the church.

Martin Luther: Monk on a Mission

In 1517, a German monk named **Martin Luther** supposedly nailed a list of 95 theses on a church door—a list that was distributed quickly and widely by aid of the new-fangled printing press. His list outlined his frustrations with current church practices, including the church's practice of selling indulgences, which he said amounted to selling salvation for profit. Luther's frustrations had been building for some time. He had traveled to Rome, and was unnerved by the worldly nature of the city and the Vatican (the seat of the Catholic Church), which was in the midst of getting a Renaissance makeover—upgrades that were clearly paid for with money from churchgoers in far-away places.

Among Luther's many complaints was his insistence that church services should be conducted in the local languages of the people, not in Latin, a language that the German people didn't understand. To help in this effort, he translated the Bible into German so that it could be read and interpreted by everyone, as opposed to making people dependent on the church for biblical understanding. Luther's most significant claim was that salvation was given directly by God through grace, not through indulgences, and not through the authorization of the church. In other words, Luther suggested that the Bible teaches that people could appeal directly to God for forgiveness for sins and salvation. This revolutionary concept significantly reduced the role of the church as the exclusive middleman between God and man. In essence, the church was marginalized to an aid for salvation as opposed to the grantor of salvation.

Pope Leo X was outraged, and ordered Luther to recant, or formally retract, his theses. Meanwhile, Luther's ideas were spreading through much of northern Europe as the printing presses continued to roll. When Luther refused to recant, he was excommunicated. When he was allowed to address church leaders and princes at an assembly in Worms (1521), he refused to abandon his convictions. The pope called for his arrest, but a nobleman from Luther's hometown protected him, and Luther continued to write and spread his ideas.

Christianity Splits Again

The consequences of Luther's actions were enormous. Luther's followers began to refer to themselves as **Lutherans**, and began to separate themselves from the Catholic Church. What's more, other theologians began to assert their own biblical interpretations, some of which were consistent with Luther's; others were wildly different. Once the floodgates were opened, Luther had no control over the consequences.

John Calvin from France led a powerful Protestant group by preaching an ideology of predestination. Calvinist doctrine stated that God had predetermined an ultimate destiny for all people, most of whom God had already damned. Only a few, he preached, would be saved, and those people were known as the Elect. In the 1530s, the city of Geneva in Switzerland invited Calvin to construct a Protestant theocracy in their city, which was centrally located and near France. From there, Calvinist teachings spread, and were as influential to successive Protestant Reformations as were the doctrines of Luther. **Calvinism**, for example, greatly influenced religious development in Scotland under John Knox, and in France with the growth of the Huguenots.

In time, the Reformation spread to England, motivated by political as well as religious reasons. **King Henry VIII** did not have a son as heir to his throne and sought to abandon his wife, Catherine of Aragon, because of it. When the pope denied an annulment of the marriage, Henry VIII renounced Rome and declared himself the head of religious affairs in England. This sat well with those in England who already were becoming Protestants, but much of England remained Catholic. Nevertheless, Henry pushed forward and presided over what was called the **Church of England**, also known as the Anglican Church. Henry VIII went on to marry five more wives and to father a son, who died young. His daughter Elizabeth, also a Protestant, rose to the throne, but more on that later when we discuss political developments in England.

Focus On: Independent Thinking

The **Protestant Reformation** was a huge deal in world history. Its significance went well beyond the religious arena. While previous skirmishes between the pope and the nobles had been about papal political authority, Luther's challenges were theologically based and directed at the pope's religious role. Luther asserted that the people did not need the Catholic Church, or its priests, in order to interact with God; they only needed their Bibles. If the religious authority of the pope could be so openly and brazenly challenged, and commonly accepted understandings of God's relationship to man could be re-evaluated and rearticulated, then people's understanding of other concepts might need to be re-evaluated as well. Put simply, by challenging the pope, Luther made it acceptable to question the conventional wisdom of the church. With newly printed Bibles available in their own languages, lay people could learn how to read and form their own relationships with God. As the common masses became literate and better educated, more and more Europeans began to question both the world around them and the authority of the church. Europeans desired to search for their own answers to the questions of the universe. In short, the Protestant Reformation paved the way for revolutions in education, politics, and science.

The Counter-Reformation: The Pope Reasserts His Authority

During the **Catholic Reformation** (also known as the **counter-reformation**) of the sixteenth century, the Catholic Church itself reformed, while also succeeding in winning back some of the souls it had lost to the fledgling Protestant denominations.

At first, the Catholic Church responded ineffectively to the new religious trends. But when Luther refused to recant and German princes started to convert to Lutheranism, the Catholic Church began to institute reforms, which were led by Spain, a dedicated Catholic country. By banning the sale of indulgences, consulting more frequently with bishops and parishes, and training its priests to live the Catholic life instead of merely preaching it, the Catholic Church regained some of its lost credibility. However, make no mistake, the counter-reformation was as much about reaffirming as it was about reforming, and the church made it clear that it was not bowing to Protestant demands, but rather clarifying its position. Weekly mass became obligatory, and the supreme authority of the pope was re-established. During this time, a former Spanish soldier and intellectual, **Ignatius Loyola**, founded the society of Jesuits, which was influential in restoring faith in the teachings of Jesus as interpreted by the Catholic Church. The **Jesuits** practiced self-control and moderation, believing that prayer and good works led to salvation. The pious example of the Jesuits led to a stricter training system and higher expectations of morality for the clergy. Because of their oratorical and political skills, many Jesuits were appointed by kings to high palace positions.

A group of church officials held a series of meetings known as the **Council of Trent** to direct the counter-reformation period from 1545 to 1563, dictating and defining the Catholic interpretation of religious doctrine and clarifying the Catholic Church's position on important religious questions, such as the nature of salvation. During this period, "heretics" were once again tried and punished, and the Catholic Church re-established Latin as the language to be used in worship.

The result? The Catholic Church staged an amazing comeback. The counter-reformation proved successful in containing the southward spread of Protestantism. By 1600, southern Europe (especially Italy, Spain, and Portugal), France, and southern Germany were heavily Catholic. Northern Germany and Scandinavia were mostly Lutheran. Scotland was Calvinist, as were pockets within central Europe and France. And England, as mentioned previously, was Anglican.

The result of the result? Wars, of course. But more on that when we discuss developments in individual countries.

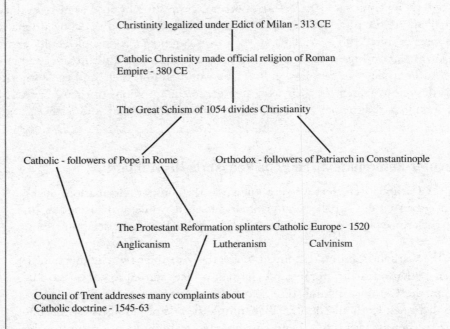

3. The Scientific Revolution: Prove It or Lose It

Prior to the Scientific Revolution, Europe and most of the world believed, as Aristotle asserted, that Earth was the center of the universe and that the sun, stars, and planets revolved around the earth. There certainly were numerous inconsistencies observed by scientists with regard to this theory, but most scientists continued to attempt explaining the inconsistency rather than investigating the theory itself.

During the Middle Ages, the Catholic Church and the political structure reinforced the lack of scientific investigation. The church focused everyone's attention on salvation, while the feudal system focused everyone's attention on mundane, local concerns. In other words, the lives of the vast majority of Europeans, in-

ing the nobility, were not engaged in big-picture concepts beyond military conquest and eternal salvation.

But as Europe changed dramatically due to the Renaissance and the Protestant Reformation, and as the growth of universities gave structure to burgeoning questions about the world, educated Europeans began to examine the world around them with new vigor. The results were revolutionary.

The Copernican Revolution: A Revolution About Revolutions

Just as the counter-reformation was gaining momentum, **Nicolaus Copernicus** developed a mathematical theory that asserted that the earth and the other celestial bodies revolved around the sun and that the earth also rotated on its axis daily. This was pretty shocking stuff to many in the "establishment." Although most educated people had accepted the world was a sphere for centuries, even well before Columbus's voyage in 1492, the earth's position at the center of the universe was widely accepted. Copernicus's heliocentric theory of the solar system brought about much debate, and much skepticism. In 1543, Copernicus published *On the Revolutions of the Heavenly Spheres* to prove his points, but it wasn't until Galileo—who discovered the moons of Jupiter with his telescope—that the Copernican model really took off.

In 1632, **Galileo** published his *Dialogue Concerning the Two Chief Systems of the World*. He wrote the work in Italian in order to reach a wide audience and hopefully defeat the defenders of Ptolemy (the scientist who promoted the earth as the center of the universe). He showed how the rotation of the earth on its axis produced the apparent rotation of the heavens, and how the stars' great distance from the earth prevented man from being able to see their changed position as the earth moved around the sun. His proofs made it difficult to continue accepting the Ptolemaic model, which just so happened to be the model sanctioned by the Roman Catholic Church. The church put Galileo on trial before the Inquisition in Rome for heresy and he was forced to recant. His book was placed on **The Index**, a list of banned heretical works (where, astonishingly, it remained until 1822!). Nevertheless, while under house arrest, Galileo continued to research and document his findings.

The Scientific Method: In Search of Truth

Recall that during the High Middle Ages and the early Renaissance, the scholastic method of reasoning was deemed the most reliable means of determining scientific meaning. Scholasticism was based on Aristotelianism and therefore used reason as the chief method of determining truth. Sometimes reason led to heresies, other times reason was used to explain and complement faith, as was the case with Thomas Aquinas.

The scientific method was born out of the scholastic tradition, but it took it to considerable new levels. Reason alone wasn't good enough. Under the scientific method, one had to prove what the mind concluded, document it, repeat it for others, and open it up to experimentation. At its highest stage, the scientific method required that any underlying principles be proven with mathematical precision.

Copernicus and Galileo, of course, were two fathers of the scientific method, but it took more than a century for the method to be widely used. There were many contributors. **Tycho Brahe** (1546–1601) built an observatory and recorded his observations, and **Francis Bacon** (1561–1626) published works on inductive logic. Both asserted that scientists should amass all the data possible through experimentation and observation and that the proper conclusions would come from these data. Then, **Johannes Kepler** (1571–1630) developed laws of planetary motion based on observation and mathematics. **Sir Isaac Newton** took it one step further. In *The Mathematical Principles of Natural Philosophy* (1697), he invented calculus to help prove the theories of Copernicus, Galileo, Bacon, and others. He also developed the law of gravity.

Together, these men and others developed a widely used system of observation, reason, experiment, and mathematical proof that could be applied to every conceivable scientific inquiry. With precise scientific instruments, like the microscope and the telescope, a scientist could retest what another scientist had originally tested. Many scientific inquires were conducted with practical goals in mind, such as the creation of labor-saving machines or the development of power sources from water and wind. Francis Bacon, for example, argued that science was pursued not for science's sake but as a way to improve the human condition.

All of this led to the Industrial Revolution, which will be discussed in the next chapter. In the meantime, however, you need to understand that the Scientific Revolution led to a major rift in society. While many Christians were able to hold on to their beliefs even as they studied science, many also began to reject the church's rigid pronouncements that conflicted with scientific findings. Many of these people either became **atheists** (who believe that no god exists) or **deists** (who believe that God exists but plays a passive role in life).

Deism: God as a Watchmaker

The Scientific Revolution contributed to a belief system known as deism, which became popular in the 1700s. The deists believed in a powerful god who created and presided over an orderly realm but who did not interfere in its workings. The deists viewed God as a watchmaker, one who set up the world, gave it natural laws by which to operate, and then let it run by itself (under natural laws that could be proved mathematically). Such a theory had little place in organized religion.

Focus On: The Church Defends Itself on Two Fronts
Both the Protestant Reformation and the Scientific Revolution challenged the absolute authority of the pope. The Reformation challenged the pope's authority on theological grounds; the Scientific Revolution challenged his authority on scientific and mathematical grounds. Don't presume that the Protestant Revolution was the main instigator of religious change during this time period. The religious implications of the Scientific Revolution were just as huge.

4. The Enlightenment: Out of Darkness, Into the Light

While the scientists put forth revolutionary ideas, the philosophers and social critics had a revolution of their own. **The Enlightenment** of the seventeenth and eighteenth centuries focused on the role of mankind in relation to government, ideas which greatly influenced the framers of the U.S. Constitution. Because the U.S. Constitution has since been a model for so many others across the globe, it's safe to say that the writers of the Enlightenment period changed the world. Keep this in mind when you move on to Chapter 9 and the Atlantic Revolutions.

First a Little Background: Divine Right

During the High Middle Ages and through the Renaissance and counter-reformation, the church allied itself with strong monarchs. These monarchs came to power by centralizing authority, uniting people under a common banner of nationalism, forming empires by promoting exploration and colonization (much more on this later), and ruling with absolute authority. Because the vast majority of their populations were Christian, the best way to rule was to align oneself with God. Monarchs became convinced that God had ordained their right to govern, and that meant that people had a moral and religious obligation to obey them. This concept was known as the **divine right** of monarchs. James I of England, who ruled from 1603 to 1625, summed it up this way: "The king is from God and the law is from the King." His statement made it pretty clear that an illegal act was an ungodly act.

Because the pope also claimed to be ordained by God, the question of ultimate authority became very confusing indeed. During the Reformation, monarchs who resented the power of the church supported the reformists (Luther, Calvin, and others). Other monarchs, particularly in Spain and France, allied themselves with the church during the counter-reformation. In both cases, monarchs claimed to have divine right. Divine right could be used to support either position because the bottom line was that God supported whatever the monarchs chose.

> ### Contrast Them: Divine Right and Mandate of Heaven
> Recall that under the Chou Dynasty in China, the emperor ruled under what became known as a **Mandate of Heaven**, which sounds a whole lot like Divine Right, and it was except for an important difference. Under the Mandate of Heaven, the emperors believed they were divinely chosen, but would only be given authority to rule so long as they pleased heaven. If they didn't rule justly and live up to their responsibility, heaven would ensure their fall. Divine Right, on the other hand, was used to justify absolute rule without any corresponding responsibilities. Monarchs who ruled under a strict theory of Divine Right saw themselves as God's personal representatives, chosen specifically for the task of ruling. In other words, Divine Right was a privilege without any corresponding responsibilities, whereas the Mandate of Heaven was upheld only so long as rulers acted justly.

The Social Contract: Power to the People

During the seventeenth century, philosophers and intellectuals began to grapple with the nature of social and political structures, and the idea of the social contract emerged. The social contract held that governments were formed not by divine decree, but to meet the social and economic needs of the people being governed. Philosophers who supported the social contract theory reasoned that because individuals existed before governments did, governments arose to meet the needs of the people, not the other way around. Still, because different philosophers looked at human nature differently, they disagreed about the role of government in the social contract.

Thomas Hobbes (1588–1679), who wrote *Leviathan*, thought that people by nature were greedy and prone to violent warfare. Accordingly, he believed the role of the government under the social contract should be to preserve peace and stability at all costs. Hobbes therefore advocated an all-powerful ruler, or Leviathan, who would rule in such a heavy-handed way as to suppress the natural war-like tendencies of the people.

John Locke (1632–1704), who wrote *Two Treatises on Government*, had a more optimistic view of human nature, believing that mankind, for the most part, was good. Locke also believed that all men were born equal to one another and had natural and unalienable rights to life, liberty, and property. Since mankind was good and rational, and thus capable of self-rule, Locke believed the primary responsibility of the government under the social contract was to secure and guarantee these natural rights. If, however, the government ever violated this trust, thus breaking the social contract, the people were justified in revolting and replacing the government.

Jean-Jacques Rousseau (1712–1778) took the social contract theory to its furthest extreme, arguing that all men were equal and that society should be organized according to the general will, or majority rule, of the people, an idea he outlined in his famous work *The Social Contract* (1762). In a rational society, he argued, each individual should subject himself to this general will, which serves as the sovereign or ruling lawmaker. Under this philosophy, the individual is protected by the community, but is also free (or as free as one can be in organized society). He argues the essence of freedom is to obey laws that people prescribe for themselves. Needless to say, Rousseau's beliefs not only had a tremendous effect on revolutionary movements in the colonies of the European empires, but also inspired the anti-slavery movement.

In addition to philosophers, there were many Enlightenment writers. **Voltaire** espoused the idea of religious toleration. **Montesquieu** argued for separation of powers among branches of government. In all cases, Enlightenment writers didn't presume that government had divine authority, but instead worked backward from the individual and proposed governmental systems that would best serve the interest of the people by protecting individual rights and liberties.

While the real fruits of the Enlightenment were the revolutionary movements in the colonies and later in Europe, the new political ideas also affected the leadership of some eighteenth-century European monarchs. The ideals of tolerance, justice, and improvement of people's lifestyle became guidelines for rulers known as **Enlightened Monarchs**, such as Joseph II of Austria and Frederick II of Prussia. To be sure, they still ruled absolutely, but they internalized the Enlightenment philosophy and made attempts to tolerate diversity, increase opportunities for serfs, and take on the responsibilities that their rule required.

B. European Exploration and Expansion: Empires of the Wind

Exploration before the late fifteenth century was largely limited to land travel. To be sure, ships were used on the Mediterranean and Indian Ocean trade routes for centuries, but they were linked up to land routes through Persia, Arabia, northern Africa, or central Asia on the Silk Road.

Eager to eliminate Muslim middlemen and discover more efficient trade routes to Asia, the Portuguese and their Iberian rivals, the Spanish, set out to sea. Advances in navigation, ship-building and the development of gunpowder weapons allowed for increased sea travel. These "floating empires of the wind" soon controlled major shipping routes in the Indian Ocean, Indonesia, and the Atlantic Ocean.

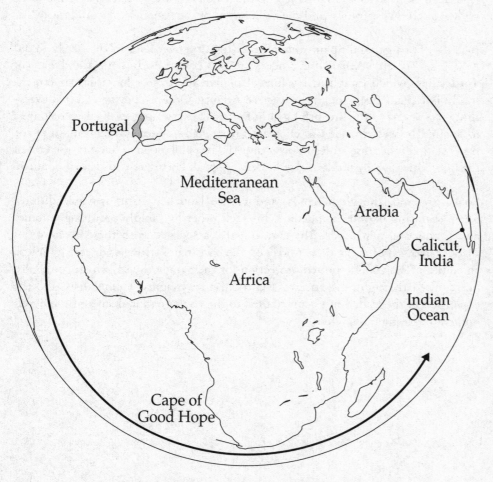

Portuguese Exploration in the 1500s

The increase in European trade encouraged by the formation of the Hanseatic League and the Crusades spawned a search for new, efficient trade routes on the seas. Portugal led the way because it was strategically situated near the coast of Africa, had long-standing trade relations with Muslim nations, and, most important of all, was led by a royal family that supported exploration (King John I of Portugal's most famous son was **Prince Henry the Navigator**). In 1488, Portugal financed a voyage by Bartholomew Dias who rounded the tip of Africa (which became known as the Cape of Good Hope). In 1497, **Vasco da Gama** rounded the Cape of Good Hope, explored the east African kingdoms, and then went all the way to India, where he established trade relations.

Shortly thereafter, Spain, which had recently been unified under Isabella and Ferdinand, wanted in on the action. As you well know, in 1492 **Christopher Columbus** convinced them to finance a voyage to reach the east by going west. While those who were educated understood that the earth was a sphere, few people understood how large it was. Despite the fact that some scholars had accurately estimated the earth's size, most people, including Columbus, thought it was smaller. As a result, Columbus thought that China and India were located where the American continents are. He sailed, found Cuba and the islands that came to be known as the West Indies, and the exploration of the Americas was underway.

By 1494, Portugal and Spain were already fighting over land in the newly found Americas. To resolve their differences, the two countries drew up the **Treaty of Tordesillas**, which established a line of demarcation on a longitudinal (north-south) line that runs through the western Atlantic Ocean. They agreed that everything to the east of the line belonged to Portugal; everything to the west belonged to Spain. The western side was enormous (they had no idea how enormous at the time) so Spain became a mega-power quickly. Brazil happened to lie to the east of the line, which is why modern-day Brazilians speak Portuguese instead of Spanish.

Soon, England, the Netherlands, and France launched their own expeditions. These seafaring nations competed with each other by rapidly acquiring colonies and conquering new lands. The cost and risk associated with these explorations made it necessary for explorers to rely on the backing of strong and wealthy states. In addition, merchants wanted protection for their trade routes, which could also be acquired through allegiance to a particular sovereignty. Colonialism and the expansion of the trade routes contributed to the rise in nationalism and the development of strong monarchies.

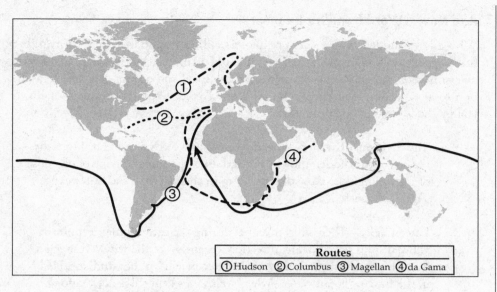

European Exploration in the Early Sixteenth Century

A quick list of other explorers

- **Amerigo Vespucci**—He explored South America on several trips around 1500; realized that the continent was huge and not part of Asia; America was named for him.

- **Ponce de Leon**—In 1513, he explored Florida for Spain in search of the fountain of youth.

- **Vasco de Balboa**—In 1513, he explored much of Central America for Spain; laid sight on the Pacific Ocean.

- **Ferdinand Magellan**—In 1519, he sailed around the tip of South America to the Pacific Ocean for Portugal. He made it as far as the Philippines, where he died; his crew continued, however, and became the first to circumnavigate the globe.

- **Giovanni da Verrazzano**—In 1524, he explored the North American coast for France.

- **Sir Francis Drake**—In 1578, he became the first Englishman to circumnavigate the globe.

- **John Cabot**—In 1597, he explored the coast of North America for England.

- **Henry Hudson**—Beginning in 1609, he sailed for the Dutch, looking for a **Northwest Passage** to Asia. He explored the Hudson River and made claims to the area for the Dutch.

And Now a Word from Our Sponsors

Why, all of a sudden, were so many explorers sailing around the globe? Why didn't this happen sooner? In the late fifteenth century, innovation was combined with determination to apply new technologies to political and economic goals. In addition to advanced mapmaking techniques, the Age of Exploration was brought to you by the following fine products:

- **The Sternpost Rudder**—Invented in China during the Han Dynasty, the sternpost rudder allowed for better navigation and control of ships of increasing size. How did it end up in the hands of the Europeans? Trade, of course.

- **Lateen Sails**—These sails, invented during the early Roman Empire, allowed ships to sail in any direction, regardless of the wind. This was a huge improvement to ships that were dependent on the wind, especially in the Indian Ocean waters, where monsoons kept ships docked for long periods of time. Once these sails were used regularly on the Indian Ocean routes, they quickly became standard on transatlantic voyages.

- **The Astrolabe**—Sailors used this portable navigation device, developed in the Hellenic world around 150 B.C.E., to help them find their way. By measuring the distance of the sun and the stars above the horizon, the astrolabe helped determine latitude.

- **The Magnetic Compass**—Borrowed from the Chinese, who developed it during the Han Dynasty, the magnetic compass traveled west through trade with Arabs and allowed sailors to determine direction without staying in sight of land.

- **Three-Masted Caravels**—These large ships employed significantly larger lateen sails and could hold provisions for longer journeys in their large cargo rooms.

To be sure, many of these inventions existed prior to the fifteenth century, but so much of history is about timing. In the late fifteenth century, these inventions had converged on one continent, a continent that was fiercely competitive about trade routes, newly wealthy, increasingly organized under strong leaders, and racing with the innovation and imagination of the Renaissance. We've said it before and we'll say it again: The events of this time period are so interrelated that you can't separate them. The era needs to be understood as one giant glob of inseparable, indistinguishable forces.

The New World: Accidental Empire

Although Columbus failed to locate gold or spices in the Americas, the next generation of Spanish explorers found great wealth in the Aztec and Inca Empires.

In 1519, **Hernan Cortes** landed on the coast of Mexico with a small force of 600 men. He found himself at the heart of the Aztec Empire, which you read about in the previous chapter. As you might recall, the Aztecs used the conquest of neighboring communities to secure humans for religious sacrifices. Many of these neighboring states loathed the Aztecs and were more than willing to co-operate with the Spaniards. Cortes alternatively subjugated or slaughtered those that were not.

Cortes, aided and guided by the resentful neighbors, first approached the magnificent Aztec capital of Tenochtitlan on horseback. Horses were as yet completely unknown in America (and in fact were introduced to the continent by Spanish conquistadores). He sent a gift of gold to appease this newcomer to his lands, but unfortunately for the Aztecs, this offering only fueled the appetite of the new conquerors. Because the Spaniards' sole motivation for exploring the New World was to acquire gold and spices, the Spanish didn't hesitate to seize Montezuma and begin a siege of Tenochtitlan.

Disease: The Ultimate Weapon of Mass Destruction

Although the Aztecs resisted the occupation and fought to rid their capital of the invaders, the Spanish had incredibly powerful weapons on their side, including diseases such as smallpox. These infections were completely new to the Americas, thanks to their geographic isolation prior to Europeans' arrival, and quickly decimated the Aztecs, who had no natural resistance to them. The combination of disease, superior weapons, and assistance from Aztec enemies reduced the native population of the region from well over 20 million in 1520 to fewer than 2 million by 1580. Because so many of the deaths occurred in the first few years, the Spaniards were able to seize control of the empire by around 1525.

A similar fate met the Inca Empire. In 1531, **Francisco Pizarro** set out in search of the Incas with a tiny force of 200 men. Disease, superior weapons, and help from enemies quickly destroyed what little resistance the Incas could mount. In addition, Pizarro happened to land shortly after a very destructive civil war that had left the current emperor of the Incas in a shaky political position. By 1535, Pizarro was in control of the region.

Contrast Them: Expansion in the Americas versus Empire-Building Elsewhere
We've talked about a lot of empires that expanded into far-reaching territories: the Romans, the Mongols, the Muslims, and the Macedonians, for example. In each of these cases, the empires either allowed existing cultural traditions to remain intact, or converted the existing population to their way of doing things, forcibly or not. By contrast, in the case of the Americas, the existing populations were largely wiped out. In addition, huge numbers of people moved in, far outnumbering the number of natives that survived. Even the Mongols, who didn't hesitate to wipe out communities in their paths, didn't totally supplant the native populations the way the Europeans did in the Americas. Never before had an empire moved into such a vast territory that was so unpopulated (or, more accurately, depopulated). All of the other empires had to merge with, convert, or be converted by the existing populations. In the Americas, the Europeans created two new continents strictly in their own image.

The *Encomienda* System: American Feudalism

Once Spain established a foothold in the New World, thousands of Spaniards arrived to build a new colonial empire. The colonial society was a hierarchical organization. At the top were the **peninsulares**, the select group of Spanish officials sent to govern the colonies. Below them, the *crillos* or **creoles**, were people born in the colonies to Spanish parents. Because they weren't born in Spain, they were looked down upon by the Spanish monarchy and were consequently barred from high positions. Yet, because they were the children of Spaniards, the creoles were educated and wealthy, and after many generations, they were able to organize and demand recognition. They later became the leaders of the independence movements (more on that in the next chapter). Below the crillos were **mestizos**, those with European and Native American ancestry, followed by the **mulattos**, those with European and African ancestry. Finally, there were the native Americans, who had little or no freedom and worked on estates or in mines.

To run the empire, the **viceroys**, who were appointed governors of each of the five regions of New Spain, established the *Encomienda* System, which was sort of like a feudal system. The system provided the peninsulares with land and a specified number of native laborers. In return, the peninsulares were expected to protect the natives and convert them to Christianity. Shocked at the treatment of some of the natives, Christian missionaries appealed to the viceroys, emperor, and the Catholic Church to improve the natives' lot. Some in the empire agreed that reform was needed, but disastrously, the reform that was viewed as most important was the need for more workers. They agreed to reduce the strain on the natives by bringing in new workers for the hardest jobs. Those new workers were African slaves. Not only was this a cruel and ironic way to solve the problem (relieve the burden on one group of victims by creating a second group), it ended up not improving the lot of the natives. Within a few decades, both slaves and natives were at the bottom of the social structure, and neither had significant rights.

The African Slave Trade: The Love of Money at the Root of Evil

Even before transatlantic voyages began, Europeans had begun exploiting a system of slavery that already existed in Africa. While many African tribes and nations practiced a form of slavery by requiring prisoners taken in battle to serve their captors for a period of time before being eventually released (when their captors judged that prisoners' honor, lost in battle, had been restored by their service), Europeans traded guns and other goods to African leaders in exchange for their surplus slaves but did not understand (or chose to ignore) the custom of eventual release. By the mid-fifteenth century, the Portuguese were also capturing slaves while exploring the coasts of Africa. When the plantations (and mines) of the New World demanded more labor, the money-hungry empire builders knew where to go. And so began a forced migration of people that would forever change the fate of millions of lives and the history of the New World.

Some African rulers cooperated with the slave trade, while others protested, but they were in a difficult position—as demand for the transatlantic slave trade increased, Europeans became increasingly ruthless in their methods, kidnapping

Africans in their own raids or pitting groups against one another through control of the weapons trade. Kings and other leaders faced the choice of cooperating with the Europeans or seeing their people seized or slaughtered. So the slave trade expanded. Africans were rounded up, forced onto ships, chained together, taken below deck, and forced to endure the brutal **Middle Passage** to the Americas. By historians' best estimates, at least 13 million Africans were taken from the continent and carried to the New World; approximately 60 percent went to South America, around 35 percent to the Caribbean, and about 5 percent to North America. Along the way, some suffocated from the hot, unventilated conditions below deck, others starved or died from outbreaks of disease, and yet others were killed attempting revolt or jumped overboard to their deaths, preferring suicide to the dishonor of slavery. Based on slave traders' existing records, historians believe average mortality rates were around 20 percent, though some voyages lost a much larger portion of their human cargo. Those that survived the journey were taken to the auction blocks, sold into slavery, and forced to work in plantation fields or in mines until their deaths, as were their children and their children's children.

Focus On: Demographic Shifts

The demographic changes of the sixteenth and seventeenth centuries were, in a word, huge. The Aztecs and Incas were wiped out. Huge cities were depopulated. Europeans moved by the hundreds of thousands. Africans were forced to migrate by the millions. Cities in Europe swelled as the feudal system evaporated and urban, middle class merchants lined their pockets with the fruits of trade and empire. By 1750, the continents of Europe, Africa, North America, and South America were unrecognizable from their 1450 portraits.

The Columbian Exchange: Continental Shift

One consequence of the Spanish and Portuguese empires in the New World was what became known as the Columbian Exchange—the transatlantic transfer of animals, plants, diseases, people, technology, and ideas among Europe, the Americas, and Africa. As Europeans and Africans crisscrossed the Atlantic, they brought the Old World to the New and back again. From the European and African side of the Atlantic, horses, pigs, goats, chili peppers, and sugar cane (and more) flowed to the Americas. From the American side, squash, beans, corn, potatoes, and cacao (and more) made their way back east. Settlers from the Old World carried bubonic plague, smallpox, typhoid, influenza, and the common cold into the New, then carried Chagas and syphilis back to the Old. Guns, Catholicism, and slaves also crossed the Atlantic. Never before had so much been moved across the oceans, as ship after ship carried the contents of one continent to another.

The American food crops (cassava, corn, peanuts, and potatoes) that traveled east made population increases possible throughout Europe, Asia, and Africa. Urban populations and commercial interests grew throughout Europe and led to increased cultivation and enclosure of land. With increased cultivation came increased use of previously rural areas. Despite some threat of famine, shortages due to a long cooling period or "little ice age," and out-migration, overall the trend throughout much of northern Europe was that of a growing population.

Two key products of the Columbian Exchange were **sugar** and **silver**. Sugarcane roots had arrived in the Caribbean from India with Columbus, who saw an opportunity to monopolize a profitable crop in a new environment. Sugarcane production resulted in the development of plantations throughout the Spanish colonies and an increased need for enslaved or forced labor once the Native populations of the islands declined. The results of the plantation system were brutal, dangerous labor and a transformation of the natural landscape.

The Spanish also monopolized the world's silver market from the mines they controlled in Mexico and in the Andes Mountain of Peru. This industry also resulted in a harsh system of forced labor: the previously mentioned encomienda. Like the sugar plantations, early silver mining depended on Native labor until that grew too scarce to make a profit, when labor shifted to African slaves provided by Portuguese traders.

More importantly, Spanish control of Latin American silver opened doors in Ming China. Spanish access to the Philippines, China and the Pacific Ocean trade routes made the world a much smaller place.

The Commercial Revolution: The New Economy

The trading, empire building, and conquest of the **Age of Exploration** was made possible by new financing schemes that now form the basis of our modern economies. Though many elements had to come together at once for the new economy to work, timing was on the side of the Europeans, and everything fell into place.

First, the church gave in to state interests by revising its strict ban on what are now standard business practices, like lending money and charging interest on loans. Once banking became respectable, a new business structure emerged: the **joint-stock company**, an organization created to pool the resources of many merchants, thereby distributing the costs and risks of colonization and reducing the danger for individual investors. Investors bought shares, or stock, in the company. If the company made money, each investor would receive a profit proportional to his or her initial investment. Because huge new ships were able to carry unprecedented cargoes, and because the goods were often outright stolen from their native countries, successful voyages reaped huge profits. A substantial middle class of merchants continued to develop, which in turn attracted more investors, and the modern-day concept of a stock market was well under way.

These corporations later secured royal charters for colonies, like the Jamestown colony in Virginia, and funded them for business purposes. Even when they didn't establish colonies, monarchies granted monopolies to trade routes. The **Muscovy Company** of England monopolized trade routes to Russia, for example. The **Dutch East India Company** controlled routes to the Spice Islands (modern-day Indonesia).

Increased trade led to an early theory of macroeconomics for the nations of Europe. Under the theory of **mercantilism**, a country actively sought to trade, but tried not to import more than it exported; that is, it attempted to create a favorable balance of trade. Trade deficits forced dependencies on other countries, and therefore implied weakness. Of course, one country's surplus had to be met with another country's deficit. To resolve this dilemma, European countries were feverish to colonize. Colonies gave the mother country raw resources (not considered imports because the mother country "owned" them), while creating new markets for processed exports. To further aid the effort, monarchies promoted domestic industry and placed tariffs on imports from competing empires. As you'll see in the next chapter, once the Industrial Revolution was under way, mercantilism really took off.

It shouldn't be surprising that mercantilism fostered resentment in colonies. The colonial resources were shipped back to Europe while the colonists were forced to pay for products from Europe. Add taxes, and you've got major resentment. You already know that the American Revolution was in part due to colonial fury over this arrangement. One by one, beginning with America, European colonies revolted against the abuses by the unforgiving mercantilist economies of the European powers.

Oh Yeah…Remember Asia?

Recall that the original Portuguese explorers were trying to figure out a short cut to India and China. Once they stumbled upon a couple of continents along the way and began wiping out native civilizations, building empires, and forcibly transporting millions of Africans to do hard labor, they forgot the original purpose of their exploration. In time, European explorers, armed with bottomless resources of energy and greed, remembered and pursued the East.

Asian colonization didn't really get rolling until the nineteenth century, so that will be covered in the next chapter. From the sixteenth through the eighteenth centuries, however, the Europeans managed to establish trade with the Asian empires, although it was more limited than they would have liked due to Asian protectionist policies and the difficulty of travel.

After making their way around the Cape of Good Hope, the Portuguese set up a trading post in Goa on the west coast of India. They also gained control over the Spice Islands by establishing naval superiority in the Straits of Malacca. In less than a century, however, other European powers coveted Asian riches. The Dutch, under the backing of the newly formed Dutch East India Company, conducted deliberate raids on Portuguese ships and trading posts. In the seventeenth century, the Dutch became the biggest power in the spice trades. Meanwhile, England and France set up trading posts in India.

As for China and Japan, both empires severely limited trade with the Europeans. Throughout this time period, the two Asian empires couldn't have been more unlike their European counterparts. They were highly isolationist. Not only did they not go out and try to find the rest of the world, they also pushed the rest of the world away when it came to find them. You'll read more about China and Japan in the next section.

IV. DEVELOPMENTS IN SPECIFIC COUNTRIES AND EMPIRES 1450–1750

It's dangerous to presume that because the Renaissance, the Protestant Reformation, the Scientific Revolution, the Enlightenment, and the Age of Exploration eventually had enormous consequences that they did so quickly, broadly, or in equal proportions. In reality, the major movements impacted different parts of Europe at different times and took a long time to penetrate all circles of society. Most people with power guarded it jealously, regardless of the intellectual or religious movements that brought their power into question. What's more, most of the peasant class didn't participate in the intellectual, scientific, or commercial developments because they weren't educated or in a position to be immediately impacted by the consequences.

Outside of Europe, the major developments of the time period also had widely varying consequences. In the previous section, we discussed the consequences on the Americas and on much of Africa. But lest you think the rest of the world remained passive in the face of European growth, it is important to note that powerful and centralized states were established (or reestablished) in the Middle East, India, China and Japan. The empires of Asia, too, had unique experiences, which are discussed in detail later in the chapter. As you review the developments in the European empires, keep in mind that most nations were led by monarchs, or sovereigns, who felt that the right to govern was ordained by God. Under this idea of divine right, it was essential for royal families to retain pure bloodlines to God, so intermarriage among royal families of different nations was common. Thus, the monarchies of one country also gained international influence as the ties of marriage and inheritance led to alliances.

Monarchies also contributed to the development of strong national loyalties, which led to many conflicts, internally and externally. The European wars of this time fall into three categories: religious fights between Protestants and Catholics, internal civil wars between a monarch and disgruntled nobles, and battles stemming from the trade disputes between rival nations. In the beginning of this era, Spain became the world's strongest nation with a powerful naval fleet and an extensive empire. As the balance of power in Europe shifted, the rival nations of England and France emerged as great powers.

A. The European Rivals

1. Spain and Portugal

As you read in the previous chapter, in 1469, **King Ferdinand**, from the Christian Kingdoms in northern Spain, and **Queen Isabella**, from the more Muslim regions of southern Spain, initiated the consolidation of Spanish authority under one house, and thereby created a nation-state that would become one of the world's most powerful forces over the next century. By aggressively supporting exploration (initially by underwriting Columbus's exploration and then later by establishing empires in the New World), Ferdinand and Isabella had a long-term impact on cultural world developments—they ensured the survival and expansion of the Spanish language and culture, including Roman Catholicism, by extending them across the Atlantic. Ferdinand and Isabella also built a formidable naval fleet, allowing Spain to rule the seas for the next century.

As Spain focused on western exploration and its empire in the New World, the Portuguese continued their domination of coastal Africa, the Indian Ocean, and the Spice Islands. A small country with limited manpower, Portugal had to be content as the middleman of a "floating empire." It was an early player in the transatlantic slave trade, controlled sea routes, and garrisoned trading posts, but was unable to exert control over large sections of the interior of Africa and India. Inevitably, Portugal could not maintain control of its far-flung colonies and lost control of them to the Dutch and British who had faster ships with heavier guns.

The international importance of Spain grew under **Charles V**, who inherited a large empire. Charles was a Hapsburg, a family that originated in Austria and, through a series of carefully arranged marriages (recall that divine right promoted intermarriage among royalty), created a huge empire stretching from Austria and Germany to Spain. While one set of Charles's grandparents were Hapsburgs, his other grandparents were Ferdinand and Isabella, who themselves had married to solidify the Spanish empire. Talk about family connections.

Anyway, in 1519, Charles was elected Holy Roman Emperor by German princes, which meant that he then held lands in parts of France, the Netherlands, Austria, and Germany in addition to Spain. These possessions, plus the new colonies in the Americas, brought wars as well as riches. Spain fought France for control of Italy and the Ottoman Turks for control of eastern Europe, which led to an expansion of Ottoman rule into much of Hungary (more on that later). In Germany, Charles defended Catholicism from the encroachment of Protestantism (recall that Spain was allied with the Catholic Church during the counter-reformation). Frustrated over trying to manage such an enormous empire at a time of expansion in the New World and revolution in Europe (the Protestant Reformation and Scientific Revolution, for example), he decided in 1556 to retire to a monastery and thereby abdicate the throne. He gave control to his brother, **Ferdinand I**, over Austria and the Holy Roman throne of Germany. To his son, **Philip II**, he conferred the throne of Spain and jurisdiction over Burgundy (in France), Sicily, and the Netherlands as well as Spain's claim in the New World. We'll talk more about Ferdinand's half of the empire later in this chapter. Phillip II also gained control over Portugal.

Under Philip II, the Spanish Empire in the west saw some of its greatest expansion in the New World and a rebirth of culture under the Spanish Renaissance, but it also started showing signs of decay. A devoutly religious man, Philip oversaw the continuation of the **Spanish Inquisition** to oust heretics, led the Catholic Reformation against Protestants, and supported an increase in missionary work in the ever-expanding empire in the New World. Increasingly Protestant and increasingly eager to develop their own empire, the Dutch (of the Netherlands) revolted. By 1581, the mostly Protestant northern provinces of the Netherlands gained their independence from Spain and became known as the Dutch Netherlands. The mostly Catholic southern provinces remained loyal to Spain (this region would later become Belgium).

Exhibiting further signs of weakness, Spanish forces fighting for Catholicism in France fared poorly, and to the shock of many Spaniards, the English defeated and devastated the once mighty Spanish Armada as it tried to attack the British Isles. The defeat invigorated the English, who by the late sixteenth century were expanding their own empire, and signaled containment of Spanish forces.

Although Spain amassed enormous sums of gold from the New World, it spent its wealth quickly on wars, missionary activities, and maintenance of its huge fleets. By the mid-seventeenth century, Spain still had substantial holdings, but its glory days had passed. England and France were well poised to replace it as the dominant European powers.

2. England

As you read above in the discussion of the Protestant Reformation, **King Henry VIII**, who ruled from 1509 to 1547, nullified the pope's authority in England, thereby establishing (under the 1534 **Act of Supremacy**) the Church of England and placed himself as head of that church. This was so that he could divorce his wife and marry Anne Boleyn in an effort to father a male heir. He didn't succeed in getting a male heir. Instead, he got another daughter, **Elizabeth I**, who oversaw a golden age in the arts known as the Elizabethan Age.

The **Elizabethan Age** (1558–1603) boasted commercial expansion and exploration and colonization in the New World, especially after the English fleet destroyed the Spanish Armada in 1588. During this time, the **Muscovy Company** was founded as the first joint-stock company, and the **British East India Company** quickly followed suit. Drake circumnavigated the globe. The first English colonists settled in Roanoke colony in present-day Virginia. And to top it all off, Shakespeare wrote his masterpieces. Simply put, England under Elizabeth experienced a golden age.

The religious battles that were unleashed by the Protestant Reformation still unsettled the region. Anglicans (Church of England) were battling Catholics, while other Protestant groups such as the Puritans were regularly persecuted. When **James I** came to power in 1607 after the death of Elizabeth, a reign that brought together the crowns of England and Scotland, he attempted to institute reforms to accommodate the Catholics and the Puritans, but widespread problems persisted. The Puritans (who were Calvinists) didn't want to recognize the power of the king over religious matters, and James reacted defensively, claiming divine right. It was at this point that many Puritans decided to cross the Atlantic. The Pilgrims cross to Plymouth colony (1620) occurred during James's reign. Jamestown colony, as you might have guessed, was also founded during the reign of James I. The English aren't known for their innovative place names.

Charles I, son of James, rose to power in 1625. Three years later, desperate for money from Parliament, he agreed to sign the **Petition of Right**, which was a document limiting taxes and forbidding unlawful imprisonment. But Charles ignored the petition after he secured the funds he needed and, claiming divine right, ruled without calling another meeting of parliament for eleven years.

In 1640, when Scotland's resentment toward Charles resulted in a Scottish invasion of England, Charles was forced to call Parliament into session. Led by Puritans, this Parliament was known as the **Long Parliament** because it sat for twenty years from 1640 through 1660. The Long Parliament limited the absolute powers of the monarchy. In 1641, the parliament denied Charles's request for money to fight the Irish rebellion, and in response he led troops into the House of Commons to arrest some of the members. This sparked a civil war. Parliament raised an army, called the Roundheads, to fight the king. The Roundheads, under the leadership of **Oliver Cromwell**, defeated the armies of Charles I, who were called Cavaliers. The king was tried and executed. Oliver Cromwell rose to power, not as a monarch, but first as leader of what was called the **English Commonwealth**, then after reorganizing the government, as **Lord Protector**.

When Cromwell ruled as Protector, he ruled with religious intolerance and violence against Catholics and the Irish. He encouraged Protestants to settle in Northern Ireland (this would cause many problems in future centuries). All of this caused much resentment, and after Cromwell died, Parliament invited Charles II, the exiled son of the now-beheaded Charles I, to take the throne and restore a limited monarchy. This is called the **Stuart Restoration** (1660–1688). A closet Catholic, Charles II acknowledged the rights of the people, especially with regard to religion. In 1679, he agreed to the **Habeas Corpus Act** (which protects people from arrests without due process). Following Charles II's death, his brother James II took over.

James II was openly Catholic, and he was unpopular. Like so many before him, he believed in the divine right of kings. In a bloodless change of leadership known as the **Glorious Revolution**, he was driven from power by Parliament, who feared he'd make England a Catholic country, and he fled to France. He was replaced in 1688 by his son-in-law and daughter, William and Mary, the Protestant rulers of the Netherlands, who promptly signed the **English Bill of Rights** in 1689. The Glorious Revolution ensured that England's future monarchs would be Anglican, and that their powers would be limited.

Focus On: The Enlightenment Writers

Keep in mind that the Enlightenment writers were busy at work by this time. Hobbes published *Leviathan* in 1651 in response to the English Civil War, a time during which the monarch, Charles I, was beheaded. Hobbes's violent view of human nature and desire for an all-powerful ruler to maintain peace are completely understandable within the context of the English Civil War. While Hobbes missed the peaceful resolution of the war in the Glorious Revolution and the English Bill of Rights (1688–1689), John Locke did not. Locke's more optimistic view of human nature can be viewed in the context of the bloodless transition of power between James II and William and Mary. In addition, Locke's writings in *Two Treatises on Government* justified this change of leadership by suggesting James II had violated the social contract. Political events in England during this time, and such events in general, cannot be separated from the development of social and political philosophy and visa versa.

3. France

After the Hundred Years' War (1337–1453) drove the English from France, the French began to unify and centralize authority in a strong monarchy. But, as elsewhere, religious differences stood in the way. France was largely Catholic, but during the Protestant Reformation, a group of French Protestants, known as **Huguenots**, developed into a sizeable and influential minority. Throughout the mid- to late-sixteenth century, Catholics and Huguenots bitterly fought each other, sometimes brutally, until, in 1598, **Henry IV** issued the **Edict of Nantes**, which created an environment of toleration. Henry IV was the first Bourbon king. The Bourbons ruled France until 1792, nearly two centuries.

> **Contrast Them: England and France During the Seventeenth Century**
> Unlike England, France was ruled by a series of strong and able monarchs under the Bourbon Dynasty. After the death of Elizabeth, England went from monarchy to Commonwealth to Restoration to Glorious Revolution. Hardly stable. On the other hand, France's Estates-General (a governing body representing clergy, nobles, merchants, and peasants) was not nearly as powerful as the English Parliament. It didn't even meet for the bulk of the seventeenth century because the French kings ruled successfully under the justification of divine right.

Cardinal Richelieu, a Catholic, played an important role as the chief advisor to the Bourbons. His primary political role was to strengthen the French crown. While clashes erupted among Catholics and Huguenots (Protestants) in France, Richelieu did not seek to destroy the Protestants; he compromised with them and even helped them to attack the Catholic Hapsburgs of the Holy Roman Empire, an empire that he wanted to end in order to make France a stronger power in Europe. A new bureaucratic class, the *noblesse de la robe*, was established under Richelieu. The bureaucracy that Richelieu and then later successor, **Cardinal Mazarin**, established prepared France to hold the strong position it would achieve in Europe under Louis XIV.

Louis XIV was four years old when he inherited the crown of France. His mother and Cardinal Mazarin ruled in his name until he reached adulthood, at which time he became one of the most legendary monarchs of European history. Louis XIV's long reign (1643–1715) exemplified the grandiose whims of an absolute monarchy. Calling himself the "Sun King" and "The Most Christian King," he patronized the arts as long as they contributed to the glorification of France and its culture, which became much admired and emulated. Ruling under divine right, he reportedly declared, "I am the State," and he built the lavish palace of Versailles to prove it. He never summoned the Estates-General, the lawmaking body, to meet. He revoked the Edict of Nantes, forcing many Huguenots to leave France. Perhaps most importantly, he appointed **Jean Baptiste Colbert** to manage the royal funds.

A strict mercantilist, Colbert wanted to increase the size of the French empire, thereby increasing the opportunity for business transactions and taxes. To accomplish this, France was almost constantly at war. For a while, warfare and mercantilist policies allowed France to increase its overseas holdings and gain the revenue needed for the extravagances of a king named for the sun. But the **War of Spanish Succession** (1701–1714) proved to be a disaster for the grand plans of France.

Recall that European royalty was intermarrying and reproducing. It turned out that the twisted branches of the royal family trees led to a situation in which, in 1701, one of Louis XIV's grandsons inherited the Spanish throne. This alarmed the rest of Europe, who feared that Spain, although substantially weaker than it had been in the previous century, and France, already quite powerful, would form an unstoppable combo-power, especially given their American holdings at the time (France owned a huge chunk of North America, Spain the bulk of Central and South America). It's a complicated story, but England, the Holy Roman Empire, and German princes all united under the perceived common threat, and thirteen years later, the question of Spanish succession was settled. **Philip V**, the grandson, was able to rule Spain, but Spain couldn't combine with France, and France had to give up much of its territory to England, a country that then became even more powerful.

The bottom line is that Colbert and Louis XIV's many territorial invasions and wars proved costly and ineffective. France remained powerful, but by the eighteenth century, its position as a military power was weakening. Nevertheless, by 1750, its position as a center for arts was firmly established.

4. German Areas (The Holy Roman Empire, Sort of)

The situation in German and Slavic areas of central Europe during this time period was complicated. The Holy Roman Empire wasn't really in Rome but rather in present-day Austria and parts of Germany and surrounding regions because Italy was controlled by ruling families in the Italian city-states. The Holy Roman Empire geographically dominated the region, but was also still very feudal with lots of local lords running their own shows. Therefore, the Holy Roman emperor was pretty weak. This is further complicated by the rise of the powerful Hapsburg family of Austria, which, as we already stated, kept intermarrying so that it dominated not only substantial territory within the Holy Roman Empire but also Spain and parts of Italy. It was complicated even more by the fact that northern Germany was essentially a collection of city-states, such as Brandenburg, Saxony, and Prussia. Finally, remember that northern Germany went Lutheran during the Protestant Reformation, while southern areas of the Holy Roman Empire stayed Catholic, along with Spain and France. Got it? It's nutty, so we're only going to hit the highlights, or else your head will be spinning.

Contrast Them: "Germany" with Spain, England, and France
Germany unified under a central government much later than Spain, England, and France did. You'll read about German unification in the next chapter. You won't read about a huge German empire in the New World or a strong German monarchy, because for centuries it remained caught in a complicated web of rulers of the Holy Roman Empire, the Hapsburgs of Austria, and the princes of city-states. It was also a tangle of religious movements, because it was at the heart of the Protestant Reformation.

You need to grasp the following three things from this time period:

- The Holy Roman Empire lost parts of Hungary to the Ottoman Turks in the early sixteenth century (this is discussed in the section on the Ottoman Empire).

- The Thirty Years' War (1618–1648) devastated the region and significantly weakened the role of the Holy Roman emperors, which in the nineteenth century would finally lead to the rise of hundreds of nation-states in the region.

- By the eighteenth century, the northern German city-states, especially Prussia, were gaining momentum and power.

Now for a few of the details.

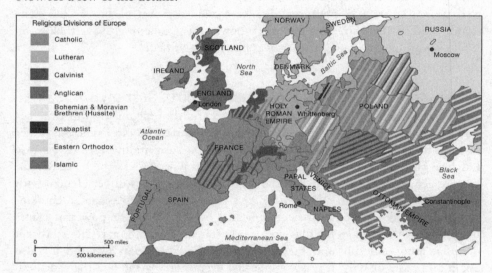

Religious Divisions Around 1550

In 1555, the **Peace of Augsburg** was intended to bring an end to the constant conflicts between Catholics and Protestants that engulfed the region during the Reformation and counter-reformation. The peace didn't last. The **Thirty Years' War** began in 1618 when the Protestant territories in Bohemia (which was under the rule of the Catholic Hapsburg clan) challenged the authority of the Holy Roman Catholic emperor, a situation that frequently arose prior to the Peace of Augsburg. This time, though, the conflict grew bigger than anything before it, and developed into a huge religious war, as well as a major political war. Everyone seemed to want a piece of the action, including other countries, like France (under Richelieu), Denmark, and Sweden. Although this grew into a war between major European powers, actual fighting stayed within the German empire, which meant that after 30 years of fighting, many parts of Germany were left depopulated and devastated. Some estimates suggest that the Holy Roman Empire lost one-third of its population during these 30 years, some 7 million people.

When the **Peace of Westphalia** was negotiated in 1648, the independence of small German states was affirmed, and Prussia became the strongest of them. The Holy Roman Empire was left barely limping along. Its territories had been reduced and its emperor, along with the Hapsburg family, was much less powerful. Somehow the Holy Roman Empire survived in name until 1806, but it hardly had any power after Westphalia.

The biggest beneficiary of the war was France. It became the most powerful country in Europe during the seventeenth century under Louis XIV, although, as you already read, by the eighteenth century it was weakened after the country overspent and overplayed its hand, particularly during the War of Spanish Succession. The other war beneficiary was Prussia, the German city-state centered in Berlin, which also controlled parts of Poland. Prussia eventually rose to dominate the German territories, unifying them into the powerful country of Germany, but you'll read about that in the next chapter.

B. Russia Out of Isolation

When the Turks conquered Constantinople and the Byzantine Empire fell, the center of Orthodox Christianity moved northward to Moscow, which was called the "Third Rome" (after Rome itself and then Constantinople). At around the same time, Russian leaders were overthrowing the Mongols. In 1480, **Ivan III** of Moscow refused to pay tribute to the Mongols and declared Russia free of Mongol rule. He, and later his grandson **Ivan IV**, established absolute rule in Russia, uniting it and expanding it ever eastward. They recruited peasants and offered them freedom from their feudal lords if they agreed to settle in new lands to the east. The catch was that these peasants had to conquer the land themselves! Known as **Cossacks**, these peasant-soldiers expanded Russian territories in the sixteenth through the eighteenth centuries well into Siberia and southward to the Caspian Sea.

Ivan IV was such a strong leader and held such absolute power that he became known as **Ivan the Terrible** (not necessarily meaning bad, but instead formidable or impressive). Taking on the title of czar (Russian for "Caesar"), Ivan the Terrible expanded Russia's holding, but not without cost to the Russian people. By the 1560s, he ruled under a reign of terror, regularly executing anyone whom he perceived as a threat to his power, including his own son (executed in 1580).

Contrast Them: Russia and Western Europe

Despite the centralization of authority under the Ivans, Russia remained very much a feudal arrangement, with local lords exercising considerable power. While western Europe basked in the glow of the Renaissance, explored and expanded its influence across oceans, and debated about religion, science, and government in a series of movements, Russia remained isolated from the west and pushed eastward instead. Its growth was territorial, but not intellectual or artistic. During the fifteenth, sixteenth, and most of the seventeenth centuries, it had nothing that could be labeled a Renaissance or Enlightenment. It wasn't part of the Renaissance because it was under the control of the Mongols at the time. It wasn't part of the Reformation because it wasn't part of the Catholic Church in the first place. So even though today we often see Russia as a European power, its history progressed along a very different path. It wasn't until the late seventeenth century that Russia turned its eyes westward.

After the death of Ivan IV in 1584, and with no strong heir to take the throne, Russia's feudal lords continually battled over who should rule the empire. The situation grew especially messy from 1604 to 1613, a period that historians refer to as the **Time of Troubles**, because one pretender to the throne would be killed by another pretender and yet another. In 1613, the madness subsided when **Michael Romanov** was elected czar by the feudal lords. The Romanov Dynasty added stability to the empire. It ruled until 1917.

Like the Ivans, the Romanovs consolidated power and often ruled ruthlessly. The peasants, now serfs, were practically slaves. By the late 1600s, the Romanovs had expanded the empire, with the help of the Cossacks, eastward through Siberia. By 1689, Russian territory spread from the Ukraine (west of Moscow) to the Pacific Ocean, north of Manchuria.

Compare Them: Forced Labor Systems

Although slavery was not a new system, the demands of the newly global economy resulted in an expansion of systems of forced labor in the empires. At the same time, Russia's attempts to control their large land mass relied on the forced labor of the peasants or serfs. All three systems took advantage of the laborers and were frequently managed by harsh and brutal overseers. In the Spanish part of the New World, *haciendas* were established in which Natives owed labor to their landlords—not unlike the feudalism of Europe. This system fell apart as the Native populations diminished due to disease, and as Natives converted to the Roman Catholic faith. The Portuguese took advantage of the already thriving intra-African slave trade and transformed it into a trans-oceanic one. The majority of transported Africans wound up on plantations in Brazil and the Caribbean where life expectancy was just three to five years. Russian serfdom differed in that the Russian economy was domestic and both the laborers and the landowners were Russian.

At around this same time, **Peter the Great**, who ruled from 1682 through 1725, came to power. He was convinced he needed to westernize Russia. He built Russia's first navy and founded St. Petersburg on the Baltic Sea as his new capital. The "window to the west," St. Petersburg became the home to hundreds of western European engineers, scientists, architects, and artists who were recruited specifically to westernize Russia. Women of the nobility were forced to dress in western fashions. Men were forced to shave their beards. Most of the hard labor of building the great new city was accomplished, of course, by serfs turned slaves.

Under **Catherine the Great**, who ruled from 1762 until 1796, more enlightened policies of education and western culture were implemented. Still, Russia suffered because Catherine fiercely enforced repressive serfdom and limited the growth of the merchant class. Catherine continued the aggressive westward territorial expansion, gaining ground in Poland and, most significantly, territory on the Black Sea. This advance ensured Russia's access to the Mediterranean to its south and west.

C. Islamic Gunpowder Empires: Ottoman, Safavid, and Mughal

The history of the **Ottoman Empire** actually extends before 1450. You might recall from the previous chapter that the territories of the former Islamic Empire were overrun by the ubiquitous Mongols in the thirteenth century. Recall also that the Byzantine Empire, centered in Constantinople, controlled most of Turkey and influenced southeastern Europe and Russia. As the Mongol Empire fell, the Muslim Ottoman Empire, founded by **Osman Bey**, rose in Anatolia (eastern parts of Turkey) to unify the region and challenge the Byzantine Empire. As it grew in the fourteenth century, the Turks (as the Ottomans were called) came to dominate most of modern-day Turkey and eventually, in 1453, invaded Constantinople, thereby ending the Byzantine Empire. Perhaps 1450 isn't such an artificial boundary after all.

> ### Focus On: Westernization of Russia
> Both Peter and Catherine are important because they positioned Russia for engagement with the rest of the world, particularly the Western world. By the late eighteenth century, Russia was in a significantly different position than it had been at the beginning of that century. It gained access to the west by both the Baltic and the Black Seas, and it gained cultural access to the West by actively seeking interaction. Unlike China and Japan, who repelled the West from their shores in the same time period, the Russians wanted to engage with and emulate the West.

The Ottomans made Constantinople their capital city, renamed it Istanbul, and converted the great cathedrals such as the Hagia Sophia into mosques. In the expanding empire, Christians and Jews were allowed to practice their religions, making the empire more tolerant than both the previous Islamic Empire and the other major regimes of the era. Within a hundred years, the Ottomans conquered the expanse of the old Byzantine Empire, save Italy, by the ancient Roman Empire, except for Italy westward. In other words, the Ottoman Empire extended from Greece eastward to Persia, and then all the way around the Mediterranean into Egypt and northern Africa.

As the empire grew, so too did religious persecution. To conquer large territories, the Ottomans enslaved children of their Christian subjects and turned them into fighting warriors, known as Janissaries. Much of this expansion occurred during the reign of **Selim I**, who came to power in 1512. Significantly, Selim claimed that he was the rightful heir to Islamic tradition under the Arab caliphs. With that claim, and with such a huge empire, Istanbul became the center of Islamic civilization.

Just eight years later, **Suleiman I** (a.k.a. Suleiman the Magnificent) rose to power. He not only built up the Ottoman military, but also actively encouraged the development of the arts. For this reason, the Ottoman Empire experienced a golden age under his reign, which lasted from 1520 until 1566. During this time, the Ottomans tried to push into Europe through Hungary. You already read that the Holy Roman Empire was weakening during the Protestant Reformation. The Ottomans took advantage of this weakness; after taking parts of Hungary, the Turks tried to move into Austria. In 1529, the empire laid siege to Vienna, a significant European cultural center. Had the Turks successfully taken Vienna, who knows what the history of western Europe would have been. From Vienna, the Turks could have easily poured into the unstable lands of the Holy Roman Empire. But it wasn't meant to be. Vienna was as far as the Turks ever got. Although Austrian princes and the Ottomans battled continually for the next century, the Ottomans were never able to expand much beyond the European territories of Byzantine influence.

Still, the Ottoman Empire lasted until 1922, making it one of the world's most significant empires. In that time, it greatly expanded the reach of Islam, while also keeping eastern Europe in a constant state of flux. This allowed the powers of western Europe to dominate, and once they started exploring the oceans, they were able to circumvent their eastern neighbors and trade directly with India, China, and their American colonies.

It is worth mentioning the chief rivals of the Ottoman were their eastern neighbors, the Safavids. This centralized state was based on military conquest and dominated by Shia Islam. Its location between the Ottomans and the Mughals, in what is modern-day Iran, resulted in often contentious relationships between the Muslim states, alliances with European against the Ottomans, and a continuation of the long-standing rift between the Sunni and Shia sects.

Remember the Mongols? After several false starts, in 1526, **Babur**, a leader who claimed to be descended from Genghis Khan but was very much Muslim, invaded northern India and swiftly defeated the Delhi Sultanate (also Muslim). Babur quickly established a new empire, known as the **Mughal Empire**, which dominated the Indian subcontinent for the next 300 years.

The Mughal Empire was distinctive for several reasons. First, within about 150 years, it had united almost the entire subcontinent, something that hadn't previously been done to the same extent. Recall that northern India experienced a series of invasions and empires, many of which you reviewed in previous chapters. The same was not true of southern India. The Deccan Plateau in southern India had remained mostly isolated. It was there that Hinduism became very firmly established.

Babur's grandson, **Akbar**, who ruled from 1556 to 1605, was able to unify much of India by governing under a policy of religious toleration. He allowed Hinduism and Islam to be practiced openly. He eliminated the jizya, the head tax on Hindus that had been a source of great anger to the people, and tried to improve the position of women by attempting to eliminate sati, the practice in which high-caste Hindu women would throw themselves onto their husbands' funeral pyres. He even married a Hindu woman, and welcomed Hindus into government positions. For nearly

100 years, Hindus and Muslims increasingly lived side-by-side and, consequently, became more geographically mixed. The result was a golden age of art, architecture, and thought. Under **Shah Jahan**, Akbar's grandson, the **Taj Mahal** was built. However, after Akbar, two developments forever changed India.

The first was that religious toleration ended. When a new emperor, Aurangzeb, who was a very pious Muslim, came to the throne, he enacted pro-Muslim policies and waged wars of expansion to try to conquer the remaining portions of India still not under Mughal control. The Muslim government reinstated the jizya; Hindu temples were destroyed. The consequences of this development were significant for later centuries, but for the moment, understand that by 1700, Muslims began to persecute Hindus and Hindus were organizing against their Muslim rulers and neighbors.

The second development was the arrival of the Europeans. In the early seventeenth century, the Portuguese and British were fighting each other for Indian Ocean trade routes. In the beginning, Portugal had established trade with the city of Goa, where it also sent Christian missionaries. By 1661, the British East India Company had substantial control of trade in Bombay. By 1691, the British dominated trade in the region and founded the city of Calcutta as a trading outpost. While the Mughal emperors were annoyed with the Europeans, they generally permitted the trade and regarded the Europeans as relatively harmless. Of course, the Industrial Revolution would turn Britain into an imperial superpower. But before 1750—the calm before the storm—India didn't feel particularly vulnerable to the Europeans, except in its port cities. It was a huge country with tons of resources united under strong Muslim rulers. It couldn't be conquered, right? At the time, Indians probably couldn't imagine that a century later, a British woman named Victoria would be crowned Empress of India.

D. Africa

Beginning in the tenth century, strong centralized states developed in southern and western Africa based on the wealth accumulated from trade. The trend of increased power continued with the trans-Atlantic slave trade and the establishment of powerful kingdoms by the **Songhai**, and in the kingdoms of **Kongo and Angola**, among others. While you are not expected to know each of these kingdoms in detail, you should recognize the pattern of state-building and the relationship of Africa to both the Islamic world and the Europeans.

The sub-Saharan empire of Songhai was mentioned briefly in the previous chapter. Like its predecessors, Ghana and Mali, this was an Islamic state with economic ties to the Muslim world through the trans-Saharan trade of salt and gold. Like other empires, this was built on conquests and military force. Sunni Ali (ruled 1464–1493) consolidated his empire in the valley of the Niger River using an imperial navy, established a central administration, and financed the city of Timbuktu as a major Islamic center. And like all great empires, Songhai fell, in this case to Moroccans with muskets, a superior military force.

On the west coast of Africa, the centralized kingdom of **Kongo** was bolstered by its trade with Portuguese merchants as early as the 1480s. The Europeans established close economic and political relationships with the king, which initially worked to everyone's advantage. The kings of the Kongo converted to Roman Catholicism, and **King Alfonso I** was particularly successful at converting his people. Over the long term, Portuguese tactics and the desire for slaves from the interior undermined the authority of the kings of Kongo and the state gradually declined. Eventually, there were outright hostilities and war between the two former allies and the kingdom was mostly destroyed.

South of Kongo, the Portuguese established a small trading post in Ndongo, or **Angola**, as early as 1575 for the sole purpose of expanding their trade in slaves from the interior. As a result, Angola grew into a powerful state and when the Portuguese attempted to further exert their authority and control, **Queen Nzinga** fiercely resisted. For 40 years, the warrior queen led her troops in battle, studied European military tactics, and made alliances with Portugal's Dutch rivals. Despite her efforts, in the end, she could not unify her rivals nor overcome the superior weaponry of the Portuguese.

E. Isolated Asia

1. China

By 1368, the Ming Dynasty booted out the last of the Mongol rulers in China and restored power over the empire to the native Chinese. The Ming Dynasty ruled until 1644. During this time, the Ming built a strong centralized government based on traditional Confucian principles, reinstated the civil service examination, and removed the Mongol influence by reinvigorating Chinese culture.

In the early fifteenth century, the Chinese also did something quite extraordinary: They built huge fleets. **Zheng He**, a Chinese navigator, led fleets throughout southeast Asia and the Indian Ocean, all the way to East Africa, a century before the Europeans did the same. Had the Chinese continued to explore and trade, they may have become the dominant colonial power. But instead, within a few decades, the Chinese abruptly stopped their naval voyages. Increasingly, Chinese society turned inward.

The Ming government attempted to prop up their failing economy by changing easily counterfeited paper money to a "single-whip" system based on silver currency. Initially, Japan supplied the silver (much to the benefit of the shoguns in Japan), but with the discovery of American silver sources, China established trade relations with the Spanish through the Philippines. Although this exchange fueled a period of commercial expansion, inevitably, the silver flooded the Chinese market and the government was unable to control the resulting inflation.

By the sixteenth century, the Ming dynasty was already in its decline, just as the Europeans were beginning to sail toward China. Pirates increasingly raided port cities, and the Portuguese set up shop in Macao. Still, the Chinese were able to keep the Europeans at a safe distance. However, internal problems persisted. By the seventeenth century, famines crippled the Chinese economy, and peasant revolts erupted against the increasingly powerless Ming rulers. In 1644, the Ming emperor invited a group of **Qing** warriors from nearby Manchuria to help him quell a peasant uprising, but instead, the Qing ousted the emperor. With that act, the Ming Dynasty ended and the Qing (or Manchu) Dynasty began. The **Manchus** ruled China until 1911.

Focus On: Environmental Change and Collapse

The new food crops that arrived in Europe, Africa, and Asia from the Americas (cassava, corn, peanuts, and potatoes) were high in calories, easy to grow in previously uncultivated areas, and, as a result, allowed for massive population increases. There crops along with new agricultural technologies, and political stability were initially a boon to China's economy and productivity. However, the new population levels could not be sustained over the long term, and a period of global cooling in the late seventeenth century put pressure on agricultural lands and hastened the collapse of the Ming Dynasty. In Europe, the arrival of potatoes finally stabilized a food supply and a population that had been devastated by centuries of cold weather, poor farming, and epidemic disease.

Because the Qing were from Manchuria, they were not ethnically Chinese. They attempted to remain an ethnic elite, forbidding the Chinese to learn the Manchu language or to marry Manchus. Yet, because the Manchus comprised a mere 3 percent of the population, they needed the help of ethnic Chinese to run the country. Therefore, the civil service examination gained new heights. Even members of the lower classes were able to rise to positions of responsibility as the Manchus opened up the floodgates to find the best talent.

Manchu emperors were well steeped in Chinese traditions. Both **Kangxi**, who ruled from 1661 to 1722, and his chief successor, **Qianlong**, who ruled from 1735 to 1796, were Confucian scholars. Both emperors not only supported the arts, but also expanded the empire. Kangxi conquered Taiwan and extended the empire into Mongolia, central Asia, and Tibet. Qianlong added Vietnam, Burma, and Nepal to the vassal states of China.

In all of this expansion, the Chinese did not aspire to conquer the rest of the world, or even interact with it very much. They stayed focused on China and its surrounding neighbors. The Manchus did trade with the Europeans, and granted rights to the Portuguese, Dutch, and British, but they were vigilant about and successful at controlling trade relations through the mid-eighteenth century. The Manchu were fierce protectors of their culture. When they felt threatened by European advances, they expelled them. In 1724, for example, Christianity was banned. In 1757, trade was restricted to just one city, Canton. Still, trade with Europeans was substantial. The Europeans bought large quantities of tea, silk, and porcelain. In exchange, the merchants received huge sums of silver, which created a new rising class of merchants in Chinese coastal cities.

2. Japan

During the sixteenth century in Japan, a series of shoguns continued to rule while the emperor remained merely as a figurehead. But as the century went on, Japanese feudalism began to wane and centralized power began to emerge. The shogun still ruled (as opposed to the emperor), but the power of the feudal lords was reduced. This coincided with Japanese exposure to the West. In 1542, the Portuguese established trade with the empire (they also introduced guns to the Japanese). Within a decade, Christian missionaries streamed in. By the end of the century, not only had a few hundred thousand Japanese converted to Christianity, but the Jesuits took control of the port city of Nagasaki and trade flourished. Japan was well on its way to westernization.

In 1600, the trend changed dramatically. In that year, **Tokugawa Ieyasu** established the Tokugawa Shogunate, a strict and rigid government that ruled Japan until 1868. The shogun further consolidated power away from the emperor and at the expense of the daimyo (feudal lords). Ieyasu claimed personal ownership to all lands within Japan and instituted a rigid social class model, inspired somewhat by Confucianism but in practice more like the caste system. Four classes (warrior, farmer, artisan, and merchant) were established and movement among the classes was forbidden.

The Tokugawa period—also known as the **Edo period** because Tokugawa moved the capital to Edo (modern-day Tokyo)—was marked by a reversal in attitudes toward Western influences. Within two decades, Christians were persecuted. By 1635, a **National Seclusion Policy** prohibited Japanese from traveling abroad, and prohibited most foreigners from visiting Japan (limited relations were kept with China, Korea, and the Netherlands). In other words, Japan became increasingly secluded. The policy remained in place for nearly 200 years.

Tokugawa was very serious about this policy. He was worried that Japan would be overrun by foreign influences. Keep in mind that Spain had claimed the nearby Philippines and that the English and Portuguese kept trying to make their way into China. So, in 1640, when a group of Portuguese diplomats and traders sailed to Japan to try to negotiate with the emperor and convince him to open up a dialogue, the shogun had every member of the Portuguese delegation executed on the spot. The message was clear. Japan was off limits.

The absence of foreign influences allowed Japanese culture to thrive. During this time period, Buddhism and Shinto remained at the center of culture, and unique Japanese art forms also prospered. **Kabuki** theatre and a new form of poetry, **haiku**, became very popular. Artists gave their lives to the creation of richly detailed scrolls, wood-block prints and paintings. In other words, under a strong central authority, Japanese culture underwent its own renaissance. Unlike the European Renaissance, however, it was strictly intended for domestic consumption.

Contrast Them: India, China, and Japan on European Aggression
No doubt about it, the Japanese under the Tokugawa Shogunate reacted most decisively against European colonialism. China and India both allowed trade and European occupation of port cities, although China increasingly limited it under the Manchus. India was the least suspecting of the Europeans, and it paid dearly. In the next chapter you'll see the consequences of these three attitudes toward the Europeans: India was overrun, China was partially overrun, and Japan, after briefly falling prey to outside influence, turned the tables and became a colonizing empire itself.

V. TECHNOLOGY AND INNOVATIONS 1450–1750

Europe became a powerful force during this time period because of their willingness to adapt and use three key innovations that existed in other parts of the world: gunpowder weapons, navigation and ship-building technology, and finally the printing press (which developed independently in Germany). But at a time when competition among the Europeans resulted in big risks and innovations, the Chinese and Japanese returned to more traditional lifestyles in order to maintain stability, and the Muslims, while retaining powerful land-based empires, allowed innovations in shipping and weaponry to pass them by.

The biggest impact of these new technologies was the expanded knowledge of the world that resulted from exploration by the European nations. Using their superior weapons and larger trading ships, the Europeans established new overseas trading empires, moved lots of plants and animals, enslaved and transported people across oceans, and generally transformed the interactions of the entire world. They fought wars with one another in Europe and—when they were unable to establish suitable trading relationships—went to war in the places they wished to conquer.

Increased contact meant the spread of new ideas and technology (such as the printing press), and the exposure to new cultures transformed both education and religion. The establishment of new Protestant churches in northern Europe increased the power of the kings and nation-states at the expense of the Catholic Church. Conversely, religious conflicts led to increased migrations from northern Europe and the resettlement of large numbers of colonists in the New World.

VI. CHANGES AND CONTINUITIES IN THE ROLE OF WOMEN

A number of powerful women took charge of the most powerful empires of this time. These included Elizabeth I of England, Isabella of Spain, and Nur Jahan of Mughal, India. With the exception of Elizabeth, who chose never to marry, most of these women shared power with their husbands. And in spite of the great power and visibility of these few elite women, for the most part, the status and freedoms of women changed little from the previous period—legally they were often considered property of their husbands, inherited less than sons or brothers, and had few rights in legal or political spheres.

The biggest change in the lives of women came from the mixing of previously unknown cultures. The result of global exploration and colonization, these new relationships produced offspring considered mixed or mestizo. Racial categories began to be more widely used in determining status or class hierarchy, and restrictions developed regarding marriages and legal relationships between classes. Changes in trade and production also placed a greater premium on male labor and jobs that women had traditionally held, like textile weaving, were increasing dominated by men.

Some regions of the world served as exceptions to these general patterns, but were still impacted by the global interactions. The forced migration of males in African societies resulted in a disproportionate number of females left behind in what were already matrilineal societies. These numbers reinforced polygyny or multiple marriages. Although large numbers of men also migrated from Europe, the predominately Christian societies did not allow multiple marriages, and as the number of unmarried women increased, this created a problem in societies that regarded marriage as the goal of all women.

The non-European areas of the world tended to regard older or widowed women with both respect and superstition. In both Africa and many Native American societies, councils of older women were part of the political decision making process. However, older women were also to be feared as they couldn't necessarily be controlled. It was this need for control that led to a continuation of Neo-Confucianism values in eastern Asia. This social philosophy designated proper roles and virtues for women within the home with the understanding that if the home were stable so was the state.

In Europe, the revolutionary new ideas of the Renaissance and the Enlightenment included women, at least nominally. Education was more widely available to all classes, but opportunities for girls lagged far behind those of boys, and the highest levels of education were only open to males. Even the less-hierarchical new Protestant religions limited the roles of women to wife and mother and did not have convents or monastic systems as alternatives to traditional roles. Eventually, the Protestant countries grew even more puritanical in their regulation of sex, marriage, and illegitimacy.

VII. PULLING IT ALL TOGETHER

In the context of the Age of Exploration, "exploration" has lots of connotations. Of course, the most obvious is that it involved European exploration of the Americas, and the beginnings of direct contact with Asia. But more than that, its exploration was also internal. In the Renaissance, Europe explored its own lost history. During the Protestant Reformation it explored its relationship with God. During the Scientific Revolution Europe explored the universe and the laws by which the universe functioned. During the Enlightenment it explored the rights of man and the appropriate role of government, even as its empire depended on slavery. And during the Commercial Revolution, Europe explored its potential.

Combined, these explorations were going in all directions—outward, upward, inward, backward to the past, forward to the future—and it was all going on simultaneously. If you're confused by the developments, you should be. It's hard to figure out which movements in which combination impacted which events. Historians haven't sorted it out either. It's open to debate.

What we can say is this: During the time period discussed in the chapter, Europe was where the energy was. There was so much change, for so many reasons, that the boundaries of the continent literally couldn't contain it. Unlike China and Japan, which largely looked inward, and unlike the Islamic world, which didn't take to the seas or radically shake up religious and social orders, Europeans were dynamic at this particular time in history. They were analyzing everything and they were full of inconsistencies. Other civilizations at other times in history had at least as much energy and unrest, but because the Europeans had the technology, the political motivation, and the financial structure, they were able to quickly explode onto the world scene. Add in the evangelical nature of Christianity (an explicit desire to convert the world) and it's clear that the desire for expansion ran deep.

Some would say that European monarchs ruled absolutely during this time period and adopted a controlling, ethnocentric attitude with regard to the cultures they dominated. Perhaps this was precisely because Europe was in such cultural chaos itself. Who knows? We'll leave that to your further studies. In any case, it's hard to deny that even as Europeans explored their own history, culture, and structures to unprecedented degrees, they had little trouble marginalizing the complexities of others.

What About the Non-European Cultures?
Why Was Their Interaction with the West So Varied?

There are lots of ways to answer these questions, but we'll get you started. China and Japan were both highly organized, confident civilizations. The contingencies of Europeans on their shores were modest. Because the Japanese and Chinese wanted desperately to preserve their own cultures, and because they had the power and sophistication to keep the Europeans, for the moment, at bay, that's precisely what they did. Why didn't the others?

In Africa, the societies were fragmented. No centralized power existed, so the Europeans were harder to fend off. What's more, the Europeans weren't initially obsessed with penetrating the entire continent. Because they didn't have to overtake entire civilizations to achieve their goals, they were able to trade goods and abduct individuals one by one, with little concern for long-term impact on the continent.

In the Americas, of course, civilizations were quickly overwhelmed by European technology and disease. And in the Ottoman Empire and Arabia, the interaction was somewhat limited because the Europeans weren't as dependent on the overland routes in their efforts to trade with India and China. This diminished the importance of the Middle East to the Europeans. What's more, because the Crusades ended unsuccessfully for the Europeans, trade with the Muslims was important but conquest of the region was off the radar.

Finally, What About the Global Economy?
How Did It Change?

In short, sailing, mercantilism, and private investment changed the global economy. In a few more words: Improvements in sailing diminished the need for the Asian land routes and connected the world like never before. Mercantilism and its dependence on the establishment of imperialism married economic and political developments. And the establishment of joint stock companies took major economic motivation out of the hands of governments and put it into the hands of the private sector. This meant that now thousands, tens of thousands, or even hundreds of thousands of people had a direct stake in trade routes and conquest. Because the benefits of economic prosperity were diffused among a larger group of individuals than ever before, governments began to lose their grip on controlling their own economies.

Important Terms

Absolute Monarch
Agrarian
Atheists
Capitalism
Cash Crop
Circumnavigate
Colonization
Commerce
Commercial
Commonwealth
Consequences
Continuity
Convent
Currency
Deists
Demography
Divine
Divine Right
Dominant
Economy
Hedonism
Hinder
Humanism
Institution
Jurisdiction
Left-Wing
Mercantilism
Monarchy
Monastic
Monk
Monopoly
Monotheism
Morality
Nun
Papacy/Papal
Parliament
Patriarch
Pope
Revolution
Right-Wing
Salvation
Sanctioned
Satire
Subsistence
Urbanization
Utopia/Utopian
Vassals
Venerate
Vernacular

People, Places, and Events

Age of Reason
Akbar the Great (Mughal India)
Batavia, Indonesia
Calvin, John
Columbian Exchange
Counter-Reformation
Dutch East India Company
Eastern Orthodox
Edict of Nantes
Edict of Fountainbleu
Elizabeth I of England
Encomienda System
English Bill of Rights
English Commonwealth
European Exploration
Floating Empires
Goa, India
Gutenberg's Printing Press
Hacienda System
Hapsburg Spain
Henry Tudor (Henry VIII)
Heliocentric Theory
Holy Roman Empire
Huguenots
Indulgences
Inquisition
Jannissary Corps
Jesuit Order
Law of Heavenly Bodies
Luther, Martin
Louis XIV (France)
Manchu (Qing Dynasty) China
Peter the Great (Russia)
Philip II of Spain
Potosi Silver Mine
Protestant Reformation
Renaissance
Roman Catholic Church
Scientific Methods
Scientific Revolution
Shogun
Silver or Single Whip System
Straits of Malacca, Indonesia
Suleiman the Magnificent (Ottoman)
Thirty Years War (1618–1648)
Tokugawa Bakufu System
Treaty of Westphalia (1648)
The Vatican
Zheng He (Ming, China)

VIII. TIMELINE OF MAJOR DEVELOPMENTS 1450–1750

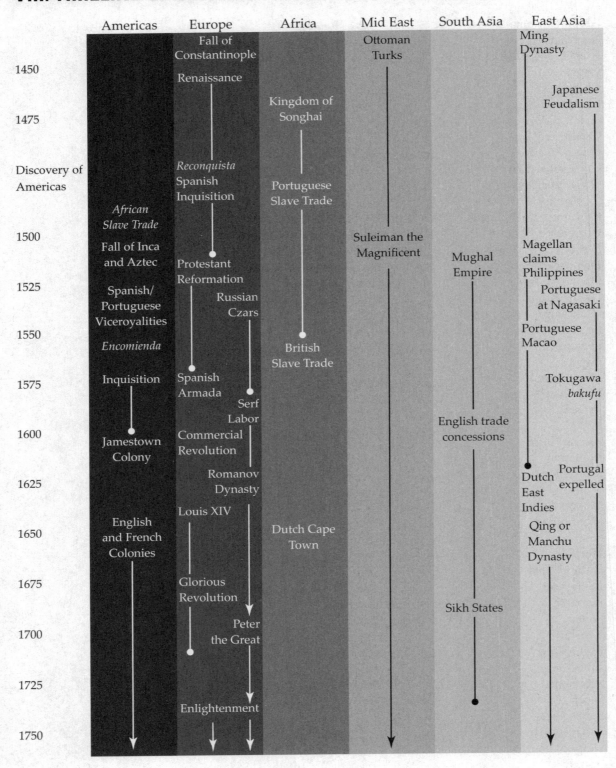

	Americas	Europe	Africa	Mid East	South Asia	East Asia
1450		Fall of Constantinople		Ottoman Turks		Ming Dynasty
		Renaissance				
1475			Kingdom of Songhai			Japanese Feudalism
Discovery of Americas		*Reconquista* Spanish Inquisition	Portuguese Slave Trade			
	African Slave Trade					
1500	Fall of Inca and Aztec			Suleiman the Magnificent		Magellan claims Philippines
1525	Spanish/ Portuguese Viceroyalities	Protestant Reformation			Mughal Empire	Portuguese at Nagasaki
		Russian Czars				
1550	*Encomienda*		British Slave Trade			Portuguese Macao
1575	Inquisition	Spanish Armada				Tokugawa *bakufu*
		Serf Labor				
1600	Jamestown Colony	Commercial Revolution			English trade concessions	
1625		Romanov Dynasty			Dutch East Indies	Portugal expelled
1650	English and French Colonies	Louis XIV	Dutch Cape Town			Qing or Manchu Dynasty
1675		Glorious Revolution			Sikh States	
1700		Peter the Great				
1725						
		Enlightenment				
1750						

REFLECT ACTIVITY

Respond to the following questions:

- For which content topics discussed in this Chapter do you feel you have achieved sufficient mastery to answer multiple choice questions correctly?

- For which content topics discussed in this Chapter do you feel you have achieved sufficient mastery to discuss effectively in an essay?

- For which content topics discussed in this Chapter do you feel you need more work before you can answer multiple choice questions correctly?

- For which content topics discussed in this Chapter do you feel you need more work before you can discuss effectively in an essay?

- What parts of this Chapter are you going to re-review?

- Will you seek further help outside of this book (such as a teacher, tutor, or AP Central), on any of the content in this Chapter—and, if so, on what content?

Chapter 9
Not So Old
Stuff: Sometime
Around 1750
to About 1914

I. CHAPTER OVERVIEW

Less than two centuries is covered in this chapter, but during that time, the world changed dramatically. Europe's influence in the West waned even as it waxed in the East. Napoleon tried to conquer Europe. Italy and Germany unified into modern nation-states. Japan became an imperial power. India was entirely overrun by the British. The United States rose to become a world power. And the Industrial Revolution—the single biggest event of the time period—seemed to impact everything it touched, from political and economic developments, to the drive for colonial holdings in Africa and Asia, to daily life.

Here's the chapter outline.

I.   Chapter Overview

        You're in it.

II.   Stay Focused on the Big Picture

        Organize the major social, political, and economic changes that occurred during this time period into some big-picture concepts.

III.   Enlightenment Revolutions in the Americas and Europe

    A. Two Revolutions: American and French
    B. Lots of Independence Movements: Latin America

IV.   Industry and Imperialism

This section focuses on the Industrial Revolution and its consequences, especially as it impacted social and economic developments in Europe and European imperialism in Africa and Asia. Here's how we've organized this section.

    A. The Industrial Revolution
    B. European Imperialism in India
    C. European Imperialism in China
    D. Japanese Imperialism
    E. European Imperialism in Africa

V.   Nationalist Movements and Other Developments

While Africa and Asia were increasingly dominated by Europe in the eighteenth and nineteenth centuries, the Europeans lost most of their holdings in the Americas due to successful revolutionary movements. In the meantime, Europe underwent continuous political restructuring, and strong centralized nation-states were formed. Here's how we've organized this section.

    A. Two Unifications: Italy and Germany
    B. Other Political Developments

II. STAY FOCUSED ON THE BIG PICTURE

As you review the details of the developments in this chapter, stay focused on some big-picture concepts and ask yourself some questions, including the following:

1. How are the events of this time period interconnected? The Industrial Revolution and imperialism are not only interconnected, but are connected to other developments in this time period as well. Stay focused on how developments in one region of the world had an impact on developments in another. Also, stay focused on how regional developments were able to have a global impact through improvements in communication and transportation, as well as through colonialism.

2. Why did nationalism grow during this time period? How did the impact of nationalism vary among different countries? Whether in the Americas, Europe, or Asia, nationalism was a huge force. It sparked rebellions, independence movements, and unification movements. It also sparked domination and colonialism.

3. How and why does change occur? Stay focused on the complexity of social, political, and economic developments, as opposed to presuming that the dominant economic or political philosophies were shared universally among people in a certain country or region. Think about change as an evolving process in which certain ideas gain momentum, while other ideas lose steam but don't entirely die out.

4. How did the environment impact industrial and economic development? In Europe, the earliest phases of the Industrial Revolution were fueled by the resources available in England, so the resulting imperialism on a global scale was driven by the need for additional resources. Keep in mind the political and economic decisions that resulted in

environmental change. At the same time, the environment impacted people. The general global cooling that began around 1500 C.E. put pressure on the populations of Europe and contributed to great poverty and peasant revolts, especially in the northern countries.

SECTION III

A. Two Revolutions: American and French

1. The American Revolution

For the most part, you won't need to know much about American history for the AP World History Exam. However, you will need to know about events in the United States that impacted developments in the rest of the world. The American Revolution is one of those events.

As you know, Britain began colonizing the east coast of North America during the seventeenth century. By the mid-eighteenth century, British colonists in America felt threatened by France's colonial settlements on the continent. France and Britain were long-time rivals (archenemies in the Hundred Years' War and since) and they carried this rivalry with them into fights in America. The French enlisted the Algonquin and Iroquois tribes to fight alongside them against the encroaching English colonists, but in 1763, England prevailed over the French in a war that was known in the colonies as the **French and Indian War**, but known in Europe as the **Seven Years' War.** The British victory changed the boundaries of the two empires' worldwide possessions, pushing French territory to the north while English territories expanded westward into the Ohio River valley.

While the colonists were thrilled with the results of the war, the British were upset about the costs, and felt that the American colonists did not adequately share in the burden. Of course, the colonists resented this, claiming that it was their efforts that made colonial expansion possible in the first place. At the same time, Britain's **George Grenville** and later **Charles Townshend** passed very unpopular laws on behalf of the British crown. These laws, including the **Revenue Act** (1764), the **Stamp Act** (1765), and the **Tea Act** (1773), were intended to raise additional funds for the British crown. In addition to generating funds, however, these laws generated unrest, not only because American colonists thought they were economically unfair but also because American colonists were not represented in England's Parliament when these laws were passed. Thus arose the revolutionary cry, "No taxation without representation."

After the colonists dumped tea in Boston Harbor to protest the Tea Act, relations between crown and colonies deteriorated rapidly. On April 19, 1775, British troops battled with rebellious colonists in Lexington and Concord, and by the end of that bloody day, nearly 400 Britons and Americans were dead. The War of Independence had begun.

Independence Can't Happen Without a Little Paine

The overwhelming majority of American colonists had either been born in England or were children of those born in England, and therefore many colonists felt ambivalent about—if not completely opposed to—the movement for independence. Even those who sought independence were worried that Britain was too powerful to defeat. But a student of the Enlightenment, **Thomas Paine**, urged colonists to support the movement. In his widely distributed pamphlet, *Common Sense*, he assailed the monarchy as an encroachment on Americans' natural rights and appealed to the colonists to form a better government. A mere six months later, Americans signed the **Declaration of Independence**. The printing press, the powerful tool of the Protestant Reformation, quickly became a powerful tool for the American Revolution.

France: More than Happy to Oblige

By 1776, as the war moved to the middle colonies and finally to the South, the Americans endured defeat after defeat. But in 1777, the French committed ships, soldiers, weapons, and money to the cause. France and England, of course, had been bickering for centuries, and so the French leapt at the opportunity to punish England. In 1781, French and American troops and ships cornered the core of the British army, which was under the command of General George Cornwallis. Finding himself outnumbered, he surrendered, and the war was over. Within a decade, the Constitution and Bill of Rights were written, ratified, and put into effect. A fledgling democracy was on display.

2. The French Revolution

After the reign of Louis XIV, the Bourbon kings continued to reside in the lavish Versailles palace, a lifestyle that was quite expensive. More costly, however, were France's war debts. The War of Spanish Succession, the Seven Years' War, the American Revolution, you name it…France seemed to be involved in every major war both in Europe and abroad. With droughts damaging the French harvests and the nobility scoffing at spending restrictions, Louis XVI needed to raise taxes, but to do that he needed to get everyone on board. So, in 1789, he called a meeting of the **Estates General**, a "governing body" that hadn't met in some 175 years. Bourbon monarchs, you'll recall, ruled under divine right, so no other input was generally seen as necessary. But the king's poor financial situation made it necessary to call on this all-but-forgotten group.

> **Focus On: Causes and Consequences of the American Revolution**
> Don't worry too much about knowing the details of the American Revolution. You certainly don't need to know battles or even the personalities. Instead, understand that the Enlightenment had a huge impact because it not only helped to inspire the revolution itself, but also the type of government that was created after it succeeded. Also remember that mercantilist policies drove the American colonists nuts, as was the case in European colonies everywhere. These same forces—the Enlightenment and frustration over economic exploitation—are common themes in the world's revolutionary cries against colonialism throughout the 1800s.

The Estates General: Generally a Mess

French society was divided into three estates (something like social classes). The First Estate comprised the clergy. Some were high ranking and wealthy; others were parish priests and quite poor. The Second Estate was made up of the noble families. Finally, the Third Estate comprised everyone else—peasant farmers and the small but influential middle class, or bourgeoisie, including merchants. The overwhelming majority (more than 95 percent) of the population were members of the Third Estate, but they had very little political power.

When Louis XVI summoned the Estates General, he was in essence summoning representatives from each of these three estates. The representative nobles of the Second Estate came to the meeting of the Estates General hoping to gain favors from the king in the form of political power and greater freedoms in the form of a new constitution. The representatives of the Third Estate (representing by far the greatest proportion of France's population), always suspicious of the nobility, wanted even greater freedoms similar to what they saw the former British colonies had in America. They went as far as suggesting to the king that the Estates General meet as a unified body—all Estates under one roof. However, the top court in Paris, the parlement, ruled in favor of the nobility and ordered that the estates meet separately.

Frustrated at the strong possibility of being shut out of the new constitution by the other two estates, the Third Estate did something drastic on June 17, 1789—they declared themselves the **National Assembly**. The king got nervous, and forced the other two estates to join them in an effort to write a new constitution. But it was too little, too late. By then, peasants throughout the land were growing restless and were concerned that the king wasn't going to follow through on the major reforms they wanted. They stormed the Bastille, a huge prison, on July 14, 1789. From there, anarchy swept through the countryside and soon peasants attacked nobility and feudal institutions.

By August, the National Assembly adopted the **Declaration of the Rights of Man**, a document recognizing natural rights and based on the ideas of the Enlightenment, the American Declaration of Independence, and particularly the writings of Jean-Jacques Rousseau. This declaration was widely copied and distributed across Europe, furthering the ideas of freedom, equality, and rule of law. The Assembly also abolished the feudal system and altered the monopoly of the Catholic Church by declaring freedom of worship. Meanwhile, the king and his family were taken to Paris, where the Third Estate revolutionaries could ensure that they wouldn't interfere with the work of the National Assembly. But perhaps most importantly, the French Revolution established the nation-state, not the king or the people (as in the United States), as the source of all sovereignty or political authority. In this sense, France became the first "modern" nation-state in 1789.

A New Constitution Causes Consternation

In 1791, the National Assembly ratified a new constitution, which was somewhat similar to the U.S. Constitution ratified just two years before, except that instead of a president, the king held on to the executive power. In other words, it was a constitutional monarchy, rather than a constitutional democracy. Those who wanted to abolish the monarchy felt cheated; those who wanted to retain the feudal structure felt betrayed.

Remember how most of the royalty in Europe intermarried? Well, it just so happened that Marie Antoinette, who was the wife of the increasingly nervous Louis XVI, was also the sister of the Emperor of Austria. The Austrians and the Prussians invaded France to restore the monarchy, but the French revolutionaries were able to hold them back. Continuing unrest led French leaders to call for a meeting to draw up a new constitution. Under the new constitution, the **Convention** became the new ruling body, and it quickly abolished the monarchy and proclaimed France a republic. Led by radicals known as the **Jacobins**, the Convention imprisoned the royal family and, in 1793, beheaded the king for treason.

Contrast Them: American and French Revolutions
The American Revolution involved a colonial uprising against an imperial power. In other words, it was an independence movement. The French Revolution involved citizens rising up against their own country's leadership and against their own political and economic system, and in that sense was more of a revolution. In other words, at the end of the American Revolution, the imperial power of England was still intact, and indeed the new United States was in many ways designed in the image of England itself. In contrast, at the end of the French Revolution, France itself was a very different place. It didn't simply lose some of its holdings. Instead, the king was beheaded and the socio-political structure changed.

That said, the word revolution aptly describes the American independence movement because the United States was the first major colony to break away from a European colonial power since the dawn of the Age of Exploration. What's more, the ideas adopted in the Declaration of Independence, the U.S. Constitution, and in the French Revolution inspired colonists, citizens, and slaves across the globe. Quite revolutionary indeed!

The Reign of Terror: The Hard-Fought Constitution Gets Tossed Aside

While Prussia and Austria regrouped and enlisted the support of Great Britain and Spain, the Convention started to worry that foreign threats and internal chaos would quickly lead to its demise, so it threw out the constitution and created the **Committee of Public Safety**, an all-powerful enforcer of the revolution and murderer of anyone suspected of anti-revolutionary tendencies. Led by **Maximilien Robespierre** and the Jacobins, the Committee of Public Safety certainly wasn't a committee of personal safety, since it was responsible for the beheading of tens of thousands of French citizens. Even though the Committee was successful at controlling the anarchy and at building a strong national military to defend France against an increasing number of invading countries, after two years the French had enough of Robespierre's witch hunt and put his head on the guillotine. France quickly reorganized itself again, wrote a new constitution in 1795, and established a new five-man government called the **Directory**.

Napoleon: Big Things Come in Small Packages

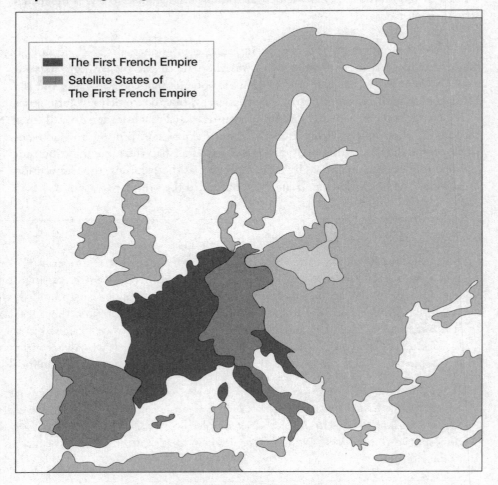

The Height of Napoleon's Empire

While the Directory was not so great at implementing a strong domestic policy, the five-man combo was good at building up the military. One of its star military leaders was a teenager named **Napoleon Bonaparte**, who was a general by age 24. After military successes on behalf of the Directory, Napoleon returned to France and used his reputation and immense popularity to overthrow the Directory in 1799. He legitimized his actions by putting them before a popular vote, and once affirmed, he declared himself the First Consul under the new constitution (if you're counting, that makes four constitutions since the Revolution began).

Domestically, Napoleon initiated many reforms in agriculture, infrastructure, and public education. He also normalized relations with the church and restored a degree of tolerance and stability. Most importantly, his **Napoleonic Codes** (1804) recognized the equality of French citizens (meaning men) and institutionalized some of the Enlightenment ideas that had served as the original inspiration for many of the revolutionaries. At the same time, the code was also extremely paternalistic, based in part on ancient Roman law. The rights of women and children were severely limited under the code. Still, the code was a huge step forward in the recognition of some basic rights and in the establishment of rules of law. The code has since been significantly modified to reflect more modern sensibilities, but it is still in effect today, and has served as the model for many other national codes, especially in Europe.

But Napoleon's biggest impact was external, not internal. In a stunning effort to spread France's glory throughout Europe and the Americas, Napoleon not only fended off foreign aggressors, but also made France an aggressor itself. Napoleon's troops conquered Austria, Prussia, Spain, Portugal, and the kingdoms within Italy. He dissolved the Holy Roman Empire, which was on its last legs anyway, and reorganized it into a confederacy of German states. In 1804, he crowned himself emperor of this huge new empire, fancying himself the new Charlemagne. By 1810, the empire was at its peak, but it didn't stay there for long. France lacked the resources to control a far-flung empire, and conflicts including an attempted blockade of powerful Britain cost it dearly. Nationalistic uprisings, such as unrest in Italy and fierce guerilla warfare in Spain and Portugal, undermined Napoleon's power.

In 1812, Napoleon's greed got the better of him. He attacked the vast lands of Russia, but was baited into going all the way to Moscow, which the Russians then set aflame, preventing Napoleon from adequately housing his troops there. As winter set in and with no place to go, the troops had to trudge back to France, and were attacked all along the way. Short on supplies, the retreat turned into a disaster. The army was decimated and the once great emperor was forced into exile.

The leaders of the countries that had overthrown Napoleon met in Vienna to decide how to restore order (and their own power) in Europe. The principal members of the coalition against Napoleon were **Prince von Metternich** of Austria, **Alexander I of Russia**, and the **Duke of Wellington** of Britain. At first, disagreements among them prevented much progress. Hearing this, Napoleon returned from exile and attempted to regain power. His enemies, of course, rallied. At **Waterloo** in 1813, the allies united against their common threat. Defeating Napoleon decisively, they sent him to permanent exile on the island of St. Helena, where he later died. The allies eventually came to an agreement, in a meeting known as the **Congress of Vienna**, over what to do with France and its inflated territories.

The Congress of Vienna: Pencils and Erasers at Work

In 1815, the Congress decreed that a **balance of power** should be maintained among the existing powers of Europe in order to avoid the rise of another Napoleon. France was dealt with fairly: Its borders were cut back to their pre-Napoleonic dimensions, but it was not punished militarily or economically. And although it rearranged some of the European boundaries and created new kingdoms in Poland and the Netherlands, the Congress also reaffirmed absolute rule, reseating the monarchs of France, Spain, Holland, and the many Italian states. While remarkably fair-minded, the Congress of Vienna ignored many of the ideals put forth by French revolutionaries and the rights established under France's short-lived republic. In other words, it essentially tried to erase the whole French Revolution and Napoleon from the European consciousness and restore the royal order.

B. Lots of Independence Movements: Latin America

The European colonies in Latin America were inspired by the success of the American Revolution and the ideas of the French Revolution. To be sure, there had been unsuccessful revolts and uprisings in the Latin American colonies for two or three centuries prior to those revolutions. In the early nineteenth century, however, the world order was different. Europe was in chaos because of the rise and fall of Napoleon, and this distracted the European powers from their American holdings, a development that gave rebellious leaders an opportunity to assert themselves more than they previously could have.

Haiti: Slave Revolt Sends France a Jolt

The first successful Latin American revolt took place in Haiti, a French island colony in the Caribbean. The French, true to their mercantilist policies, exported coffee, sugar, cocoa, and indigo from Haiti to Europe. French colonists owned large plantations and hundreds of thousands of slaves, who grew and harvested these crops under horrible conditions. By 1800, 90 percent of the population was slaves, some of whom had been freed, but the vast majority of whom worked on the plantations.

In 1801, as Napoleon was gaining momentum in Europe, **Pierre Toussaint L'Ouverture**, a former slave, led a violent, lengthy, but ultimately successful slave revolt. Enraged, Napoleon sent 20,000 troops to put down the revolt, but the Haitians were capable fighters. They also had another weapon on their side—yellow fever—that claimed many French lives. The French did succeed, however, in capturing L'Ouverture and imprisoning him in France, but by then they couldn't turn back the revolutionary tide. L'Ouverture's lieutenant **Jacques Dessalines**, also a former slave, proclaimed Haiti a free republic in 1804 and named himself governor-general for life. Thus, Haiti became the first independent nation in Latin America.

South America: Visions of Grandeur

In 1808, when Napoleon invaded Spain, he appointed his brother, Joseph Bonaparte, to the Spanish throne. This sent the Spanish authorities in the colonies into a tizzy. Who should they be loyal to? The colonists decided to remain loyal to their Spanish king and not recognize the French regime under Bonaparte. In Venezuela, they ejected Bonaparte's governor and, instead, appointed their own leader, **Simon Bolivar**. Tutored on the republican ideals of Rousseau during his travels to Europe and the United States, Bolivar found himself in the midst of a great opportunity to use what he learned. In 1811, Bolivar helped establish a national congress, which declared independence from Spain. Royalists, supporters of the Spanish crown, declared civil war. But Bolivar proved to be a wily and effective military leader, and during the next decade, he won freedom for the area called Gran Colombia (which included modern-day Colombia, Ecuador, and Venezuela). Bolivar envisioned a huge South American country spanning across the continent, similar to the growing United States in North America, but it wasn't meant to be. In the following decades, the individual nation-states of northwestern South America formed their own governments.

Meanwhile, farther south in Argentina, the conflict between the French governor and those who still wanted to support the Spanish crown created another opportunity for liberation. **Jose de San Martin** was an American-born Spaniard (or Creole) who served as an officer in the Spanish army. In 1814 he began to put his extensive military experience to use—but for the rebels—taking command of the Argentinian armies. San Martin joined up with Bernardo O'Higgins of Chile and took the revolutionary movement not only through Argentina and Chile, but also to Peru, where he joined forces with Bolivar. The Spanish forces withered away. By the 1820s, a huge chunk of South America had successfully declared its independence from Spain.

Brazil: Power to the Pedros

Brazil, of course, was a Portuguese colony, and so when Portugal was invaded by Napoleon's armies in 1807, **John VI**, the Portuguese king, fled to Brazil and set up his royal court in exile. By 1821, Napoleon had been defeated and it was safe for John VI to return to Portugal, but he left behind his son, Pedro, who was 23 years old at the time, and charged him with running the huge colony. Pedro, who had spent most of his childhood and teenage years in Brazil and considered it home, declared Brazilian independence and crowned himself emperor the next year. Within a few more years, Brazil had a constitution.

In 1831, Pedro abdicated power to his son, **Pedro II**, who ruled the country through much of the nineteenth century. While he reformed Brazilian society in many ways and turned it into a major exporter of coffee, his greatest single accomplishment was the abolition of slavery in 1888 (which actually occurred under the direction of his daughter, Isabel, who was running the country while Pedro II was away). This action so incensed the land-owning class that they revolted against the monarchy and established a republic in 1889.

Mexico: A Tale of Two Priests

As in other parts of Latin America, a revolutionary fervor rose in Mexico after the French Revolution, especially after Napoleon invaded Spain and Portugal. In 1810, **Miguel Hidalgo**, a Creole priest who sympathized with those who had been abused under Spanish colonialism, led a revolt against Spanish rule. Unlike in South America, however, the Spanish armies resisted effectively, and they put down the revolt at Calderon Bridge, where Hidalgo was executed.

Hidalgo's efforts were not in vain, however, because they put the revolution in motion. **Jose Morelos** picked up where Hidalgo left off and led the revolutionaries to further successes against the loyalists. But similar to what later happened in Brazil, the land-owning class turned against him when he made clear his intentions to redistribute land to the poor. In 1815, he was executed.

It wasn't until 1821, after the landowning class bought into the idea of separation from Spain, that independence was finally achieved. In the **Treaty of Cordoba**, Spain was forced to recognize that its 300-year-old domination of Latin America was coming to an end. Mexico was granted its independence and Central America soon followed.

The Effects of the Independence Movements: More Independence than Freedom

While Europe was effectively booted out of many parts of the American continents during a 50-year time span beginning in about 1780, in some Latin American countries the independence from colonial power wasn't accompanied by widespread freedom among the vast majority of citizens. As in the United States, slavery still existed for decades. Peasants still worked on huge plantations owned by a few landowners. But unlike in the United States, a significant middle class of merchants and small farmers didn't emerge, and many of the Enlightenment ideas didn't spread to populations other than the land-owning male class.

There were several reasons for this. The Catholic Church remained very powerful in Latin America, and while many of the priests advocated on behalf of the peasants and of the slaves (some martyred themselves for that cause), the church hierarchy as a whole protected the status quo. The church, after all, was one of the largest landowners in Latin America.

What's more, the economies of Latin America, while free of Europe, were still largely dependent on Europe. Latin American countries still participated in European mercantilism, often to their own detriment. They specialized in a few cash crops, exported almost exclusively to Europe, and then bought back finished products. In other words, most Latin American economies didn't diversify, nor did they broaden opportunities to a larger class of people, so innovation and creativity rarely took root.

There are notable exceptions. Chile diversified its economy fairly successfully, and Brazil and Argentina instituted social reform and broadened their economies to include a growing middle class. But ultimately, the hugely successful independence movements in Latin America didn't result in noticeable changes for a majority of the population for more than a century.

	American 1764–1787	French 1789–1799	Haitian 1799–1804	Latin America 1810–1820s
Causes	Unfair Taxation/War Debt Lack of Representation	Unfair Taxation/War Debt Social Inequalities Lack of Representation	French Enlightenment Social and Racial Inequalities Slave Revolt	Social Inequalities Removal of Peninsulares Napoleon's Invasion of Spain
Key Events	Boston Tea Party Continental Congress Declaration of Independence Constitution and Bill of Rights	Tennis Court Oath National Assembly Declaration of Rights of Man Storming Bastille Reign of Terror 5 Man Directory	Civil War Slave Revolt Invasion of Napoleon	Peasant revolts Creole revolts Gran Colombia
Major Players	George III Thomas Paine Thomas Jefferson George Washington	Louis XVI Three Estates Jacobin Party Robespierre	Boukman Gens de Couleur Toussaint L'Overture Napoleon Bonaparte	Miguel Hidalgo Simon Bolivar José de San Martin Emperor Pedro I
Impacts	Independence Federal Democracy Spreads-France, Haiti, Mexico	Rise of Napolean Congress of Vienna Constitutional Monarchy	Independence Destruction of Economy Anti Slavery Movements	Independence Continued inequalities Federal Democracy (Mexico) Creole Republics Constitutional Monarchy (Brazil)

IV. INDUSTRY AND IMPERIALISM

The Industrial Revolution, which began in the mid-eighteenth century in Britain and spread rapidly through the nineteenth century, is inseparable from the Age of Imperialism, which reached its peak in the late nineteenth and early twentieth centuries. Industrial technology had two enormous consequences: (1) Countries with industrial technology by definition had advanced military weapons and capacity, and were therefore easily able to conquer people who did not have this technology; (2) To succeed, factories needed access to raw materials to make finished products, and then markets to sell those finished products. Colonies fit both of these roles quite well.

Because the bulk of the western hemisphere freed itself from European control by the early nineteenth century (a lot more on this later), the industrial imperialists turned their eyes toward Africa and Asia, where exploitation was easy and markets were huge.

A. The Industrial Revolution

The Industrial Revolution began in Britain, helping to propel the country to its undisputed ranking as the most powerful in the nineteenth century. But Britain wasn't the only country that industrialized. The revolution spread through much of Europe, especially Belgium, France, and Germany, as well as to Japan and ultimately to the country that would eclipse Britain as the most industrialized—the United States. Still, since most of the developments occurred in Britain first, and since the social consequences that occurred in Britain are representative of those that occurred elsewhere, this section will focus heavily on the revolution in Britain. References to other countries will be made where warranted.

Agricultural Revolution Part II

Hopefully you remember that early civilizations came about, in part, because of an Agricultural Revolution that resulted in food surpluses. This freed some of the population from farming, and those people then went about the business of building the civilization. In the eighteenth century, agricultural output increased dramatically once again. This time, it allowed not just some people, but as much as half of the population to leave the farms and head toward the cities, where jobs in the new industrial economy were becoming available.

Keep in mind that agricultural techniques had been slowly improving throughout history. Since so many developments happened so quickly in the eighteenth century this period was considered a revolution. Agricultural output increased for a whole host of reasons. Potatoes, corn, and other high-yield crops were introduced to Europe from the colonies in the New World. Farmers started rotating their crops, rather than leaving one-third of their land fallow (as they had done in the Middle Ages under the three-field system), which allowed them to farm all of their land each season without stripping the land of its nutrients. Through a process known simply as **enclosure**, public lands that were shared during the Middle Ages were enclosed by fences, which allowed for private farming and private gain.

But what really cranked up the efficiency and productivity of the farms was the introduction of new technologies. New machines for plowing, seeding, and reaping, along with the development of chemical fertilizers, allowed farmers to greatly increase the amount of land they could farm, while decreasing the number of people needed to do it. **Urbanization** was a natural outgrowth of the increased efficiencies in farming and agriculture. In short, cities grew. In 1800, there were only 20 cities in Europe with a population of more than 100,000. By 1900, 150 cities had similar populations, and the largest, London, had a population of more than 6 million.

Cities developed in areas where resources such as coal, iron, water, and railroads were available for manufacturing. The more factories that developed in favorable locations, the larger cities would grow. In 1800, along with London, the Chinese cities of Beijing (Peking) and Canton ranked in the top three, but just 100 years later, nine of the ten largest cities in the world were in Europe or the United States.

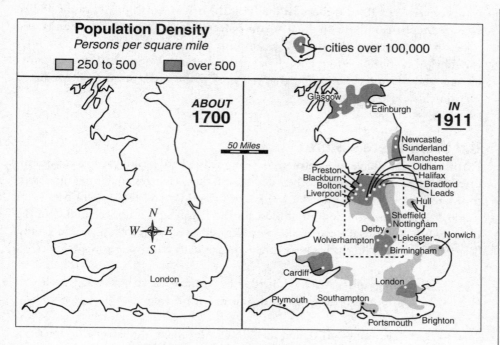

Population Density
Persons per square mile

250 to 500   over 500   cities over 100,000

ABOUT 1700

IN 1911

50 Miles

Glasgow
Edinburgh
Newcastle
Sunderland
Manchester
Preston
Blackburn
Bolton
Liverpool
Oldham
Halifax
Bradford
Leads
Hull
Sheffield
Derby
Nottingham
Wolverhampton
Leicester
Norwich
Birmingham
Cardiff
London
Plymouth
Southampton
Portsmouth
Brighton
London

Population Density in Great Britain

Technological Innovations: The Little Engine That Could

Prior to the Industrial Revolution, most Europeans worked on farms, at home, or in small shops. Even after Britain started importing huge amounts of cotton from its American colonies, most of the cotton was woven into cloth in homes or small shops as part of an inefficient, highly labor-intensive arrangement known as the **domestic system**. Middlemen would drop off wool or cotton at homes where women would make cloth, which would then be picked up again by the middlemen, who would sell the cloth to buyers. All of this was done one person at a time.

However, a series of technological advancements in the eighteenth century changed all this. In 1733, John Kay invented the **flying shuttle**, which sped up the weaving process. In 1764, John Hargreaves invented the **spinning jenny**, which was capable of spinning vast amounts of thread. When waterpower was added to these processes, notably by Richard Arkwright and Edward Cartright in the late eighteenth century, fabric-weaving was taken out of the homes and was centralized at sites where waterpower was abundant. In 1793, when **Eli Whitney** invented the **cotton gin**, thereby allowing massive amounts of cotton to be quickly processed in the Americas and exported to Europe, the textile industry was taken out of the homes and into the mills entirely.

Although industrialization hit the textile industry first, it spread well beyond into other industries. One of the most significant developments was the invention of the **steam engine**, which actually took the work of several people to perfect. In the early 1700s, Thomas Newcomer developed an inefficient engine, but in 1769, **James Watt** dramatically improved it. The steam engine was revolutionary because steam could not only be used to generate power for industry but also for transportation. In 1807, **Robert Fulton** built the first **steamship**, and in the 1820s, **George Stephenson** built the first **steam-powered locomotive**. In the hands of a huge, imperial power like Britain, steamships and locomotives would go a long way toward empire-building and global trade. Because Britain had vast amounts of coal, and because the steam engine was powered by coal, Britain industrialized very quickly.

But Wait, There's More

During the next 100 years, enormous developments changed how people communicated, traveled, and went about their daily lives. These changes are far too numerous to list entirely, but we've picked a few major inventions and listed them below. It's unlikely you'll need to know all of these for the exam, but an understanding of the impact of the Industrial Revolution is perhaps best grasped by looking at the details. There isn't one item on the list below that you can deny has changed the world.

- **The Telegraph**—Invented in 1837 by Samuel Morse. Allowed people to communicate across great distances within seconds.

- **The Telephone**—Invented in 1876 by Alexander Graham Bell. Don't answer it while you're studying.

- **The Lightbulb**—Invented in 1879 by Thomas Edison. Kind of a big deal: now factories can run all night.

- **The Internal Combustion Engine**—Invented in 1885 by Gottlieb Daimler. If you've ever been in a car, you've personally benefited from the internal combustion engine.

- **The Radio**—Invented in the 1890s by Guglielmo Marconi, based on designs by Thomas Edison.

- **The Airplane**—Invented in 1903 by Orville and Wilbur Wright. It travels ever so slightly faster than a steamship (invented just one hundred years prior).

At the same time, there were huge advances in medicine and science. Pasteurization and vaccinations were developed. X-rays came onto the scene. **Charles Darwin** developed the concept of evolution by means of natural selection. The developments of this time period go on and on and on.

Compare Them: The Scientific Revolution and the Industrial Revolution

Both changed the world, of course. One was about the process of discovering, learning, evaluating, and understanding the natural world. The other was about applying that understanding to practical ends. In both cases, knowledge spread and improvements were made across cultures and across time. Even though patents protected individual inventions, one scientist or inventor could build on the ideas of colleagues who were tackling the same issues, thereby leading to constant improvement and reliability. This same collaborative effort is used today. Universities and research organizations share information among colleagues across the globe. The Internet, of course, allows data to be analyzed almost instantaneously by thousands of like-minded individuals.

The Factory System: Efficiency (Cough), New Products (Choke), Big Money (Gag)

The Industrial Revolution permitted the creation of thousands of new products from clothing to toys to weapons. These products were produced efficiently and inexpensively in factories. Under Eli Whitney's system of **interchangeable parts**, machines and their parts were produced uniformly so that they could be easily replaced when something broke down. Later, Henry Ford's use of the **assembly line** meant that each factory worker added only one part to a finished product, one after another after another. These were incredibly important developments in manufacturing, and they made the factory system wildly profitable, but they came with social costs. Man wasn't merely working with machines; he was becoming one. Individuality had no place in a system where consistency of function was held in such high esteem.

The factories were manned by thousands of workers, and the system was efficient and inexpensive primarily because those workers were way overworked, extremely underpaid, and regularly put in harm's way without any accompanying insurance or protection. In the early years of the Industrial Revolution, 16-hour workdays were not uncommon. Children as young as six worked next to machines. Women worked long hours at factories, while still having to fulfill their traditional roles as caretakers for their husbands, children, and homes.

This was a huge change from rural life. Whereas the farms exposed people to fresh air and sunshine, the factories exposed workers to air pollution and hazardous machinery. The farms provided seasonal adjustments to the work pattern, while the factories spit out the same products day after day, all year long. The despair and hopelessness of the daily lives of the factory workers were captured by many novelists and social commentators of the time (for example, Charles Dickens).

Focus On: The Family

The biggest social changes associated with industrialization were to the family. Both women and children became part of the work force, albeit at lower wages, and in more dangerous conditions than their male counterparts. Factory-run boardinghouses housed workers dependent on the company for housing, food, and personal items. These new living arrangements removed workers from families and traditional structures. In many ways, this lessened the restrictions on young women and men. They were able to live away from home, manage their own incomes, and pursue independent leisure activities—theatres, dance halls, recitals, dining out in restaurants—all of which developed to support the new urban working class.

The emergence of a middle class also brought changes to the family. Home and work were no longer centered in the same space. Middle- and upper-class women were expected to master the domestic sphere and to remain private and separate from the realities of the working world. This was a time of great consumption as desirable products were mass produced and women were expected to arrange parlors and dining rooms with fancy tea cups and serving trays.

New Economic and Social Philosophies: No Shortage of Opinions

Industrialization created new social classes. The new aristocrats were those who became rich from industrial success. A middle class formed, made up of managers, accountants, ministers, lawyers, doctors, and other skilled professionals. Finally, at the bottom of the pyramid was the working class—and it was huge—made up of factory workers in the cities and peasant farmers in the countryside.

Contrast Them: Social Class Structures Before and After Industrialism

Keep in mind that throughout history, the wealthy class was small and the poorest class was huge, but industrialism gave it a new twist. Because of urbanization, people were living side by side. They could see the huge differences among the classes right before their eyes. What's more, the members of the working class saw factory owners gain wealth quickly—at their expense. The owners didn't inherit their position, but instead achieved success by exploiting their workers, and the workers knew it. In the past, under feudalism, people more readily accepted their position because, as far as they knew, the social structure was the way it had always been, and that's the way it was meant to be. If your dad was a farmer, you were a farmer. If your dad was the king, you were a prince. After industrialism, people literally saw for the first time the connection between their sacrifices and the aristocracy's luxuries.

The rise of the industrial class had its origins in the concept of private ownership. **Adam Smith** wrote in *The Wealth of Nations* (1776) that economic prosperity and fairness is best achieved through private ownership. Individuals should own the means of production and sell their products and services in a free and open market, where the demand for their goods and services would determine their prices and availability. A **free market system** (also known as **capitalism**), Smith argued, would best meet the needs and desires of individuals and nations as a whole. When governments remove themselves entirely from regulation, the process is called **laissez-faire capitalism**.

Smith wrote his book in response to the western European mercantilist practices that had dominated during the Age of Exploration. In the New World, monarchies—which were not only corrupt, but also highly inefficient—closely managed their economies. In the nineteenth century, European countries continued to develop their mercantilist philosophies (especially using colonies as a way of obtaining raw materials without having to import them from other countries and as a way of increasing exports). European countries also permitted and encouraged the development of private investment and capitalism. Hence the rise of factory workers and the rise of major investment firms like the British East India Company.

While Adam Smith believed that free market capitalism would lead to better opportunities for everyone, **Karl Marx**, a German economist and philosopher who spent a good part of his adult life living in poverty, pointed out that the factory workers had genuine opportunities but were being exploited as a consequence of capitalism. In other words, the abuses weren't merely the result of the way in which capitalism was practiced, but an inherent flaw in the system. In *The Communist Manifesto* (1848), Marx and Friedrich Engels wrote that the working class would eventually revolt and take control of the means of production. All the instruments of power—the government, the courts, the police, the church—were on the side of the rich against the workers. Once the class struggle was resolved by the massive uprising of the exploited, Marx predicted that the instruments of power wouldn't even be needed. The impact of Marxism was enormous, and served as the foundation of **socialism** and **communism**.

Marx and Engels were not just theorizing, they were also observing, and there was much discontent to support their view. In England in the early 1800s, groups of workers known as **Luddites** destroyed equipment in factories in the middle of the night to protest working conditions and pitiful wages. The government unequivocally sided with the business owners, executing some of the workers, while also enacting harsh laws against any further action.

At the same time, however, a greater number of people with influence (the middle class and the aristocracy) began to realize how inhumane the factory system had become and started to do something about it. These reformers believed that capitalism was a positive development, but that laws were needed to keep its abuses in check. In other words, they believed that the government needed to act on behalf of the workers as well as the factory owners. By the mid-nineteenth century, there was a major split in thought among intellectuals and policymakers.

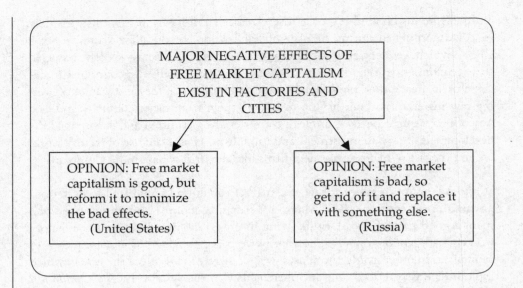

In Britain and the United States, where the impact of the Enlightenment was strong, democracy was developing, and the middle class was growing, reforms to the free market system that lessened the negative impact of capitalism on workers took root. In other countries like Russia where absolute rule was strong and the peasant class extremely oppressed, reform was almost nonexistent. There, Marxist ideas grew popular among a small group of urban intellectuals, eventually including Vladimir Lenin, who believed they could lead a worker revolution and end the tyranny of the czars. Elsewhere, Marxism impacted social thought and intermixed with capitalist thought to create economic systems that were partly socialist (in which the government owned some of the means of production) and partly capitalist (in which individuals owned some of the means of production). Most of Europe, including Britain after World War II, mixed socialist and capitalist ideas.

Capitalism and Enlightenment Combine: Reform Catches On

In the second half of the nineteenth century, after the abuses and social consequences of the Industrial Revolution became clear, a series of reforms occurred. The British Parliament passed laws, such as the **Factory Act of 1883**, which limited the hours of each workday, restricted children from working in factories, and required factory owners to make working conditions safer and cleaner. Meanwhile, **labor unions** were formed. The unions were vehicles through which thousands of employees bargained for better working conditions, or threatened to strike, thereby shutting down the factory. In addition, an increasing number of factory owners realized that a healthy, happy, and reasonably well-paid workforce meant a productive and loyal one.

All of these developments combined, though slowly and sporadically, to improve not only the conditions in the factories and cities, but also the standard of living on an individual family level. The middle class became substantially larger. Public education became more widely accessible. **Social mobility**—the ability of a person to work his way up from one social class to the next—became more commonplace. In 1807, the slave trade was abolished, which meant that no new slaves were transported from

Africa, though the ownership of existing slaves continued. In 1833, the British outlawed slavery, and three decades later, it was outlawed in the United States.

As men earned more money, women left the factories and returned to their traditional roles in the home, which limited their influence socially, politically, professionally, and intellectually, even as democratic reforms greatly increased the power of most men, especially through the right to vote. In response, women began organizing to increase their collective influence. It wasn't until 1920 in the United States, and 1928 in Britain, however, that the **women's suffrage movement** fully succeeded in giving women the right to vote.

Despite improvements in the overall standards of living in industrialized nations, by 1900 extreme hardships persisted. In many cases, Europeans dreamed of starting over somewhere else, or escaping cruelties at home. From 1800 to 1920, 50 million Europeans migrated to North and South America. Millions fled from famine in Ireland, or anti-Semitism in Russia, or poverty and joblessness in general.

In Search of Natural Resources: Stealing Is Cheaper than Dealing

The factories of the Industrial Revolution created useful products, but to do so they required natural resources. Europe had its share of coal and iron ore used to provide power and make equipment for the factories, but raw materials such as cotton and rubber had to be imported because they didn't grow in the climates of western Europe.

Industrial nations amassed incredible wealth by colonizing regions with natural resources, and then taking those resources without compensating the natives. The resources were sent back to Europe, where they were made into finished products. Then, the industrial nations sent the finished products back to the colonies, where the colonists had to purchase them because the colonial powers wouldn't let the colonies trade with anyone else. In short, the colonial powers became rich at the expense of the colonies. The more colonies a nation had, the richer it became.

Soon, Europe colonized nations on every other continent in the world. Europe became a clearinghouse for raw materials from around the globe while the rest of the world increasingly became exposed to Europe and European ideas. What's more, the need for raw materials transformed the landscape of the conquered regions. Limited raw materials depleted faster than at any time in human history. The Industrial Revolution, in addition to creating pollution, began to have an impact on the environment by gobbling natural resources.

The European Justification: Superiority Is a Heavy Burden

Even as progressives argued for an end to the slave trade and better working conditions in the factories, a huge number of Europeans—not just the industrialists—either supported or acquiesced in the colonization of foreign lands. Most Europeans were very ethnocentric and viewed other cultures as barbarian and uncivilized. Ironically, this ethnocentrism may have driven some of the social advancements within European society itself—after all, if you think of yourself as civilized, then you can't exactly brutalize your own people.

Two ideas contributed to this mindset. First, **social Darwinists** applied Charles Darwin's biological theory of natural selection to sociology. In other words, they claimed that dominant races or classes of people rose to the top through a process of "survival of the fittest." This meant that because Britain was the most powerful, it was the most fit, and therefore the British were superior to other races.

Second, many Europeans believed that they were not only superior, but that they had a moral obligation to (crassly said) dominate other people or (politely said) teach other people how to be more civilized—in other words, how to be more like Europeans. **Rudyard Kipling** summed it up in his poem "**White Man's Burden**." As European nations swallowed up the rest of the world in an effort to advance their economies, military strategic positioning, and egos, Kipling characterized these endeavors as a "burden" in which it was the duty of Europeans to conquer each "half-devil and half-child" so that they could be converted to Christianity and civilized in the European fashion. Never mind if the non-Europeans didn't want to be "civilized." The Europeans supposedly knew what was best for everyone.

Contrast Them: Ethnocentrism in Europe and Elsewhere

To be sure, many cultures were ethnocentric. The Chinese, for example, believed their kingdom to be the Middle Kingdom, literally the "center of the world," and themselves ethnically superior to other races. Similar attitudes existed in Japan and in most major civilizations. So the Europeans were hardly unique in their self-important attitudes. However, in their ability to act on those attitudes, they were dangerously unique. Armed with the most technologically advanced militaries and strong economic motives, the Europeans were quite capable of subjugating people whom they considered to be inferior, barbaric, or dispensable. Their success at doing so often reinforced the ethnocentric attitudes, leading to further colonialism and subjugation.

B. European Imperialism in India

As you know from the previous chapter, the Indian subcontinent had long been a destination of European traders eager to get their hands on India's many luxuries, such as tea, sugar, silk, salt, and jute (an extremely strong fiber used for ropes). By the early eighteenth century, the Mughal Empire (remember that?) was in decline following decades of fighting wars and by renewed religious conflict between Muslims and Hindus. Lacking a strong leader and a unified people created an opening (as it so often does) for external powers to move in. And that is precisely what Britain and France decided to do.

In the 1750s, the rivalry between France and England reached fever pitch. During the Seven Years' War (more on it later), the two countries battled each other in three theaters: North America, Europe, and India. England won across the board. The **British East India Company**, a joint-stock company that operated like a multinational corporation with exclusive rights over British trade with India, then led in India by **Robert Clive**, raised an effective army that ridded the subcontinent of the French. During the next two decades, Clive successfully conquered the Bengal region (present-day Bangladesh), quite a feat given that the East India Company was a corporation. It wasn't British troops who conquered the region, but corporate troops!

Over the next hundred years, the company took advantage of the weakening Mughals and set up administrative regions throughout the empire. In 1798, the large island of Ceylon (present-day Sri Lanka) fell to the British. In the early 1800s, the Punjab region in northern India came under British control, and from there the Brits launched excursions into Pakistan and Afghanistan.

The Sepoy Mutiny: Too Little, Too Late

To help it administer the regions under its control, the East India Company relied on Sepoys, Indians who worked for the Brits, mostly as soldiers. By the mid-1800s, the Sepoys were becoming increasingly alarmed with the company's insatiable appetite for eating up larger and larger chunks of the subcontinent. What's more, the company wasn't very good about respecting the local customs of the Sepoys, and respected neither Muslim nor Hindu religious customs. When, in 1857, the Sepoys learned that their bullet cartridges (which had to be bitten off in order to load into the rifle) were greased with pork and beef fat, thus violating both Muslim and Hindu dietary laws, the Sepoys rebelled. The fighting continued for nearly two years, but the rebellion failed miserably.

The consequences were huge. In 1858, the British parliament stepped in, took control of India away from the East India Company, and made all of India a crown colony. The last of the Mughal rulers, **Bahadur Shah II**, was sent into exile, thereby ending the Mughal Empire for good. Nearly 300 million Indians were suddenly British subjects (that's as many people as currently living in the United States). By 1877, Queen Victoria was recognized as Empress of India.

Full-Blown British Colonialism: England on the Indus

In the second half of the nineteenth century, India became the model of British imperialism. Raw materials flowed to Britain; finished products flowed back to India. The upper castes were taught English and were expected to adopt English attitudes. Christianity spread. Railroads and canals were built. Urbanization, as in Europe, increased dramatically. But all of this came at the expense of the Indian culture and Indian institutions. Still, as the upper castes were Anglicized, they gained the education and worldly sophistication to begin to influence events. Increasingly, they dreamed of freeing India from British rule.

In 1885, a group of well-educated Indians formed the **Indian National Congress** to begin the path toward independence. It would take the impact of two world wars before they would get it. In the meantime, Indians, especially those that lived in the cities, continued to adapt to British customs while trying to hold on to their traditions.

C. European Imperialism in China

As you know, for much of its history, China was relatively isolationist. It traded frequently, but it didn't make exploration a high priority. It also expanded by conquering its neighbors, but never took this expansion beyond its own region of the globe. Up until the 1830s, China allowed the European powers to trade only in the port city of Canton, and it established strict limitations on what could be bought and sold. But as the European powers, particularly the British, gained industrial muscle, they came barging in, this time with weapons and warships.

The Opium Wars: European Drug Pushers Force Their Right to Deal

In 1773, British traders introduced opium to the Chinese. By 1838, the drug habit among the Chinese had grown so widespread and destructive that the Manchu Emperor released an imperial edict forbidding the further sale or use of opium. Consistent with this edict, the Chinese seized British opium in Canton in 1839.

The British would have none of it. From 1839 to 1842, the two countries fought a war over the opium trade. This was known as the first **Opium War**. Overwhelmed by British military might, China was forced to sign the **Treaty of Nanjing**, the first of what came to be known as the "**unequal treaties**," by which Britain was given considerable rights to expand trade with China. And, of course, the right to create more opium addicts.

In 1843, Britain declared Hong Kong its own crown possession, a significant development because that went beyond trading rights and actually established a British colony in the region. In 1844, the Manchu Dynasty was forced to permit Christian missionaries back into the country.

When China resisted British attempts to expand the opium trade even further, the two countries fought a second Opium War for four years beginning in 1856. The Chinese defeat was humiliating. It resulted in the opening of all of China to European trade. Still, other than in Hong Kong, European imperialism in China was quite different from what it was in India and what it would be in Africa. In China, Britain fought more for trading concessions than for the establishment of colonies.

The Word Is Out: China Is Crumbling

The Opium Wars had a huge impact on the global perception of China. For centuries, the world knew that China was one of the more advanced civilizations. With the clear-cut British defeat of China with relatively few troops, the world realized that China was an easy target. What's more, the Chinese themselves knew that their government was weak, and so they, too, started to rebel against it. Internal rebellion started at the beginning of the nineteenth century with the **White Lotus Rebellions** led by Buddhists who were frustrated over taxes and government corruption. It continued through the middle of the century with the **Taiping Rebellion**. The Taipings, led by a religious zealot claiming to be the brother of Jesus, recruited an army nearly a million strong and nearly succeeded in bringing down the Manchu government. The rebels failed, but the message was clear. China was crumbling from within, and unable to stop foreign aggression from outside.

In the 1860s, the Manchu Dynasty tried to get its act together in what became known as the **Self-Strengthening Movement**, but it did no good. In 1876, Korea realized China was weak and declared its independence. Later, in the **Sino-French War** (1883), the Chinese lost control of Vietnam to the French, who established a colony there called French Indochina. If that wasn't enough, a decade later the Chinese were defeated in the **Sino-Japanese War**, when the rising imperial power of Japan wanted in on the action. In the **Treaty of Shimonoseki** (1895), China was forced to hand over control of Taiwan and grant the Japanese trading rights similar to those it had granted the Europeans. Japan also defeated the Koreans and took control of the entire peninsula.

Meanwhile, the European powers were rushing to establish a greater presence in China. By establishing **spheres of influence**, France, Germany, Russia, and of course Britain carved up huge slices of China for themselves. These spheres were not quite colonies. Instead, they were areas in which the European powers invested heavily, built military bases, and set up business, transportation, and communication operations. The Manchu Dynasty was still the governmental authority within the spheres.

By 1900, the United States, which had its own trading designs on Asia, was worried that China would become another India or Africa, and that the United States would be shut out of trade if the Manchu government fell and the Europeans took over the government. Through its **Open Door Policy**, the United States pledged its support of the sovereignty of the Chinese government and announced equal trading privileges among all imperial powers (basically Europe and the United States).

The Boxer Rebellion: Knocked Out in the First Round

By the twentieth century, nationalism among the Chinese peasants and local leadership was festering. Anti-Manchu, anti-European, and anti-Christian, the Society of Righteous and Harmonious Fists, or **Boxers** as they came to be known, organized in response to the Manchu government's defeats and concessions to the Western powers and Japan. Infuriated, the Boxers' goal was to drive the Europeans and Japanese out of China. Adopting guerilla warfare tactics, the Boxers slaughtered Christian missionaries and seized control of foreign embassies. Ultimately, however, they were not successful in achieving their aims. Instead, their uprising resulted in the dispatch of foreign reinforcements who quickly and decisively put down the rebellion. The Manchu government, already having made great concessions to the Europeans and Japanese, was then even further humiliated. As a result of the rebellion, China was forced to sign the **Boxer Protocol**, which demanded that China not only pay the Europeans and the Japanese the costs associated with the rebellion but also to formally apologize for it as well.

Contrast Them: European Imperialism in China and in India

Multiple European countries originally traded with India, but the British won out and established exclusive control. In China, the British dominated trade early on, and as they succeeded, more and more countries piled on.

In India, the British established a true colony, running the government and directing huge internal projects. In China, Europeans and the Japanese established spheres of influence, focusing on the economic benefits of trade with no overall governmental responsibilities. Therefore, when independence movements began in India, the efforts were directed against Britain, the foreign occupier. In contrast, when the people wanted to change the government in China, they targeted the Manchu Dynasty.

On its last legs, the Manchu Dynasty couldn't prevent the forces of reform from overtaking it from both within and without, and as a consequence, Chinese culture itself started to crumble. In 1901, foot binding was abolished. In 1905, the 2,000-year-old Chinese Examination System was eliminated. By 1911, the government was toppled and imperial rule came to an end. For the first time, under the leadership of Sun Yatsen, a republic was established in China. But more on this in the next chapter.

D. Japanese Imperialism

During the seventeenth and eighteenth centuries, Japan succeeded in keeping European influences away from its shores. It consequently built a highly ethnocentric, self-involved society that didn't even allow its own citizens to travel abroad. But by the nineteenth century and the Industrial Revolution, the Europeans and the United States became so powerful and so crazed for markets that Japan found it hard to keep the westerners at bay. In 1853, **Commodore Matthew Perry** from the United States (not the one from *Friends*) arrived in Japan on a steamboat, something the Japanese had never seen before, and essentially shocked the Japanese, who quickly realized that their isolation had resulted in their inability to compete economically and militarily with the industrialized world.

For a time, the West won concessions from Japan through various treaties such as the **Treaty of Kanagawa** (1854). These treaties grossly favored the United States and other countries. As in China, the nationalists grew resentful, but unlike the Chinese, the Japanese were organized. Through the leadership of the samurai, they revolted against the shogun who had ratified these treaties, and restored Emperor Meiji to power.

The Meiji Restoration:
Shogun Out, Emperor In, Westerners Out

The **Meiji Restoration** ushered in an era of Japanese westernization, after which Japan emerged as a world power. By the 1870s, Japan was building railways and steamships. By 1876, the samurai warrior class as an institution had been abolished, and universal military service among all males was established.

The relative isolation of Japan during the Tokugawa and the deliberate attempt to westernize while strengthening Japanese imperial traditions during the Meiji led to a period of increased cultural creativity with rituals aimed at developing national identity. Much of this new identity was centered on military pageantry that celebrated Japanese victories over China and Russia in the early twentieth century.

In the 1890s, Japanese industrial and military power really started to roll. It was now powerful enough to substantially reduce European and U.S. influence. It maintained trade, but on equal footing with western powers. Japan went through an incredibly quick Industrial Revolution. In 1895, Japan defeated China in a war for control of Korea and Taiwan. Japan was now an imperial power itself. Later, after the **Russo-Japanese War** of 1904, the victorious Japanese kicked Russia out of Manchuria and established its own sphere of influence there. As if demonstrating that Japan was now an equal among European states, the British offered them an alliance in 1905, a treaty the Japanese gratefully accepted. Japan was now not just an imperial power but a world power.

Compare Them: The Industrial Revolution in Europe and in Japan

The industrialization of Europe and Japan followed very similar paths, but Japan's was on fast forward. It managed to accomplish in a few decades what had taken Europe more than a century, in large part because it didn't have to invent everything itself—it just needed to implement the advances of Western industrialization. Still, the pattern was remarkably similar. Private corporations rose up, industrialists like the Mitsubishi family became wealthy, factories were built, urbanization increased dramatically, and reform was instituted. Japan learned from the Europeans quite well. If you can't beat an industrialized power, become one yourself.

E. European Imperialism in Africa

Unlike India and China, and to a certain degree Japan, Africa held little interest for most Europeans prior to the Industrial Revolution. To be sure, north of the Sahara, in Egypt and along the Mediterranean, Europeans had historical interest and impact. But the vast interior of the continent remained unknown to the outside world. During the Age of Exploration, coastal regions of Africa became important to Europeans for limited trade, and also for strategic positioning, as stopping-off points for merchant ships en route to India or China. Most significantly, of course, Africa became the center of the slave trade.

The Slave Trade Finally Ends

As Enlightenment principles took root in Europe, larger and larger numbers of people grew outraged at the idea of slavery. Between 1807 and 1820, most European nations abolished the slave trade, although slavery itself was not abolished until a few decades later. In other words, no new slaves were legally imported from Africa, but those already in Europe or the New World continued to be enslaved until emancipation in the mid-nineteenth century. In some cases, former slaves returned to Africa. Groups of former American slaves, for example, emigrated to Liberia, where they established an independent nation.

It's a terrible irony that as the slave trade ended in the nineteenth century, Europeans turned their greedy eyes to the continent of Africa itself. Within 50 years, the Africans were subjugated again, but this time in their own homeland.

South Africa: Gold Rings, a Diamond Necklace, and a British Crown

Prior to the discovery of gold and diamonds in South Africa in the 1860s and 1880s, South Africa was valuable to the Europeans only for shipping and military reasons. The Dutch arrived first and settled Cape Town as a stopping point for ships on the way from Europe to India. In 1795, the British seized Cape Town, and the South African Dutch (now known as Boers or Afrikaners) trekked northeast into the interior of South Africa, settling in a region known as the Transvaal. When the Boers later discovered diamonds and gold in the Transvaal, the British quickly followed, fighting a series of wars for the rights to the resources. After years of bloody battles, known as the **Boer War** (1899–1902), the British reigned supreme, and all of South Africa was annexed as part of the ever-expanding British Empire. Of course, throughout this entire process, Africans were not allowed claims to the gold and diamonds, and were made to work in the mines as their natural resources were sent abroad.

South Africa became a significant British colony, complete with extensive investment in infrastructure and institutions. In 1910, the colony had its own constitution, and it became the Union of South Africa, still part of the British Commonwealth, but exercising a considerable amount of self-rule. Under the constitution, only white men could vote, so the native Africans had few rights. In 1912, educated South Africans organized the **African National Congress** in an effort to oppose European colonialism and specific South African policies. This organization, of course, was similar to the Indian National Congress, which was established for similar ends.

Egypt: A New Waterway Makes a Splash

In theory, the Ottomans ruled Egypt from 1517 until 1882, although throughout the nineteenth century, Ottoman rule was extremely weak. Local rulers, called beys, had far more influence over developments in Egypt than the rulers in Istanbul. When Napoleon tried to conquer Egypt during his tireless attempt to expand

France into a mega-empire at the turn of the nineteenth century, **Muhammad Ali** defeated the French and the Ottomans, and gained control of Egypt in 1805. Egypt technically remained part of the Ottoman Empire, but as viceroy, Ali wielded almost exclusive control. During the next 30 years, he began the industrialization of Egypt and directed the expansion of agriculture toward cotton production, which was then exported to the textile factories of Britain for substantial profit.

Ali's westernization attempts were temporarily halted by his grandson, **Abbas I**, but were reinvigorated under subsequent rulers, who worked with the French to begin construction of the **Suez Canal**. The canal, when completed in 1869, connected the Mediterranean Sea to the Indian Ocean, eliminating the need to go around the Cape of Good Hope. Because Britain had a huge colony in India, the canal became more important to the British than to anyone else. As Egypt's finances went into a tailspin because of excessive government spending, Egypt started selling stock in its canal to raise money, stock that the British government eagerly gobbled up. By 1882, Britain not only controlled the Suez Canal, but had maneuvered its way into Egypt to such a degree that it declared it a British protectorate, which was essentially a colony except that Egyptians remained in political power.

Pushed out of Egypt, France focused on other parts of North Africa, particularly Nigeria. The Italians, once they had unified as a country, also became interested in North Africa. The race for control of Africa was on.

The Berlin Conference: Carving Up the Continent

In 1884, Otto von Bismarck hosted the major European powers at a conference in Berlin intended to resolve some differences over various European claims to lands in the African Congo. By the end of the conference, the delegates had set up rules for how future colonization rights and boundaries would be determined on that continent. With rules in hand, the Europeans left the conference in haste. Each country wanted to be the first to establish possession in the various parts of Africa. Within three decades, almost the entire continent of Africa was colonized by Britain, France, Germany, Italy, Spain, Portugal, and Belgium. Only Ethiopia and Liberia remained independent of European rule by 1914.

While the Europeans added substantial infrastructure to the continent by building railroads, dams, and roads, they stripped Africa of its resources for profit and treated the natives harshly. Every colonial power except Britain exercised direct rule over its colonies, meaning Europeans were put in positions of authority and the colonies were remade according to European customs. The British, having their hands full with the huge colony in India and massive spheres of influence in China and elsewhere, permitted the native populations to rule themselves more directly and to more freely practice their traditional customs (similar to how the Roman Empire handled its far-flung territories).

Because the Berlin Conference of 1884 encouraged colonialism solely based on bargaining for political and economic advantage, the boundary lines that eventually separated colonial territories were based on European concerns, not on African history or culture. Therefore, in some situations, tribal lands were cut in half between two colonies controlled by two different European nations, while in other situations two rival tribes were unwillingly brought together under the same colonial rule. For a time, the disruption of traditional tribal boundary lines worked to the Europeans' advantage because it was difficult for the native Africans to organize an opposition within each colony. But it did much more than thwart opposition; it disrupted the culture. Add in European schools, Christian missionaries, and western business practices, and traditional African culture, as elsewhere in the global colonial swirl, started breaking apart.

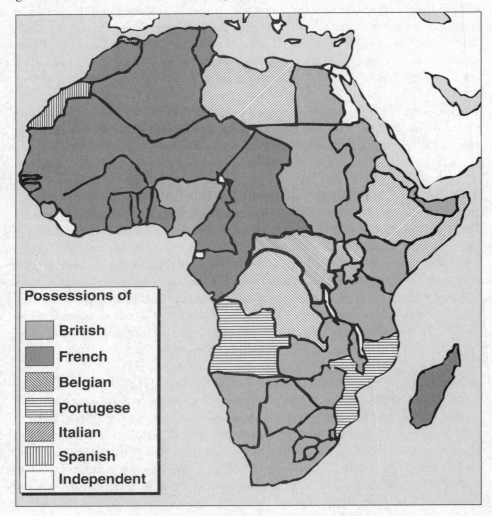

Possessions of

- British
- French
- Belgian
- Portugese
- Italian
- Spanish
- Independent

European Colonies in Africa, 1914

Compare Them: European Colonialism in Africa and in Latin America

Colonialism in Africa was similar to that in the Americas in that boundary lines were determined by European agreements from abroad. In other words, there was total disregard for the societies that existed beforehand. Colonialism in Africa was similar to colonialism in America because multiple countries held claims to the land. Except for the colonies controlled by the British, the African colonies were governed by direct rule, similar to European rule of colonies in the Americas. This meant they sent European officials to occupy all positions of authority. Native traditions were overcome, not tolerated, and certainly not developed. This, of course, was in contrast to spheres of influence in China, for example, in which Europeans were generally more interested in making money rather than changing the entire culture.

V. NATIONALIST MOVEMENTS AND OTHER DEVELOPMENTS

A. Two Unifications: Italy and Germany

One of the consequences of the Napoleonic era was that it intensified nationalism, or feelings of connection to one's own home, region, language, and culture. France, Spain, Portugal, Britain, and Russia, of course, had already unified and, in some cases, built enormous empires. But the Italian and German city-states were still very feudal, and were constantly at the center of warfare among the European powers. In the second half of the nineteenth century, however, all of that changed. With the wave of industrialization and all the changes that it inspired, as well as the nationalist sentiments that were still lingering decades after Napoleon's defeat, a drive to unify Italy and Germany resurfaced. Italy and Germany unified, and with unification, they eventually altered the balance of European power.

The Unification of Italy: Italians Give Foreign Occupiers the Boot

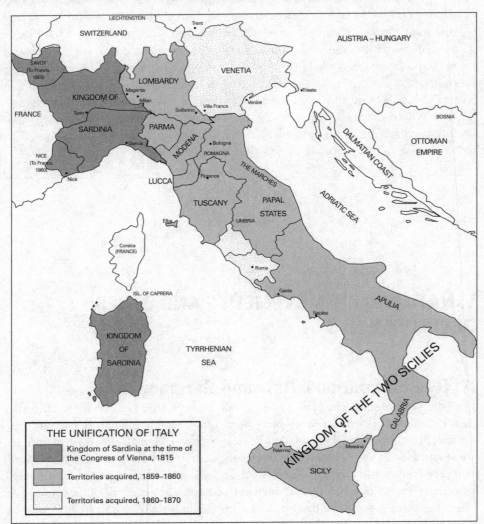

The Unification of Italy

In the mid-nineteenth century, Italy was a tangle of foreign-controlled small kingdoms. Austria controlled Venetia, Lombardy, and Tuscany in the north. France controlled Rome and the Papal States in the mid-section. Only the divided kingdom of Sardinia (part of which was an island in the Mediterranean) was controlled by Italians.

In 1849, the king of Sardinia, **Victor Emmanuel II**, named **Count Camillo Cavour** his prime minister, and nationalism in Italy took off. Both Emmanuel and Cavour believed strongly in Italian unification. Through a series of wars in which Cavour sided with European powers that could help him boot out Austria from Italy, he managed to remove Austrian influence from all parts of Italy (except Venetia) by 1859. Meanwhile, **Giuseppe Garibaldi**, another Italian nationalist, raised a volunteer army and and in 1860 his army overthrew the kingdom whose citizens pledged allegiance to Sardinia. So, by 1861, a large chunk of present-day Italy was unified, and it declared itself a unified kingdom under Victor Emmanuel.

In the following decade, the Italians managed to gain control of Venetia after siding with Prussia in its war against Austria (which previously controlled Venetia) and finally won control of Rome in 1870 when the French withdrew. Still, even though Italy was essentially unified, the boundaries of Europe were still very shaky. Some Italians thought that southern provinces of Austria and France were far more Italian than not and that those provinces were rightly part of Italy. What's more, Italy had a hard time unifying culturally because for centuries it had developed more regionally. Still, now unified, Italy was more able to assert itself on the world stage, a development that would impact Europe in the next century.

The Unification of Germany: All About Otto

The provinces that comprised Germany and the Austrian Empire (the Hapsburgs) hadn't been truly united since the decline of Charlemagne's Holy Roman Empire in the Middle Ages. Since the Peace of Westphalia (1648), which asserted the authority of regional governments, two areas in the region of the former Holy Roman Empire had politically dominated it: Prussia and Austria. Prussia, under the enlightened monarch Frederick the Great and his successors, achieved economic preeminence by embracing the Industrial Revolution. They also strongly supported education, which created a talented work force.

Many in Prussia wanted to consolidate the German territories into a powerful empire to rival the great powers of Europe, particularly Britain, France, and increasingly Russia. So, in 1861, the new king of Prussia, **William I**, appointed **Otto von Bismarck** prime minister with the aim of building the military and consolidating the region under its authority.

In order to achieve this consolidation, Bismarck had to defeat Austria, which he did in only seven weeks, after he won assurances from the other European powers that they would not step in on Austria's behalf. Through further war and annexation, Bismarck secured most of the other German principalities, except for heavily Catholic regions in the south. So, the crafty Bismarck formed an alliance with the Catholic German states against aggression from France, and then, in 1870, provoked France to declare war on Prussia, starting the **Franco-Prussian War**—a war which, once won, consolidated the German Catholic regions under Prussian control. In 1871, the victorious Bismarck crowned King William I as emperor of the new German Empire, which was also known as the Second Reich ("second empire," after the Holy Roman Empire, which was known as the First Reich).

After unification, Germany quickly industrialized and became a strong economic and political power. But Otto was not popular with everyone, especially socialists. In 1888, Germany crowned a new emperor, **William II**, who wanted to run the country himself. In 1890, he forced Bismarck to resign as prime minister and re-established authority as the emperor. With the Industrial Revolution in Germany now running full throttle, he built a huge navy, pursued colonial ambitions in Africa and Asia, and oversaw the rise of Germany into one of the most powerful nations in the world. By 1914, Germany felt capable of taking on any other power.

D. Other Political Developments

Russia: Life with Czars

In the nineteenth century, Russia consolidated power over its vast territory by giving absolute power to its Romanov czars. The vast majority of the citizens were serfs with no rights, living an almost slavelike existence. Alexander I and Nicholas I frequently used the secret police to quash rebellions or hints of reform, despite the fact that an increasing number of Russians demanded change.

By the 1860s, long after the Enlightenment had had an effect on most developments in the West, **Alexander II** began some reforms. He issued the **Emancipation Edict**, which essentially abolished serfdom. It did little good. The serfs were given very small plots of land for which they had to give huge payments to the government to keep, so it was difficult for them to improve their lot. Some peasants headed to the cities to work in Russia's burgeoning industries, but there, too, the reforms that softened some of the harsher working conditions in the West hadn't made their way eastward. Whether in the fields or in the factories, the Russian peasants continued to live a meager existence, especially when compared to many of their western European counterparts.

Still, during the second half of the nineteenth century, a small but visible middle class started to grow, and the arts began to flourish. In a span of just a few decades, Russian artists produced some of the greatest works of all time: Tolstoy wrote *Anna Karenina* and *War and Peace*, Dostoyevsky authored *The Brothers Karamazov*, and Tchaikovsky composed *Swan Lake* and *The Nutcracker*. Meanwhile, an intellectual class well-acquainted with political and economic thought in the rest of Europe began to assert itself against the monarchy. In 1881, Alexander II was assassinated by a political group known as **The People's Will**.

Alexander III reacted fiercely by attempting to suppress anything that he perceived as anti-Russian. Through a policy known as **Russification**, all Russians, including people in the far-flung reaches of the Empire that did not share a cultural history with most of Russia, were expected to learn the Russian language and convert to Russian Orthodoxy. Anyone who didn't comply was persecuted, especially Jews. Meanwhile, terrible conditions in the factories continued, even as production capacity was increased and greater demands were put upon the workers.

By the time **Nicholas II** reigned (1894–1917), revolution was in the wind. The Socialists began to organize. Nicholas tried to rally Russians around the flag by going to war with Japan over Manchuria in 1904, but the Russians suffered a humiliating defeat. On a Sunday in 1905, moderates marched on the czar's palace in a peaceful protest, an attempt to encourage him to enact Enlightened reforms, but Nicholas felt threatened and ordered his troops to fire on the protestors. The day has since been known as **Bloody Sunday**.

For the next decade, resentment among the working classes festered. In 1906, the czar attempted to enact legislative reforms by appointing a Prime Minister, **Peter Stolypin**, and by creating the **Duma**, a body intended to represent the Russian people, but every time the Duma was critical of the czar, he immediately disbanded it. In the end, the attempts at reform were too little, too late. The Romanov Dynasty would soon come to an end.

The Ottoman Empire: Are They Still Calling It an Empire?

The Ottoman Empire began its decline in the sixteenth century and never was able to gain a second wind. Throughout the seventeenth and eighteenth centuries, the Ottomans continually fought the Russians for control of the Balkans, the Black Sea, and surrounding areas. Most of the time, the Russians were victorious. So by the nineteenth century, not only was the Ottoman Empire considerably smaller and less powerful, but it was in danger of collapse. Greece, Egypt, and Arabia launched successful independence movements. This worried Britain and France, who feared that if the Ottoman Empire fell entirely, the Russian Empire would seize the chance to take over the eastern Mediterranean. So, for the next century, Britain and France tried to keep the Ottoman Empire going if only to prevent Russian expansion, as they did in the Crimean War in 1853. At the same time, of course, Britain and France increased their influence in the region. In 1882, for example, Britain gained control of Egypt.

U.S. Foreign Policy: This Hemisphere Is Our Hemisphere

After the wave of independence movements swept Latin America in the early nineteenth century, Europe found itself nearly shut out of developments in the entire western hemisphere—even as European countries were swiftly colonizing Africa and Asia.

To ensure that Europe wouldn't recolonize the Americas, U.S. President Monroe declared in his 1823 State of the Union Address that the western hemisphere was off-limits to European aggression. The United States, of course, wasn't the superpower then that it is today, so it was hardly in a position to enforce its declaration, which became known as the **Monroe Doctrine**. But Britain, whose navy was enormous and positioned all over the globe, was fearful that Spain wanted to rekindle its American empire, so it agreed to back up the United States. As a result, the European powers continued to invest huge sums of money in Latin American business enterprises but didn't make territorial claims. In 1904, after European powers sent warships to Venezuela to demand repayment of loans, President Theodore Roosevelt added what came to be known as the **Roosevelt Corollary**, which provided that the United States would intervene in financial disputes between European powers and countries in the Americas, if doing so would help to maintain the peace. While Latin American nations have at times benefited from the protection and oversight of their North American neighbor, the Monroe Doctrine also gave rise to anger and resentment in many

Latin Americans, who sometimes saw the United States as exercising its own brand of imperialism in the region. This became clear when the United States incited Panamanians to declare their independence from Colombia, so that the United States could negotiate the right to build the **Panama Canal** in the Central American nation. Construction began in 1904 and finished in 1914.

In 1898, a European power was dealt another blow in its efforts to maintain its footing in the Western Hemisphere. Spain, which at that time still controlled both Cuba and Puerto Rico, was embroiled in conflict with Cuban revolutionaries when the United States, which sympathized with the Cubans, intervened and launched the **Spanish-American War** of 1898. In a matter of a few months, it was all over. The United States quickly and decisively destroyed the Spanish fleets in Cuba and in the Philippines, and thereby gained control of Guam, Puerto Rico, and the Philippines. Cuba was given its independence, in exchange for concessions to the United States, including allowing the creation of two U.S. naval bases on the island. The United States, henceforth, was considered to be among the world powers.

VI. TECHNOLOGY AND INTELLECTUAL DEVELOPMENTS 1750–1914

Economic, political and social changes occurred so rapidly in this 150 year period that is difficult to keep track of them all. The flow chart in section VII of this chapter provides a good outline of the causes and effects of these changes. Advances in power and transportation drove the Industrial Revolution. Steam provided consistent power for new factories. In transportation news, millions of miles of rail lines were laid through out Europe, India, Africa, and throughout eastern Asia. This facilitated the movement of resources and manufactured goods. The new industrial world required large numbers of laborers. In the latter half of the nineteenth century, this need, along with the abolition of slavery, resulted in large-scale migrations around the world. Europeans and east Asians immigrated to the Americas, and south Indians moved into other British-controlled territories.

This rapidly transforming world also resulted in the creation of new forms of entertainment for the urban working-class, new literature and revolutionary new ideas, exhibitions, fairs and amusement parks, professional sports, as well as the first department stores with widely available consumer goods. Both English and Japanese women published novels, some of which were indictments of working class life. The rapid industrialization also created the need for new forms of job protection including unions and new ideas about the relationships between the social classes.

With industrialization came new imperialism and interactions. The arts and culture of Europe were influenced by contact with Asia and Africa, and new more modern forms developed. Meanwhile, the Japanese started to integrate Western styles into traditional art forms. The seemingly radical Impressionist period in nineteenth-century European painting was based on depictions of real life, while the modernist art movements included cubism, surrealism, and art nouveau.

New industrialization and imperialism also resulted in new reasons and new ways to make war. This period saw the development of automatic weapons, including the Maxim gun of the 1880s. The assembly line allowed for mass production of gasoline-powered automobiles and eventually the first tanks, which led to the massive destruction wrought on the battlefields of World War I.

VII. CHANGES AND CONTINUITIES IN THE ROLE OF WOMEN

With all the dramatic transformations that took place in the nineteenth century, this was actually a low point in terms of women's rights. Education, real wages, and professional opportunities continued to be mostly inaccessible; however, the new intellectual and economic opportunities available to men did open doors for women, and movements began throughout the world to rally for women's political and legal rights.

Although women continued to be heavily restricted with few freedoms, political and legal barriers for men based on class or racial categories were mostly eliminated. Yet women were not unaffected by the new Enlightenment ideals of freedom, equality and liberty, and the earliest feminist writers emerged in western Europe during this period. Both middle- and working-class women joined reform movements, labor unions, and socialist parties. Most important to these women was access to education which was still denied to the majority of them due to ideas of mental inferiority based on social Darwinism.

Although most Western countries opened university education to women, literacy rates in China and India—countries with long histories of secluding women—remained shockingly low well into the twentieth century. However, male literacy in these regions was also low, and despite Christian missionary schools, it was not in the interest of the imperial powers to have a well-educated colonial populace.

VIII. PULLING IT ALL TOGETHER

From 1750 to 1914, so much happened in so many different places that it's easy to get lost unless you focus on major developments and trends. We suggest that you try to link up many of the events and movements in a flowchart. Once you start, you'll be amazed at how much is interconnected.

We've put together a sample flowchart for you. You may choose to connect developments quite differently from the way we have—there's certainly more than one way to link events together. That said, take a look at the chart and use it to help you begin to make your own.

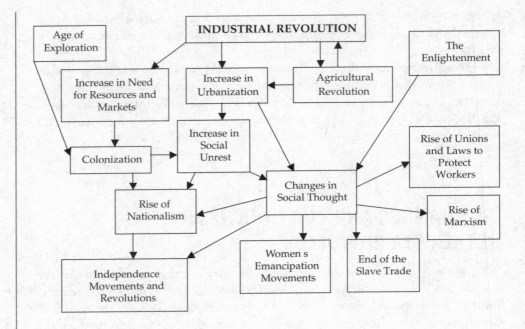

Of course, the chart above doesn't begin to address many of the developments covered in this chapter. To include everything would require an enormous chart. In addition, developments were complicated and not entirely sequential. For example, there were two big rounds of independence movements and revolutions because there were two rounds of colonialism. The first round occurred after the Age of Exploration when the United States and Latin America declared their independence. The second round occurred after the Industrial Revolution and led to a race for new colonies in Asia and Africa. Those independence movements didn't occur until after 1914, so they are not included this chapter.

Notice also that there are arrows going in both directions between the Agricultural Revolution and the Industrial Revolution—they each led to more of the other. The greater the food surplus, the more a country could industrialize. The more it industrialized, the more it developed efficient machines and tools that could be used to increase agricultural production.

The Growth of Nationalism: Me, Myself, and My Country

Nationalism was an enormous force on all continents during the time period covered in this chapter. Nationalism, broadly defined, is the desire of a people of a common cultural heritage to form an independent nation-state and/or empire that both represents and protects their shared cultural identity. It drove movements in Germany and Italy to unify. It drove movements in the Americas to declare independence. It drove resistance against European colonialism in India, China, and Africa, while it drove Europeans to compete with each other to promote national pride and wealth by establishing colonies in the first place. In China, it even drove peasant movements against the Manchu government, which was targeted for not representing the Han majority. It drove the French to unite behind Napoleon to attempt to take over Europe, and it drove the British to unite to try to take over the world. Nationalism drove the Japanese to quickly industrialize and the Egyptians to limit the power of the Ottomans.

In short, by 1914, the world had become one of strong identification with one's own nation, or with the dream of the creation of one's own nation. Even in the European colonies, and perhaps especially there, nationalism was growing. The oppressors used nationalist feelings to justify their superiority. The oppressed used nationalistic feelings to justify their rebellion.

The Complex Dynamics of Change: Enough to Make Your Head Spin

During the time period covered in this chapter, there were many forces of change. Exploration. Industrialization. Education. The continuing impact of the Enlightenment. The end of slavery. Military superiority. Nationalism. Imperialism. Racism. Capitalism. Marxism. It's mind-boggling.

What's more, these changes were communicated more quickly than ever before. Trains and ships raced across continents and seas. Telegraph cables were laid. By 1914, planes were in the air and telephones were ringing. Think about how much more quickly Japan industrialized than England. Think about how much more quickly Africa was colonized than Latin America. Increases in transportation and communication had far-reaching consequences.

Urbanization, too, fueled change. As people came in closer contact with each other, ideas spread more quickly. Like-minded people were able to associate with each other. Individuals had contact with a greater variety of people, and therefore were exposed to a greater variety of ideas. Increasingly, developments in the cities raced along at a faster pace than those in villages and on farms. In India, for example, British imperialism greatly impacted life in the cities. Indians learned to speak English and adopted European habits. In the countryside, however, Hindu and Muslim culture continued along largely uninterrupted.

Of course, most change—even "revolutionary" change—didn't entirely supplant everything that came before it. For example, the Scientific Revolution challenged some assertions made by Roman Catholicism, but both survived, and many people learned to be both scientific and Christian. Slavery was successfully outlawed, but that didn't mean that former slaves were suddenly welcomed as equals. Racism, both social and institutional, continued.

It's also important to keep in mind that individuals, even those who were the primary agents of change, acted and reacted based on multiple motives, which were sometimes at odds with each other. The United States declared its independence eloquently and convincingly, and then many of the signers went home to their slaves. Factory workers argued tirelessly for humane working conditions, but once achieved, happily processed raw materials stolen from distant lands where the interests of the natives were often entirely disregarded.

Change is indeed very complex, but it's also impossible to ignore. Life for virtually everyone on the globe was different in 1914 than in 1750. If you can describe how, you're well on your way to understanding the basics. If you can describe why, you're on your way to doing well on the exam.

Important Terms

Abolish
Absolute Monarch
Assembly Line
Balance of Power
Capital
Capitalism
Cartel
Commercial
Communism
Constitution
Corporation
Doctrine
Domestic
Emancipation
Enclosure
Enlightenment
Estates-General
Factory
Free Market
Free Trade
Immigration
Imperialism
Indemnity
Industrial Revolution
Laissez-Faire
Labor Union
Leisure
Marxism
Monopoly
Nationalism
Nation-State
Natural Resources
Revolution
Rural
Social Class

Social Darwinism
Socialism
Suffrage
Trade Union
Universal Suffrage
Urbanization
Utopia/Utopian
Wage Labor

People, Places, and Events

American Revolution
Assembly Line
Berlin Conference 1884
Bloody Sunday
Boer Wars (Africa 1899–1902)
Boxer Rebellions
British East India Company
Capitulations
Charles Darwin
Communist Manifesto
Congress of Vienna
Declaration of Independence
Declaration of the Rights of Man
The Diet of Japan
Emancipation of Serfs
Empress Cixi (China)
Frederich Engels
Execution of Louis XVI (France)
Miguel Hidalgo (Mexico)
Indian National Congress

Intolerable Acts
The Jewel in the Crown
Mahmut II (Ottoman)
Karl Marx
Maxim Guns
Meiji Restoration
Monroe Doctrine
Muhammad Ali (Egypt)
Muslim League
Napoleon Bonaparte
Open Door Policy
Opium Wars
Panama Canal
The Raj
Reign of Terror
Cecil Rhodes
Rudyard Kipling
Russification
Russo-Japanese War
Scramble for Africa
Sepoy Mutiny (1857)
Seven Years War (French and Indian)
Sino-Japanese War
Social Darwinism
Spanish American War
Spheres of Influence
Suez Canal
The State Duma of Russia
Steam Engine (James Watts)
Taiping Rebellion
Unequal Treaties
Otto von Bismarck
Wealth of Nations (Adam Smith)
"White Man's Burden"
Witte Industrialization Program
Young Turks Party

VIII. TIMELINE OF MAJOR DEVELOPMENTS 1750–1914

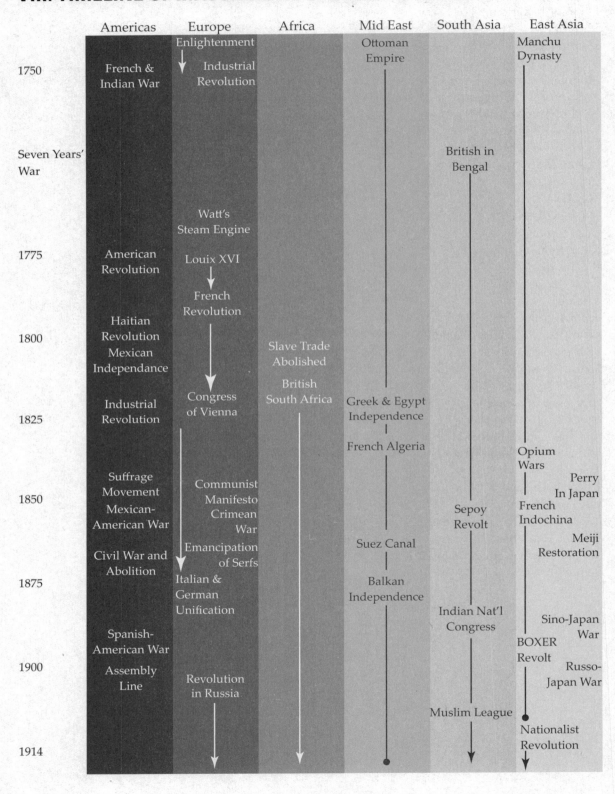

	Americas	Europe	Africa	Mid East	South Asia	East Asia
1750	French & Indian War	Enlightenment · Industrial Revolution		Ottoman Empire		Manchu Dynasty
Seven Years' War					British in Bengal	
		Watt's Steam Engine				
1775	American Revolution	Louix XVI · French Revolution				
1800	Haitian Revolution · Mexican Independance		Slave Trade Abolished · British South Africa			
1825	Industrial Revolution	Congress of Vienna		Greek & Egypt Independence · French Algeria		Opium Wars
1850	Suffrage Movement · Mexican-American War	Communist Manifesto · Crimean War · Emancipation of Serfs		Suez Canal	Sepoy Revolt	Perry In Japan · French Indochina · Meiji Restoration
1875	Civil War and Abolition	Italian & German Unification		Balkan Independence	Indian Nat'l Congress	Sino-Japan War
1900	Spanish-American War · Assembly Line	Revolution in Russia				BOXER Revolt · Russo-Japan War
1914					Muslim League	Nationalist Revolution

REFLECT ACTIVITY

Respond to the following questions:

- For which content topics discussed in this Chapter do you feel you have achieved sufficient mastery to answer multiple choice questions correctly?

- For which content topics discussed in this Chapter do you feel you have achieved sufficient mastery to discuss effectively in an essay?

- For which content topics discussed in this Chapter do you feel you need more work before you can answer multiple choice questions correctly?

- For which content topics discussed in this Chapter do you feel you need more work before you can discuss effectively in an essay?

- What parts of this Chapter are you going to re-review?

- Will you seek further help outside of this book (such as a teacher, tutor, or AP Central), on any of the content in this Chapter—and, if so, on what content?

Chapter 10
Recent Stuff:
Around 1914
to the Present

I. CHAPTER OVERVIEW

From 1914 onward, everything seemed to have global significance. Wars were called "world wars." Issues were thought of in terms of their worldwide impact, such as "global hunger" or "international terrorism." Organizations formed to co-ordinate international efforts, such as the United Nations. And economies and cultures continued to merge to such a degree that eventually millions of people communicated instantaneously on the World Wide Web, feeding a massive cultural shift known simply as "globalization."

It's a complex 100 years. We'll help you sort through it. Here's how we organized this chapter.

I.   Chapter Overview

You're reading it now.

II.   Stay Focused on the Big Picture

This section will help you think about and organize the huge number of global events that have occurred over the past century.

III.   The Twentieth Century in Chunks

This is the largest section of the chapter. In it, we plow through historical developments in four massive chunks. If you're totally clueless on any part of this section, you might consider also reviewing the corresponding topic in your textbook. As you can see from the section titles, and as you hopefully remember from your history class, there were a bunch of very significant wars in the twentieth century. As you study, worry more about the causes and consequences than about particular battles, although with regard to World War II, it's important to understand the general sequence of military and political events, so we've included quite a bit. Here's how we've organized the information.

   A.   The World War I Era
   B.   The World War II Era
   C.   Communism and the Cold War
   D.   Independence Movements and Developments in Asia and Africa
   E.   Globalization and the World Since 1980

IV.   Changes and Continuities in the Role of Women

Finally, equal rights (in some places).

V.   Pulling It All Together

Refocus on big-picture concepts after you review the specific developments in the previous two sections.

VI.   Timeline of Major Developments Since 1914

II. STAY FOCUSED ON THE BIG PICTURE

As always, connections, causation, and big-picture concepts are important. As you review the details of the twentieth-century developments in this chapter, stay focused on the big picture, and ask yourself some questions, including the following:

1. How do nationalism and self-determination impact global events? As you review, notice how nationalism impacts almost every country that is discussed in this chapter. It serves as both a positive force in uniting people, and a negative force in pitting people against one another. Self-determination is closely linked with nationalism because it is the goal of most nationalists.

2. Are world cultures converging? If so, how? There's plenty of evidence that world cultures are, in fact, converging, especially with regard to technology, popular culture, and the Internet. But on the other hand, there seems to be no shortage of nationalism or independence movements, which suggests that major differences exist. As you read the chapter, think about the forces that are making the cultures of the world converge and those that are keeping cultures separated.

3. How do increasing globalization, population growth, and resource use change the environment? Which resources are renewable and which are not? As the world grows ever more interconnected in trade and consumption of resources, think about what political, economic, and environmental decisions are made to maintain those trade relations.

III. THE TWENTIETH CENTURY IN CHUNKS

A. The World War I Era

By 1914, most of the world was either colonized by Europe, or was once colonized by Europe, so everyone around the world was connected to the instability on that small but powerful continent. Tragically, that meant that when European powers were at war with each other, the colonies were dragged into the fight. To be sure, European rivalries had had a global impact for centuries, particularly during the colonial period. The Seven Years' War in the eighteenth century between the French and British, for example, impacted their colonial holdings everywhere. France, too, jumped in to help the U.S. in its revolution against the British.

But in 1914, a major fight among European powers had a far more substantial and destructive effect. The Industrial Revolution had given Europe some powerful new weapons plus the ships and airplanes that could be used to deliver them. Large industrial cities had millions of people, creating the possibility of massive casualties in a single bombing raid. A rise in nationalism fed a military build-up and the desire to use it. And after the unifications of Germany and Italy, Europe simply had too many power-grabbing rivals. Not a good combination of factors if you like, well, peace.

Shifting Alliances: A Prewar Tally of European Countries

In the decades leading up to World War I, the European powers tried to keep the balance of power in check by forming alliances. The newly unified Germany quickly gained industrial might, but it was worried that France, its archenemy since the Franco-Prussian War in 1870, would seek revenge for its defeat. So, before he resigned from office, Otto von Bismarck created and negotiated the **Triple Alliance** among Germany, Austria-Hungary, and Italy in the 1880s. On the side, Bismarck also had a pact with Russia. Otto played to win.

Over the next few decades, the major players of Europe became so obsessed with a possible war that their generals were already putting plans into motion in the event of an outbreak. After William II ousted Bismarck from power in 1890, he ignored Russia and allowed previous agreements between the two countries to wither. With Russia now on the market for friends, France jumped at the chance to make an alliance. Because France is to the west and Russia is to the east of Germany, a Franco-Russo alliance helped keep Germany in check. Meanwhile, Germany's 1905 **Schlieffen Plan** called for a swift attack on France through Belgium, an officially neutral country that had a growing relationship with Britain. By 1907, Britain had also signed friendly agreements with France and Russia, creating what became known as the Triple Entente. Clearly, everyone was anticipating the possibility of war, which was a pretty safe bet considering the contentious climate.

Trouble in the Balkans: Europe in a Tizzy

Remember the Ottoman Empire? In the first two decades of the twentieth century, it was still around, but it was in such bad shape that Europeans were calling it the "sick man of Europe." It kept losing territory to its neighbors. After Greece won its independence in 1829, the Slavic areas to the north of Greece, including Romania, Bulgaria, Serbia, and Montenegro, began to win their independence as well. Bosnia and Herzegovina, however, were under the control of Austria-Hungary, as decided by the Berlin Conference of 1878, the same conference that led to the European scramble to colonize Africa. Serbia wanted Bosnia and Herzegovina for itself. To complicate matters, Russia was allied with Serbia, a fellow Slavic country.

It was in this political climate that **Archduke Franz Ferdinand** of Austria-Hungary visited Sarajevo, the capital of Bosnia, in 1914. While there, **Gavrilo Princip**, a Serbian nationalist, shot and killed the Archduke and his wife. In an age when Europe was so tightly wound in alliances, suspicion, and rivalry that a sneeze could have set off a war, the dominos quickly started to fall. Austria-Hungary declared war on Serbia. Russia, allied with Serbia, then declared war on Austria-Hungary. Because Russia and Austria-Hungary were on opposite sides of the Triple Entente–Triple Alliance divide, the pressure mounted on France, Italy, Germany, and Britain to join in. Britain was reluctant to honor its commitments at first, but when Germany implemented the Schlieffen Plan and stormed through Belgium toward France, Britain joined the fray in order to protect France. Italy, on the other hand, managed to wiggle out of its obligations and declared itself neutral, but the Ottoman Empire took its place, forming with Germany and Austria-Hungary an alliance called the **Central Powers**.

World War I: The War to End All Wars?

Europe on the Eve of World War I

Since the European powers had colonies or strong economic ties with most of the rest of the world, the original gunshot by a Serbian nationalist resulted in widespread casualties across the globe. More than 40 countries found themselves taking up arms, including Japan, which fought on the side of Britain, France, and Russia, now known as the Allies. In 1915, Italy managed to complete its about-face and joined the Allies as well.

The United States declared its neutrality at first, preferring to focus on its own internal affairs, a policy known as **isolationism**. But when a German submarine (wow, technology came a long way quickly) sank the British passenger liner *The Lusitania* in 1915, killing more than 100 Americans who happened to be on board, public opinion in the United States shifted away from isolationism. The next year, as Germany tried to cut off all shipments to Britain, thereby starving the island country, it attacked U.S. merchant ships en route to Britain, further fueling American sentiment toward war. Then the **Zimmermann telegram**—a secret message sent between German diplomats suggesting that Mexico might want to join forces with Germany and thereby regain the territory it had lost to the United States in the Mexican-American War of 1846—was intercepted by the United States. The public and President Wilson flipped out. On April 2, 1917, America entered the war on the side of the Allies. On November 11, 1918, after brutal battles, trench warfare, and enormous loss of life, Germany and the Central Powers finally gave up.

The consequences of the war were staggering. Eight-and-a-half million soldiers were killed. Around 20 million civilians perished. The social impact on the home front was substantial as well. Most governments took over industrial production during the war, while instituting price controls and rationing of products that were needed on the front lines. With huge numbers of men taking up arms, women moved into the factories to fill empty positions. This experience revved up the women's suffrage movement, and became the basis for a successful push by women in Britain and the United States to gain the vote after the war.

Of course, World War II hadn't happened yet, so no one referred to the war as World War I. Instead, most people called it the Great War, mistakenly thinking that there would never again be one as big or bloody. Indeed, the war was so horrendous that commentators called it "the war to end all wars."

The Treaty of Versailles: Make the Germans Cry

Signed in 1919, the **Treaty of Versailles** brought an official end to World War I. France and Britain wanted to cripple Germany economically, so that it could never again rise to power and threaten to invade other sovereign states of Europe. The resulting treaty was extremely punitive against Germany, which was required to pay war reparations, release territory, and downsize its military. It also divided Austria-Hungary into separate nations, and created other nations such as Czechoslovakia. The treaty was a departure from President Wilson's **Fourteen Points**, which was more focused on establishing future peace and a workable balance of power. However, Britain and France, for example, needed to justify the human and financial cost of the war and the duration of the war to their own demoralized populations and so found Wilson's proposal unacceptable. So the victors blamed the war on Germany and then forced Germany to sign an extremely punitive treaty over the objections of the United States. The victors hoped that as a result, Germany would never threaten the security of Europe again. Instead, the treaty greatly weakened Germany's economy and bred resentment among the German population, laying the groundwork for the later rise of nationalistic Adolf Hitler.

The League of Nations: Can't We All Just Get Along?

President Wilson was the voice of moderation at Versailles. He had hoped that the postwar treaties would be an opportunity to establish international laws and accepted standards of fairness in international conduct. His Fourteen Points speech addressed these issues and called for the creation of a joint council of nations called the **League of Nations**. The leaders at Versailles agreed with the idea in principle, and they set out to create the organization to preserve peace and establish humanitarian goals, but when they got around to actually joining the league, many nations refused to do so. England and France were tepid, while Germany and Russia initially scoffed at the idea (though later joined). Worse, the United States openly rejected it, a major embarrassment for President Wilson, who couldn't persuade the isolationist U.S. Congress that the league was a step toward lasting peace.

The Russian Revolution: Czar Out, Lenin In

The **Russian Revolution** occurred even before the war had ended. Russia entered the war with the world's largest army, though not the world's most powerful one, because the nation was not nearly as industrialized as its Western neighbors. Very quickly, the army began to suffer large-scale losses and found itself short on food, munitions, and good leadership. In February 1917, in the face of rising casualties and food shortages, **Czar Nicholas** was forced to abdicate his throne. The Romanov Dynasty came to an end. Under **Alexander Kerensky**, a provisional government was established. It was ineffectual, in part because it shared power with the local councils, called soviets, which represented the interests of workers, peasants, and soldiers. Although the provisional government affirmed natural rights (such as the equality of citizens and the principle of religious toleration—changes that were inconceivable under the czar), it wanted to continue war against Germany in the hope that Russia could then secure its borders and become a liberal democracy. But the working classes, represented by the soviets, were desperate to end the suffering from the war. The idealism of the provisional officials caused them to badly miscalculate the depths of hostility the Russian people felt for the czar's war.

By 1918, the soviets rallied behind the socialist party, now called the **Bolsheviks**. Amid this turmoil, **Vladimir Lenin**, the Marxist leader of the party, mobilized the support of the workers and soldiers. He issued his **April Theses**, which demanded peace, land for peasants, and power to the soviets. Within six months, the Bolsheviks took command of the government. Under his vision of mass socialization, Lenin rigidly set about nationalizing the assets and industries of Russia. In March 1918, the soviets signed an armistice with Germany, the **Treaty of Brest-Litovsk**, which ceded a huge piece of western Russia to Germany, so Russia dropped out of World War I. It therefore wasn't part of the negotiations during the Treaty of Versailles.

In the Baltic republics of what would soon be called the **Soviet Union**, and in the Ukraine, Siberia, and other parts of the former Russian Empire, counterrevolutionary revolts broke out. The Bolsheviks faced nonstop skirmishes between 1918 and 1921. To put down these struggles, the Bolsheviks created the **Red Army**, a military force under the command of **Leon Trotsky**. By 1918, the Red Army was a sizeable force, and with the support of the peasants, it defeated the counterrevolutionaries. But the counterrevolution had two lasting implications. First, the prolonged civil war deepened the distrust between the new Marxist state and its Western neighbors, who had supported the counterrevolutionaries. And second, the Bolsheviks now had a very powerful army, the Red Army, at its disposal.

Here Come the Turks: The Sick Man of Europe Is Put Out of His Misery

The Ottoman Empire, already on its last legs, made a fatal mistake by joining the losing Central Powers of World War I. In the peace negotiations, it lost most of its remaining land, and was therefore ripe for attack from the Greeks, who picked up arms in 1919. **Mustafa Kemal**, who later became known as **Ataturk**, "the Father of the Turks," led successful military campaigns against the Greeks, and then overthrew the Ottoman sultan. In 1923, Ataturk became the first president of modern Turkey. He successfully secularized the overwhelmingly Muslim nation, introduced Western-style dress and customs (abolishing the fez), changed the alphabet from Arabic to Latin, set up a parliamentary system (which he dominated), changed the legal code from Islamic to Western, and set Turkey on a path toward Europe as opposed to the Middle East. However, he instituted these reforms against opposition, and sometimes was ruthless in his determination to institute change.

B. The World War II Era

Even though World War II didn't get started until 1939, its causes were already well underway in the 1920s. In some ways, World War II isn't a separate war from World War I, but instead the Great War Part II.

Stalin: The Soviet Union Goes Totalitarian

Once the Soviets removed themselves from World War I, they concentrated on their own domestic problems. Lenin first instituted the **New Economic Policy (NEP)** in the early 1920s, which had some capitalistic aspects, such as allowing farmers to sell portions of their grain for their own profit. The plan was successful in agriculture, but Lenin didn't live long enough to chaperone its expansion into other parts of the Soviet economy. When Lenin died, the leadership of the Communist Party shifted to **Joseph Stalin**.

Stalin believed the NEP was ridiculously slow, so he discarded it. Instead, he imposed his **Five Year Plans**, which called for expedient agricultural production by ruthlessly taking over private farms and combining them into state-owned enterprises, a process known as **collectivization**. The plans also advocated for the construction of large, nationalized factories. This process was achieved in the name of communism, but it was really totalitarianism. The people didn't share in the power or the profits, and had no choices regarding participation. Untold numbers died fighting to protect their farms. Even more died in famines that resulted when Stalin usurped crops to feed government workers at the expense of the farmers themselves.

Stalin's plans successfully industrialized the **USSR** (Union of Soviet Socialist Republics), the formal name for the Soviet Union, and improved economic conditions for the country as a whole, but Stalin relied on terror tactics, such as a secret police force, bogus trials, and assassinations. These murders peaked between 1936 and 1938. Collectively, they are sometimes referred to as the "Great Purge" because the government systematically killed so many of its enemies. Stalin also established labor camps to punish anyone who opposed him. It's hard to know for sure how many Soviet citizens were imprisoned or killed during the 1930s, especially because so many died of famines during the collectivization process, but historians agree that millions of Soviets were slaughtered under Stalin's direction.

The Great Depression: Capitalism Crashes, Germany Burns

World War I was shockingly expensive. Countries spent more than $180 billion on armaments, boats, and trench warfare. Europe spent an additional $150 billion rebuilding. The massive scale of the war meant massive spending, at a level that nations had never experienced previously, and in the years following World War I, capitalism financed most of the recovery. As a consequence, the financial headquarters of the world shifted from London to New York, which had become a major center of credit to Europe during and after the war. In other words, Americans lent Europeans money, and lots of it.

In particular, the economies of two countries relied on American credit: France and Germany. France had loaned huge sums of money to Russia, its prewar ally, but the Bolshevik government refused to honor the czar's debts, leaving France almost out of luck, except that Germany owed it a bunch of cash as well. Germany experienced extreme financial hardship because of the wartime reparations they were required to make under the Treaty of Versailles. Germany's answer was to use American credit to pay its reparations by issuing I.O.U.s to countries like France. France took these "payments," backed up by American credit, and spent them on rebuilding its economy. From 1924 to 1929, this arrangement looked great on paper due to growth in both the United States and European economies. But in many ways, the growth was artificial, based on loans that were never going to be repaid.

When the U.S. stock market crashed in October 1929, a spiral of monetary and fiscal problems called the **Great Depression** quickly escalated into an international catastrophe, and shattered the illusion of financial health in Europe. American banks immediately stopped extending credit. The effect was that Europe ran out of money, which it never really had in the first place. Germany couldn't pay its reparations without American credit, so France had no money either.

The depths of the depression were truly staggering. The United States and Germany were hit hardest. In both countries, almost one-third of the available workforce was unemployed. In the United States, out-of-work Americans rejected the dominant political party and in 1932 elected **Franklin Roosevelt** as president in a landslide election. But other countries had much more fragile political structures. In places where democracy had shallow roots, such as Germany and Italy, whose shaky elective assemblies had been created only a decade earlier after World War I, the crisis resulted in the triumph of a political ideology that was anathema (look it up!) to the very spirit of democracy—fascism.

Fascism Gains Momentum

Between the First and Second World Wars, fascist parties emerged across Europe. They did not possess identical sets of beliefs, but they held a few important ideas in common. The main idea of **fascism** was to destroy the will of the individual in favor of "the people." Fascists wanted a unified society (as did the communists), but they weren't concerned with eliminating private property or class distinctions (the principal aim of communists). Instead, fascists pushed for another identity, one rooted in extreme nationalism, which often relied on racial identity.

Fascism is a subset of totalitarianism. A totalitarian dictator rules absolutely, attempting to control every aspect of life. Fascist rulers are a particular kind of totalitarian ruler, often regarded as extremely right-wing because they rely on traditional institutions and social distinctions to enforce their rule, and are extremely nationalistic. Their particular brand of nationalism is often based on racism. Communist totalitarian leaders like Stalin are often referred to as extreme left-wing because they seek to destroy traditional institutions and class distinctions, even as they retain absolute power themselves. Therefore, they're not referred to as fascist, but they're just as militaristic and controlling. Put another way, in their extreme forms, right-wing (fascist) and left-wing (communist) governments use the same tactics: totalitarianism. In both cases, all power rests in the hands of a single militaristic leader.

Fascism in Italy: Another Step toward Another War

Italy was the first state to have a fascist government. The founder and leader was **Benito Mussolini**, who created the National Fascist Party in 1919. The Party paid squads, known as **Blackshirts**, to fight socialist and communist organizations, an action that won over the loyalty of both factory owners and landowners. By 1921, the party seated its first members in the Italian parliament.

Although the fascists held only a few seats in the legislature, Mussolini demanded that King Victor Emmanuel III name him and several other fascists to cabinet posts. To rally support, Mussolini organized his paramilitary thugs to march to Rome and possibly attempt to seize power. If the king had declared martial law and brought in the army, most believe that the fascists would have scattered. However, the king was a timid man—facing economically troubling times—who was not unsympathetic to the fascist program. So, he named Mussolini prime minister, and the fascist march on Rome turned into a celebration.

As the postwar economy failed to improve, Italy was demoralized. Mussolini faced very little opposition to his consolidation of political power. He dabbled as a parliamentary leader for several months before completely taking over Parliament in 1922. He then implemented a number of constitutional changes to ensure that democracy no longer limited his actions, and, by 1926, Italy was transformed into a totalitarian fascist regime. To rally the people in a nationalistic cause, Italy started to focus on expansion, specifically in North Africa.

The Rise of Hitler

Immediately following the end of World War I, a revolt occurred in Germany when the emperor abdicated. Germany might well have become socialist at this point. Workers' and soldiers' councils (not unlike Russian soviets) formed in cities like Berlin. Yet, because the middle class in Germany was quite conservative and a large number of Germans had been relatively prosperous before the war, a socialist or communist system was rejected in favor of a fairly conservative democratic republic, called the **Weimar Republic**.

At the same time, Germany was in economic crisis, and Mussolini's success influenced Germany in many ways. The **National Socialist Party (Nazis)** rose to power in the 1920s, ushered in by the worldwide depression. As Germany's economy collapsed under the harsh reparations dictated by the Treaty of Versailles and the faltering world economy, German people increasingly rejected the solutions of the Weimar Republic's elected body, the **Reichstag**.

During this period **Adolf Hitler** rose to power as head of the Nazi Party. Like Mussolini's fascism, Hitler's Nazism inspired extreme nationalism and the dreams of renewed greatness for a depressed and divided country. But Hitler's philosophies differed from Mussolini's in their emphasis on the superiority of one race over others. Well versed in social Darwinism, Hitler was convinced that the Aryan race was the most highly evolved race, and that inferior races, such as Slavs and Jews, had "corrupted" the German race. He argued that Jews should be deported (later that changed to "eliminated") and that Germans should take over Europe.

The Nazi Party gained political power in the 1920s with Hitler as its guide, or fuhrer. At first, the Nazis received votes democratically and participated in the Reichstag. In the early 1930s, as the Great Depression devastated the German economy, Hitler received increasing support. In the election of 1930, the Nazi Party increased its seats in Parliament tenfold. By 1932, the Nazis dominated German government and many who disagreed with Hitler still backed him, thinking he was the country's only hope. In 1933, Hitler became chancellor, or leader of the Reichstag. He then seized control of the government, known under his fascist rule as the **Third Reich**, and set his eyes on conquering Europe.

> ### Contrast Them: Nationalism in Europe and Nationalism in Its Colonies
> Nationalism was a driving force throughout much of the nineteenth and twentieth centuries, but it had a very different flavor in Europe and Japan than in most European and Japanese colonies. In Europe and Japan, nationalism fueled extreme racism, fascism, and domination. National pride became almost synonymous with national expansion and conquest of other peoples. In the colonies, nationalism meant self-determination, the ability to free the nation from rule by another and determine one's own destiny. National pride meant national sovereignty, not colonial or territorial expansion.

Appeasement: "Peace for Our Time," or Just Wishful Thinking?

Rhineland

Europe on the Brink of World War II

In 1933, Hitler began to rebuild the German military. This was a clear violation of the Treaty of Versailles—which was specifically intended to limit future German aggression—but the other nations of Europe, especially Britain and France, chose not to object, fearing another war. Later that year, Germany again snubbed world opinion by withdrawing from the League of Nations.

Meanwhile, Spain, which had established a parliamentary democracy in 1931, was falling apart following the fall of the Spanish monarchy. In the summer of 1936, a group of army officers under the leadership of General **Francisco Franco** took control of large parts of Spain. Democratic loyalists organized to defend the state, and a brutal and divisive civil war ensued. Germany and Italy supported Franco's troops, called "nationalists." Although Franco was not a fascist, the Germans and Italians believed that the defeat of democracy in Spain was a step in the right direction.

France and Great Britain, still scarred from the loss of life and money in the Great War, adopted a nonintervention policy and refused to aid the supporters of the Spanish democracy. By 1939, Franco's troops captured Madrid and installed a dictatorship in Spain that managed to stay neutral throughout the war that soon erupted in Europe. The message was clear: Germany and Italy were more than willing to exercise their influence and support antidemocratic uprisings.

Meanwhile back in Germany in 1935, Hitler continued his policy of restoring Germany to its former world-power status by taking back the **Rhineland**, a region west of the Rhine River that had been taken away from Germany after World War I. Still, the rest of Europe stayed quiet. In 1937, he formed an alliance with the increasingly militant Japan. Then, in 1938, he annexed Austria and moved to reclaim the Sudetenland from Czechoslovakia. At the **Munich Conference of 1938**, which included Hitler, Mussolini, and Prime Minister **Neville Chamberlain** of England, Hitler was given the Sudetenland, without the consent of Czechoslovakia, in return for the promise to cease his expansionist activities. This incredibly optimistic (some would say stupid) policy is known as **appeasement**. Chamberlain agreed to give Hitler what he wanted as a means of avoiding war, believing German claims that it would be satisfied with Austria and the northern half of Czechoslovakia and would not expand further. And Hitler, in fact, did stop his expansion—for one whole year. In 1939, Hitler invaded the remaining territories in Czechoslovakia.

The rest of Europe was shocked, but they didn't do anything to kick the Nazis out of Czechoslovakia. Instead, in March 1939, while Italy was invading Albania, Britain and France signed a non-aggression pact with Greece, Turkey, Romania, and Poland that provided that if any one of them were attacked, they'd all go to war.

Meanwhile, the Germans signed the **Nazi-Soviet Pact** in August of 1939. Stalin and Hitler agreed that Germany would not invade the Soviet Union if the Soviets stayed out of Germany's military affairs. Furthermore, the countries determined how Eastern Europe would be divided among them, giving Lithuania and eastern Poland to Germany and the remainder of Poland and Finland and the Baltic States to Russia. So Stalin got a measure of security, and Hitler got a clear path by which to take Poland. With a secure agreement with the Soviet Union, German forces marched into Poland. Two days later, Britain realized that all diplomacy had failed and declared war on Germany, and France reluctantly followed suit. World War II had begun.

Need to Read About Some More Aggression? How About Japan?

You should remember that after the Meiji Restoration in Japan, the country kicked out the Europeans and started industrializing quickly. You should also remember that by 1905, they had already defeated the Chinese and the Russians in wars for territory in and around Korea.

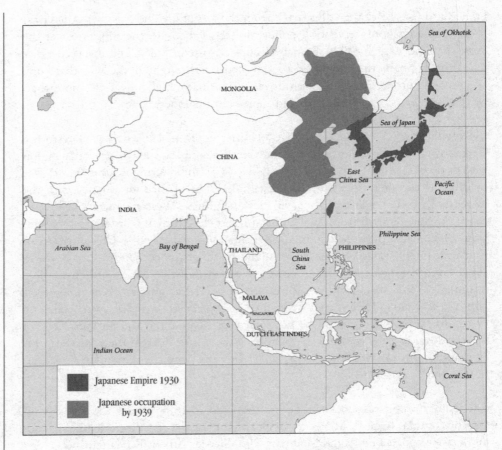

Japanese Territory by 1939

After World War I, in which Japan fought on the side of the Allies and was therefore one of the victors, Japan's economy and military really started to thrive. In 1915, during World War I, Japan sent a list of twenty-one demands to China, requiring China to give it trading rights and outright control over aspects of the government and economy, an act that was even more aggressive than some of the spheres of influence that had been established (and were still in effect) by the Europeans. In the 1920s, the country backtracked a little bit and focused on internal developments, softening its position toward China. But by 1930, the Great Depression began to severely affect Japan and the Japanese militarists gained momentum, claiming that an empire would pull them out of the economic doldrums. In 1931, Japan invaded Manchuria, renaming it **Manchukuo** and establishing a colony there. After withdrawing from the League of Nations, Japan signed the **Anti-Comintern Pact** (against communism, specifically in Russia) with Germany in 1936, thereby forming the beginnings of an alliance that would eventually lead to a more formal one during World War II. In 1937, Japanese troops invaded China, pillaging towns and cities as they made their way down the eastern shore. One of the worst offenses was the aptly named, "Rape of Nanjing," where in the city of Nanjing nearly 250,000 Chinese were slaughtered in a matter of a few weeks by occupying Japanese forces. Japan's war with China eventually merged into the global conflagration of World War II that later started to burn in Europe.

A Quick Review of World War II: Tens of Millions Dead

Hitler's forces were devastating. Their war tactic, known as **blitzkrieg** (literally "lightning war"), destroyed everything in its path with historically unprecedented speed. Poland's flat open plains were tragically well-suited for the German run. The swiftly moving German forces acquired so much territory in the west of Poland that Stalin was forced to mobilize quickly lest he lose the entire country to the German Reich. Within ten days, Germany and Russia had divided Poland between them. Hitler then focused on the western front. In early 1940, Germany assaulted Holland and Belgium. Two days later, German forces entered France. Within a year, the Axis power controlled most of continental Europe.

Hitler assumed that Great Britain would crumble quickly after the fall of its ally, France. But a new leader, **Winston Churchill**, replaced Britain's more diplomatically minded Chamberlain. Churchill proved to be a resolute and fierce prime minister. He refused to cut a deal with Germany, so Hitler launched a massive air bombing campaign in 1940 known as the **Battle of Britain**, which pitted the superior numbers of the German air force against the smaller numbers of the Royal Air Force. The British succeeded in keeping the German army out, and with their newly devised handy tool known as radar, they managed a successful, though costly, defense of the island.

In the meantime, Italy attacked Greece but was unable to defeat the country until April 1941, when German armies rushed in to help out. The Nazi-Soviet Pact tacitly gave the Balkan state to Russia, so the takeover of Greece had serious consequences. Now that Germany had taken control of the Balkans, their previous agreement was moot, so they invaded the Soviet Union too for good measure, advancing quickly. The resulting movement of men and supplies into the Soviet Union relieved pressure on the desperate British, the only Allied nation still fighting (other than the Soviet Union, of course).

Meanwhile in the Pacific, Japan continued its expansion in China and invaded Indochina (Vietnam). For trade reasons, the United States viewed this action as hostile, but the United States still didn't want to get involved in the war, so it froze Japanese assets in the United States and imposed sanctions instead. At the same time, Japan entered into the **Tripartite Pact** with Rome and Berlin, ensuring worldwide implications for a war that had, up until that time, been two regional wars. Japan also made war plans against the United States if the United States refused to lift sanctions against Japan. The United States didn't, and on December 7, 1941, the Japanese bombed a U.S. naval station in Hawaii at **Pearl Harbor**. The United States was stunned, and promptly declared war against Japan, and in response, Germany declared war against the United States.

It took a while for the United States and Great Britain to coordinate a land attack against Germany because they needed a foothold in Europe from which to begin their assault. In the meantime, the Allies fought the Japanese in the Pacific and Germans and Italians in Africa while the United States also secretly worked on its **Manhattan Project**—the development of an atomic bomb. By 1943, the United States and Britain were ready for their European offensive, and they started it by taking control of Italy. The next year, English, American, and Canadian forces launched their biggest offensive, landing on the French beaches of Normandy on June 6, 1944, which is now known as **D-day**. With the help of French resistance forces, Allied Forces battled their way across northern France in the summer of 1944 and liberated France.

On the opposite side of Europe, the Red Army won a stunning victory against the Germans at Stalingrad in 1942 and advanced steadily west for three years. By May 1945, the Allied forces closed in on Hitler's troops from the eastern and the western fronts until they reached Berlin, ending the European theater of World War II. Hitler committed suicide.

The war in the Pacific continued to drag on for a few months. At great cost, the American forces defeated Japan from island to island in the South Pacific. But the Japanese refused to surrender, even though their fate was sealed. Believing that dropping an atomic bomb on Japan would end World War II quickly and result in fewer casualties than a prolonged war, **President Truman** of the United States ordered the dropping of an atomic bomb on the city of **Hiroshima** on August 6, 1945. The event marked the first time such a bomb had been used in warfare. The result was horrendous. More than 100,000 people were killed or injured and the city was completely leveled for miles. When the Japanese vowed to fight on, President Truman authorized the dropping of a second bomb on **Nagasaki** on August 9 with similar consequences. Japan finally surrendered and World War II was brought to a close.

The Consequences: So Much Changed!

The close of World War II brought with it enormous global changes. Since they are so numerous, it's best to think about them in broad categories.

The Holocaust Revealed

Outside of Germany, few knew just how horrible the Nazi regime was until after the war was over. In an ongoing slaughter known now as the Holocaust, but known in Nazi Germany as "The Final Solution," millions of Jews who lived in Germany and German-occupied lands were rounded up, blamed for every conceivable problem in society, and methodically killed in gas chambers and firing lines, their bodies disposed of in ovens and mass graves. As many as 6 million Jews were killed, making the Holocaust one of the largest acts of genocide in history (in addition, as many as 6 million Poles, Slavs, Gypsies, homosexuals, disabled people, and political dissidents were killed in the Holocaust). When the news of the atrocity spread after the war, public sympathy for the creation of Israel as a homeland for Jews rose sharply. More on that later.

The Peace Settlement

The United States and the Soviet Union became superpowers. Germany was occupied by the Allies—more on that later too. War crimes tribunals were established to prosecute and sentence Nazi officials. Japan was forced to demilitarize and establish a democracy. It did. It also embraced capitalism and became an economic powerhouse within a decade, but this time was friendly to the West.

Europe Torn to Shreds

In addition to a staggering loss of life (the Soviet Union alone lost more than 20 million soldiers and civilians), the infrastructure and communities of Europe were devastated. To help in the rebuilding effort, the United States instituted the **Marshall Plan** (named for George C. Marshall, the secretary of state who conceived of it) in 1947. The plan, in which billions of dollars of American money was made available for reconstruction, was offered to all European countries but only accepted by Western European nations. The plan worked: The economies of Western Europe recovered in less than a decade.

The Decline of Colonialism

European imperialism was already on the wane before World War II, but the war affected attitudes about empire, and inspired native populations to rise up against their oppressors. Much more on the decline of colonialism later in this chapter.

Big Changes for Women

Just as in World War I, in many countries, women worked outside the home during the war, raising money to support themselves or their families, while also helping the war effort. In Britain alone, more than three-fourths of adult women under age 40 were employed during the war. After the war, many women kept their jobs, or sought higher education, or otherwise began to broaden their horizons.

The Creation of International Organizations

After World War II, the Allies believed that a network of international organizations could reduce the probability that such a great war would break out again. The first of these international organizations was the **United Nations**, established in 1945 to replace the failed League of Nations. Given more muscle than the League of Nations, the primary goal of the UN was simple: to mediate, and if necessary to intervene in, international disputes between nations. As time passed, the UN expanded beyond the realm of political conflicts and increasingly involved itself in the monitoring of human rights and other social problems. But in addition to the UN, the World Bank, International Monetary Fund, and the General Agreement on Trade and Tariffs (now known as the World Trade Organization), were formed to create and manage a more integrated global economy. The Allies believed that countries that were more connected economically would be less likely to invade one another.

The Start of the Cold War

Although they were allies during the war, the United States and the Soviet Union had very different worldviews. One was democratic and capitalist, the other totalitarian and communist. Neither wanted the other to spread its influence beyond its borders, so even before the war ended, they were strategizing on how to contain each other. This strategizing lasted for nearly 50 years, and the following section in this chapter explains the consequences.

C. Communism and the Cold War

The Cold War in Europe

The **Cold War** lasted from 1945 through the early 1990s. Very few areas of the globe were unaffected. The two superpowers that emerged after World War II, the United States and the Soviet Union, not only vied for global domination, but also tried to pull the rest of the world into their standoff. Every time a government in any country across the globe changed hands, the Americans and Soviets evaluated it based on its leanings toward one side or the other, and in many cases actually tried to militarily influence the position it would take. All of this took place in the context of an arms race between the two superpowers in which nuclear arsenals became so massive that global holocaust became possible at the touch of a button.

In 1945, no one would have predicted how polarized the world would become during the Cold War, or even that a cold war would develop in the first place.

Power Grab:
Soviets and Americans Want Everyone to Take Sides

After Germany was defeated, the U.S.-Soviet struggle immediately influenced the chain of events. The biggest conflict was over future security. Both superpowers wanted arrangements in Europe that made it more likely for their worldview to dominate. The U.S. promoted capitalism and variations on democracy. The Soviet Union promoted communism, which, as practiced by the Soviets at the time, also meant totalitarianism. A good chunk of Western Europe was solidly in the American camp, but the bigger question was Germany and parts of Eastern Europe.

According to plans drawn up by the Allies during conferences at **Yalta** and **Potsdam**, in February and July 1945 respectively, Germany and other parts of Eastern Europe were divided into temporary "spheres of influence," each to be occupied and rebuilt by respective members of the Allied forces. Germany was divided into four regions, each under the influence of one of four Allies: France, Britain, the United States, and the Soviet Union. Determined to protect its borders and ideology, the Soviet Union demanded that its neighboring states, places like Poland, Czechoslovakia, Hungary, Romania, and Bulgaria, be under its influence as well. The United States wanted those nations to have free elections. The Soviet Union refused and simply set up puppet states in those countries. This was the first hint of the beginning of the Cold War.

Meanwhile, in Germany in 1948, the French, British, and American regions merged into one, forming a democratic West Germany, while the Soviet Union's region became East Germany. The capital, Berlin, was on the eastern side, and within that city, an eastern and western zone were created. The Soviets wanted all of Berlin to be within its control, so they cut off land access to Berlin from the west, an action known as the **Berlin Blockade**. The West retaliated by flying in food and fuel to the "trapped" western half of the city, an action known as the **Berlin Airlift**. Eventually, the Soviets relented and Berlin was divided in half. In 1961, the Soviets built a wall between the two halves, preventing East Berliners access to the West until the wall fell in 1989 (more on that later).

East versus West: Let's Point Our Weapons at Each Other

By the late 1940s, Europe was clearly divided into East and West, each under the influence of their respective superpowers.

East Germany, Poland, Czechoslovakia, Romania, and Hungary became part of the Eastern bloc, also called the **Soviet bloc** or Soviet satellites. Yugoslavia was communist as well, but established its own path, having testy relations with Moscow. Western Europe, including Britain, France, Italy, Belgium, the Netherlands, Norway, West Germany, and eventually Greece and Turkey, became part of the **Western bloc**.

Under the **Truman Doctrine** of 1947, the United States explicitly stated that it would aid countries threatened by communist takeovers. This policy is known as **containment**, as in "containing" your enemy. To this end, the Western bloc formed a military alliance of mutual defense called **NATO** (the North Atlantic Treaty Organization). In response, the Eastern bloc formed a military alliance known as the **Warsaw Pact**. For more than 40 years, the two alliances loaded their borders with weapons, first conventional, then nuclear, and dared the other to strike first. Churchill called the line between East and West the **Iron Curtain** because Western influence couldn't penetrate it and Easterners were rarely allowed to go to the Western bloc.

As for the rest of the world, the two superpowers quickly tried to influence developments to tip the balance of world power in their favor. Some countries allied with one side or the other (more on this later), but other countries, such as India, refused to take sides and sometimes accepted investment from both, a policy known as nonalignment.

Focus on: Nuclear Proliferation

Ever improving weapons technology was the force behind political strength in the twentieth century. This was true from the devastated battlefields of World War I to the hot spots and standoffs of the Cold War. Beginning with the atomic bombs dropped on Japan in 1945, the Eastern and Western superpowers raced to develop superior weapons and defensive technologies. Despite attempts to limit nuclear technology to just five powers (China, Russia, U.S.A., Great Britain, and France) through the **Nuclear Nonproliferation Treaty** (1968) and the watchdog **International Atomic Energy Agency or IAEA** (1957), weapons development continued even after the collapse of the Soviet Union. Israel, India, and Pakistan chose not to participate in the treaty and now each has some nuclear weapons capacity. North Korea has continued to develop nuclear material in violation of treaty terms and both Iraq and Iran have attempted to build uranium enrichment programs. Only South Africa has voluntarily dismantled its nuclear weapons program.

The Cold War affected different countries in different ways. On the next several pages, you'll review how it impacted China, Korea, Vietnam, Cuba, and Europe.

China: Communists Make Huge Gains

China changed a lot after the fall of the Manchu Dynasty in 1911. Under the leadership of **Sun Yat-sen**, who led the **Chinese Revolution of 1911**, China became more Westernized in an effort to gain power and boot out the Europeans and Japanese, who had established spheres of influence in the country. Sun Yat-sen promoted his **Three Principles of the People**—nationalism, socialism, and democracy. It was hoped that nationalism would unite the people against foreign interests and give them a Chinese identity, state capitalism, or industrialization financed by the government, was useful in order to improve economic productivity and efficiency while not necessarily redistributing wealth, something Sun did not agree with. Although he advocated for a democratic system, Sun Yat-sen established a political party, the **Kuomindang (or KMT)**, which was dedicated to his own goals.

Sun Yat-sen didn't live long enough to see his plans implemented. His successor, however, **Chiang Kai-shek**, established the KMT as the ruling party of China, but only for a while. Throughout the 1920s and 1930s, two forces wreaked havoc on Chiang's plans. The Japanese Empire invaded Manchuria and made an effort to take over all of China in the late 1930s. Meanwhile, the communists, allied with the Soviet Union, were building strength in northern China. The communists joined the KMT in its fight against the Japanese, but at the same time were bitter rivals of the Kuomindang in the struggle to control the future of China.

During World War II, the United States pumped money into the KMT's efforts against Japan, while the Soviets weren't as active in their support for the communists' efforts against Japan, partly because they were focused on Germany. As you know, Japan was defeated. As in Europe, after the war, the powers of democracy and communism clashed, and the KMT and communists continued to fight the Chinese Civil War for the next four years.

By 1949, the communists under **Mao Zedong** had rallied millions of peasants in northern China and swept southward toward the Kuomindang strongholds, driving the Kuomindang farther and farther south until they finally fled to the island of Taiwan, where they established the **Republic of China**. The impact for mainland China was enormous. It became the **People's Republic of China**, the largest communist nation in the world under the leadership of Mao Zedong. The two Chinas have been separate ever since, and both claim to be the "real" China. Taiwan eventually developed into an economic powerhouse, but it lost its credibility as the true China when the United Nations and eventually the United States recognized the People's Republic of China as China in 1973. Taiwan has rejected China's efforts toward reunification, but nevertheless the two nations have grown close together, especially as the economies of both nations have grown stronger and stronger.

Mao Zedong: His Own Way

After the success of the Communist Revolution in China in 1949, its leader, Mao Zedong, collectivized agriculture and industry, and instituted sweeping social reform using policies that were not unlike Stalin's five-year plans. Most of these plans were relatively successful, and China greatly increased its productivity, especially in the steel industry. By the late 1950s, Mao implemented his **Great Leap Forward**, in which huge communes were created as a way of catapulting the revolution toward its goal of a true Marxist state. In reality however, the local governments that ran the communes couldn't produce the ridiculously high agricultural quotas demanded by the central government. So they did what any fearful local government would—they lied about their production, leading to the starvation deaths of nearly 30 million Chinese people. By all accounts, it was more like a Great Stumble Backward. The successes of Mao's initiatives in the early 1950s were erased, and agriculture and industry failed to produce results. Part of the problem was that the Soviet Union, up until that time the only foreign supporter of China, pulled away and eventually withdrew its support. The Soviet Union not only wanted the world to become communist, but it wanted the world to be communist under its control. China wasn't following orders, so Soviet support for China cooled. The Sino-Soviet split left China on its own with its communal system in disarray.

Mao stepped back to focus on building the military—something that was essential if the country couldn't rely on Soviet support—while more moderate reformers tried to turn the country around. The progress was quick and substantial; elements of capitalism were introduced into the economy and, in 1964, China tested its first atomic bomb, adding to the global arms race that was quickly building around the world. Mao was unimpressed, however. A purist, Mao was upset that the country was straying from its communist path, and so, in 1966, he jumped back to the forefront of his government and promoted his most significant domestic policy, the **Cultural Revolution**. Mao's goal in the Cultural Revolution was to discourage anything approaching a privileged ruling class, as it existed in the West as well as among the Soviet communist elite. To accomplish this, Mao instituted reforms meant to erase all traces of a Western-influenced intelligentsia. Many universities were shut down for four years. The students and faculty, along with other "elites" including doctors, lawyers, and classically trained musicians, were sent to work on collective farms for "cultural retraining." In addition, many political dissidents were either imprisoned or killed. When the universities were reopened, the curriculum was reorganized to include only communist studies and vocational training. During this time, Mao's *Little Red Book*, a collection of his teachings on communism, became a popular symbol of the forced egalitarianism of the Cultural Revolution.

The whole plan failed miserably in advancing China economically or socially. By the early 1970s, China realized it needed to open itself up to Western ideas. In 1976, the new leadership under Deng Xiaoping quickly changed the education policy and began to focus on restructuring the economic policies.

Note the Change: Dynastic China to Communist China

For more than 2,000 years, Confucianism and a class structure dominated China. With the Communist Revolution, however, all traces of a class-based system were nearly erased. Traditional Chinese society valued large families, both because children were able to help on the farm and because Confucian philosophy gave identity to people based on their relationships—the parent/child relationship was one of the most important. When the communists took over, however, their program of collectivization made family farms obsolete. In addition, communists were not sympathetic to traditional values based on religious or philosophical beliefs that competed with the authority of the state. As the population of China continued to grow dramatically through the late twentieth century, the communists took a practical approach to the overpopulation problem and began a propaganda campaign aimed at the use of contraception and abortion. By the late 1980s, faced with ever-increasing population figures, the Chinese government instituted a one-child-per-family policy. Reactions to the policy were severe. Many refused to abide by the policy in the first place. Others followed the law, but some of them killed their firstborn female infants in the hope of getting a male child the second time around. Opposition became more widespread and the government relaxed its policy.

The equality demanded in a classless society resulted in considerable advances for women. Husbands and wives were treated equally, at least as far as the law was concerned. Women gained the right to divorce their husbands. They obtained property rights. They received equal pay for equal work and were encouraged to pursue professional and vocational careers.

China Looks West: Likes the Money, Not So Sure About the Freedom

More recently, China's economy has been transformed from a strict communist command economy to one that includes elements of free-market capitalism. Deng Xiaoping's government entered into joint ventures with foreign companies in which the profits and business decisions were shared. In addition, Deng allowed for limited business and property ownership to stimulate hard work and innovation. The reforms have been wildly successful. China's economy is expanding faster than most of the economies of the world and reforms continue to be introduced slowly, which gives the economy time to adjust to the changes. However, despite the economic reforms, the government continues to remain strictly communist in the political sense, and has frequently resisted government and social reforms. In 1989, one million demonstrators converged on Tiananmen Square, calling for democratic reform. In an event known as the **Tiananmen Square massacre**, the government sent troops and opened fire. Hundreds were killed. Today, while China continues to reform its economy and is rapidly becoming a major economic powerhouse, the possibility for democratic reforms is still unknown.

Division of Korea: The Cold War Turns Hot and Now Possibly Nuclear

Prior to World War II, Korea was invaded by Japan and annexed as part of the expanding Japanese Empire. After Japan was defeated in World War II, Korea was supposed to be re-established as an independent nation, but until stability could be achieved and elections held, it was occupied by the Soviet Union and the United States in two separate pieces—the Soviet Union north of the 38th parallel and the United States south of it. This was very much like the way that Germany was split, and, just like in Germany, the two superpowers couldn't agree on the terms of a united Korea.

In 1948, two separate governments were established—a Soviet-backed communist regime in North Korea and a U.S.-backed democracy in South Korea. Both superpowers withdrew their troops in 1949, but in 1950, North Korea attacked South Korea in an attempt to unite the two nations under a single communist government. The United Nations condemned the action and soon a multinational force, largely consisting of U.S. and British troops, went to the aid of the South Koreans. The UN forces made tremendous headway under **General MacArthur**, nearly reaching the Chinese border, but when it looked as if the North Koreans would be defeated, China entered the war on behalf of the communist North. The two sides battled it out along the 38th parallel, eventually leading to an armistice in 1953.

Today, the two nations remain separate and true to the political philosophies under which they were formed 50 years ago. The United States maintains a large military presence in South Korea, which has become an economic powerhouse. North Korea, meanwhile, has suffered through isolationist and just plain nutty rulers and massive food shortages, but has built up a huge military and acquired the technology to develop a nuclear bomb. It has already developed missiles capable of delivering those bombs to South Korea, Japan, China, or possibly even as far as the west coast of the United States. In October 2006, North Korea declared its first nuclear weapons test a success. Western scientists doubted their claims of success, but did confirm that some type of test had taken place. In response, the United Nations imposed additional, but largely symbolic, sanctions on North Korean imports (though China and Russia disagreed with the policy). Six Party Talks (including the U.S., North Korea, South Korea, China, Russia, and Japan) resumed, for the fifth time, and concluded with the agreement that North Korea was to shut down its reactor in July 2007 in return for extensive fuel aid. As of 2009, North Korea pulled out of the Six Party Talks for good, and has continued its nuclear enrichment program, and, as of February of 2013, has detonated three nuclear devices. The failure of the international community to reach a resolution on the Korean peninsula in the early 1950s has created a modern-day crisis of nuclear proportions. The secretive nature of the North Korean regime has made it harder for international observers to gauge the communist nation's intentions, an especially frightening prospect for foreign observers who feared the instability the transfer of power could bring when Kim Jong-Il passed away in December of 2011. However, their fears were not realized as his son Kim Jong-un seems to be pursuing similar militaristic and aggressive policies towards the West as his father did.

Vietnam: The Cold War Turns Ugly

After World War II, the French tried to hold on to their colony of **Indochina**, but nationalists known as the **Vietminh** fought them back. By 1954, the Vietminh's guerilla warfare techniques succeeded in frustrating the French, and an accord was signed in Geneva dividing the nation—you guessed it—into two pieces. The communists, under the leadership of **Ho Chi Minh**, gained control of the land north of the 17th parallel while **Ngo Dihn Diem** became the president of the democratic south. Under its new constitution, North Vietnam supported reunification of Vietnam as a communist state. Ho Chi Minh supported communist guerrillas in the south, and soon war broke out. France and the United States came to the aid of South Vietnam. Ho Chi Minh prevented them from taking over the north, but not before years of fighting led to hundreds of thousands of deaths. As United States forces finally withdrew in 1975, North Vietnamese Army and communist **Viet Cong** fighters took control throughout South Vietnam. A peace agreement eventually led to the reunification of Vietnam as a communist state under the leadership of Ho Chi Minh. The long-range impact was significant for the region, the world, and the United States. The world witnessed the defeat of a superpower by a small but determined nation. Communism took a major step forward in the region. And for the United States, the defeat affected foreign policy for decades, as the American public remained fearful of involving itself in "another Vietnam."

Contrast Them: High-Tech Warfare and Guerilla Warfare

High-tech warfare, such as fighter jets, missiles, and tanks, are not only sophisticated and effective, but also costly and logistically complicated. Generally, nations that have mastered high-tech warfare, like the United States, take months to position their weaponry and put together a war plan. Once implemented, high-tech warfare can be devastatingly efficient. Guerilla warfare, on the other hand, is behind the scenes, stealthy, and much lower tech. Individuals or small groups fight site-to-site, disrupting their enemies' supply chains, or targeting seemingly random sites with small bombs and munitions. Each individual attack is generally less deadly, but since the attacks are flexible, random, and hard to predict, they can be very effective against a cumbersome, less flexible, high-tech opponent.

The Cuban Revolution:
Communism on the American Doorstep

After Cuba won its independence from Spain during the Spanish-American War of 1898, the United States remained involved in Cuban affairs under the terms of the **Platt Amendment**, which also provided for the presence of U.S. military bases. During the following decades, the Americans invested heavily in Cuban businesses and plantations, but those investments generally only made the wealthy very rich with little or no benefit for the masses of peasants. From 1939 to 1959, the United States supported the **Batista Dictatorship** in Cuba, which continued the policies that benefited the wealthy landowners. In 1956, the peasants began a revolt under the leadership of **Fidel Castro**. Even the United States eventually withdrew its support of Fulgencio Batista. Using guerilla warfare techniques, the revolutionaries made tremendous advances, and by 1959, Batista fled. The **Cuban Revolution** was hailed as a great success against a dictator.

But then, Castro, the great promoter of democracy, took control of the government, suspended plans for an election, and established a communist dictatorship. By 1961, he had seized the industries and nationalized them, and executed his rivals. The United States, concerned about the communist dictatorship on its borders, freaked, especially when Castro established strong ties with the Soviet Union after the United States imposed an economic embargo on Cuba. In an attempt to overthrow Castro, the United States trained and supported a group of anti-Castro Cuban exiles living in the United States. The U.S. was convinced that an invasion by these exiles would lead to a popular revolt against Castro. But it didn't work out that way. In 1961, **President Kennedy** authorized the **Bay of Pigs Invasion**, not with the full force of the mighty U.S. military, but with the small force of Cuban exiles, who were quickly captured after they landed, their revolt over before it began.

After the Bay of Pigs debacle, Cuba and the Soviet Union realized the United States might try something bigger next time around, so they mobilized. In 1962, U.S. spy planes detected the installation of Soviet missiles in Cuba, and Kennedy immediately established a naval blockade around the island, refusing to allow any more shipments from the Soviet Union. Kennedy made it clear to the world that if missiles were launched from Cuba, the United States would retaliate against the Soviet Union itself. The standoff became known as the **Cuban Missile Crisis**. For three months the world waited to see who would back down, and on October 28, the Soviets said that they would remove the missiles in exchange for a promise from the Americans that they would not invade Cuba. The Americans agreed to the settlement. This was the closest brush the world has had with full-out nuclear war.

When the Soviet Union collapsed in the early 1990s, the Cubans lost their main financial backer. This was a huge loss because it amounted to billions of dollars of aid. Still, Castro managed to hang on to his power, but economic conditions in Cuba deteriorated sharply after the fall of communism in Europe. From 2006 to 2011, Fidel Castro transferred his powers and responsibilities to his younger brother, Raúl, in stages, handing over first the presidency and then his position as First

Secretary of the Communist Party of Cuba, which he had held since 1965. The elder Castro stepped down due to illness but has periodically resurfaced in videos demonstrating his continued presence as a political force in his brother's regime.

Conflicts with "Good Neighbors:" Cold War Tensions and Democratization in Latin America

Despite independence movements, democratic elections, and developing economies, the United States maintained a heavy hand in Latin America whenever possible (remember the Roosevelt Corollary to the Monroe Doctrine?). But some of this was also the product of Cold War tensions. Marxism's anti-capitalist message had great appeal in less-developed countries and increased as U.S. investment in copper-mining and oil-drilling in the region intensified in the 1920s. Radical political parties developed in Mexico, Peru, Venezuela, Brazil, and much of Central America as complaints about imperial policies of the "**Good Neighbor**" to the north increased. As the U.S. confronted two world wars and the Great Depression, however, and Latin America became less of a priority, the region's nations took the opportunity to explore alternative paths to economic development. These took various forms: the stability of single-party rule (Mexico's **PRI**), the brutality of militaristic leaders (Argentina's Juan Peron) or the development of socialist democracies (Nicaragua and Guatemala). It was the latter that garnered the most attention from the United States—still in the midst of an ideological war with the Soviet Union—resulting in U.S.-backed coups, the use of Nicaragua as a staging ground for the Bays of Pigs invasion, and the targeting of the **Sandinista** guerillas in Nicaragua and El Salvador during the 1980s.

Perhaps the biggest issues Latin America continues to face are their **export economies**. Reliance on products such as coffee, fruit, sugar, and oil has resulted in weak domestic economies and tremendous debt. So while there is a long history of democracy throughout the region, the lag in economic development, increasing debt payments from loans dating back to 1970s and 1980s, and out-migration continue to challenge the region. However, in the first years of the twenty-first century, there has been tremendous growth throughout Latin America. Some is based on rising oil prices, but much can also be attributed to the development of new industries and trade agreements, both within Latin America and with the U.S. and Canada. Both Chile and Brazil are among the fastest-growing economies in the world.

Democracy has also taken interesting turns in Mexico and Venezuela in the last decade. The year 2000 was the first time a true multi-party election was held in Mexico since the formation of the state under the 1917 Constitution. The opposition, **PAN** or **National Action Party** candidate won the presidency. Mexico had a second national election with an opposition slate in 2006 and again, the PAN candidate won, though the PRI won the most recent election in 2012. Venezuela, on the other hand, has amended its constitution to allow its Socialist president Hugo Chavez a third term as the country has nationalized a number of industries including telephone and steel.

Europe: The Cold War Finally Ends

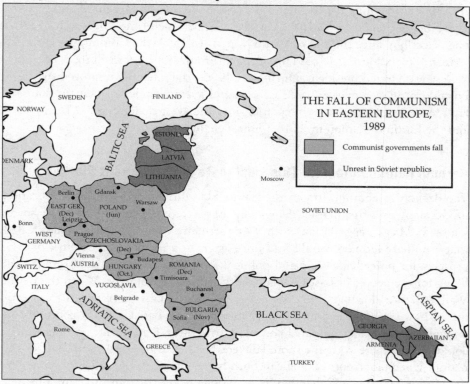

The Fall of Communism in Eastern Europe

During the Cold War, the standard of living in Western Europe improved dramatically, despite economic swings. In Eastern Europe, behind the iron curtain, the massive state-run industries couldn't keep up with the innovations in the West. A growing divide between the "rich" West and the "poor" East was becoming obvious, and as it became obvious to the people who lived within the Eastern bloc, they began to revolt.

The revolt was as much about democracy and self-determination as it was about the economy. The Soviet Union was a huge patchwork of many different nationalities, many of which wanted to control their own destinies. What's more, an increasing number of people in the Eastern bloc countries that were controlled by the Soviet Union, such as Poland, were also itching for democratic and economic reform. By the 1980s, groups of reform-minded individuals began scratching that itch.

Poland: Solidarity Grows in Popularity

The decline of communism brought sweeping reform to Poland and its government, which had been trying for years to prevent the spread of anticommunist sentiment. In 1980, more than a decade before the fall of communism in the Soviet Union, a group of workers began the Solidarity movement under the leadership of Lech Walesa. Thousands of workers joined a strike for reform of the communist economic system. The government reacted by imposing martial law and arresting

Lech Walesa, as well as other Solidarity leaders. Throughout the early- and mid-1980s, the government tried to suppress Solidarity. But in 1988, the reform-minded Rakowski became the Premier of Poland. Solidarity was legalized and in 1989, a member of Solidarity, **Tadeusz Mazowiecki**, became Prime Minister in the first open elections since the end of World War II. In 1990, the Communist Party fell apart in Poland, just as it was falling apart throughout Eastern Europe, and Lech Walesa was elected president. During the 1990s, the economy improved swiftly as Poland introduced market-based reforms and a new democratic constitution. Poland formally completed its integration into the West by joining NATO in 1999 and the European Union in 2004. Quite a change.

German Reunification: All This, Just to Be Back Where It Started

The decline of communism in the Soviet bloc directly led to the reunification of Germany as a free market democracy. East Germany cut ties with the Soviet Union and began negotiations with West Germany. Many Western nations feared that a united Germany would lead once again to a nationalistic regime, but the prospect for peace, economic and political reform, and an improved standard of living for the people of East Germany outweighed the concerns. When the Berlin Wall was torn down in 1989, signaling the fall of East Germany, a mass exodus of East Germans fled to the West. Businesses in East Germany continued to struggle because their outdated corporate structures, equipment, and machinery could not compete with the more efficient businesses in the western half of the nation. Unemployment was high in both halves of the newly united nation. Yet, the government did not abandon its ambitious reconstruction program aimed at the modernization of the former East Germany and the establishment of nationwide communication and transportation lines. Germany has therefore continued to press forward and has since emerged as a leading economy in Europe.

Just in case you haven't been keeping track, in the last 90 years Germany went from being crushed in World War I, to being built up under fascist Nazis, to being crushed in World War II, to being occupied by four former enemies, to being divided in two, to being at the epicenter of the Cold War, to being reunified as a modern, capitalist-leaning, democratic nation. That's some pretty extreme historical whiplash!

The Soviet Union Collapses: Glasnost, Perestroika, Kaput

When **Mikhail Gorbachev** came to power in the Soviet Union in 1985, he instituted policies of *glasnost* (openness) and urged a *perestroika* (restructuring) of the Soviet economy. He may not have realized it at the time, but he set in motion a tidal wave of change that he wouldn't be able to reverse. Legislation was passed to add elements of private enterprise to the economy. Nuclear arms treaties were signed with the United States. Gorbachev publicly and officially denounced the Great Purge, a huge deal because it showed that the Soviet Union was re-evaluating itself. The list of reforms and changes goes on and on, but the bottom line is that within six years, Poland and other former Soviet satellites declared their separation from the USSR. The Soviet Union itself disintegrated in 1991. Russia became its own country again, while the other parts of the old Soviet Empire, such as the Ukraine, Belarus, and Georgia, became independent nations.

Some observers were shocked by the degree to which so many different nationalities within the former Soviet Union wanted to form their own countries, and further shocked that most of the shifts in power happened relatively peacefully. But there were exceptions. In the same region that sparked World War I 80 years prior—the Balkans—nationalistic movements within the former Yugoslavia led to "**ethnic cleansing**" in which Bosnian and Albanian Muslims were raped and slaughtered by Christian Serbians in what was simply the latest horrific chapter in a centuries-long regional and ethnic conflict. The violence eventually led to the involvement of UN troops during much of the 1990s. Even in Russia itself, nationalists in different regions, especially in Muslim-dominated **Chechnya**, want to break away, and have used guerilla warfare and terrorist methods to advance their cause.

During the 1990s, most of the new countries in the former Soviet bloc, especially those in Eastern Europe, created constitutional democracies with economic systems based on variations of capitalism. While the reform movements have been faster in some countries than in others, and while believers in communism make themselves heard and the transition from state-owned industries to privately owned industries has caused high unemployment and corruption in many countries, democracy seems to be taking a foothold in the region. Though much is uncertain about the future of the former Soviet bloc, a few things can be said for sure: by the end of 1991, the Cold War was over, the Warsaw Pact had disbanded, and the United States found itself as the world's only superpower.

Democracy and Authoritarian Rule in Russia (yes, it's Russia again!)

The new (old) country of Russia was (re)formed under a 1993 Constitution. Although, it had lost its Soviet satellite countries, this new Russian Federation was formidable in size, plentiful in natural resources, and full of corrupt Soviet bureaucrats looking to get rich under the new rules. On paper, the new Russia looks very much like a perfect **Federal** state with three branches, checks and balances and an independent court. But in reality, Russia's abrupt introduction to both democracy and capitalism resulted in a ten-year period of corruption, high-unemployment, deep poverty, wide-spread crime and a nostalgia for Soviet-style control and discipline. The challenge for Russia's first president, **Boris Yeltsin**, was to reform the structures of both state and society. This is an enormous task, requiring completely new systems of government and trade.

Yeltsin actually resigned in 1999 and for the next eight years, former **K.G.B.** agent **Vladimir Putin**, headed the Russian state. He was elected president twice, in 2000 and 2004, and was appointed Prime Minister in 2008 by the newly elected president Dmitry Medvedev. This new style of Russian democracy has been marked by corruption and an authoritarian strengthening of the executive branch, limits on opposition candidates, and a crackdown on a free press. In a move that alarmed international observers, Putin announced in 2011 that he would run for a third presidential term in 2012, stretching his leadership to 16 years (and perhaps beyond?). Despite some protests in Russia, Putin defeated several challengers in March 2012 to return to the presidency. Russia's twenty-first-century economic growth has been considerable, helped by the rising price of oil (sold at great profit to western Europe), but old habits die hard and conflicts with the U.S. continue over plans for expansion of NATO, the placement of missiles in eastern Europe, and the sale of technology to Iran.

Contrast Them: "West" and "East"

During the Cold War, the two terms were frequently used to describe much of the world, especially the northern hemisphere. The "West," led by the United States, was generally democratic, generally capitalist, and generally prosperous. The "East," led by the Soviet Union, was communist, generally totalitarian, and generally substantially less prosperous in terms of per capita standard of living. Japan, incidentally, was part of the "West," because after World War II it developed along pro-Western, capitalist, generally pro-democracy lines. After the fall of communism in most of the world in the early 1990s, the terms began to lose their relevance. A bipolar description no longer seemed to fit the complexities. The West grew dramatically, but should Russia be considered part of the "West"? Clearly, most of its former satellites wanted to be considered as such. What's more, China, still communist, is transforming its economy and possibly irrevocably opening up its doors to the world, a movement called "Westernizing" but so far not leading to democratic reforms. As for the "East," nobody's sure what that refers to any more. Today, a new, perhaps overly general division between the "Western World" and the "Islamic World" is being used to describe world relations.

D. Independence Movements and Developments in Asia and Africa

After World War II, a wave of independence movements marked the beginning of the end of European imperialism. In an era when the United States and Western Europe were fighting a Cold War in part to defend people's right to choose their own futures (self-determination) under democratic systems, it became difficult for Western colonial powers to reconcile their post-World War II principles with their imperialist policies. More importantly, it was increasingly difficult for the subjugated peoples to tolerate their treatment, so they rose up and demanded independence.

The Indian Subcontinent

After the **Indian National Congress**, a mostly Hindu political party, was established in 1885 to increase the rights of Indians under colonial rule, and then the **Muslim League** in 1906 to advance the causes of Islamic Indians, it took years for momentum to build into an organized resistance to colonial power. In 1919, the **Amritsar massacre** catapulted the movement.

In Amritsar, 319 Indians, some Hindu and some Muslim, were slaughtered by British General Dyer during a peaceful protest in a city park. They were protesting the arrest of two of their leaders who also were doing nothing other than protesting, were unarmed, and entirely surprised by the attack. Because the park was walled, there was no way to escape from the attackers. By all accounts, the slaughter was unprovoked and entirely unwarranted. When news of the massacre spread, Indians joined the self-rule cause by the millions. It was now a full-fledged movement.

During the 1920s, **Mohandas Gandhi** became the movement's most important voice and organized huge protests against colonial rule. Gandhi's philosophy of **passive resistance**, or civil disobedience, gained popular support in the struggle against British colonial rule. Instead of fighting with weapons, Gandhi's followers staged demonstrations and refused to assist the colonial governments. This included massive boycotts of British imperial goods as well as strikes, such as when hundreds of thousands of workers refused to act as labor for the British colonial government's salt factories. Gandhi's nonviolent teachings, and his success, became enormously influential. They also partly inspired the civil disobedience of the U.S. civil rights movements led by Dr. Martin Luther King Jr.

At the same time, there was an increase in violence between Hindus and Muslims. While both groups worked together peacefully against the British, radical members of each group found it hard to tolerate the other. This disturbed Gandhi, who was raised Hindu but yearned for mutual respect among people of both religions. In the late 1920s, Gandhi began to call for Indian unity above religious considerations. Instead, the Muslim League actively pushed for the creation of a Muslim nation, and even bounced around a name for their future country: Pakistan.

Independence Won: Nations Two

After World War II, Britain finally granted independence to the Indian subcontinent. The long and relatively nonviolent struggle for independence had finally paid off. The terrible irony was that once independence was granted, the real bloodshed began. Radical Hindus and Muslims started killing each other.

There were two schools of thought regarding the newly independent subcontinent. The first, promoted by Mohandas Gandhi and, at first, the British, called for the establishment of a united India where both Hindus and Muslims could practice their religions. The second was a movement by **Muhammad Ali Jinnah**, whose aim was to partition the subcontinent and form a separate Muslim nation in the northern region, where Islam had become the dominant religion. The British eventually were convinced that a partition would save lives by separating people who seemed intent on killing each other, so when the British turned over the reigns to new leaders of independent India in 1947, it separated the country into thirds: India in the south and Pakistan in two parts, one to the northwest of India (Pakistan) and the other to the east (East Pakistan, currently Bangladesh).

Both parts of Pakistan were Muslim, while India was predominately Hindu, although officially secular. The result was chaotic. Millions of people moved or were forced to flee due to religiously motivated violence. Essentially, India and Pakistan exchanged millions of citizens, with practitioners of each religion moving to the nation where their religion was dominant. Gandhi's worst nightmares were realized. Nearly half a million people were killed as they migrated to their respective "sides." The move of so many people along religious lines only served to create an international conflict between Pakistan and India. Within a year, Gandhi himself was assassinated by a Hindu who was upset with Gandhi's secular motivations. Today, the two nations are still fighting, especially in Kashmir along their borders, where religious self-determination still remains the big issue. What's more, both countries have since become nuclear powers, and 2008 saw a significant increase in terrorism between the two nations as Pakistan became less stable.

Africa

After World War II, African nations also began to assert their independence. They were partly inspired by events in India and the rest of the world, but they were also motivated by the war itself. Hundreds of thousands of Africans fought for their colonial powers during the war. Many of them felt that if they were willing to die for their governing countries, then they had earned the right to live free.

Other than South Africa, which had been independent before World War II, the nations north of the Sahara were the first colonies to win independence. These nations had strong Islamic ties, and the mostly Muslim Middle East had already won its freedom in the decades prior (more on that later). Egypt, too, had won its independence early, in 1922, although it kept extremely close ties to Britain. In the 1950s, as the independence movement gathered steam in Africa, **Gamal Nasser**, a general in the Egyptian army, overthrew the king and established a republic. He nationalized industries, including the Suez Canal, and then became embroiled in Middle Eastern conflicts. Nasser's actions emboldened other Islamic nationalists to seek independence, and soon the African nations along the Mediterranean were free.

South of the Sahara, independence was a trickier issue. The problem was that while nearly everyone wanted independence, most of the colonies had been raped of their resources. There had been little investment in human beings. The vast majority of Africans were uneducated, or only educated through grammar school. Unlike in India, where a substantial number of upper-caste Indians were highly educated and even attended universities in Britain, many African nations had few natives who were skilled professionals: doctors, scientists, lawyers, diplomats, businesspeople. This meant that once the colonial powers left, there would be few people left with the education and skills to immediately take charge and begin to build a productive, self-sufficient society.

As mentioned in the previous chapter, national unity among the natives was also hard to foster because the boundaries of so many African colonies had been drawn according to European needs, and took no account of African history or needs. Africans within the same colony spoke different native languages and had differing, sometimes opposing, customs, histories, and loyalties. For all of these reasons, even after attaining their hard-won independence, many African nations struggled to build strong, stable, independent countries.

Decolonization and nation building occurred in a variety of ways across Africa. The **Algerians** fought a bitter war for independence from France (1954–1962) while in the early 1960s Nigeria and **Ghana** negotiated their freedom into a Parliamentary governing style borrowed from England, but after a series of military coups, have adopted presidential systems. **Kenya**, under the leadership of Jomo Kenyatta, negotiated their constitution with Great Britain after a brutal crack-down engineered by coffee planters unwilling to lose such profitable property. Others, such as **Angola** and **Belgian Congo**, overthrew colonial governments, only to become embroiled in civil wars or in Cold War tensions. **Zimbabwe** was among the last to establish African majority rule in 1980 (see following section on South Africa).

Fifty-three of Africa's 54 nations belong to the **African Union**, a political and economic confederation formed in 2001 to replace the **Organization of African Unity** or **OAU**. But success and stability is not guaranteed for any of these nations. **Chad**, **Sudan**, **Uganda**, **Somalia**, and **Rwanda** (see on the next page) as well as the newly renamed **Democratic Republic of Congo** (former Zaire) have been wracked by on-going and devastating civil wars since the turn of the twenty-first century. Attempts to form stable democracies have been thwarted by a reversion to "big man" politics, corruption, military coups, and escalating debt payments (to IMF and World Bank—see Alphabet Soup later in chapter). Even relatively stable governments such as Kenya's have seen political violence escalate in recent years.

Economically, most of Africa is still rich in natural resources, albeit different ones than the colonial powers were interested in. Palm oil and rubber have given way to petroleum and metals including nickel, cadmium and lithium—prized for batteries to power cell phone, laptop computers, and hybrid cars. So the former colonial powers plus some new industrial players (China!) remain interested and invested in the nations of Africa.

Note the Change: Globalization and the Rise of NGOs

NGOs, or nongovernmental organizations, have become an ever-increasing presence in our modern world. NGOs are typically private, often nonprofit, agencies that provide relief services and/or advocacy for groups that are generally not serviced or represented by their governments. Some familiar examples of NGOs include the International Committee of the Red Cross (ICRC), Doctors Without Borders, Amnesty International, and even the American Civil Liberties Union. It is often NGOs that lead relief efforts following natural disasters and during wars, particularly to countries and people who cannot afford to pay for such efforts. Organizations such as the World Wildlife Fund provide advocacy for the world's animals, which of course do not have any representation in the world's governments. But why have most of these organizations formed only in the years since World War II? Well, the major international governmental organizations that formed after World War II, such as the UN and World Bank, were criticized for only representing the interests of the world's wealthier and more powerful nations (as they had been created by the victors of the war), and so many well-meaning individuals formed private companies to fill needs that were not being met by the world's governments. Globalization, which has increasingly made it easier to communicate and travel around the world, has not only made it easier for NGOs to provide their services on a global scale, but has also made it much easier for them to raise the money needed to fund their operations.

Rwanda: Ethnic Genocide

The difficulties of establishing stable nations in Africa are exemplified by the situation in Rwanda. Ethnic strife, genocide, and human rights violations in Rwanda stem from conflicts between two groups: the **Tutsi** (15 percent of the population in Rwanda) who governed the **Hutu** (85 percent of Rwanda) during German and Belgian colonial occupation. Belgian rule in particular exacerbated interethnic tensions, setting the stage for bloodshed as soon as colonial authorities withdrew. Upon Rwanda's independence in 1962, the Hutu revolted against the Tutsi leadership, leaving thousands dead and the two groups locked in bitter, bloody conflict. In 1973, a military coup by Juvenal Habyarimana unseated the government and eventually established a one-party republic in 1981. The military government worked to keep peace but encountered only modest success. That, too, was destroyed when Habyarimana's personal airplane was shot down over his presidential palace in 1994, assassinating the Hutu general. Almost immediately, conflict escalated, with the Hutu needing little encouragement to exact revenge on the Tutsi population whose leadership they blamed for the assassination. One hundred days of genocide left as many as 800,000 Tutsi dead, and by the following year more than 2 million mostly Hutu refugees were sent or fled to neighboring Zaire, where many died from disease. Because the entire country has only 7 million people, the genocide and displacement in Rwanda ranks among the most devastating in recent history.

Compare Them: Independence in Africa and India

Both India and Africa successfully gained independence in the years following World War II, and both areas were tragically torn apart by ethnic and religious strife shortly following independence. In India, the tensions between Hindus and Muslims, which existed before the British colonized the subcontinent, re-emerged as they departed. In many African nations, independence served only as an opportunity for long-held tribal hatreds to resurface in power struggles. The colonial powers, of course, were no better. They had been killing each other for thousands of years.

It is a mistake to think that the colonial powers assimilated the native peoples entirely or completely eradicated the underlying cultures. While there's no doubt they raped the colonies of their resources and in many cases ruthlessly subjugated the natives, they couldn't erase the native people's memories. Even after generations of colonial rule, Africans remembered old rivalries and hatreds and, in many cases, acted on them.

Developments in South Africa: The Rise and Fall of Apartheid

The year after the **South Africa Act** of 1909, the **Union of South Africa** was formed by combining two British colonies with two Dutch Boer republics, and although the British and Dutch colonists were given considerable rights to self-government, black people were entirely excluded from the political process. In 1923, residential segregation was established and enforced. In 1926, blacks were banned from work in certain skilled occupations that whites wanted for themselves. When South Africa won independence from Britain in 1931, the racial policies didn't improve. In fact, a system of **apartheid** ("separation of the races") was established in South Africa in 1948 as an all-encompassing way of dividing black (80 percent of the population) and white. By the late 1950s, apartheid was extended to the creation of homelands, areas of the country that were "set aside" for blacks. The homelands were in the worst part of the country, and comprised less than 15 percent of the nation's land. The whites were given the cities, the resource-rich mines, and the best farmland. While many blacks were compelled to move to the homelands, others stayed in the cities, where they were segregated into black slums. If this starts to sound like District 9 (2009), there's a reason a sci-fi movie about segregating aliens was set in South Africa.

In response, the black community organized. In the 1950s, **Nelson Mandela** became leader of the **African National Congress**, an organization determined to abolish apartheid. At first, he advocated peaceful protest, following the example of Gandhi. But in 1960, after the **Sharpeville massacre** in which 67 protesters were killed, the African National Congress supported guerrilla warfare. At Sharpeville, blacks were protesting a policy that forced them to carry passes to be in the cities in order to go to their jobs. The passes were issued at places of employment. This meant that if you worked and your wife didn't, you couldn't go into the city with her because she wouldn't have a pass. The massacre rallied the anti-apartheid movement. Mandela was arrested in 1964 for his role in anti-apartheid violence and sentenced to life imprisonment.

After decades of increasing pressure from the black majority and the international community, South Africa finally released Mandela in 1990 and agreed to negotiate on the policy of apartheid. The government more than negotiated, it crumbled. In 1994, after apartheid was abolished, Mandela was elected president in the first free and open election in the nation's history.

The Middle East

After the fall of the Ottoman Empire and the creation of the modern nation of Turkey at the close of World War I, the Middle East, which was largely comprised of old Ottoman lands, was temporarily put under the control of the League of Nations. As if the two European powerhouses didn't already control enough of the world, France was put in charge of Syria and Lebanon, while Britain got Palestine, Jordan, and Iraq. Persia (Iran) was already carved up into spheres of influence between Britain and Russia during the nineteenth century. As for Arabia, it united as a Saudi kingdom immediately following the fall of the Ottoman Empire.

The Middle East during the twentieth century is complicated stuff, but a good chunk of the essential information involves the creation of the modern nation of Israel, so that's where we'll start.

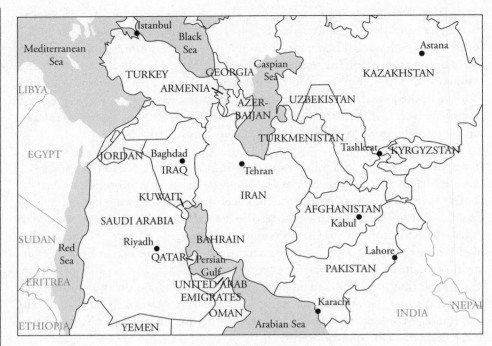

The Middle East

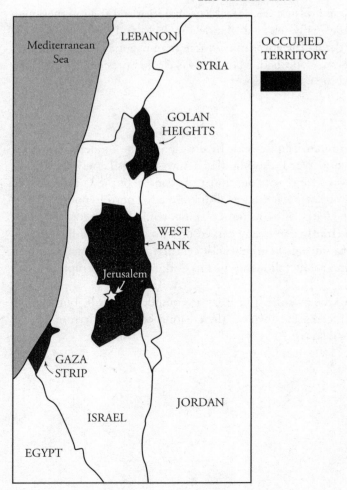

OCCUPIED
TERRITORY

Modern Israel

Israel: Balfour Declares a Mess

If you remember way back four chapters ago, the Hebrews (Jews) occupied lands in Palestine at the time of the ancient Roman Empire. As is the case everywhere else on the globe, between that chapter and this chapter a series of conquests shifted power over the region a mind-numbing number of times. While a few Jews managed to stay in the region, most bolted for Europe or other areas as Palestine became increasingly entrenched in Islam. All the while, however, many Jews had wanted to return to what they believed was the "promised land." But in the meantime, generation after generation of Muslim Palestinians had made that land home.

During World War I, **Zionists** (Jewish nationalists) living in Britain convinced **Arthur Balfour**, Britain's foreign secretary, that a Jewish homeland in Palestine was both desirable and just. He issued what became known as the **Balfour Declaration of 1917**, which explicitly stated the right for a home in Palestine for the Jewish people, but he also stated that it should in no way displace the Palestinians who currently lived there. As history would have it, Britain gained control of Palestine in 1920 as a mandate from the League of Nations—which meant that it was to govern on behalf of the League of Nations—and was therefore in a position to make good on its declaration.

But the declaration was messy because it essentially provided that the Palestinians and Jews were to divide land that they both claimed. Not long after, many Jews, mainly Russian Jews fleeing violent, anti-Semitic mobs (**pogroms**), began streaming into Palestine. As their numbers grew, the Palestinians started to get uneasy. In the 1930s, huge numbers of Jews flooded the region to escape Germany as Hitler came to power. By the beginning of World War II, nearly 500,000 Jews had emigrated to Palestine. While Palestinians still outnumbered Jews, the Jewish population was now large enough to pull some serious weight, especially because money was pouring into the region from Jewish communities worldwide.

The Jewish Wait for a State Ends in 1948

In 1948, the United Nations (which had replaced the ineffectual League of Nations) officially created two Palestines, one for Jews and the other for Muslims (Palestinians). Sound familiar? It should. The same arrangement was made with India and Pakistan. The Indians and Pakistanis have been fighting ever since. This should give you a clue for what's coming in the next paragraph.

As soon as **David Ben-Gurion**, the first prime minister of Israel, announced the official creation of the Jewish homeland on May 14, 1948, Muslims from six Arab countries attacked Israel in what became known as the **1948 Arab-Israeli War**. But the Israelis shocked and awed them with their quick organization and military capability. Within months, the Israelis controlled most of Palestine, including the Palestinian parts, while Jordan held the remaining portions (the **West Bank**). Suddenly, Palestinians were without a home. They had no land to call their own.

As Jews flocked to Israel from all over the world, Israel and Arab countries continued to have skirmishes. In 1967, the amazingly short **Six Days' War** resulted in total victory for the Israelis who took control of the West Bank from Jordan, the Sinai Peninsula and **Gaza Strip** from Egypt, and the **Golan Heights** from Syria. With the West Bank came control of the city of Jerusalem, Judaism's historical homeland. However, Muslims throughout the region resented Israeli control of the Dome of the Rock, a revered Islamic shrine dating back to the Abbasid caliphate which is also the site of the Temple Mount, an important Jewish historical site. The territorial gains resulted in new waves of Palestinian refugees to Jerusalem. In 1977, Israeli **Prime Minister Begin** and Egyptian **President Sadat** signed the **Camp David Accords**, an agreement that did not mention Golan Heights, Syria, or Lebanon, but which led to Israel pulling out of the Sinai and Egypt becoming the only Arab country yet to recognize Israel's right to exist. This was a huge blow to the Palestinians and other Arab nations. Sadat was assassinated and the lands gained in the Six Days' War remain some of the most contested in the region.

In the years since, the Israelis and the Palestinians have been fighting over the Israeli occupation of the West Bank, Golan Heights, and Gaza Strip. The **Palestine Liberation Organization (PLO)**, a group dedicated to reclaiming the land and establishing a Palestinian state, has so far been unsuccessful in negotiating a homeland. The efforts are complicated by the intifada (uprising), an on-again off-again movement that sometimes uses terrorism against Israeli citizens in an attempt to either destroy Israel or force it into withdrawal from the occupied territories.

In 2000, a new intifada reignited violence between Palestinians and the occupying Israeli forces. As suicide bombings became more frequent, newly elected Israeli prime minister **Ariel Sharon** approved the construction of a wall to be built between the Palestinian West Bank and Israel in order to protect Israelis against suicide attacks. Often compared to the Berlin Wall, Israel has been criticized by the international community for employing such a draconian measure to fight terrorist attacks.

Not limiting itself to criticism, however, in 2003 the international community, led by the United States, the European Union, the UN and Russia, proposed a "Roadmap to Peace," which outlined a set of goals to achieve peace in the region. Progress on the Roadmap remained stalled until the death of Palestinian president (and former PLO leader) **Yassir Arafat** in November 2004. Arafat had been consistently blamed by Israel and the United States for blocking such progress. Following his January 2005 election, Palestinian president **Mahmoud Abbas** quickly signed a cease-fire with Israel that effectively ended the *intifada* that began in 2000.

Under a "disengagement plan" adopted by the Israeli government, all Israeli settlers were supposed to have vacated the Gaza Strip by August 2005. Residents of the settlements who did not leave were forcibly removed by the Israeli army, a military action which greatly divided the Israeli public. Additional settlements were disbanded in the West Bank as part of the same plan. It is likely, however, that lasting peace will remain elusive until the Israelis and Palestinians can reach agreement on issues such as movement into and outside of the Palestinian Authority-controlled territories, the disarmament of militant groups, and the potential independence of a Palestinian state.

The situation is made even more complicated by limited financial stability and political divisions among Palestinians. The governing Palestinian Authority is divided into two factions: Fatah, a branch of the former Palestinian Liberation Organization, and Hamas.

Translating to "Islamic Resistance Movement," Hamas was founded as an offshoot of the Muslim Brotherhood in 1987. Because of their open willingness to support terrorist tactics, Hamas is frequently the target of Israeli military attacks. Despite similar goals for a Palestinian state, Hamas and Fatah are deeply divided, and violent clashes occur with increasing frequency. After the creation of a unity government in 2006, Hamas led a coup in 2007 which concluded with a Hamas-imposed government in the Gaza Strip and a Fatah-run West Bank. Further complicating governance, in retaliation, President Mahmoud Abbas (Fatah) named Salam Fayyad Prime Minister. Hamas contends that Fayyad's appointment is illegitimate, as he was not voted into office. Israel's current government, led by Prime Minister Benjamin Netanyahu, and the United States show willingness to work with Fatah; the United States and a number of European countries list Hamas as a terrorist organization and so do not negotiate with that party.

Israel's border with Lebanon and Syria is another hotspot. Hezbollah, a militant Shia group backed by Syria and Iran, operates in the region. In 2006, Israel launched a major offensive against Hezbollah after two Israeli soldiers were captured in Israeli territory. These new hostilities threatened the stability of a country which had been the scene of intense fighting between Syrian, Israeli, and PLO forces throughout the 1980s and 1990s. Syria is widely seen to have a controlling hand in Lebanese politics. In 2005, when Prime Minister Rafiq Hariri was assassinated, fingers quickly pointed to Hezbollah and Syrian sources. A UN Special Tribunal was formed to investigate the assassination and the newest announcements state that findings can be expected in 2015. The Tribunal has already issued arrest warrants for four Hezbollah operatives.

The Iranian Revolution: The Shah Gets Shooed

Reza Shah Pahlavi rose to power in 1925 by ousting the then-ruling shah, who had allowed Persia to fall under European spheres of influence. Taking a stance similar to the Japanese during the Meiji Restoration, Reza Shah decided that the best way to beat the Westernizers was to join them. Iran (formerly Persia) modernized slowly at first, but once the Europeans left after World War II, the Westernization efforts gained momentum, and in the 1960s, the shah instituted land reform and education reform, and increased the rights of women, including the right to vote. Women also pursued higher education and careers, and began to adopt Western dress. All of this infuriated many Islamic fundamentalists who wanted to make the teachings of the Qu'ran the law of the land. Believing that the influence of the West was too strong, they sought to reverse the economic and social changes. Others believed that the shah was not reforming enough, especially with regard to the political system, which lacked significant democratic changes.

The shah reacted violently against dissent from both sides, pressing forward with his own mix of social and economic reform even in the face of strong public opposition. When **President Carter** of the United States visited Iran to congratulate it on its programs of modernization and Westernization, the Islamic fundamentalists had had enough. In 1979, the shah was ousted from power during the **Iranian Revolution**, which sent Iran back to a theocracy led by *Ayatollah* ("Mirror of God") **Khomeini**. Iran is primarily Shia, and the ayatollah is the Shiite caliph (this was important during the Iran-Iraq war, as Iraq was ruled by Sunni Muslims). Immediately, modernization and Westernization programs were reversed, women were required to wear traditional Islamic clothing and to return to their traditional roles, and the Qu'ran became the basis of the legal system.

In 1980, soon after the revolution, Iraq invaded Iran following a series of border disputes between the two countries. Iran's position was further complicated by Iraqi leader Saddam Hussein's quiet support from the United States, which was still quite furious over Iran's taking of U.S. hostages during the revolution. Even with some U.S. support, the **Iran-Iraq war** turned into an eight-year war of attrition with neither side gaining much ground until a cease-fire was signed in 1988.

Since the Ayatollah Khomeini's death in 1989 (watch out—he was succeeded by the differently-spelled **Ayatollah Khamenei**!), Iran has been characterized by a power struggle between powerful Islamic fundamentalist clerics and an increasingly vocal reform-minded and somewhat pro-Western minority. Most recently however, Iran has caused international concern (particularly in the United States) by pushing ahead with efforts to develop what they deemed "peaceful" nuclear technologies, claiming they have a right as an independent nation to develop such technology as they see fit. Along with the International Atomic Energy Agency and the European Union, the United States is currently calling on Iran to sign an international agreement limiting or even eliminating its nuclear programs.

In 2005, Tehran's ultra-conservative mayor, **Mahmoud Ahmadinejad**, was elected president. The American-led war in Iraq that began in 2003, the relationship of Iran and Iraq's Shia populations, and Iran's development of weapons programs and nuclear research have only complicated matters further.

Compare Them: Role of Women After Chinese Revolution and Before Iranian Revolution

In the West, women have benefited from substantial societal and legal changes, but the change has been gradual, over many generations. In China and Iran, the changes were quick. Within a single woman's lifetime, she went from an extremely traditional, oppressive society to one in which she could vote (in the case of Iran), dress less traditionally, divorce her husband, become educated, and pursue a career. Of course, after the Iranian Revolution, those reforms were reversed immediately. At that point, women in China and Iran were in completely different situations.

Oil: Enormous Amounts of Goo

The Industrial Revolution was a huge bonanza for the Middle East. That's because they'd been sitting on over two-thirds of the world's known oil reserves since the beginning of civilization. Prior to the Industrial Revolution, it was goo. After the Industrial Revolution, it was fuel. As multinational corporations rushed to the Middle East throughout the twentieth century to obtain drilling and production rights, Middle Eastern governments like Saudi Arabia, Kuwait, Iran, and Iraq started to earn billions of dollars annually. But the goo also meant that the rest of the world had become very, very interested in the Middle East, because oil allowed the West to do one of its favorite things: drive. This world interest sometimes led to intervention and war.

Once the oil-producing nations of the Middle East realized how much power they wielded, they organized. In 1960, the region united with a few other oil-exporting nations, like Venezuela, to form a petroleum cartel known as **OPEC** (Organization of Petroleum Exporting Countries). With three-quarters of the world's petroleum reserves, OPEC members collectively cut supply dramatically in the 1970s, sending the price of oil through the roof. Billions of extra dollars flowed into OPEC member nations' coffers. Nations like Saudi Arabia used the extra money to modernize their infrastructures, and spent billions on attempts to improve their agricultural sectors. Since the 1970s, OPEC hasn't been able to keep its members in line, and is therefore a much less powerful organization, but the individual members who make up the organization continue to wield huge power over the world economy.

E. Globalization and the World Since 1980

International Terrorism and War

Since World War II and the formation of the United Nations, there has been increased interest in maintaining international security. Some of the organizations that are charged with this task are from Cold War era: NATO, the United Nations, and the International Atomic Energy Agency. Others, such as the International Criminal Court in The Hague (formed in 2002) were formed to prosecute war crimes and crimes against humanity, no matter who committed them. Still others, including Amnesty International and NGOs, such as Human Rights Watch and Doctors Without Borders, serve to publicize issues that threaten human health and safety and provide aid to those in need.

War in the Gulf: Oil and Saddam Hussein

Iraq invaded Kuwait in August 1990 under the leadership of **Saddam Hussein** because Iraq wanted to gain control of a greater percentage of the world's oil reserves. Iraqi control of Kuwait would have nearly doubled Iraq's oil reserves to 20 percent of the world's total, and would have put it in good position to make advances on Saudi Arabia and the United Arab Emirates, actions that would have given Iraq control of more than half of the world's oil reserves. The world, especially the industrialized West, reacted immediately. In January 1991, the United Nations, and particularly the United States, sent forces to drive the Iraqis out of Kuwait in what we now call the **Persian Gulf War**. The immediate impact of their success was the liberation of Kuwait and the humiliation of Iraq, which was subjected to UN monitoring, severe limitations on its military activities, and economic sanctions. Nevertheless, Hussein remained in power, and the UN forces left the region without moving forward to oust him. Hussein held on to his brutal dictatorship for another ten years while also, many argue, ignoring key elements of the peace treaty that allowed him to keep his power after his invasion of Kuwait.

In April 2003, a coalition of countries consisting primarily of the United States and Great Britain invaded Iraq to oust Saddam from power. Saddam's government quickly fell to coalition forces but Hussein himself was not captured until December of that year. Sovereignty was returned to a transitional government in June of 2004, and a new democratically elected government was formed in May 2005. However, since the initial invasion, Iraq has been increasingly plagued with sectional conflicts among Sunni, Shiites, and Kurds, the conflicts defined by suicide bombings against coalition forces and more and more against Iraqi forces and civilians of rival sects. Even amidst the violence, the Iraqi government ratified a new constitution in October 2005, followed by a general election in December 2005, with legislative seats distributed according to "proportional representation." This system allotted percentages of seats to women, Sunni Muslims, Kurdish Iraqis, as well as to the Shia majority. Despite delays in certifying the results of the December 2005 election, the newly elected government took office in May 2006, with **Jalal Talabani**, who is Kurdish, as president, and **Nouri al-Maliki**, who is Shia, as Prime Minister. The government has faced a number of challenges, and it remains to be seen whether it can successfully bring a violent insurgency to peaceful engagement in the political process. Even with the end of U.S. combat operations and the withdrawal of most coalition troops by the end of 2011, Iraq must also still contend with a number of opposing domestic and international interests as it tries to find stability in its new incarnation.

Taliban, Al Qaeda, Osama bin Laden

During the early 1980s, the Soviet Union sent thousands of troops to Afghanistan at the request of Marxist military leader **Nur Muhammad Taraki**, who had engineered a military coup against the previous government. Many Afghans opposed communism and Soviet intervention, however, and soon a massive civil war raged. Some of the resistors called themselves "holy warriors" and, with the aid of weapons from the Western powers who supplied the Cold War on every front, launched guerilla attacks against the superior military might of the Soviet Union. As internal problems escalated in the Soviet Union, Gorbachev agreed to withdraw Soviet troops from the region and a peace accord was signed. While communism fell apart in the Soviet Union and Eastern Europe, the problems in Afghanistan continued. The decline of communism removed the Soviet threat, but warring factions vied to fill the power void.

The power that finally triumphed after 14 years of fighting and more than 2 million deaths was called the **Taliban**, an Islamic fundamentalist regime that captured the capital of Kabul in 1996. The new government imposed strict Islamic law and severe restrictions on women. It also provided safe haven for **Osama bin Laden**, the Saudi leader of an international terrorist network, known as **Al Qaeda**, which has a serious distaste for Saudi Arabia and the United States. It's believed that Al Qaeda's main issue with Saudi Arabia is that the ruling family is too cozy with the United States and that they have allowed U.S. troops to remain in the country since the Persian Gulf War, which amounts to the presence of infidels in a kingdom that is home to Islam's most holy sites. Al Qaeda despises the United States for what many believe are at least three reasons. First, the United States supports Israel, which the organization would like to see removed from the planet. Second, it has troops stationed in Saudi Arabia, and third, the United States is the primary agent of globalization, which Al Qaeda believes is infecting Islamic culture.

On **September 11, 2001**, Al Qaeda operatives managed to take control of four American passenger jets and fly two of them into the **World Trade Center** in New York City, one into the Pentagon in Washington, D.C., and one (presumably unintentionally) into a field in Pennsylvania. The towers of the World Trade Center fell to the ground, killing more than 2,500 civilians. The deaths of the people on all four planes and those killed at the Pentagon bring the total number of casualties to almost 3,000. The United States immediately launched a war on terrorism, targeting Al Qaeda and the Taliban. Within months, the Taliban was removed from power and U.S. and UN forces occupied the country of Afghanistan. Al Qaeda, on the other hand, still survives, though its leadership is being directly attacked and eliminated, most notably with the death of Osama bin Laden in May of 2011.

Although smaller in scale, suicide bombing and terrorist attacks (many linked to Al Qaeda and similar groups), continue regularly. They are a problem throughout the Israeli territories, between Sunni and Shia factions in Iraq, targeting tourists in the cities of Saudi Arabia, Egypt, and Turkey, and among Muslim separatists in Russia. Coordinated attacks occurred throughout Lebanon in 2004 and 2005, killing the former Prime Minister Rafiq Hariri (among others), while larger-scale attacks occurred in March 2004 on commuter trains in Madrid, Spain, in July 2005 on the London subway system, and the following July on trains in Mumbai (Bombay), India. While the Madrid attacks were attributed to Basque separatists, the remainder of the attacks were credited to Islamic fundamentalists.

World Trade and Cultural Exchange

The end of the Cold War removed the last obstacles to true global interaction and trade. Currencies were no longer tied to old alliances, and new business opportunities emerged. This deregulation, along with the development of systems of instantaneous communication such as the Internet, resulted in globally integrated financial networks. Commercial interdependence intensified in the 1980s as eastern Asia began to flex its industrial and commercial muscles.

Competition further drove global developments, and regional trading blocks were created such as **North American Free Trade Agreement** (NAFTA) in the early 1990s. The European Economic Community (EEC), originally formed in 1957, transformed into the modern **European Union** (EU) tied to a single currency, the euro. The ease with which goods and ideas are transported across the world has resulted in cultures being more homogenous and integrated. This does not mean that local culture is lost, but it does mean that one can satisfy a craving for a Starbucks mocha latte inside Beijing's Forbidden City. It also means almost instantaneous access to a wider range of music, art, literature, and information. Much of this is facilitated by the spread of English as the language of business and communication across the globe. This began in the eighteenth century with the far-flung colonies of the British Empire and continued with the emergence of the United States as a global power after World War II.

E.U.

The **European Union** or EU was formed to give the United States some economic competition by banding Europe together in a single market. The real impetus to expand the powers of the EU came in the early 1990s when the collapse of the Soviet Union simultaneously opened Europe and left the U.S. unchallenged as the world's superpower. In 1989, the EU had 12 members; by 2011, it had 27, of which 10 were former Soviet satellite nations. The EU has three branches: executive, legislative, and judicial. Elections are held throughout Europe every five years. The formation of a monetary union, the **Eurozone**, in 1999, led all but three nations (UK, Sweden, and Denmark) to adopt a unified currency, the euro, in 2002.

While economic integration initially seemed relatively easy and produced a few boom years, in the crisis of the late 2000s (which began slightly earlier in Europe than in the U.S.), it became clear that stronger economies such as Germany's had borne the freight of weaker, over-extended economies such as Greece's, and by 2010, economic collapse in states such as Greece, Ireland, and Portugal threatened to destabilize the entire Eurozone. This has provoked sharp debates about economic integration that have now piled onto existing concerns about political and judicial integration, putting national interests and questions of sovereignty at stake.

Note the Change: The Threat of "McDonaldization"
Consider for a moment since the first McDonalds restaurant opened in California in the late 1930s just how far and to how many people the company and the fast-food culture has come. Take a quick jump over to McDonalds' website and you can view the list of over 100 countries in which McDonalds has restaurants today, including Saudi Arabia, Pakistan, and Egypt. But why point out these Muslim countries? The so-called "McDonaldization" of the world can be used as both an example and a metaphor for the spread of what is predominantly a Western popular culture to the rest of the world. Many countries, such as India and even China, have embraced the fruits of Westernization, integrating and assimilating aspects of Western culture into their own. Other groups however, including fundamentalist movements in some Muslim countries, have rejected this "invasion" of modern Western culture, which they see as a threat to their traditional Islamic ways. Responses to the perceived threat of globalization have included many acts of international terrorism in an effort to fight the encroachment of the West as symbolized by the international spread of such Western cultural icons as Starbucks, Wal-Mart, and Disney.

To Be Rich Is Glorious: The Rise of China and India

"Socialism with Chinese Characteristics" or "To Be Rich Is Glorious" sum up Deng Xiaoping's plans for China after the death of Chairman Mao. Since normalized trade relations with the United States in the 1990s and acceptance into the World Trade Organization in 2001, China has become an industrial and economic juggernaut. What began with the creation of special economic zones exempt from the strict controls of communism in the late 1980s has become the world's warehouse and discount store! In the last ten years, China's imports have increased from $82 billion (1999) to $338 billion (2008) built on a wide array of everyday consumer goods, toys, and apparel. This new and profitable industrial revolution has funded a building boom throughout China, brought the 2008 Olympic games to Beijing, and contributed to a rising and educated middle class who now shop and eat at 300 Starbucks and 800 McDonalds stores. But economic success has also led to a crack-down on Internet freedom. Politically, it is pretty much the same old China. The CCP allows some local elections and the New York Times is available on-line, but one party is clearly in charge and watching what you Google.

India, the world's largest democracy and one of its fastest growing economies, has spent the past two decades making itself indispensible to the globally connected world. In 1991, India was broke, the leading contender for Prime Minister had been assassinated and the country desperately needed a way to reinvent its economy and industries. Since loans from the IMF required economic reforms and austerity measures, major industries were privatized and others were publicly traded. India's greatest advantage is its highly educated and skilled population, yet the focus on traditional industry advocated by Gandhi had left India isolated and unable to compete globally. The desperation of 1991, at a time when technology and computer chip industries were developing in the United States was a moment of opportunity for Indian investors and workers, many of whom had migrated to Silicon Valley. Indian entrepreneurs brought these new ideas back to Indian companies such as Infosys and Tata, developed technology to route global calls, and built on the global demand for software, new technology, and support.

Both India and China are nuclear powers with two of the world's largest armies. Both are currently dealing with belligerent neighbors (Pakistan and North Korea), both have complicated relationships and history with Western powers, both have yet to deal with tremendous economic inequality and poverty within their borders, and as members of the G20 (see Alphabet Soup) both have figured out a way to keep growing while much of the industrialized world is in an economic slowdown.

Global Alphabet Soup

With globalization of trade come many agencies and organizations designed to protect and facilitate trade. The earliest of these were the International Monetary Fund or IMF (1945) with 185 members and the World Bank (also founded in 1945). Both organizations were formed to stabilize world economic relationships and to loan financial assistance when needed. At the same time, The General Agreement on Tariffs and Trade, or **GATT**, was agreed upon to reduce barriers to international trade. GATT became the World Trade Organization, or WTO, in 1994. The WTO boasts 153 member states—most of the world's active trading nations—who adhere to the WTO's rules and regulations regarding trade relationships.

An organization of note is the **Group of Six**, or **G6**, created in 1975 as a forum for the world's major industrialized democracies. Its original members included U.S., Great Britain, West Germany, Italy, Japan, and Poland. They have since been joined by Canada in 1977, and by Russia in 1997, and are now know as the **G8**. This informal summit of the world's most powerful leaders meets annually to discuss issues of mutual or global concern such as climate change, terrorism, and trade.

In addition to the G8, a group of 19 nations plus EU representatives make up the **G20** or the Group of 20 Finance Ministers and Central Bank Governors. Beginning with the financial crises of the late 1990s, this group represents key industrialized as well as developing economies.

Environmental Change

Until the 1980s, environmental issues focused on localized pollution or waste management, but along with global integration in every sector came global environmental concerns. Most recently, these concerns have focused on food; as suppliers become ever more distant from their consumers and trade agreements open up supply routes, safety regulations may not follow.

The "green revolution" of the 1950s and 1960s led to increased agricultural productivity through industrial means—chemical fertilizers and pesticides, biologically engineered foods, more efficient means of harvesting, and more marginal lands available for agriculture. While this resulted in inexpensive and plentiful food supplies, it destroyed traditional landscapes including rainforests in Indonesia and South America, reduced species diversity, and fostered social conflicts that might not have otherwise existed. As has been true throughout history, marginal lands can not sustain the population increases they initially produce with new industrial technologies. This is especially notable in eastern and sub-Saharan Africa, where political and financial mismanagement contributed to widespread famines in the 1970s and 1980s.

Bottled water has become ubiquitous and widespread, but water is a crucial natural resource that is often carelessly managed by cities at the expense of their hinterlands. This is not a rapidly renewable resource and needs to be regulated for drinking and for agriculture. A similar pattern is seen with industrialized countries consumption of oil—they want more and they want it cheap! Oil fuels industry, transportation, and heating of homes and businesses. The insatiable appetite for oil reserves on the part of industrialized democracies can lead to strange political and economic alliances (see the previous section on the Middle East). Although some progress has been made in developing alternative fuel options, like ethanol, there are big drawbacks to them as well. Clearly, much more research into viable alternatives to fossil fuel is needed.

Finally, a quick note on global warming. It's getting warmer and human activities, including fuel consumption, heating, and cooling, are contributing to this. What the results of these warming trends will be is uncertain. On the positive side, there will be longer growing seasons in temperate parts of the world, but the negative will be more extreme conditions in marginal areas—longer periods of drought in some, flooding and disappearance of coastlines in others. The first Earth Summit on global climate change was held in 1992 in Rio de Janeiro. Five years later, the Kyoto Protocol was an attempt to make a global agreement on ways to reduce environmental damages, but because the United States has refused to ratify the

Protocol (and Canada denounced it in 2011), it remains controversial and unable to function to its full potential. Industrialized nations continue to struggle with balancing potential damage to the environment with the growth potential of their business sector, and it is the business of production and consumption that has been of primary importance to policymakers.

Global Health Crises

Within globalization efforts, the relief of health crises is a primary focus. Non-profit organizations like the WHO (World Health Organization) work to lower infant mortality as well as to combat various diseases, such as influenza, which kill millions in third-world countries due to a lack of appropriate medical care and medicine. This problem has existed as far back as 1918, when a flu epidemic killed millions across the globe, but is still important today. Recent outbreaks of bird flu and swine flu, two strains of influenza passed from animals to humans, show that such epidemics, especially in countries without the U.S.'s high level of sanitation, are still an issue.

AIDS is another notable global health crisis, especially in sub-Saharan Africa, where almost 25 percent of adults in some countries live with HIV (the virus that causes AIDS). While AIDS treatments can help those with the disease to live relatively normal lives, there is no cure as yet for this fatal illness, and only those in wealthier countries tend to have access to the most advanced treatments. Currently, global efforts to combat this health crisis are focused on prevention, and the WHO and other organizations are working on changing the social norms and behaviors of at-risk populations, particularly in Africa where the AIDS crisis is at its worst.

Other notable global health issues today include diseases which, in developed countries, are not a threat, such as cholera. New treatments for cholera, such as oral rehydration therapy, have drastically lowered mortality rates associated with the disease in Bangladesh, India, and neighboring countries. Global health issues highlight the disparities that, despite the ongoing process of globalization, still exist between first-world, industrialized countries and those that are not.

The Age of the Computer

The single most important technological advance since the 1980s has been the rise of computers and, in turn, the internet. Beginning in the 1970s, new hardware was developed by American companies such as Compaq and IBM, which allowed computers to radically shrink in size (by using a silicon chip to store data). The PC, or personal computer, became a reality, since this advance meant that computers no longer took up entire rooms. By the late 1980s, an early version of the World Wide Web existed, though only those with advanced technical knowledge had access.

In the 1990s, more homes got computers; commercial software, such as web browsers and the services and programs offered by America Online, introduced the internet to the American population at large, transforming both the home and the workplace. The Y2K scare, which involved a possible glitch in computers caused by the switch of dates to the new millennium, pointed out how dependent industry and society were on computers and the internet. Y2K did not cause an actual crisis, and personal computers and similar technologies, including cell phones, are all the more crucial today to the personal and global business lives of many.

More recently, social media and the spread of the internet have had huge ramifications worldwide. Social media, such as Twitter, has changed the way news is reported and has played a huge role in political developments in Middle Eastern countries where, during the "Arab Spring" of 2011, oppressive regimes in several nations were toppled due in part to the exposure—via social media—of the problems in those countries. Internet censorship exists in many nations, notably India and China, but overall this technology has served to bring people together both in business and in other aspects of life, changing the way we receive our news, take classes, and even shop. One current concern, however, is the growing gap in access between those in developed and those in undeveloped countries. The importance of the internet and computer technology may serve as a barrier to globalization in countries without the infrastructure to join this "digital revolution."

IV. CHANGES AND CONTINUITIES IN THE ROLE OF WOMEN

Finally, the upheavals and changes of the twentieth century resulted in really dramatic changes in women's social, political, and economic roles. The integration and global connectedness of the world made access to education and political freedoms far more widespread, especially among the middle and upper classes. Change came more slowly to the lower and working classes, but still it came.

Politically, women gained the right to vote in many parts of the world by the first quarter of the twentieth century. By 1930, that right had been gained by women in much of Latin America, Indian, China, Japan, and most of Europe. After World War II, most of the newly independent African countries included women's suffrage in their constitutions, and it is only in the most fundamentalist of the Middle Eastern countries that women still do not have the right to vote. However, having the right to vote differs significantly from having the education and opportunity to vote. In most Asian and African countries, female access to formal political power continues to be limited.

Contradictions also exist between theory and practice in communist and formerly communist countries. Under communism, everyone was equal, women played key roles in the Communist Revolutions in Russia, China and Cuba, and educational opportunities were opened especially in professions such as medicine. Women were also generally given equal legal rights including those of inheritance, divorce, and child-rearing. However, in reality, discrimination and gender issues continue. Almost all key positions within the Communist parties were and are held by men. In China, the one-child policy and mandatory sterilization disproportionately impact women and female children. State-sponsored sterilization was also common in Puerto Rico and India. Additionally, the end of communism and the loosening of economic restrictions seems to present more opportunities for men than for women.

Family structure changed dramatically in the twentieth century, especially in the industrialized world. Birth rates dropped, birth control was widely available, and marriage rates declined as divorce and second marriages became more common. The twentieth century also saw dramatic changes in the role of women at work. Beginning with wage labor in factories during the World Wars, women's presence in the workforce has become more widely accepted. A shift to profitable industries in chemicals, textiles and electronics, has provided further economic opportunities for women. By the mid-1980s, education and access in Westernized and industrialized countries allowed women to participate fully in the work force. But women in agricultural economies continued to have their labor under-enumerated and throughout the world, women's pay has yet to fully equal that of her male counterparts, nor are women compensated for the time they spend on a "second shift" as primary caregivers of young children.

V. PULLING IT ALL TOGETHER

You've read about a lot of stuff in this chapter. Two world wars. A cold war and all its consequences. The end of European imperialism. The rise of the United States as a superpower. Islamic fundamentalism in the Middle East. These are all huge issues. And it's hard to discern immediately how you can connect them all together, other than to say that there were a lot of wars and a lot of hatred. Yet, beyond the morbidity and feelings of helplessness that a careful study of history can engender, there are also a lot of ways to think about history that can help you evaluate how people and the world function.

In the last chapter, we talked a lot about nationalism, and it certainly didn't stop in the twentieth century. Nationalism not only led to fascism in Nazi Germany, but also to independence movements after World War II in India and Africa, and in Europe and Asia after the fall of the Soviet Union. Sometimes it was based on broad cultural characteristics—Gandhi, for example, unsuccessfully wanting everyone to look at themselves as Indians, not as Hindus or Muslims—and other times it was very narrowly defined—Serbs, for example, or Nazis.

Regardless of its forms, nationalism affected all of the major global events in the twentieth century. In both World War I and II, the aggressors were highly nationalistic. The independence movements following World War II were nationalistic. And the Cold War, because it pitted two opposing worldviews that were so strongly identified with the nations of the Soviet Union and the United States, was arguably a nationalist struggle as well. National pride was on the line. And in the end, superpower status was on the line, too.

By the late twentieth century, whether because of nationalism or not, there were a huge number of independent nation-states. Each former colony in Africa was independent. Lots of new countries formed from the old Soviet Union. What's more, most of the countries were developing along democratic lines, though some along militaristic or Islamic theocratic lines, and capitalism seemed to be making huge gains after the fall of the Soviet Union, which leads us to the next question.

Is There Currently a Convergence of Cultures?

This is a tough question to answer. It could go either way, and if you study history enough, you can argue for both sides.

On the one hand, globalization is clearly occurring, and it's been occurring for a long time. It's just that now it's getting a lot faster and it's penetrating more and more hidden parts of the globe. Centuries ago, trade, conquest, and exploration were forms of globalization because they brought people together, essentially "making the world smaller." Big movements like the Scientific Revolution, the Enlightenment, and the Industrial Revolution can certainly be categorized as movements toward globalization because they weren't culturally specific, but rather could be applied nearly anywhere around the globe. They brought people closer together because they led to certain ways of thinking that were attractive and accepted by different kinds of people. If people start to agree on how the universe is organized or how governments should be organized, that is most certainly a convergence of cultures.

In the twentieth century, globalization really got going. Aided by transportation, communication, and imperialism, anything produced in one country could be received in another. Popular examples of globalization are the appearance of the same multinational companies everywhere (seeing a McDonalds in Istanbul) and certainly the use of the Internet, but globalization is much broader than even these examples. Globalization led to and continues to lead to an interconnectedness of entire economies. The Great Depression in the 1930s proved that the economies of most industrialized nations were heavily intertwined. Today, the economies are so intertwined that a fall in stock prices in Tokyo will have an instantaneous impact on the stock market in the United States.

As more and more countries start to look the same (independent, democratic, constitutional), their economies function in similar ways (stock market, low barriers to trade, strong banking system), and their cultures look the same (educated people who know English, Hollywood movies playing at theaters, cell phone in their hands), it can be strongly argued that there is a convergence of cultures.

On the other hand, globalization doesn't necessarily mean convergence. Globalization just means that everything is spread all around the globe all the time. It doesn't mean that people accept, like, or want what's being hurled at them. It just means that it's available. Some argue that globalization will lead to an increase in the number of people who lash out against it, sometimes aggressively or violently. Globalization isn't well received in Islamic fundamentalist countries, or in countries that are trying hard to maintain a historical cultural identity, like France.

But more significantly, it can't be denied that the biggest movements of the twentieth century were rooted in self-determination and nationalism. The whole point of self-determination is for nations to chart their own course. If self-determination and nationalism mean that a country is going to use its independence to do what every other country does, then why be independent in the first place? Clearly, people want to chart their own course. They fought wars for the right to do so. They must have been doing so for a reason. So it makes sense that globalization will have its limits. And isn't the world a whole lot less consolidated today than it was under European imperialism, when that small continent ruled the world? Doesn't that suggest the opposite of global convergence?

In the end, there's no right answer to this question. The challenge is not to accurately predict the future, but to have an understanding of history to make a reasonable, defendable argument about the direction that history seems to be taking. If you can discuss globalization, nationalism, and self-determination in the same essay or conversation without totally losing your mind, you have command enough of the issues and complexities to be confident in yourself. Keep reading, keep studying, and keep thinking.

Important Terms

Abdicate

Allies

Armaments

Armistice

Atomic Energy

Capitalism

Cold War

Collective/Collectivization

Communism

Conservative

Containment

Decolonization

Deposed

Democratization

Doctrine

Egalitarian

Ethnic Cleansing

Exodus

Fascism

First World

Front Line

Globalization

Global Warming

Guerilla

Intervention

Isolationism

Jihad

Legislature

Liberal

Militarism

Nationalism

Nationalize

Nation-State

Natural Resources

National Socialist Party (Nazi)

Nuclear

Radical

Recession

Reform

Reparations

Revolution

Rivalry

Secular

Sectarian

Terrorism

Third World

Totalitarian

Westernization

People, Places, and Events

Apartheid
Asian Tigers
Aswan Dam
Ataturk, Kemel Mustafa
    (Turkey)
Ayatollah Khomeini (Iran)
Balfour Declaration
Berlin Airlift
Berlin War
Bolshevik Party
Castro, Fidel (Cuba)
Chiang Kai Shek (China)
Churchill, Winston
    (England)
Cuban Missile Crisis
Cultural Revolution
Deng Xioaping (China)
Eastern Bloc
European Economic
    Community
European Union
Fourteen Points
Gandhi, Mahatmas (India)
Garvey, Marcus
Great Leap Forward
Hitler, Adolph (Germany)
Ho Chi Minh (Vietnam)
Holocaust
Hussein, Saddam (Iraq)
IAEA (International Atomic
    Energy Agency)
IMF (International
    Monetary Fund)
Intifada
Iran-Iraq War
Iron Curtain
Israel
Korean War
League of Nations
Lenin, Vladimir (Russia)
Mao Zedong (China)
Marshall Plan
NAFTA (North American Free
    Trade Agreement)

NATO(North Atlantic Treaty
    Organization)
OPEC (Organization of
    Petroleum Exporting
    Countries)
Pahlavi, Shah Reza (Iran)
Palestine
Rape of Nanjing
Six Days War
Stalin, Josef (Soviet Union)
Sun Yat Sen (China)
Third Reich
Treaty of Versailles (1919)
Trench Warfare
Trotsky, Leon (Russia)
Truman Doctrine
Union of the Soviet Socialist
    Republics (USSR)
United Nations
Vietnam War
War on Terror
Warsaw Pact
Wilson, Woodrow (USA)
WTO (World Trade
    Organization)
World War I
World War II
Young Turks Party

VI. TIMELINE OF MAJOR DEVELOPMENTS SINCE 1914

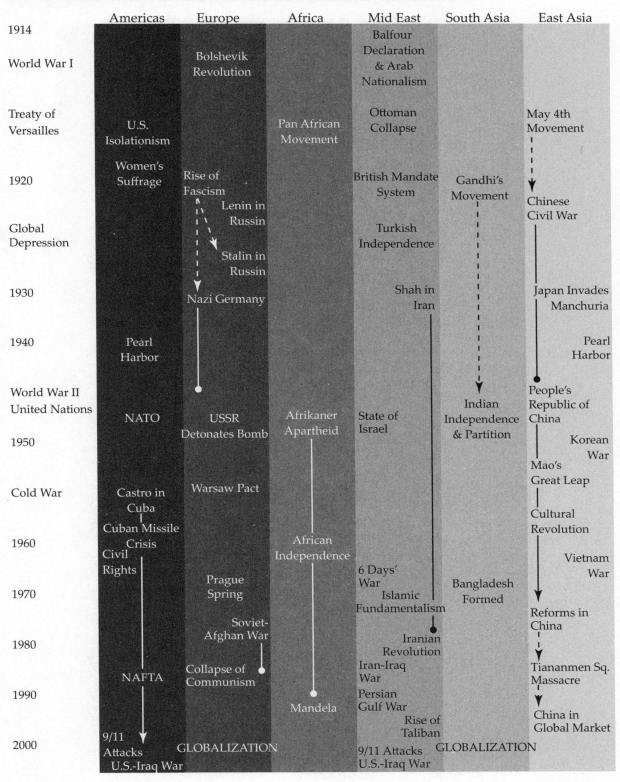

	Americas	Europe	Africa	Mid East	South Asia	East Asia
1914				Balfour Declaration & Arab Nationalism		
World War I		Bolshevik Revolution				
Treaty of Versailles	U.S. Isolationism		Pan African Movement	Ottoman Collapse		May 4th Movement
1920	Women's Suffrage	Rise of Fascism		British Mandate System	Gandhi's Movement	Chinese Civil War
Global Depression		Lenin in Russin / Stalin in Russin		Turkish Independence		
1930		Nazi Germany		Shah in Iran		Japan Invades Manchuria
1940	Pearl Harbor					Pearl Harbor
World War II United Nations						People's Republic of China
	NATO	USSR Detonates Bomb	Afrikaner Apartheid	State of Israel	Indian Independence & Partition	
1950						Korean War
						Mao's Great Leap
Cold War	Castro in Cuba	Warsaw Pact				Cultural Revolution
	Cuban Missile Crisis		African Independence			
1960	Civil Rights					Vietnam War
1970		Prague Spring		6 Days' War	Bangladesh Formed	
		Soviet-Afghan War		Islamic Fundamentalism		Reforms in China
1980				Iranian Revolution		
	NAFTA	Collapse of Communism		Iran-Iraq War		Tiananmen Sq. Massacre
1990			Mandela	Persian Gulf War		China in Global Market
				Rise of Taliban		
2000	9/11 Attacks U.S.-Iraq War	GLOBALIZATION		9/11 Attacks U.S.-Iraq War	GLOBALIZATION	

REFLECT ACTIVITY

Respond to the following questions:

- For which content topics discussed in this Chapter do you feel you have achieved sufficient mastery to answer multiple choice questions correctly?

- For which content topics discussed in this Chapter do you feel you have achieved sufficient mastery to discuss effectively in an essay?

- For which content topics discussed in this Chapter do you feel you need more work before you can answer multiple choice questions correctly?

- For which content topics discussed in this Chapter do you feel you need more work before you can discuss effectively in an essay?

- What parts of this Chapter are you going to re-review?

- Will you seek further help outside of this book (such as a teacher, tutor, or AP Central), on any of the content in this Chapter—and, if so, on what content?

Part V
Practice Tests

YOU KNOW THE SAYING...

Practice, practice, practice! Now that you have reviewed the high points of world history and learned some strategies for cracking each type of question on the AP World History Exam, it's time to put your knowledge into action. The final step to being totally prepared for your AP exam is to do some trial runs.

Part V of this book comprises two full-length practice tests and explanations for each of the multiple-choice sections. During the weeks leading up to your exam, set aside time to take each of these practice tests (not on the same night, of course). Try to simulate real testing conditions. Once you have completed a practice test, go back over it and use the explanations for further review. Also, ask a classmate to score your essays using the scoring rubrics contained in Chapters 3 and 4.

While you cannot convert your raw score to a score on the 1 to 5 scale, remember our rough guidelines for making sure you are on track.

AP World History Raw Score Goals to Get a 3 or Above

Section	Raw Score Points
Multiple-Choice	50 or more
DBQ	7 or above
Change-Over-Time Essay	6 or above
Comparative Essay	6 or above

Good luck!

Chapter 11
Practice Test 1

AP® World History Exam

DO NOT OPEN THIS BOOKLET UNTIL YOU ARE TOLD TO DO SO.

At a Glance

Total Time
55 minutes
Number of Questions
70
Percent of Total Grade
50%
Writing Instrument
Pencil required

Instructions

Section I of this examination contains 70 multiple-choice questions. Fill in only the ovals for numbers 1 through 70 on your answer sheet.

Indicate all of your answers to the multiple-choice questions on the answer sheet. No credit will be given for anything written in this exam booklet, but you may use the booklet for notes or scratch work. After you have decided which of the suggested answers is best, completely fill in the corresponding oval on the answer sheet. Give only one answer to each question. If you change an answer, be sure that the previous mark is erased completely. Here is a sample question and answer.

Sample Question   Sample Answer

Chicago is a   Ⓐ ● Ⓒ Ⓓ
(A) state
(B) city
(C) country
(D) continent

Use your time effectively, working as quickly as you can without losing accuracy. Do not spend too much time on any one question. Go on to other questions and come back to the ones you have not answered if you have time. It is not expected that everyone will know the answers to all the multiple-choice questions.

About Guessing

Many candidates wonder whether or not to guess the answers to questions about which they are not certain. Multiple choice scores are based on the number of questions answered correctly. Points are not deducted for incorrect answers, and no points are awarded for unanswered questions. Because points are not deducted for incorrect answers, you are encouraged to answer all multiple-choice questions. On any questions you do not know the answer to, you should eliminate as many choices as you can, and then select the best answer among the remaining choices.

GO ON TO THE NEXT PAGE.

This page intentionally left blank.

GO ON TO THE NEXT PAGE.

WORLD HISTORY

SECTION I

Time—55 minutes

70 Questions

Directions: Each of the questions or incomplete statements below is followed by four suggested answers or completions. Select the one that is best in each case and then fill in the corresponding oval on the answer sheet.

Note: This examination uses the chronological designations B.C.E. (before the common era) and C.E. (common era). These labels correspond to B.C. (before Christ) and A.D. (anno Domini), which are used in some world history textbooks.

1. Which of the following is NOT a characteristic of all early civilizations?

   (A) Written communication
   (B) Agricultural surplus
   (C) Some economic specialization
   (D) Water resources

2. "The books of those heresiarchs…are absolutely forbidden. The books of other heretics, however, which deal professedly with religion are absolutely condemned. Those on the other hand, which do not deal with religion…are permitted. Likewise, Catholic books written by those who afterward fell into heresy…may be permitted…"

   Source: *Internet Modern History Sourcebook*, Council of Trent, "Rules on Prohibited Books."

   Why was the above ruling issued by the Council of Trent in 1545?

   (A) It was a response to the scientific advances made by Copernicus and Galileo.
   (B) It was part of the reforms to Roman Catholicism called for by Luther and Calvin.
   (C) It was part of the strict behavioral code endorsed by Calvinists.
   (D) It was an attempt during the Catholic Reformation to respond to Protestantism.

3. Which of these were considered the Gunpowder Empires in the Islamic world?

   (A) Ming China, Mughal India, Seljuk Turks
   (B) Tokugawa Shogunate, Ming China, Yuan China
   (C) Ottoman Turkey, Delhi Sultanate, Khmer Cambodia
   (D) Safavid Persia, Ottoman Turkey, Mughal India

4. All of the following were features of the civilizations in Mesopotamia, Mesoamerica, the Indus River Valley, and the Yellow River Valley EXCEPT

   (A) a degree of craft specialization
   (B) development of irrigation systems
   (C) construction of architectural monuments
   (D) religious systems that included sacrifice rituals

5. Which of the following statements about the rule of Peter the Great is accurate?

   (A) Under Peter the Great, Russia became a strong military nation but failed to modernize or industrialize.
   (B) Peter the Great was able to build a strong, centralized government based on militaristic principles.
   (C) The lives of ordinary Russian citizens were greatly improved as a result of the Western influences imported by Peter the Great.
   (D) Peter the Great was considered the first enlightened despot in the history of Russia.

6. The factors destabilizing the balance of power in Europe in the late 1800s and early 1900s included all of the following EXCEPT

   (A) the strong sense of nationalism held by many European nations
   (B) European colonial rivalries in Africa and Asia
   (C) German aggression on the continent under Bismarck
   (D) the rise of socialist and communist movements in European nations

GO ON TO THE NEXT PAGE.

7. Which of the following terms is NOT associated with the Cold War?

   (A) Brinkmanship
   (B) Peaceful coexistence
   (C) Mutual assured destruction
   (D) Appeasement

8. A major difference between Spanish and French colonization efforts was

   (A) only the Spanish were interested in resource extraction in their colonies
   (B) while Spain sent expeditions around the world, French exploration was limited to North America
   (C) the French did not form as many permanent settlements in their colonies as the Spanish
   (D) the French were less successful than the Spanish at religious conversion of people in their colonies

9. One major difference between European and Japanese feudalism during the Middle Ages was that

   (A) there was no Japanese equivalent to the position of the European lord
   (B) European feudalism was far more militaristic than Japanese feudalism
   (C) while Japanese emperors maintained power during feudalism, European kings were symbolic leaders only
   (D) there were far fewer agricultural workers in the Japanese feudal system than in the European system

10. The Glorious Revolution was unique because it

   (A) was the first time England had seen a leader deposed
   (B) was the first instance of the removal of a sitting monarch
   (C) resulted in Europe's first completely secular government
   (D) did not involve a significant amount of violence

11. The globalization of American culture has resulted in

   (A) anti-Western backlash in some developing nations
   (B) increased access to health care and education
   (C) additional tariffs on American-made goods
   (D) more cultural tolerance around the world

12. The major impact of the Delhi Sultanate on India was the

   (A) introduction of a new religion into Indian culture
   (B) decline in importance of sub-Saharan trade routes
   (C) elimination of the caste system
   (D) decline in importance of overland trade routes

13. As a result of Bismarck's Berlin Congress' plan to partition Africa

   (A) Germany controlled a substantial portion of Africa
   (B) the United States entered the scramble for Africa
   (C) the slave trade with Europe, North America, and South America was halted
   (D) only two African nations remained free at the beginning of the twentieth century

14. The ability of nations to industrialize required all of the following conditions EXCEPT

   (A) a reliable source of fuel
   (B) surplus population
   (C) improved farming techniques
   (D) a network of colonies

GO ON TO THE NEXT PAGE.

15. In which of the following ways was the Hindu Upanishad movement similar to the Protestant Reformation?

    (A) Neither was considered a significant threat to the established religion and its authorities.
    (B) Over time, both became more concerned with rituals and dogma than with individualistic expression.
    (C) Neither involved episodes of violence.
    (D) A factor behind both movements was the perceived exploitation of power by religious leaders.

16. The Four Noble Truths are associated with

    (A) Buddhism
    (B) Legalism
    (C) Judaism
    (D) Islam

17. Which of the following is an accurate characterization of both the Incan and Yuan dynasties?

    (A) Both civilizations developed strict social class hierarchies, in which upward mobility was difficult.
    (B) Peasant uprisings were responsible for the establishment of both civilizations.
    (C) Both the Yuan and the Inca depended on trade as their primary economic activity.
    (D) Both civilizations flourished under the control of outside invaders.

18. The movement to industrialize Russia was most dependent on

    (A) emancipating serfs to provide a substantial labor pool for industry
    (B) becoming more active in colonizing other lands to obtain raw materials and develop new markets
    (C) importing coal and other fuel sources plus the equipment necessary to build manufacturing factories
    (D) developing a capitalistic system with laissez-faire and free market economic policies

19. Which of the following was NOT a result of the Black Death?

    (A) Labor shortages in agriculture and industry in England
    (B) Population decline in China
    (C) Scarcity of goods throughout Europe
    (D) Rise of feudalism in western Europe

20. Which of the following was NOT a Cold War strategy?

    (A) The United States supported totalitarian dictatorships in some Latin American and Middle Eastern countries.
    (B) The Soviet Union enforced strict immigration controls, keeping its populations behind an "iron curtain."
    (C) The United States and the Soviet Union built up huge arsenals of traditional, biological, and nuclear weapons in order to prevent war.
    (D) Both the Soviet Union and the United States renewed colonization of lands in Latin America and the Middle East.

GO ON TO THE NEXT PAGE.

Population Pyramids for Botswana 2000-2050

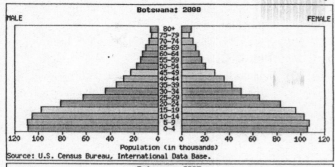

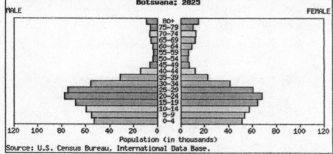

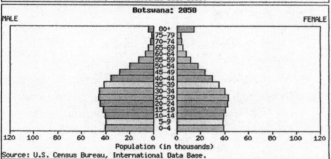

21. In the chart above, the reason for the predicted population decline between 2000 and 2050 could be attributed to any of the following reasons EXCEPT

   (A) increased use of birth control and reproductive planning
   (B) increased economic development activities
   (C) more women entering the workforce
   (D) better access to medical care

22. The Mongol Empire was divided into four Khan-ates, which governed all of the following lands EXCEPT

   (A) Russia
   (B) Persia
   (C) Japan
   (D) Ukraine

23. Which of the following is an accurate statement about the Heian period in Japan in the ninth century?

   (A) The Heian period was a time of exploration and conquest for Japan.
   (B) The focus of Heian civilization was on cultural independence.
   (C) Mongol invaders, under the rule of Ghengis Khan, ruled Japan during the Heian period.
   (D) Shintoism was replaced by Confucianism in Japan during the Heian period.

24. The changes brought about by the Council of Trent did NOT include

   (A) outlawing the sale of indulgences
   (B) the commissioning of art and architecture
   (C) the rejection of predestination
   (D) less emphasis on saints in religious ceremonies

25. "The capacities of women are supposed to be greater, and their senses quicker than those of the men; and what they might be capable of being bred to, is plain from some instances of female wit, which this age is not without."

   Source: Daniel Dafoe, *On the Education of Women*, 1719

   The author of this passage would agree most with which of these statements?

   (A) Because of their ability, women are stronger than men.
   (B) It is acceptable for women to display humor in public.
   (C) The intelligence of women is hypothetical only and not supported by evidence.
   (D) With the proper education, women have the ability to be as smart as men.

GO ON TO THE NEXT PAGE.

26. The concept of "total war" in World War I refers to the

    (A) use of troops from African colonies by England, France, and Germany
    (B) entry of Pacific Rim nations into the Triple Alliance
    (C) involvement of the United States and Canada in a conflict that did not take place within their borders
    (D) mobilization of economic, natural, and human resources for the war effort

27. In order to hold onto their territory, the Ottomans instituted the Tanzimat Reforms, which included

    (A) access to western education
    (B) universal suffrage
    (C) nationalization of private industries
    (D) emancipation of slaves

28. Which of the following statements is NOT true about Akbar the Great?

    (A) Despite gaining power through military might, he was known for being a benevolent ruler.
    (B) He expanded Mughal control over all of north India.
    (C) He tried to establish a new religion, Divine Faith, to unite Muslim, Hindu, and Christian tenets.
    (D) He constructed the Taj Mahal as a Muslim holy place.

29. The Magna Carta

    (A) created a system of common law in Anglo-Saxon England
    (B) established a Model Parliament with advisory powers
    (C) eliminated heredity as a requirement to hold the throne
    (D) did little to stop the growth of centralized government in England

30. Both Gandhi and Mao Zedong

    (A) agreed on the desirability of effecting change nonviolently
    (B) worked to reform the social order in their respective nations
    (C) believed that change must begin at the level of the individual and would involve a spiritual component
    (D) believed in unity among different religious groups

31. One similarity between the Vikings and the Mamluks was

    (A) both groups had been slaves in the lands they eventually conquered
    (B) neither group was able to move into western Europe
    (C) both groups converted to the dominant religion of the land that they conquered
    (D) both groups were known for their seafaring prowess

32. A similarity between Song China and the Italian states was that

    (A) both were able to support numerous large cities
    (B) neither had a strong, centralized government
    (C) both had strong secular and religious leaders
    (D) neither was home to a major religious movement

GO ON TO THE NEXT PAGE.

33. Which of the following is an accurate example of Hellenism?

    (A) The adoption of gothic architecture in India
    (B) Constructing buildings and monuments in stone in southwest Asia
    (C) The spread of monotheism through central Eurasia and the Far East
    (D) The expansion of international trade into northern Africa and western Mediterranean lands

34. Monasticism is a characteristic of which of the following religions?

    (A) Judaism
    (B) Hinduism
    (C) Confucianism
    (D) Catholicism

Good-by. You Certainly Have Been Good to Me.

35. Which of the following statements is an accurate interpretation of this political cartoon?

    (A) Labor unions could not have arisen in the nineteenth century without specific economic and social policies and problems.
    (B) The workplace problems that gave rise to labor unions in the 1800s had mostly been remedied by the end of the century.
    (C) By the end of the nineteenth century, labor union membership was declining.
    (D) Labor union leaders were anxious for the start of the twentieth century.

GO ON TO THE NEXT PAGE.

36. Which of the following statements about neo-Confucianism is NOT correct?

    (A) Additional restrictions were placed on the power of the merchant class.
    (B) It gained prominence not only in China but also in Korea and Japan.
    (C) It synthesized elements of Confucianism, Daoism, and Buddhism.
    (D) Loyalty to government became more important than familial ties.

37. Rachel Carson's book *Silent Spring* increased international awareness of

    (A) ethnic cleansing in Bosnia
    (B) environmental degradation
    (C) gender rights in Africa
    (D) drought and famine in Biafra

38. Which of the following statements about Spanish colonies in the New World is accurate?

    (A) The Spanish did not engage in mercantilism with their colonies.
    (B) Spanish immigration to colonies in Central and South America was low.
    (C) The main economic contribution of Spain's colonies came from gold and salt.
    (D) Sugarcane production was the primary economic activity in Spanish colonies.

39. Which of the following is accurate about the T'ang Dynasty and the Byzantine Empire?

    (A) While the Byzantine Empire had a large urban center, the T'ang Dynasty was more decentralized with small towns along trading routes.
    (B) Both of their governments consisted of bureaucrats who received a standardized education.
    (C) There was considerable overlap between church and state both in governmental affairs and everyday life in both societies.
    (D) Silk weaving was the major industry only in the T'ang Dynasty.

40. Which of the following is NOT an accurate statement about the Middle East in the late twentieth century?

    (A) The discovery of new sources of petroleum diluted the political power and military importance of OPEC member nations.
    (B) A resurgence of religious fundamentalism was responsible for the political revolutions in a number of nations, such as Iran.
    (C) There was increased tension between efforts to modernize and basic tenets of Islamic law and practice.
    (D) Nationalistic extremism was responsible for genocide and civil war in numerous nations.

GO ON TO THE NEXT PAGE.

41. Marxism found few supporters in the late nineteenth century in Europe because

    (A) working conditions in factories improved due to union demands
    (B) the middle class gained additional political representation
    (C) improvements in farming technology increased crop yields
    (D) union organizing was outlawed in a majority of industries

42. Which of the following statements about Sun Yat-sen is accurate?

    (A) The People's Republic of China founded by Sun Yat-sen was based on a Five Year Plan for economic growth.
    (B) The Chinese Republic was successful in expelling the British from China and creating an economically and politically strong nation.
    (C) One of Sun Yat-sen's first tasks as ruler was to purge communists from high-ranking government positions.
    (D) Sun Yat-sen was the first leader of China who was neither a foreign invader nor part of an imperial dynasty.

43. Which of the following statements about the Code of Hammurabi and the Justinian Code are accurate?

    (A) Both sets of laws derived their core philosophies from the Bible.
    (B) The importance of each was that they attempted to organize laws in ways that people could understand.
    (C) While the Justinian Code contained harsh provisions for those convicted of crimes, the Code of Hammurabi was less punitive.
    (D) Neither Code applied to women, foreigners, peasants, or slaves.

44. Which of these factors played the greatest role in European interest in South Africa in the late 1800s?

    (A) The need for additional sources of African slaves
    (B) The desire for new markets for European goods
    (C) The discovery of precious metal resources
    (D) Political turmoil along northern European trade routes

45. "It is the highest impertinence and presumption, therefore, in kings and ministers, to pretend to watch over the economy of private people, and to restrain their expense, either by sumptuary laws, or by prohibiting the importation of foreign luxuries."

    Source: Adam Smith, *An Inquiry into the Nature and Causes of the Wealth of Nations*, 1775.

    The author of this quotation would most likely agree with which of the following governmental programs?

    (A) Increased tariffs on imported items
    (B) Laissez-faire economic policies
    (C) Institution of social welfare systems
    (D) Minimum wage laws for unionized workers

GO ON TO THE NEXT PAGE.

African Colonization 1890-1910

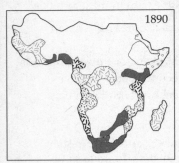
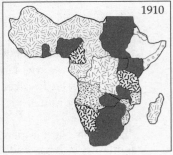

Independent
Britain
France
Belgium
Portugal
Italy
Germany
Spain

46. From the two maps above, what conclusion can you draw about the change in colonization activities between 1890 and 1910?

(A) By 1910, Belgium had become the dominant colonizer on the African continent.

(B) By 1910, more colonized lands were gaining their independence from European colonizers.

(C) While Britain and France expanded their imperial holding between 1890 and 1910, Portugal lost territory during that time period.

(D) Advances in technology and medicine allowed colonization efforts to shift geographically.

47. The European event that had the most direct impact on the growth of civilizations such as Mali and Ghana was the

(A) split between the Roman Catholic and Eastern Orthodox churches

(B) revival of the Silk Route during the rule of Kublai Khan

(C) Slav migration into the Balkans and Greece

(D) establishment of a money-based economy with minted coins

48. Before World War II, both Japan and Germany

(A) withdrew from the League of Nations over land disputes

(B) embraced social reform movements such as universal suffrage

(C) rebuilt their economies from the impacts of the Great Depression and significant war debts

(D) had been penalized for their roles in World War I

49. The *encomienda* system in Spanish colonies was most similar to

(A) mercantilism

(B) feudalism

(C) a corporate colony

(D) chattel slavery

50. Which of the following was NOT a direct outcome of the Reconquista?

(A) Spanish invasion of northern Africa and southern Italy

(B) Sometimes-violent persecution of other religions

(C) Creation of small, independent states within Spain

(D) A civil war over succession to the throne

51. In which of these societies were merchants and traders placed in a lower social class than farmers and artisans?

(A) Han China

(B) Tudor England

(C) Japan

(D) Rome

GO ON TO THE NEXT PAGE.

52. Which of the following is a major difference between the classic periods in Rome and the Islamic civilizations?

    (A) While Roman society had strict social class delineations and little mobility, Islam was egalitarian with few barriers to social mobility.

    (B) The Islamic civilization was more dependent on agriculture and therefore more susceptible to fluctuations in food supply.

    (C) While the Roman Empire fell as a result of internal warfare over succession to the throne, Islamic dynasties faced few internal divisions.

    (D) Islamic scientific thought and art forms borrowed heavily from Hellenistic sources, while Rome's scientific, philosophical, and artistic advancements were unique to its culture.

53. After the Peloponnesian War, the Macedonians took control of Greece and spread Greek culture throughout much of the known world under the leadership of

    (A) Alexander the Great
    (B) Julius Caesar
    (C) Pericles
    (D) Socrates

54. Which of the following is NOT a correct generalization about Islamic societies between 1500 and 1700 ?

    (A) There was no intellectual movement corresponding to the Renaissance and Islamic political and scientific progress lagged behind the Europeans.

    (B) Economic depression and government corruption led to the weakening of many Islamic states during the sixteenth century.

    (C) The Ottoman Empire, Safavid Turks, and Mughal India were linked by their common faith in Islam, as well as by historic trade routes.

    (D) By the late 1700s, Islamic influence had ended everywhere except in North Africa.

55. Which of the following is a true statement about the French Revolution of 1789?

    (A) It failed to instill a sense of nationalism in France.

    (B) Women gained suffrage as part of the revolution.

    (C) The Revolution turned radical with the involvement of the peasants.

    (D) It officially ended with the Constitution of 1791.

56. Which of the following is an accurate statement about modern sub-Saharan independence movements?

    (A) In most nations, cultural and ethnic harmony was achieved when imperialism ended.

    (B) In a majority of new nations, European whites dominated the governmental system.

    (C) The process of gaining independence was easier in nations that did not have a large European minority.

    (D) Substantial foreign investment helped the transition from colony to independent nation.

57. Which of the following was an impact of the theory of Social Darwinism?

    (A) Industrialization led to worker revolts.
    (B) Rulers were obligated to protect their citizens.
    (C) Europeans justified their domination of colonized people.
    (D) Science was viewed as more important than religious belief.

GO ON TO THE NEXT PAGE.

58. Which of the following did NOT happen in China during the Ming Dynasty?

    (A) China was no longer under the control of Mongol leaders.
    (B) Contact with other nations increased with the creation of a Chinese navy.
    (C) Buddhism became the official state religion of China.
    (D) Chinese foreign policy was based on collecting tribute instead of waging war.

59. Which of the following was an impact of modernization efforts in Egypt during the twentieth century?

    (A) Egypt accumulated tremendous debt to European nations such as England and France.
    (B) A Western-style democratic government was installed, although voting rights were not extended to women.
    (C) A liberalization movement among the working and middle class began to remove Muhammad Ali from power.
    (D) State-built infrastructure and public investment in industrialization enabled Egypt to withstand European imperialism.

60. The Chinese Communist Party adapted Marxist communism to

    (A) accommodate a large peasant population
    (B) allow for capitalistic economic programs
    (C) prevent Russian-style education programs
    (D) justify imperialistic policies in Japan, Taiwan, and Mongolia

61. In the Zhou dynasty, the Mandate of Heaven meant that rulers

    (A) were allowed to keep their power if they ruled justly and wisely
    (B) were appointed by Buddhist leaders
    (C) rulers were required to make human sacrifices in order to keep their power
    (D) were encouraged to spread Buddhism through the building of monasteries

GO ON TO THE NEXT PAGE.

"IT'S THE SAME THING WITHOUT MECHANICAL PROBLEMS"

63. Which of the following is an accurate statement about Islamic art and architecture?

   (A) Islamic art focused on abstract geometric patterns and ornate calligraphy in Arabic.

   (B) Elaborate miniatures of historical figures and historical battles were created during the Abbasid and Umayyad Dynasties.

   (C) The most important architectural contributions were elaborate pyramids and sculptures.

   (D) Most Islamic art forms were derived from classic Greek and Roman examples.

64. In China, Confucianism emphasized the idea that

   (A) equality should exist among all members of society

   (B) salvation could be attained by prayer, meditation, and good deeds

   (C) individual goals should be placed ahead of the needs of the group

   (D) harmony could be achieved by the proper behavior of each member of the family or society

62. Which of the following is the best explanation of this political cartoon?

   (A) While the Marshall Plan was aimed at military assistance, the Council for Mutual Economic Assistance (COMECON) was directed at agricultural production.

   (B) Marshall Plan participants were "imprisoned" by their association with Western political interests.

   (C) Stalin could not offer farmers in Russia and its satellite states the level of technology offered by the Marshall Plan.

   (D) Critics were unhappy with both the cost and the disappointing results of the Marshall Plan.

65. All of the following were impacts of the Industrial Revolution EXCEPT

   (A) the rise of social and political reform movements

   (B) a manufacturing system based on division of labor

   (C) an increased demand for African slaves in North America

   (D) an increase in the number of independent nations

GO ON TO THE NEXT PAGE.

66. The most direct result of the Protestant Reformation was

(A) Christianity spread into the Ottoman Empire and Southeast Asia

(B) the printing press was invented

(C) interest in the arts and scientific inquiry increased

(D) literacy rates across Europe rose

67. The Second Age of Islamic conquest, which began in the 1200's, was a result of

(A) the translation of the Qu'ran into the vernacular that allowed Islam to move farther into Africa and Europe

(B) a period of peace and prosperity that enabled Islamic trade routes to spread farther north and west

(C) the Crusades and other invasions that led to the formation of new militaristic dynasties

(D) disorganization among western European nations that allowed for further Islamic empire-building

68. In which of these colonies did a private company have political authority?

(A) India

(B) Brazil

(C) Cuba

(D) Benin

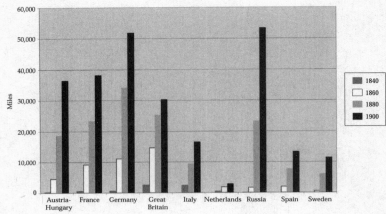

European Railroads 1840-1900

69. Based on the information in the above chart, which of the following conclusions is accurate?

(A) Eastern Europe lagged behind western Europe in the development of national railroad systems.

(B) There were approximately the same number of people living in Germany in 1900 as in Russia.

(C) Russia's Industrial Revolution occurred later than Great Britain's.

(D) The greatest proportionate growth in miles of rail occurred in Germany between 1880 and 1900.

70. Which of the following is an accurate statement about trends in art and literature after World War I?

(A) Modernism and experimental methods and materials dominated the art world.

(B) The development of new materials and technology revolutionized architecture.

(C) The anxiety and uncertainty of the postwar period influenced literature and art.

(D) Governmental censorship of literature during the war resulted in a cultural backlash of anti-government writing.

END OF SECTION I

WORLD HISTORY
SECTION II

You will have 10 minutes to read the contents of this green insert. You are advised to spend most of the 10 minutes analyzing the documents and planning your answer for the document-based question essay in Part A. You may make notes in this green insert. At the end of the 10-minute period, you will be told to break the seal on the pink free-response booklet and to begin writing your answers on the lined pages of the booklet. Do not break the seal on the pink booklet until you are told to do so. Suggested writing time is 40 minutes for the document-based essay question in Part A and 40 minutes for each of the essay questions in Part B and Part C.

BE SURE TO MANAGE YOUR TIME CAREFULLY.

Write your answers in the <u>pink</u> booklet with a <u>pen</u>. The green insert may be used for reference and/or scratchwork as you answer the free-response questions, but no credit will be given for the work shown in the green insert.

DO NOT OPEN THIS BOOKLET UNTIL YOU ARE TOLD TO DO SO.

GO ON TO THE NEXT PAGE.

WORLD HISTORY
SECTION II
Part A
(Suggested writing time—40 minutes)
Percent of Section II score—33 1/3

Directions: The following question is based on the accompanying Documents 1-7. (The documents have been edited for the purpose of this exercise.) Write your answer on the lined pages of the Section II free-response booklet.

This question is designed to test your ability to work with and understand historical documents. Write an essay that:

- Has a relevant thesis and supports that thesis with evidence from the documents.
- Uses all of the documents.
- Analyzes the documents by grouping them in as many appropriate ways as possible. **Does not simply summarize the documents individually.**
- Takes into account both the sources of the documents and the authors' points of view.
- Explains the need for one type of additional document.

You may refer to relevant historical information not mentioned in the documents.

1. Using the following documents, discuss the barriers women have faced for more equal treatment in society. Consider the goals and methods of such campaigns. What additional kinds of documents would be useful in attempting to answer these questions?

GO ON TO THE NEXT PAGE.

Document 1

Source: Anna Manning Comfort, *The Public 2*, 1899.

Home Burdens of Uncle Sam

"Take up the white man's burden" –

The Negro, once our slave!

Boast lightly of his freedom,

This problem still is grave.

We scoff and shoot and lynch him,

And yet, because he's black,

We shove him out of office

And crowd him off the track.

"Take up the white man's burden" –

Yes, one of them is sex.

Enslaved are your brave women,

No ballot, while you tax!

Your labors and your conflicts,

Columbia's daughters share,

Yet still denied the franchise,

Quick give! be just! deal fair!

GO ON TO THE NEXT PAGE.

Document 2

Source: From the *Women's Charter*, adopted at the Founding Conference of the Federation of South African Women, Johannesburg, 1954.

This organisation is formed for the purpose of uniting women in common action for the removal of all political, legal, economic, and social disabilities. We shall strive for women to obtain:

1. The right to vote and to be elected to all State bodies, without restriction or discrimination.

2. The right to full opportunities for employment with equal pay and possibilities of promotion in all spheres of work.

3. Equal rights with men in relation to property, marriage and children, and for the removal of all laws and customs that deny women such equal rights.

4. For the development of every child through free compulsory education for all; for the protection of mother and child through maternity homes, welfare clinics, crèches and nursery schools, in country-side and towns; through proper homes for all, and through the provision of water, light, transport, sanitation, and other amenities of modern civilisation.

5. For the removal of all laws that restrict free movement, that prevent or hinder the right of free association and activity in democratic organizations, and the right to participate in the work of these organisations.

6. To build and strengthen women's sections in the National Liberatory movements, the organisation of women in trade unions, and through the peoples' varied organisation.

7. To cooperate with all other organisations that have similar aims in South Africa as well as throughout the world.

8. To strive for permanent peace throughout the world.

Document 3

Source: Livy, a Roman Historian, wrote the following description of the women's demonstration supporting the repeal of the Oppian Law, 195 B.C.E., which limited women's use of expensive goods.

The matrons, whom neither counsel nor shame nor their husbands' orders could keep at home, blockaded every street in the city and every entrance to the Forum. As the men came down to the Forum, the matrons besought them to let them, too, have back the luxuries they had enjoyed before, giving as their reason that the republic was thriving and that everyone's private wealth was increasing with every day. This crowd of women was growing daily, for now they were even gathering from the towns and villages. Before long they dared go up and solicit consuls, praetors and other magistrates.

When the speeches for and against the law had been made, a considerably larger crowd of women poured forth in public the next day; as a single body they besieged the doors of the tribunes, who were vetoing their colleagues' motion, and they did not stop until the tribunes took back their veto. After that there was no doubt that all the tribes would repeal the law.

GO ON TO THE NEXT PAGE.

Document 4

Source: Ban Zhao, leading female Confucian and imperial historian under Emperor Han Hedi, from *Lessons for a Woman*, an instructional manual in feminine behavior, c. 100 C.E.

Whenever the mother-in-law says, "Do not do that," and if what she says is right, unquestionably the daughter-in-law obeys. Whenever the mother-in-law says, "Do that," even if what she says is wrong, still the daughter-in-law submits unfailingly to the command. Let a woman act not contrary to the wishes and the opinions of the parents-in-law about right and wrong; let her not dispute with them what is straight and what is crooked. Such docility may be called obedience which sacrifices personal opinion. "A Pattern for Women" says: "If a daughter-in-law who follows the wishes of her parents-in-law is like an echo and shadow, how could she not be praised?"

Document 5

Source: *The Plight of Women's Work in the Early Industrial Revolution in England and Wales*, evidence taken by Children's Employment Commission, 1841.

Miss—has been for several years in the dress-making business. The common hours of business are from 8 A.M. 'til 11. P.M. in the winters; in the summer from 6 or half past 6 A.M. 'til 12 at night. During the fashionable season, that is from April 'til the later end of July, it frequently happens that the ordinary hours are greatly exceeded; if there is a drawing room or grand fete, or mourning to be made, it often happens that the work goes on for 20 hours out of the 24, occasionally all night. . . . The general result of the long hours and sedentary occupation is to impair seriously and very frequently to destroy the health of the young women. The digestion especially suffers, and also the lungs: pain to the side is very common, and the hands and feet die away from want of circulation and exercise.

Miss—is sure that there are some thousands of young women employed in the business in London and in the country. If one vacancy were to occur now there would be 20 applicants for it. Thinks that no men could endure the work enforced from the dress-makers.

Document 6

Source: Aung San Suu Kyi, Nobel Prize Laureate, excerpts from keynote address at APC Conference, 1995.

For millennia women have dedicated themselves almost exclusively to the task of nurturing, protecting, and caring for the young and old, striving for the conditions of peace that favour life as a whole. To this can be added the fact that, to the best of my knowledge, no war was ever started by women. But it is women and children who have always suffered most in situations of conflict. Now that we are gaining control of the primary historical role imposed on us of sustaining life in the context of the home and family, it is time to apply in the arena of the world the wisdom and experience thus gained in activities of peace over so many thousands of years. The education and empowerment of women throughout the world cannot fail to result in a more caring, tolerant, just, and peaceful life for all.

GO ON TO THE NEXT PAGE.

Document 7

Source: Raja Rammohan Roy, *A Second Conference Between an Advocate for, and an Opponent of the Practice of Burning Widows Alive*, 1820.

Advocate:

I alluded. . . to the real reason for our anxiety to persuade widows to follow their husbands, and for our endeavors to burn them pressed down with ropes: viz., that women are by nature of inferior understanding, without resolution, unworthy of trust, subject to passions, And void of virtuous knowledge; they, according to the precepts of the Sastra, are not allowed to marry again after the demise of their husbands, and consequently despair at once of all worldly pleasure; hence it is evident, that death to these unfortunate widows is preferable to existence; for the great difficulty which a widow may experience by living a purely ascetic life, as prescribed by the Sastras, is obvious; may bring disgrace upon her paternal and maternal relations, and those that may be connected with her husband. Under these circumstances, we instruct them from their early life in the idea of the beatitude of their relations, both by birth and marriage, and their reputation in this world. From this many of them, on the death of their husbands, become desirous of accompanying them; but to remove every chance of their trying to escape from the blazing fire, in the burning them we first tie them down to the pile.

END OF PART A

GO ON TO THE NEXT PAGE.

WORLD HISTORY
SECTION II
Part B
(Suggested planning and writing time—40 minutes)
Percent of Section II score—33 1/3

Directions: You are to answer the following question. You should spend 5 minutes organizing or outlining your essay. Write an essay that:

- Has a relevant thesis and supports that thesis with appropriate historical evidence.
- Addresses all parts of the question.
- Uses historical context to show change over time and/or continuities.
- Analyzes the process of change and/or continuity over time.

2. Discuss how technological changes since 1750 have had an impact on family structure in one of the following nations. Be sure to include continuities as well as changes.

    China
    Japan
    India
    Great Britain

END OF PART B

GO ON TO THE NEXT PAGE.

Part C
(Suggested planning and writing time—40 minutes)
Percent of Section II score—33 1/3

Directions: You are to answer the following question. You should spend 5 minutes organizing or outlining your essay. Write an essay that:

- Has a relevant thesis and supports that thesis with appropriate historical evidence.
- Addresses all parts of the question.
- Makes direct, relevant comparisons.
- Analyzes reasons for similarities and differences.

3. Karl Marx asserted, "Religion is the opiate of the masses." Using ONE of the religions below, compare and contrast the role the religion has played in promoting or impeding societal change. Consider specific revolutions, texts, and religious leaders in answering the question.

  Christianity
  Buddhism
  Hinduism
  Islam
  Judaism

STOP

END OF EXAM

Chapter 12
Answers and Explanations for Practice Test 1

ANSWER KEY TEST 1

1.	A	36.	D
2.	D	37.	B
3.	D	38.	D
4.	D	39.	B
5.	B	40.	A
6.	D	41.	A
7.	D	42.	D
8.	C	43.	B
9.	D	44.	C
10.	D	45.	B
11.	A	46.	D
12.	A	47.	D
13.	D	48.	A
14.	D	49.	D
15.	D	50.	D
16.	A	51.	A
17.	A	52.	A
18.	A	53.	A
19.	D	54.	D
20.	D	55.	C
21.	D	56.	C
22.	C	57.	C
23.	B	58.	C
24.	D	59.	A
25.	D	60.	A
26.	D	61.	A
27.	A	62.	C
28.	D	63.	A
29.	D	64.	D
30.	B	65.	D
31.	C	66.	D
32.	A	67.	C
33.	B	68.	A
34.	D	69.	C
35.	A	70.	C

1.   A   This question is a broad generalization about early societies. Remember to read the question carefully because you need to eliminate the three answer choices that are characteristics of early societies. And, be careful when you see the word all—that means you should be critically searching for the exception to the rule. The correct answer is (A). Not all early societies developed written communications. For example, while Sumer and Mesopotamia had a system of writing, pre-Columbian civilizations such as the Inca did not. You should use POE to get rid of (B) and (D). The Neolithic Revolution brought about sweeping changes in technology that allowed for irrigated agricultural activities in river valleys. (C) is not the correct answer because as permanent settlements arose, some people worked primarily as farmers, while others worked on monument building or as artisans.

2.   D   The Council of Trent (1545) was an attempt by the Roman Catholic Church to institute its own "reformation." The Council upheld many of the church's practices and beliefs (in opposition to Protestant faiths). However, it did outlaw some of the more heinous practices, such as selling indulgences.

              Using POE, you can eliminate (B) and (C) because Luther and Calvin were both Protestant. (A) is a smart guess, yet while Copernicus and Galileo did come up against strong church opposition, the Council of Trent's edict was written before either of those scientists published their works.

3.   D   Even if you are not sure what a Gunpowder Empire is, the question asks you about something that pertains to the Islamic world. Using this information, eliminate any answer choices that include non-Muslim empires. Ming China was not Muslim so get rid of (A) and (B).

              The Gunpowder Empires are associated with nations who had been able to take advantage of new military technologies. Those who had guns included the following:

                     The Czars of Muskovy Russia
                     The Ottoman Turks
                     The Tokugawa Shogunate
                     Safavid Persia
                     Mughal India
                     The Ming Dynasty
                     The Spanish and the Portuguese

4.   D   While Mesoamerican religious rites were known to include sacrifice, the ceremonial use of sacrifice in the other civilizations is either unknown or untrue. To use POE on an EXCEPT question, first remember that you need to eliminate the three features that are true of all of the societies mentioned. You can get rid of (B) because all of these early societies developed ways to provide a constant source of water for agriculture. Likewise, they all developed specialization in craftwork, built monuments (pyramids, temples, ziggurats), and divided labor duties by gender, so (A) and (C) are also not the right answer.

5.   B   Peter the Great modernized eighteenth-century Russia by adopting Western-style culture and ideas, establishing a central bureaucratic government, building a strong military, and increasing agricultural and industrial productivity. He was also a strict dictatorial ruler, willing to use force to achieve his ends.

Using POE, you can eliminate (A) because Peter's economic reforms were successful, and (D) because Peter the Great could not be considered categorically enlightened during his rule. (C) is also incorrect because ordinary citizens' lives were not greatly improved. There were few civil rights, increased restrictions were placed on organized religion, and people in the lower classes still had few opportunities to improve their status.

6.   D   Although socialism and communism were on the rise in the late eighteenth and early nineteenth centuries, they were not factors that destabilized the balance of power. They were certainly factors that led to the destabilization of internal developments in countries like Russia near the end of World War I, but during the time period in question, European balance of power was more greatly impacted by the developments listed in the other three answer choices.

Using POE, you can eliminate any answer choice that describes a reason that one country became more or less powerful than another country in Europe during the late 1800s. You should definitely know that nationalism was impacting the balance of power, so eliminate (A). Nationalism led to unification in Italy and Germany, for example. The newly unified country of Germany quickly became an industrial power and eyed its neighbors enviously, so eliminate (C). The European powers also eagerly gobbled up Africa and Asia, extending their collective influence across the globe even as they individually competed with each other and felt threatened by the increasing size of each others' empires, so get rid of (B). The peoples of the Ottoman Empire and Austro-Hungarian Empires, in particular, channeled their sense of nationalism into sometimes violent attacks against the imperial authorities.

7.   D   Using POE, remember that (A), *brinksmanship*, refers to the period when each side brandished its massive powers in a game of military chicken, such as in Cuba. (B), *peaceful coexistence*, is also a Cold War term. Based on the recognition that the world was never going to be 100 percent democratic or communist, either way, the goal was to *peacefully coexist* (fully armed, of course), because the alternative was (C), *mutual assured destruction*, which justified the massive investment in weapons and war machines on both sides of the conflict. (D), *appeasement*, was the term used to describe European leaders' willingness to allow Adolf Hitler to seize territory in Europe without repercussions prior to World War II.

8.   C   In general, all Europeans played the colonization game for the same reasons: wealth, power, and racial and religious superiority. However, while the Spanish established large, permanent settlements in their colonies and encouraged Spaniards to move to the Americas through land grants, the French either had less success or less interest in these activities.

Using POE, you can eliminate (A) because everyone was interested in resource extraction. You can also eliminate (B) once you recall that France also held colonies in Africa (Guinea, Upper Volta, and Congo) and Southeast Asia (Indochina), plus "shared custody" of India for a time. The French encountered fewer natives than the Spanish because their mode of colonization usually did not involve expansive land-based development, meaning the French may even have converted a larger percentage of the (smaller number of) natives they encountered—so cross out (D).

9.   D   Feudalism was the primary political system in western Europe and Japan during the medieval period. Its main characteristic was a decentralized power structure that stressed alliances between nobles and monarchs. The main difference between Japanese and European feudalism was that the size of the peasant population in Japan was considerably smaller than that in European nations.

Use POE and common sense to eliminate (B) (Think of one word: *samurai*.). (A) is not the correct answer because there was a hierarchy of power in Japan similar to that in Europe. The Japanese *daimyo* was similar to the European *lord*. (C) is also incorrect. In both Europe and Japan, feudalism represented a decentralized system of governance, and, in both, the power of the ruler was inextricably tied to the bonds he forged with lords. In Japan, the emperor probably had even less power with the rise of the shogunate (a military government).

10. D   The Glorious Revolution (1688) represented a change in political power that occurred as a result of a peaceful coup. James II, the Catholic brother of Charles II, dissolved Parliament over religious differences. Parliamentary leaders led an uprising against James, and, in his place, installed a dual monarchy held by James' Protestant daughter, Mary, and her husband, William.

Using POE, you can immediately eliminate (B) because wars of succession were the norm in many European nations. It certainly wasn't the first time a monarch had ever been deposed, so it isn't (A). (C) is also incorrect because the new government was not secular—it replaced a Catholic monarchy with a Protestant one.

11. A   Make sure you read the question carefully. While certain Western knowledge and technology have probably contributed to better health care and education, (B), this is not a by-product of the spread of American culture. American *culture* is responsible for the proliferation of fast food restaurants in Kenya and weekly broadcasts of *Sex & the City* in Russia. The influence of multinational corporations also spreads Western culture. And, in a significant number of nations, Western culture has replaced, or conflicts with, religion and local culture. Protests at World Bank meetings and acts of terrorism against Western interests are some of the ways in which this anti-American backlash has been expressed. But wouldn't it be nice if (D) were true?

12. A   The Delhi Sultanate did not leave a long-lasting political or economic legacy after the fourteenth century. Its one contribution was the introduction of Islam into Indian society. There was a tremendous migration of Muslims into India as a result of instability in other Islamic lands, and many Indians embraced Islam. (For one thing, women had more rights under Muslim rule as opposed to Hindu rule.)

Use POE and common sense to eliminate (B) and (D). African and central Eurasian trade routes grew under Muslim occupation of India, and the Mamluks consolidated India into a strong, centralized state. The caste system remained an important part of Indian life into the twentieth century, so (C) is also incorrect.

13. D   The outcome of Bismarck's plan was that every nation in sub-Saharan Africa fell into foreign hands, except Ethiopia and Liberia. It was Bismarck's goal to maintain that elusive "balance of power" among European nations, and the orderly division of African land was seen as one way of averting war. The Berlin Conference of 1884 and 1885 laid down the rules for future colonization. Using POE, you can eliminate (B) because, while the United States attended the meetings where decisions about Africa were made, America did not participate in imperialism in that part of the world. You can also eliminate (A) because while Germany did gain some lands in Africa (Togoland, Cameroon, German Southwest Africa), the French and British held much more territory in Africa. (C) is out because economic and social pressures led to an end to slavery, not the plan to partition Africa.

14. D   While many European nations relied on their colonies to be a steady source of raw materials and cheap labor and a ready market for manufactured goods, imperialism was not a necessary component of industrialization, so (D) is the answer. Remember on EXCEPT questions, three of the choices are true while the one that is not is the answer.

15. D   The Upanishad movement was prompted by the focus of religious leaders on ritual instead of substance. The Protestant Reformation was sparked by the sale of indulgences and other perceived abuses among religious leaders.

          If you know nothing of the Upanishad movement but know a little about the Protestant Reformation, you can use POE to eliminate (A), (B), and (C) because none of these was entirely true of the Protestant Reformation.

16. A   The Four Noble Truths are associated with Buddhism. (C), Judaism, has the Ten Commandments. (D), Islam, has Five Pillars. (B), Legalism, is not a religion.

17. A   First, look at each choice and make sure that the statement is true for both the Inca and the Yuan. If it's only true for one or the other, it cannot be the correct answer. In the 1200s, Mongol invasion of China led to the Yuan Dynasty. (Remember Kublai Khan? He was a Yuan ruler.) During this period, the territory of China expanded greatly, as did its economy as trade routes expanded. While China flourished under Yuan rule, the Mongols established what amounted to a caste system with native Chinese having little ability for advancement. In the late thirteenth century, Yuan rule ended with a successful Chinese uprising.

          The Inca began as a small city-state, which, under militaristic native rulers, eventually conquered much of western South America. The Incan dynasty was most known for its extensive system of roads, sophisticated farming techniques, and lack of a system of writing. Another feature was the strict class system established by the Incan ruler. The Incan empire remained strong until the mid-1500s when the Spanish arrived in South America.

          Using POE, eliminate (B) because it is not true of either society. The Inca began as a small settlement in Peru and the Yuan was formed through the Mongol invasion (although the Yuan did *fall* as a result of a peasant uprising). While the Yuan Dynasty relied heavily on trade, there is little evidence that trade played a large role in Incan society, so (C) is incorrect. While (D) is true of the Yuan (China did flourish under Mongol rule in terms of size of territory, economic growth, and peace), you know what happened to native cultures once the explorers found their way to the Americas.

18. A   The Emancipation Act of 1861 "freed" the serfs and allowed them to work in nonagricultural jobs. It was this pool of labor that made industrialization possible in Russia. Use POE and common sense to eliminate (D). You know that Russia did not embrace capitalism, even during the nineteenth century, and you also know that the improvement in the standard of living realized in Western nations was never achieved in Russia. While Russia did become more interested in expansionism, it was primarily to gain access to water routes, not develop new markets so eliminate (B). If you didn't remember that Russia had large deposits of coal within its own borders and also a significant steel industry, (C) is a smart guess.

19. D   The Black Death was an important historical event because of the number of European deaths and because of its impact on other parts of the world. It serves as an illustration of how the world became more interdependent during the late medieval period and how trade routes were responsible not only for moving goods and ideas, but also for spreading disease. However, the Black Death occurred as feudalism was ending in western Europe. During this period there was more urbanization, more proto-industrialization, and more contact with other lands through trade and conquest.

The other three choices are true and therefore not the answer. Starting with the plague's impact on Europe, (A) and (C) are tied together. The staggering number of deaths in Europe did have a negative (albeit temporary) impact on productivity, which would then obviously have an impact on supply. The bubonic plague actually originated in China and then spread through central Eurasia before finally landing in Sicily in 1347. (B) was a result of the Black Death's arrival in China, and therefore cannot be the correct answer.

20. D   Direct colonization of less-developed countries did not occur during the Cold War. The other three answers are true and therefore not correct. Common sense tells you (C) is true, as is (A)—support for dictatorial regimes in Nicaragua (Somoza) and Panama (Noriega) and the support for rebel groups in Cuba and post-Somoza Nicaragua show the United States' determination to prevent the spread of communism to Latin America. In 1946, Winston Churchill used the phrase "iron curtain" to describe the Soviet lockdown of its peoples within Eastern Europe, so (B) is also true and therefore wrong.

21. D   Better access to medical care would mean that more people would live longer, there would be fewer infant deaths, and so on. If you use POE, you don't need the chart to answer this question. Just cross off the answer choices that *could* be responsible for a declining population in a developing, sub-Saharan nation. Eliminate (A), as reproductive planning generally means fewer births, then eliminate (B) and (C) because more prosperous nations where women are involved in the work force tend to have lower birth rates anyway.

22. C   Japan was one of the few nations able to withstand foreign dominance during the thirteenth and fourteenth centuries. Use POE to get rid of the nations that you know were part of the Empire. The Mongol Empire included China (Yuan), Ukraine and Russia (Muscovy), India (Delhi and Mughal), and Persia (Safavid).

23. B   During this period, the Japanese cut ties with China and focused on the study of art and literature. As a result, Japan developed its own cultural identity. Use common sense and POE to eliminate (C) because Japan was never occupied by the Mongols, and (D) because Japan never adopted Confucianism as a state religion/philosophy but rather embraced Shintoism and Buddhism, both of which remain major influences in Japan today. As for (A), Japan didn't start to explore and conquer until after the Meiji Restoration, but if you're unsure when the Meiji Restoration was in relation to the Heian period, guess and go.

24. D   The Council of Trent was formed as part of the Catholic Counter-Reformation to combat the rise of Protestantism by instituting reforms in the Catholic Church. While it failed to end the spread of Protestant beliefs, certain fundamental changes were adopted. Because (D) was not a result of the Council, it is the correct answer, but the other three choices are true. The Council outlawed the sale of indulgences, (A), in response to Luther's attacks. In order to reinforce the perception of its power and majesty, the church commissioned religious art and architecture, (B), much of it in the baroque style. One of the most significant actions of the Council of Trent came in its affirmation of all of the church doctrines, including the rejection of the Calvinist belief in predestination, (C).

25. D   This quote deals with the potential of women, which was clearly not being realized under the contemporary social and governmental restrictions. Using POE, don't be misled by bits and pieces of the quote. While "senses quicker" might imply strength and "female wit" could insinuate humor, neither (A) nor (B) are correct.

         While Dafoe is saying that women's true abilities are not well documented, he does not mean to say that no evidence has been offered to show such intelligence. Instead, he is rallying against the policies that have prevented women from realizing their potential, and he deems the best way to allow women to demonstrate their abilities will be through education. (C) is a smart guess but incorrect.

26. D   While more nations and soldiers were involved in World War I than in any previous military action, the term "total war" does not apply to answer choices (A), (B), or (C). Instead, it refers to the massive mobilization of resources necessary to carry out a military action of this size. Some of the tools nations used to achieve this level of mobilization were: nationalization of key industries, central economic planning, and wartime rationing.

27. A   The Tanzimat Reforms were a vast set of changes instated in the Ottoman Empire between 1839 and 1876. Overall, these reforms were meant to modernize the empire, and their goal was to save the empire. However, they were not ultimately successful. Among the changes were modernizing industry, granting more political and religious freedom, expansion of the nation's physical infrastructure, and the introduction of Western-style education. Women had access to education, there was more tolerance of non-Muslim citizens, and the government was secularized. However, (B), (C), and (D) were not part of the Tanzimat Reforms.

28. D You need to select the answer choice that is *not* a true statement about Akbar the Great. The Taj Mahal was built by Shah Jahan as a tribute to his wife, not by Akbar the Great. Jahan ruled after Akbar, from 1628 to 1658.

Even if you don't know who built the Taj Mahal, you can use POE to eliminate things that you know are true about Akbar. If you remember that he was a military leader who built powerful civilizations based on prosperity and tolerance, you should be able to eliminate (A) and (B), if you remember where the Mughal empire was located. If you aren't sure about the remaining answer choices, you should take your best guess and move on. If you recall that Akbar accepted the practice of all religions during his reign and even attempted to create a new faith, Divine Faith, in which he tried to combine elements of Zoroastrianism, Jainism, Hinduism, and Christianity, you can eliminate (C).

29. D Here is the important point to remember: In 1215, King John needed money to wage his war with France. The only way to "persuade" the nobles to fund his military campaign was to sign the Magna Carta, which guaranteed basic rights to nobility and restricted the ability of the king to increase taxes. While the Magna Carta did place additional restriction on the powers of the king, it did little to reverse the trend toward a more centralized and stronger national government.

Using POE, you can eliminate (A) because English common law (and the institution of grand and petit juries) was codified under Henry II in 1166. While the idea of greater rights and representation was contained in the Magna Carta, it wasn't until later in the thirteenth century, under Edward I, that the first Parliament was convened, so (B) is not the answer. You know that there were plenty of English kings after John and that conflict over succession is a common theme in English history, so eliminate (C).

30. B Both Gandhi and Mao worked to reform the social order of their respective societies albeit in different ways. Gandhi spoke often of both the suffering and the great potential of the peasant classes and even promoted the abolition of the "untouchable" caste. And Mao was clearly driven to tap the great potential of China's peasants and to create an egalitarian society during the Cultural Revolution. Use POE and be sure to select the answer choice that is true of *both* Gandhi and Mao. Choice (A) is incorrect because Mao wasn't shy about promoting change from "the barrel of a gun," but Gandhi actively practiced nonviolence. Both (C) and (D) are incorrect as Mao actively worked to eliminate religion from Chinese society whereas Gandhi promoted religious unity between Muslims and Hindus.

31. C In Kiev, Prince Vladimir I converted to Christianity, thereby fostering the spread of that religion through eastern Europe. The Mamluks became Muslims and helped protect Islamic society and culture from attacks from Mongols and Crusaders.

To use POE, remember that the correct answer will be the statement that is true about *both* the Vikings and the Mamluks. The Vikings, descendents of Germanic warrior tribes, were known for their plundering raids of western Europe (England, Normandy) and for establishing Kiev and Novogrod in Russia. Viking invasions in eastern Europe linked Slavs to the rest of the world through expanded trade routes. Remember, too, that the Vikings were excellent open-seas navigators (they were believed to be the first Europeans to cross the Atlantic). Armed with this information, you can eliminate (A) and (B). The Mamluks were former Turkish military slaves in the Islamic Empire—not known for their seafaring skills, so cross out (D)—who overthrew the Ayyubad dynasty in the thirteenth century and ruled parts of Egypt, Syria, and Arabia for two centuries.

32.   A   On the surface, it would not appear that these two societies would have much in common, but think about more general comparisons and you'll find that they do share some important features. The only answer that works for both is (A). Mercantile states (Genoa, Pisa, Venice) grew in Italy as a result of industry and trade, and owing to a strong economy and new agricultural techniques, the Song were the most urbanized society of their time.

Eliminate (D) immediately because of Italy's long history with Catholicism and its various movements and traditions, even if you don't recall that the Song were all about neo-Confucianism, which is not a religion. Conversely, (B) is true for the Song, but not for Italy. China continued to be ruled by a strong emperor, supported by neo-Confucianism and a strong central bureaucracy. On the other hand, each Italian city-state was ruled by the dominant family and not subject to any national authority.

POE will help you eliminate (C) because China, having a state philosophy instead of a state religion, did not have a spiritual leader. (Italy, on the other hand, did have a spiritual leader in the pope, but, as noted above, no single secular ruler.)

33.   B   Hellenism refers to the adoption of various elements of Greek civilization by other parts of the world. Greek architecture relied heavily on using marble and other hard stones in building construction, and the spread of this style to southwest Asia is an example of Hellenism. (A) is incorrect because gothic architecture was a feature of medieval western Europe, not ancient Greece. While monotheism did spread beyond the Mediterranean and trade expanded south and west, neither are uniquely Greek, so (C) and (D) are incorrect.

34.   D   Even if you are not sure what monasticism is you can still use POE to eliminate at least answer choice (C) because Confucianism is not a religion, but rather a philosophy. Monasticism refers to the establishment of communities, called monasteries, where monks could withdraw from the secular world to lead lives devoted to their religion. The correct answer is (D). Christian monasticism began in the third century in Egypt.

35.   A   More than other questions on the test, political cartoons allow you to use common sense to eliminate incorrect answers. You know that the problems facing workers at the end of the nineteenth century did not magically disappear with the beginning of the twentieth century. American labor unions (such as the AFL and the CIO) did not arise until the 1900s, and labor union membership continued to grow until the late 1900s. Therefore, (B) and (C) can be eliminated. While (D) is true, it's not an accurate interpretation of the cartoon.

36. D Neo-Confucianism was a movement that synthesized Confucianism, Buddhism, and Daoism. Developed during the Song Dynasty, it became the dominant philosophy during the Ming Dynasty. While loyalty to government was an important feature of neo-Confucianism, family structure was the foundation for all other relationships in one's life.

The other three choices are true and therefore not the answer. With an emphasis on moral behavior, filial piety, and social order, neo-Confucianism is not all that different from Confucianism. Therefore, (C) is a correct statement about neo-Confucianism. Because neo-Confucianism blended Dao and Buddhist elements, it was more widely accepted outside of China. Indeed, it became an influential philosophy in Japan and Korea, especially with the adoption of meritocracy, so (B) is not the answer. The Ming resurrected the examination system, and, as Confucianist scholars rose to higher positions of power in the bureaucracy, they worked to limit the power of groups whom they perceived as threats—the military and the merchant classes. Choice (A) is a correct statement, so it is not the answer.

37. B *Silent Spring* was published in 1962 and outlined the environmental dangers associated with the use of DDT. It ushered in an era of increased environmental concern and greater awareness of the interconnectedness of biological systems and world economies.

38. D Spanish plantations were established to grow sugarcane (and other cash crops). Using POE and common sense you can eliminate both (A) and (B). All mother countries engaged in mercantilism; it was one of the primary reasons for colonization. Also, you know that many Spaniards came to the New World, many under the auspices of a papal mandate for conversion of the natives to Catholicism. But Spain's true goals were more about land and profits, which meant complete control of the land and its people, regardless of what religion they followed.

To decide between (C) and (D), you need to remember what the primary source of economic gain was in Spain's colonies. Half of answer (C) is correct—the Spanish exploited the natural deposits of gold in the Americas. However, salt was not one of the resources that made Spain rich off the New World. (C) is a smart guess even though the answer is (D).

39. B Both civilizations developed strong central governments run by bureaucrats. In Byzantium, bureaucrats were trained at the University of Constantinople. In the T'ang Dynasty, the bureaucrats (mandarins) had to pass civil service exams to enter government service.

To use POE on this question, remember you need to select the answer that is true for both of these civilizations. (A) is true for the Byzantine Empire (Constantinople), but not for the T'ang. The capital city, Changan, grew into the largest city in the world at the time. (C) is true of Byzantium only, in which the emperor was considered a representative of God and Greek Orthodoxy was the foundation of the civilization. While Buddhism was still popular during the T'ang Dynasty, Confucianism was far more influential in government and private life. (D) is a tricky answer choice. While you know that silk weaving was important to the Chinese economy, it also became the primary industry in Byzantium after two monks smuggled silkworm eggs out of China on a missionary visit.

40. A   Remember you are looking for the answer that is not true—common sense can tell you that (A) doesn't make sense, so it is the answer. Even if you don't know very much about the history of the Middle East, wouldn't the discovery of something as important as petroleum lead to an increase in political power? Of course it would. As long as you know that most OPEC countries are in the Middle East, you can get this question right. As for the wrong answers, the Iranian Revolution was all about religious fundamentalism, so (B) is true; modernization and the basic tenets of any religion tend to come into conflict with each other, so (C) is true; nationalism led to civil war in Afghanistan and to genocide against the Kurds in Iraq, so (D) is true.

41. A   With better conditions, there was less reason for the level of revolt called for by Karl Marx. Moreover, many of these reforms came because of the demands made by labor unions. Many workers chose to join unions rather than stage communist revolts.

42. D   Sun Yat-sen was considered the father of modern China. As the founder of the Revolution-ary Alliance, he ousted the ruling Qing Dynasty and formed the Nationalist Party in 1911 and 1912. The goal of the Nationalists was to create a representative democracy based on the People's Principles: nationalism, democracy, and livelihood.

Using POE, you can eliminate (A) and (C). The Five Year Plan is associated with Mao Zedong, not Sun Yat-sen. Plus, the communist party had not yet been formed at the time of Sun Yat- sen's administration. (The communists took over in 1949.) Sun Yat-sen overthrew the Qing, not the British, which makes (B) incorrect. Taiwan became a territory of Japan at the end of the Sino-Japanese War in 1895.

43. B   The importance of both codes was that they attempted to organize existing laws into formats that could be understood and applied fairly to everyone. Use common sense and POE to elimi-nate (A) and (D). (A) is incorrect because the Code of Hammurabi was created before the Bible. (D) is incorrect because both sets of laws applied (however unevenly) to all members of their respective societies. (C) is also incorrect. Remember that the concept of "an eye for an eye" is derived from the Code of Hammurabi, which also contained other strict punishments.

44. C   The discovery of huge diamond and gold deposits in South Africa made it one of the most sought-after territories. Use POE to eliminate (A). By the late 1800s, the slave trade had been abolished. While industrialized nations were always looking for new markets for their goods, (B) is incorrect because this did not play the greatest role in European interest in South Africa. Nor did (D). By the late 1800s, the trade routes around southern Africa had been well estab-lished, and the opening of the Suez Canal in 1869 made the water route around the Cape of Good Hope less relevant.

45. B   If you'll remember, Adam Smith is arguably the father of modern-day economics. In *The Wealth of Nations*, he notes that economies work best with the least possible interference. This quote states that governmental leaders should not interfere with the economy and further notes that there should be no restrictions on imports. (A) is clearly incorrect. Ideas about social welfare systems, (C), and minimum hourly wages, (D) are not mentioned in this quote, plus all three ideas run counter to Smith's laissez-faire economics.

46. D   The invention of malaria-resistant drugs, better methods and tools to cut through forests, and larger and faster ships allowed colonization of once-remote areas. To use POE, let the map do most of the work. According to the map, the dominant imperial power in Africa was Great Britain, not Belgium, so (A) cannot be the correct answer. As for (B), there were only two nations in sub-Saharan Africa who remained independent by 1910: Ethiopia and Liberia. Using the map will help you eliminate that choice. (C) begins with a true statement; Britain and France did gain more land during this time period. However, so did Portugal, although not to the same extent. (C) is incorrect.

47. D   Both Mali and Ghana had substantial deposits of gold, and with the minting of coins (in gold and silver), these two societies grew in importance. If you know that Mali and Ghana are both in sub-Saharan Africa, you can use POE to eliminate (A) and (C). The split between the churches, invasions in central Europe, and military conquests in the Middle East did not have a direct impact on Mali and Ghana. (B) would be a better choice if it were about the *decline* of the Silk Route; however, it's unlikely that the revival of this trade route would have had a positive impact on the growth of these two lands.

48. A   Japan's invasion of Manchuria was condemned by the League of Nations, so Japan withdrew its membership in 1931. Germany left the League in 1933. Use POE and be sure to pick the answer that is true of both Japan and Germany. One of the reasons for Hitler's ascendancy was the Weimar Republic's failure to bring economic prosperity to Germany after the heavy penalties imposed at the end of World War I—penalties imposed on Germany but *not* on Japan (which was actually on the other side in that conflict), so cross out (D). While Japan did have a strong economy, control of the wealth rested in the hands of the elite. Choice (C) is not correct. Given the human rights violations perpetrated by Hitler's administration, you can eliminate (B) as a correct answer choice.

49. D   The *encomienda* system, a part of Spanish imperialism in the Americas, gave colonial land-owners the right to use native labor. The results were a system not very different than (D), chattel slavery. The enslavement of Native Americans declined in the mid-sixteenth century as a result of Church and governmental edicts and the growth of the African slave trade.

          You can use POE to eliminate (B): feudalism was never used in the colonies (it ended about two centuries before the Age of Discovery!). While you might think that Spain might have governed its colonies under an enlightened monarch (not true), it has nothing to do with the *encomienda* system. Also, while mercantilism was an essential part of the relationship between colonies and colonizers, it involved economic constraints. (A) is not the right answer. Corporate colonies were those established by nongovernmental bodies, such as the Dutch East India Company and the British East India Company. Spanish colonies, on the other hand, were firmly under royal control. (C) is not the right answer.

50. D   Beginning in the late 700s, Muslim invaders (Moors) inhabited parts of Spain and Portugal. In the thirteenth century, the Reconquista began, which was an attempt to remove Islamic influence from the Iberian Peninsula. The Reconquista was completed in 1492. Remember to choose the answer that is not true about the Reconquista. (A) is true and is, therefore, not the correct answer. A strong military, an expansionist government, and a fear of future Muslim incursions led Spain to invade northern Africa and southern Italy.

The Spanish Inquisition arose from the Reconquista. Probably as a backlash to Islamic domination, the Catholic Church in Spain was extremely intolerant. Muslims and Jews were required to renounce their faith and convert to Christianity or leave the country. Choice (B) was an outcome of the Reconquista, so it is not the correct answer. (C) also occurred. Because freedom came to different areas at different times, Spain developed as a group of independent states; some of them, like Castille and Aragon, were quite strong. It took the marriage of Ferdinand (of Aragon) and Isabella (of Castille) to finally unite the nation. The formation of this powerful monarchy means that (D) is the correct answer. Civil war did not occur as a direct result of the Reconquista.

51. A   In Han China, merchants had less status than farmers and artisans because they produced no substantial products. Use POE to eliminate the societies that held merchants in high esteem and where the merchant class participated in political and social activities: (B), Tudor England, and (D), Rome. In Japan, the rise of international trade led to organized guilds of merchants, which formed an influential class in Japan, so (C) is also incorrect.

52. A   Islamic society was relatively egalitarian, and there were no formal class barriers. In contrast, Roman society was very structured with numerous class differentiations and barriers to upward mobility. You can eliminate (B) using POE. Common sense tells you that the survival of both of these civilizations was dependent on agricultural production. While Rome did fall for political reasons (as well as a host of other causes), the Islamic civilization also collapsed due to internal divisions. Persia and Egypt broke away from the empire in the 900s, and by the 1200s the Islamic Empire was overthrown by the Turks and then the Mamluks and was never again as united as it was during the Abbasid Dynasty. (C) is incorrect. (D) is also incorrect. While Islamic scientific achievements might have built on earlier Greek findings, the contributions in mathematics, astronomy, chemistry, and medicine were not derived from other cultures. Nor was Islamic art, which focused on elaborate geometric shapes and patterns and ornate calligraphy (Greek art focused on the human form, which was not allowed to be depicted according to the Qu'ran). As a matter of fact, Rome's art, literature, and scientific thought were also based on Hellenistic forms.

53. A   Alexander the Great spread Hellenism (Greek culture) throughout much of the known world. He conquered the Persian Empire and expanded his empire all the way into India.

There are a couple ways you can approach this question even if you aren't 100 percent sure of the answer. First, even if you aren't sure who the leader of the Macedonians was, you can eliminate people who you remember led other empires. Second, you can focus on the names of people who you remember were major world conquerors, even if you can't remember what culture they were from. You can eliminate (B) because Julius Caesar was from Rome not from Greece or Macedonia. As for (C) and (D), Pericles and Socrates were both Greek, but neither were major world conquerors. Pericles led Greece through a golden age, and Socrates was a philosopher, not a fighter.

54. D   Even though the Islamic world lost power during this period, it continued to exert influence in the Balkans, Turkey, India, Malaysia, and areas in sub-Saharan Africa. Eliminate those answer choices you know are *true* about Muslim societies during this time period. The intellectual growth represented by the Renaissance did not spread to the Islamic world. While certain Muslim nation-states (Mughal India, Safavid Persia) became known for their artistic contributions, there was no corresponding growth in scientific, political, or technological intellectualism in the Islamic world. (A) is true, and is therefore not the answer. (B) is also a true statement. By the mid-1700s, the Mughal state failed as warlords competed for power and Islamic and Hindu factions engaged in civil war. In the late 1700s, the Safavid Empire was weakened through a succession of incompetent rulers. Even the Ottomans, turned away at Vienna, were weakened (although their empire did persist until the end of World War I). This failure of political units also led to economic disunity and depression.

A combination of the factors outlined in (A) and (B) resulted in the Muslim world's inability to compete with European nations in world trade or the race to colonize other lands. Choice (C) is also an accurate generalization and therefore not the answer.

55. C   When the Jacobins took power in 1792, King Louis and Marie Antoinette were executed. But before that—as a direct result of the 1789 Revolution—the goal was to create a constitutional monarchy modeled on that of Great Britain. Using POE, eliminate (A); the French Revolution did indeed engender strong nationalist feelings among the entire citizenry. While the French Revolution resulted in the declaration of equal rights for all citizens (in the Declaration of the Rights of Man and of the Citizen), equal rights were not granted to women, so eliminate (B). (D) can also be eliminated.

That leaves (C): The radical stage of the French Revolution began as the urban working class or *sans-culottes*, unhappy with the limited power they had, became more involved in public protests. This was in response to counter-revolutionary actions on the part of the king and the clergy, but outside of the control of the legislative body, the National Assembly. By September 1792, Paris was in turmoil, the King and Queen forced to flee, and the monarchy was abolished. The revolution was now in the hands of the people.

56. C   While maintaining independence and building strong nations was difficult almost everywhere, the process of gaining freedom was more difficult in South Africa, Rhodesia, and the Belgian Congo. Eliminate answers that are too broad because they cannot apply to all of the independence movements in sub-Saharan Africa. (A) is not a true statement. Imperial rule had suppressed conflicts between rival tribes in Nigeria, Zaire, and the Congo, but ethnic clashes arose once the tribes were independent. In other nations, dictatorial governments carried out terror campaigns against opposition and minority groups (Uganda, Central African Republic). While South Africa and Rhodesia (Zimbabwe) retained white rule until well into the twentieth century, most other nations of sub-Saharan Africa were not governed by whites after gaining independence. (B) is not correct.

Foreign investment might have made the transition easier; however, it is hard to tell because there was so little of it. One of the biggest problems every new nation faced was how to build economies that had been weakened through monoculture and mercantilism for generations. Unfortunately, much of this aid was tied to military strategy, as in Angola where the West backed the National Union and the Soviets supported the National Front. This brand of "foreign investment" resulted in years of civil war and economic instability. (D) is not the correct answer.

57. C The correct answer is (C) because you are looking for an *impact*. Since Social Darwinism applies Darwin's theories of natural selection to the social realm, (B) can be eliminated. (A) and (D) can be eliminated since neither is relevant to the question. Remember that Darwin's theories of evolution were used to make racial distinctions based on natural selection and competition. By the late nineteenth century, this theory was used to explain the superiority of the Europeans over those they had conquered in Africa and Asia.

58. C The Ming Dynasty (beginning in 1368) represented a time when China prospered economically, socially, and culturally. While neo-Confucianism meshed Confucian, Buddhist, and Daoist thought, China did not embrace *any* official state religion. (Confucianism and neo-Confucianism are considered philosophies, not religions.)

The other three choices are true and therefore not the answer. After years of Mongol rule, the Chinese expelled all Mongols, (A), and restored an examination-based, Confucianist government system. During the Ming era, China embraced an expansionistic foreign policy and sought to increase its influence through increased conquest and trade, (B). The Ming dynasty realized that attempting to directly govern such a large (and somewhat diverse) geographic area would be impossible; they instead chose to impose a system of paying tribute on these lands, (D). The naval ships sailed to these faraway lands to collect the tribute.

59. A Muhammad Ali became the ruler of Egypt in 1805 after the French were expelled from the country in 1801 and power was taken from the Ottomans. He is best known for ushering Egypt into the modern age through industrialization, imperialism, and by adopting Western political and educational systems (and for boxing! Just kidding). Under his rule, Egypt became more prosperous and independent, and he ruled Egypt until his death. (C) is not the correct answer. (B) is incorrect for a number of reasons. First, the Egyptians did not adopt a democratic form of government. Second, they did not extend suffrage to women. One purpose of modernization efforts was to strengthen Egypt to withstand foreign influence during a time when the rest of the continent was being partitioned among European nations. Isma'il decided to build a canal to link the Mediterranean and Red Seas, and the Suez Canal was a marvel of engineering and became an important economic and military link between Asia, Africa, and Europe. However, enormous debts forced Egypt to sell its shares in the canal to England in 1875, and with control of the Suez Canal, the British also assumed power over Egypt. Therefore (D) is incorrect.

60. A Karl Marx believed that the proletariat revolution would occur when industrial workers recognized the oppressive ways of the bourgeoisie industrialists and bankers. His argument was based on a class conflict that would arise as a natural outcome of industrialization. Neither Russia (in 1917) nor China (in 1921) were industrialized. So, in both nations, Marxism was adapted to accommodate a nonurban population. In China the Communist Party organized peasants, and under Mao Zedong the land was given to agricultural workers.

(B) and (C) aren't true either because capitalist policies were cautiously adopted in the 1980s and 1990s. The Chinese did not have to adapt Marxism to accommodate imperialism, (D). Marx noted that imperialists (as well as capitalists) were the enemy, so it was the job of all good communists to remove imperialists from their holding (and replace them with communists, of course).

61. A Under the concept of Mandate of Heaven, Chinese rulers were perceived to have the blessing of heaven so long as they ruled justly and wisely. If society crumbled and rulers were defeated or overthrown, it was believed to be so because the rulers had lost their mandate by ruling unjustly or unwisely. This concept led to stability within many Chinese dynasties because it encouraged people to obey the ruler as someone who was rightfully in the position of authority.

It should immediately occur to you that the Chinese did not practice human sacrifice, so cross out (C). If you remember the approximate time period of the Zhou (or Chou) Dynasty, you can eliminate even more answer choices. The Zhou Dynasty lasted for about 900 years starting around 1100 B.C.E. If you recall that Buddhism didn't even begin in India until around 500 B.C.E. and didn't spread to China until a few centuries later, you can immediately eliminate (B) and (D). During the latter Zhou dynasty, Daoism and Confucianism impacted China, but not Buddhism.

62. C The cartoon is meant to show that Stalin was giving his satellite nations a program that could not provide the same level of support as the Marshall Plan. COMECON, the Council for Mutual Economic Assistance, was a Soviet plan that offered economic assistance to communist bloc nations. It was established to compete with the Marshall Plan.

Using POE and the cartoon itself, eliminate (B) and (D) because neither of these can be interpreted from this graphic. COMECON was not limited to agricultural production (although you might think this from the cartoon). (A) is not the correct answer.

63. A Artistic expression took the form of geometric shapes and patterns and elaborate calligraphy, also known as arabesque. Most art from the Islamic Empire is religious in nature, and since Islam prohibited the representation of people and animals in artwork, you can eliminate (B) because it involves these forms of expression. (C) can also be eliminated because pyramids are associated with ancient Egyptian society, not Islam. (D) is also incorrect for a number of reasons. First, Greek and Roman art depicted human and animal forms, which would not have been adopted by Islam. Second, Islamic artistic expression was unique to the region and culture and not derived from other cultures.

64. **D** Confucianism is a belief system that holds the needs of the group above the needs of the individual and declares that if each person lives up to the responsibilities inherent to their role in life (parent, to child, to ruler, subject), society will function in an orderly way.

You can use POE to get the right answer even if you only remember the basics of Confucianism. (C) has to go because it is almost the opposite of Confucianism, which stresses societal obligations. (A) can be eliminated because Confucianism seeks to maintain a class system and hierarchy, not equality, by encouraging corresponding sets of obligations between levels (such as ruler and subject, or older brother and younger brother). Eliminate (B) because Confucianism is a social belief system concerned with social order, not a religion concerned with salvation.

65. **D** Industrialization led to increased demand and competition for resources and markets, as well as to a need to transport those resources (and the products they became) to and from those markets. European nations (and Japan) found imperialism to be the most effective way of securing these needs. The other choices are true and therefore not the answer. Working conditions in early factories were abhorrent, as were the living conditions in urban areas. Reform movements to limit child labor, protect workers rights, and provide sanitary conditions did arise, (A). Eliminate (B) because division of labor is intrinsically associated with the Industrial Revolution, and (C) since the invention of equipment like the gin mill and the growth of plantations in the western hemisphere, there were increased demands for slaves.

66. **D** The translation of religious texts into native languages made people more eager to learn how to read. Using POE, eliminate (B) because the printing press was a valuable tool used during the Reformation but was not invented as a result of the movement. (C) is tricky because the Reformation did spur questioning in other fields, but we cannot say that these inquiries were a direct result of the movement. Although Protestantism spread throughout many European nations (Switzerland, France, the Netherlands), the Ottoman Empire and Southeast Asia were not prime areas for conversion. (Although in later years, missionaries did try to spread religion throughout the rest of Europe and Asia.) (A) is incorrect.

67. **C** Before the Crusades, the Islamic Empire was in a state of fragmentation and decline. A succession of weak and/or corrupt rulers and political feuding between rival states led to the breakup of the larger empire (however, regional Islamic kingdoms formed and flourished in some places). The Islamic Empire was vulnerable to outside attacks from Mongols, Byzantines, Turks, and Crusaders. One result was the formation of strong militaristic dynasties (such as the Ayyubids and their leader, Saladin, who took Jerusalem back from Westerners), which gave rise to new conquests and conversions in eastern Europe and Africa.

Use POE to eliminate (A) because you know that the language of the Qu'ran is Arabic. Although (B) and (D) seem like reasonable answers, remember what was happening in the eastern hemisphere after 1100 or so. This was a time of tremendous economic and political growth throughout Europe, which was in sharp contrast to the declining fortunes of the Islamic Empire. So (B) is incorrect because of the turmoil in the Muslim world and the discovery by Europeans of new, non-Islamic trade routes. (D) is incorrect because western European nations were becoming more politically centralized and more interested in conquest and conversion.

68. A   Until the mid-nineteenth century, the British East India Company governed India. You can eliminate (B) and (C) using POE. While the English and the Dutch established private corporations for the purpose of carrying out exploration, the Portuguese (Brazil) and the Spanish (Cuba, the Philippines) directly governed their colonies. If you're not sure about Benin, then (D) is a smart guess. Benin was a kingdom in West Africa that reached it dominance in the fifteenth and sixteenth centuries. It engaged in trade with European nations, but none colonized it during the Age of Discovery.

69. C   Russia was still primarily an agricultural nation when Britain was industrializing. To use POE, study the graph to help eliminate wrong answers. Eastern Europe exceeded western Europe in miles of railway by 1880, so (A) is incorrect. There was considerable growth in rail miles in Germany between 1880 and 1900, but examination of the chart will show that the growth in Russia was larger in both absolute and relative terms…but while we're in the chart, note what it doesn't indicate about Germany and Russia—anything about population. (D) is incorrect, and so is (B).

70. C   The important thing to remember here is the tremendous impact the war had on people around the world. The human and economic costs were huge, and there was a sense of lost innocence and waning optimism. The broad trends in art and literature reflected this gloom. The disillusionment can be seen in the works of T. S. Eliot, Hemingway, Steinbeck, and Kafka.

HOW TO SCORE PRACTICE TEST 1

Section I: Multiple Choice

$$\underline{\hspace{4cm}} \times 0.8571 = \underline{\hspace{4cm}}$$

Number of Correct   Weighted
(out of 70)   Section I Score
            (Do not round)

Section II: Free Response

(See if you can find a teacher or classmate to score your essays using
the guidelines in Chapters 3 and 4.)

Question 1 $\underline{\hspace{3cm}} \times 2.2222 = \underline{\hspace{3cm}}$
                 (out of 9)   (Do not round)

Question 2 $\underline{\hspace{3cm}} \times 2.2222 = \underline{\hspace{3cm}}$
                 (out of 9)   (Do not round)

Question 3 $\underline{\hspace{3cm}} \times 2.2222 = \underline{\hspace{3cm}}$
                 (out of 9)   (Do not round)

AP Score Conversion Chart World History	
Composite Score Range	AP Score
77–120	5
64–76	4
48–63	3
34–47	2
0–33	1

Sum $= \underline{\hspace{4cm}}$
           Weighted Section II
           Score (Do not round)

COMPOSITE SCORE

$$\underline{\hspace{3cm}} + \underline{\hspace{3cm}} = \underline{\hspace{3cm}}$$

Weighted   Weighted   Composite Score
Section I Score   Section II Score   (Round to nearest
                                    whole number)

Chapter 13
Practice Test 2

AP® World History Exam

DO NOT OPEN THIS BOOKLET UNTIL YOU ARE TOLD TO DO SO.

At a Glance

Total Time
55 minutes
Number of Questions
70
Percent of Total Grade
50%
Writing Instrument
Pencil required

Instructions

Section I of this examination contains 70 multiple-choice questions. Fill in only the ovals for numbers 1 through 70 on your answer sheet.

Indicate all of your answers to the multiple-choice questions on the answer sheet. No credit will be given for anything written in this exam booklet, but you may use the booklet for notes or scratch work. After you have decided which of the suggested answers is best, completely fill in the corresponding oval on the answer sheet. Give only one answer to each question. If you change an answer, be sure that the previous mark is erased completely. Here is a sample question and answer.

Sample Question   Sample Answer

Chicago is a
(A) state
(B) city
(C) country
(D) continent

Use your time effectively, working as quickly as you can without losing accuracy. Do not spend too much time on any one question. Go on to other questions and come back to the ones you have not answered if you have time. It is not expected that everyone will know the answers to all the multiple-choice questions.

About Guessing

Many candidates wonder whether or not to guess the answers to questions about which they are not certain. Multiple choice scores are based on the number of questions answered correctly. Points are not deducted for incorrect answers, and no points are awarded for unanswered questions. Because points are not deducted for incorrect answers, you are encouraged to answer all multiple-choice questions. On any questions you do not know the answer to, you should eliminate as many choices as you can, and then select the best answer among the remaining choices.

GO ON TO THE NEXT PAGE.

This page intentionally left blank.

GO ON TO THE NEXT PAGE.

WORLD HISTORY

SECTION I

Time—55 minutes

70 Questions

Directions: Each of the questions or incomplete statements below is followed by four suggested answers or completions. Select the one that is best in each case and then fill in the corresponding oval on the answer sheet.

Note: This examination uses the chronological designations B.C.E. (before the common era) and C.E. (common era). These labels correspond to B.C. (before Christ) and A.D. (anno Domini), which are used in some world history textbooks.

1. Before 800 B.C.E. Indo-European steppe tribes were different from Chinese, Indian, and Middle Eastern societies in which of these ways?

   (A) Steppe societies were more likely to have built architectural monuments with religious symbolism.
   (B) Indo-European societies were ruled by oligarchies, while the other societies were governed by monarchies.
   (C) Indo-European tribes did not develop a common religion on which to base social bonds.
   (D) Chinese, Indian, and Middle Eastern societies formed permanent settlements with wealth based on land.

2. A major factor in the spread of Eastern Orthodoxy was

   (A) the Mongol invasions of the Balkans and Kiev Russia
   (B) the development of the Cyrillic alphabet
   (C) the use of icons and symbols in religious ceremonies
   (D) integration of folk customs and practices into religious doctrine

3. During the Medieval period, the dominant ethnic group in Eastern Europe was the

   (A) Vikings
   (B) Slavs
   (C) Normans
   (D) Russians

4. Which of the following nations was NOT impacted by genocide in the twentieth century?

   (A) Bosnia
   (B) Cambodia
   (C) Rwanda
   (D) Mexico

5. Feudal states arose in both Europe and China directly as a result of

   (A) the decline of the Roman and Byzantine Empires
   (B) the fragmentation of central government units
   (C) poor living and unsanitary conditions in larger towns and cities
   (D) economic changes brought about by new technologies

6. Which of the following was NOT a result of the Opium Wars?

   (A) Chinese port cities were open to foreign trade and Britain took possession of Hong Kong.
   (B) Lower tariffs were set on goods manufactured in Western nations.
   (C) Churches were permitted in port cities and Christian missionaries could travel freely within China.
   (D) China was able to successfully end the importation and sale of opium.

GO ON TO THE NEXT PAGE.

7. Feudalism and manorialism were different in which of the following ways?

   (A) Trade and commerce were more important in the feudal system.
   (B) Feudalism was a political system while manorialism was an economic system.
   (C) Advances in agricultural technology had a more positive impact on feudalism than on manorialism.
   (D) While feudalism involved the exchange of military services, only manorialism involved a social hierarchy.

8. "People send to one another to know if any of their family has a mind to have the small-pox; they make parties for this purpose, and…the old woman comes with a nut-shell full of the matter of the best sort of small-pox, and asks what vein you please to have opened."

   Source: Lady Mary Wortley Montagu, *Smallpox Vaccine in Turkey*, written while on a trip with her husband, the British Ambassador to the Ottoman Empire, 1717.

   The medical procedure Lady Montagu witnessed in the Ottoman Empire led to which of the following medical advances?

   (A) The use of leeches to remove toxins from patients' bloodstreams
   (B) The use of live viruses in preventing contagious diseases
   (C) The advent of the Hippocratic Oath
   (D) The ability of nurses, not just doctors, to administer vaccines and injections

9. The split between Sunni and Shi'a Muslims occurred as a result of

   (A) divergent interpretations of religious texts
   (B) conflict over the translation of liturgy into native languages
   (C) disagreement over leadership succession issues
   (D) a rift between more fundamentalist and more liberal branches of Islam

10. Which of the following nations is NOT a declared nuclear state?

    (A) People's Republic of China
    (B) Great Britain
    (C) France
    (D) Argentina

11. The Eastern Question concerned

    (A) how European nations would fairly partition the continent of Africa
    (B) the manner in which Prussia, Austria, and the Ottoman Empire would maintain the balance of power in Europe
    (C) the opening of port cities in China, Japan, and Korea to foreign trade
    (D) how to fill the void left by the decline of the Ottoman Empire

12. The reasons for intense imperialism among European nations included all of the following EXCEPT

    (A) industrialization generated the demand for new sources of raw materials
    (B) the military need to establish strategic bases around the world
    (C) there was a belief in the racial superiority of Europeans
    (D) population decline in European nations required new sources of labor

GO ON TO THE NEXT PAGE.

13. Which of the following statements about slavery in the pre-modern world is NOT accurate?

    (A) In Greece, slaves were most often foreigners or prisoners of war.
    (B) In the Islamic world, slaves of kings could rise to high-level positions.
    (C) All pre-modern societies except those in India and China traded slave labor.
    (D) Slavery was not always a lifetime commitment, and many slaves were taken as prisoners of war.

14. One major difference between the Inca and the Aztec civilizations was

    (A) while the Inca were agrarian, the Aztecs were nomadic
    (B) the Aztecs built religious monuments while the Inca did not
    (C) Incans were monotheistic while the Aztecs worshipped many gods
    (D) the Aztec developed a system of writing while the Inca did not

15. Which of the following resulted from to revolutionary movements in Latin American colonies?

    (A) Social inequality continued to exist.
    (B) Key industries were nationalized.
    (C) Widespread economic reforms were instituted.
    (D) Representative democracies were formed.

16. The changes that took place in Russia in the 1990s demonstrated

    (A) that modernization is a requirement for long-term social and political stability
    (B) that cultural and ethnic differences between segments of the population will undermine attempts at nationalism
    (C) that there are inherent problems in an economy governed through central planning
    (D) that the development of a substantial middle class can bring about political change

17. The Columbian Exchange involved which of the following?

    (A) Sugarcane from Europe; olive trees from the Caribbean
    (B) Peanuts from South America; rice from Africa
    (C) Pigs from South America; coffee from Europe
    (D) Sheep from Europe; slaves from North America

18. One key difference between the Ottoman Empire and the Tokugawa Shogunate was that

    (A) while the Ottoman Empire established Christianity as its state religion, the Tokugawa banned Catholicism
    (B) the Tokugawa Shogunate governed over a decentralized, feudalistic system while the Ottomans were able to centralize and govern using a neo-Confucianism model
    (C) the Ottoman Empire was less interested in expansionism than the Tokugawa Shogunate
    (D) the Tokugawa Shogunate was less influenced by other cultures than the Ottoman Empire was

GO ON TO THE NEXT PAGE.

19. The three major mercantile city-states in medieval Italy were

    (A) Genoa, Sicily, Rome
    (B) Rome, Sicily, Pisa
    (C) Genoa, Pisa, Venice
    (D) Vienna, Genoa, Rome

20. Which of the following was NOT an outcome of World War I?

    (A) The League of Nations called for disarmament and global security.
    (B) The Treaty of Versailles required Germany to pay war reparations.
    (C) France and Great Britain granted independence to their colonial lands in India and Africa.
    (D) A policy of isolationism within the U.S. Congress prevented the United States from aggressively becoming involved in world affairs.

21. Which of the following is NOT an accurate statement about Confucianism?

    (A) The ethical system is primarily concerned with relationships.
    (B) Specific duties are tied to one's status in society.
    (C) It prescribes the correct organization of the state to achieve the maximum benefits for the most members of society.
    (D) Only those who are devout and lead moral lives will be saved.

GO ON TO THE NEXT PAGE.

The Cold War 1960-1991

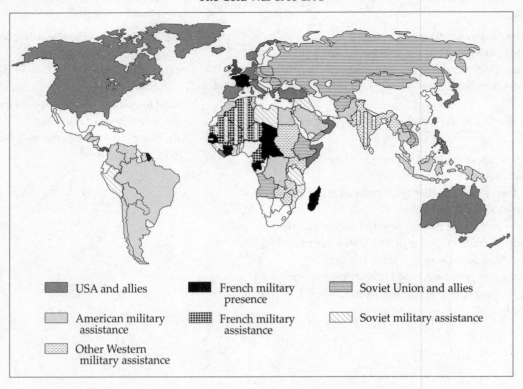

USA and allies

French military presence

Soviet Union and allies

American military assistance

French military assistance

Soviet military assistance

Other Western military assistance

22. Which of the following statements about the information in the above map is accurate?

(A) The Soviet Union was the primary source of military aid throughout South and Central America.

(B) During the Cold War, England played a greater role in African politics than the United States or the Soviet Union.

(C) United States military aid had little impact on Western European political structure.

(D) China maintained a military presence in southern African nations during the Cold War.

23. Which of these was NOT an outcome of the Bronze Age?

(A) The rise of an aristocratic military class

(B) The fall of centralized governments

(C) Additional outlets for artistic expression

(D) Advances in seafaring technology

GO ON TO THE NEXT PAGE.

24. Which of these is a true statement about Mongol invasions between 1100 and 1500 C.E.?

    (A) While Mongols were able to convert Russia to Islam, they failed to spread Muslim beliefs throughout India.
    (B) Mongols adopted elements of Chinese culture, which were then spread to other parts of Asia.
    (C) Mongol invasions were successful in China and Japan, but unsuccessful in Korea.
    (D) Mongol rule in Russia helped build a peaceful society based on Russian traditions.

25. In the 1100s, manorialism began to end in European nations for all of the following reasons EXCEPT

    (A) the development of a money-based economy
    (B) the formation of towns and cities
    (C) peasant rebellions against nobles
    (D) severe floods that destroyed fields and crops

26. Which of the following is an example of cultural synthesis?

    (A) Translation of the Bible into French
    (B) The tea ceremony in Japan
    (C) Construction of galleons by the Spaniards
    (D) Papermaking in China

27. Which of the following is NOT an accurate statement about British rule in India?

    (A) British rule led to the modernization of India's infrastructure.
    (B) India's cotton market declined due to the mercantilist practices of the British East India Company.
    (C) The caste system was not eliminated with the introduction of Western culture.
    (D) The Sepoy Rebellion of 1857 was successful in ousting the British from India.

28. Which advancement from the Scientific Revolution is matched correctly with its inventor?

    (A) Morgagni: philosophy
    (B) Copernicus: chemistry
    (C) Newton: physics
    (D) Kepler: botany

29. In the mid-1300s, Mansa Musa created a strong centralized Islamic government in

    (A) Kush
    (B) Ethiopia
    (C) Axum
    (D) Mali

30. The Hague was originally created to

    (A) administer Scandinavian bureaucracy
    (B) resolve regional differences among Austria, Prussia, and Russia
    (C) regulate the trade activities of Dutch merchant and craft guilds
    (D) handle the foreign affairs of the Netherlands' provinces

GO ON TO THE NEXT PAGE.

31. Which of the following statements illustrates the difference between English and Portuguese colonization efforts?

    (A) England generally governed its territories in a less invasive fashion than Portugal did.

    (B) While Portugal introduced the concept of monoculture in its African colonies, England was less concerned with exploiting natural resources.

    (C) Portuguese territories were limited to Africa and Asia, while England held more colonies around the world.

    (D) While English colonies depended on slaves for agricultural labor, Portugal relied on native populations to work on plantations.

32. Which of the following is NOT a true statement about the Holy Roman Empire?

    (A) The empire did not have one common language or nationality.

    (B) The empire granted citizenship to men in some conquered territories.

    (C) The empire had a decentralized government with strong local autonomy.

    (D) The empire split into Germany, Austria, and Italy in the late 1300s.

33. Which of the following was a cause of both World War I and World War II?

    (A) Political instability in the nations of eastern Europe

    (B) The complicated network of secret alliances forged by European nations

    (C) The massive debt owed by Germany to other parts of the world

    (D) The inability of the League of Nations to enforce its decisions

Japan in Corea

Japan—"Does It Hurt Up There?"

34. The main idea of this cartoon is that

    (A) Japan was becoming a stronger player in expansionism and imperialism in Asia

    (B) European colonialism was destroying Asian nations and cultures one piece at a time

    (C) Japan was content to accept smaller nations like Formosa, leaving the larger Asian nations for European colonialism

    (D) Japanese colonialism was aimed primarily at southern Asia, while European nations focused on central and northern Asia

GO ON TO THE NEXT PAGE.

Population Pyramids for Botswana 2000-2050

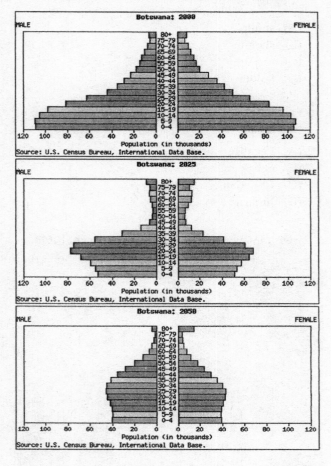

35. Which of the following trends is accurately represented on these charts?

(A) Between 2000 and 2025, fewer Botswanans will live to reach old age.
(B) In the time period shown, the ratio of men to women will remain roughly consistent.
(C) By 2025, the largest group of people will be 14 years old and under.
(D) Between 2025 and 2050 the infant mortality rate is expected to drop significantly.

36. It is thought that early Bantu migrations circa 1000 B.C.E. through Africa were caused by

(A) growth in the African slave trade, which caused people to migrate farther inland and south
(B) establishment of trade routes along coastal west Africa, which created more routes by which to migrate
(C) environmental changes, which disturbed the ecosystem people relied on for hunting, gathering, and farming
(D) advances in gold and salt mining technologies and improved transportation routes to Mali and Ghana

37. In comparing the Han Dynasty with the Roman Empire, which of the following statements is NOT correct?

(A) Both the Han Dynasty's and Roman Empire's economies suffered as a result of military spending.
(B) While Rome was successful at spreading its culture across a wide area, the Han were unable to diffuse their culture to neighboring lands.
(C) While both societies were run by centralized governments, Rome gave significant autonomy to local officials.
(D) While the Chinese were able to re-establish their imperial empire, Rome was never restored to its former status.

GO ON TO THE NEXT PAGE.

38. Which of the following actions had the most direct impact on the dissolution of the Soviet Union?

    (A) The official unification of Germany and the demolition of the Berlin Wall.
    (B) Public awareness of the human rights atrocities committed by the regime of Nicolae Ceausescu in Romania.
    (C) Labor disputes and working-class resistance to communist rule in Poland.
    (D) The imposition of martial law in Czechoslovakia after the Velvet Revolution.

39. A major difference between industrialization in England and Japan was that

    (A) while England had a well-developed rail system, Japan depended on water transportation
    (B) Japan was more dependent than England on foreign imports to establish and operate industrial facilities
    (C) working conditions were better in Japan than in England
    (D) class tensions between workers and owners were an issue in England but not in Japan

40. The Congress of Vienna led to which of the following?

    (A) The exile of Napoleon Bonaparte to Elba
    (B) The destruction of the Ottoman Empire and independence of its former territories
    (C) The division of eastern Europe among Great Britain, Italy, and Germany
    (D) The restoration of the monarchy in France and the Netherlands

41. Japanese feudal society comprised all of the following positions EXCEPT

    (A) shinto
    (B) shogun
    (C) samurai
    (D) taikun

42. Overt syncretism is an essential feature of which of these religions?

    (A) Legalism
    (B) Greek paganism
    (C) Christianity
    (D) Judaism

Jewish Immigration to Poland-Lithuania until 1600

43. The primary catalyst for the Jewish migrations from Germany, Hungary, and Crimea was probably

    (A) the impact of the Crusades on Jewish settlements in eastern Europe
    (B) more tolerant policies towards immigrants and minorities in Poland and Russia
    (C) the Ottoman Empire's expansionist policies in western European and Mediterranean lands
    (D) the development of pogroms and the establishment of ghettos where Jewish people were forcibly sent to live

GO ON TO THE NEXT PAGE.

44. Which of these scientific and cultural achievements are INCORRECTLY matched with the civilization in which they developed?

    (A) Cyrillic alphabet and engineering: Rome
    (B) Poetry and algebra: Islam
    (C) Astronomy and the idea of zero: Maya
    (D) Geometry and drama: Greece

45. Which of the following did NOT play a role in the Crusades?

    (A) Militaristic and expansionistic European monarchies
    (B) The promise of salvation to Christian crusaders
    (C) The desire of nobility to become more involved in trade
    (D) The establishment of a Jewish state in Palestine

46. The Renaissance did not have a great impact on Spain because

    (A) language differences prevented the spread of Renaissance thinking
    (B) Spain was geographically isolated from other parts of Europe
    (C) the Spanish government strictly censored humanistic ideas and writers
    (D) Islamic influence in Spain prevented the adoption of many of the art forms of the Renaissance

47. Which of the following is the most important factor in bringing about the end of the Cold War?

    (A) The breakdown of diplomatic relations between the Soviet Union and China
    (B) The economic costs to both the United States and the Soviet Union required to sustain the conflict
    (C) The end of civil conflicts in Southeast Asian nations such as Cambodia, the Koreas, and Vietnam
    (D) The spread to other nations of nuclear technology and the ability to create weapons of mass destruction

48. The ability of developing nations to establish stable economies is compromised by all of the following EXCEPT

    (A) problems attracting foreign investment and multinational corporations
    (B) cultural, tribal, and ethnic differences that threaten political stability
    (C) the inability to attract a sufficient workforce to urban areas
    (D) unstable currency and unmitigated inflation

49. Which of the following is an accurate statement about Ethiopia and Thailand before 1915?

    (A) They both remained the only free nations in their regions.
    (B) They both gained their freedom in peaceful revolutions.
    (C) Civil wars in each country toppled monarchies and installed democracies.
    (D) The citizens of both nations were converted to Islam before 1915.

50. Which of the following is an accurate statement about the Treaty of Nanking and the Monroe Doctrine?

    (A) The purpose of both the treaty and the doctrine was to maintain trade relationships and prevent foreign interference in local affairs.
    (B) While the treaty opened Chinese trade to various nations, the doctrine protected trade relationships between the United States and Latin American countries.
    (C) China and Latin American nations both experienced internal rebellion and weakened central governments as a result of the treaty and the doctrine.
    (D) Both documents were intended to limit European interference with former colonies.

GO ON TO THE NEXT PAGE.

51. Which of the following statements about the slave trade between 1450 and 1750 is NOT true?

    (A) New ethnic and racial categories grew as a result of contact among Europeans, Africans, and Native Americans.
    (B) In some African nations, slavery strengthened existing monarchies.
    (C) New crops and agricultural technology improved the diet and health of Africans.
    (D) By the late 1700s, the slave trade had been abolished in Asian and Islamic nations.

52. African goods traded on the Trans-Saharan Route included

    (A) tea and cloth
    (B) tea and gold
    (C) salt and gold
    (D) rice and sugar cane

53. All of the following were features common to the success of early nation-states in Europe EXCEPT

    (A) a common language
    (B) geographically distinct territory
    (C) a set of common laws
    (D) a feudal system

54. Roman law was most significant for which of the following reasons?

    (A) It was the first set of laws written down for easy transmission.
    (B) It was arranged systematically for easy reference.
    (C) It was a combination of Roman law and foreign law.
    (D) It served as the basis for laws in Western Europe after the Roman Empire vanished.

55. "The ordinary means therefore to increase our wealth and treasure is by Foreign Trade, wherein wee must ever observe this rule; to sell more to strangers yearly than wee consume of theirs in value."

    Source: Thomas Mun, *England's Treasures by Foreign Trade*, c. 1630.

    Thomas Mun's observations are consistent with

    (A) laissez-faire economics
    (B) colonialism policies
    (C) mercantilism policies
    (D) manorialism economics

56. The most important impact of the demilitarization of Japan after World War II was the

    (A) restoration of the Meiji Empire and a return to a more traditional society
    (B) reassignment of Japan's colonies to the United States
    (C) ability to devote a significant share of Japan's budget to industrialization
    (D) sudden lack of resources to deal with nuclear fallout

57. The only nation that did NOT engage in mercantilism during the 1600s and 1700s was

    (A) Portugal
    (B) Italy
    (C) Spain
    (D) England

GO ON TO THE NEXT PAGE.

58. Which of these statements about women's rights *before* 800 C.E. is accurate?

    (A) Hindu law and custom extended property rights to women in the upper castes only.
    (B) Confucianism gave women a limited role; however, they could become members of the meritocracy.
    (C) Women in the Jewish faith were allowed to hold positions in the religious hierarchy, but they could not own land or divorce.
    (D) According to Islamic law, women could own property, inherit belongings, and have dowries.

59. During the Middle Ages, in which of these societies did invasion and migration NOT play a significant role in social, cultural, and economic change?

    (A) Great Zimbabwe
    (B) Byzantium
    (C) Kievan Russia
    (D) Song China

The English World Kingdom, or Bloody Cartography

Queen Victoria: "The lowest corner down yonder, must be painted red!"

60. The "lowest corner" Queen Victoria refers to is most likely

    (A) New Zealand
    (B) South Africa
    (C) the Suez Canal
    (D) Argentina

GO ON TO THE NEXT PAGE.

61. The Neolithic Revolution was characterized by the

    (A) change from nomadic herding to settled farming
    (B) growth of iron toolmaking technology
    (C) migration of early peoples to the Americas
    (D) decline of the Roman Empire

62. In which of these nations was the Truman Doctrine first put to use?

    (A) Turkey and Czechoslovakia
    (B) Poland and West Germany
    (C) Yugoslavia and Turkey
    (D) Greece and Turkey

63. Population trends in industrialized nations between 1800 and 1900 included all of the following EXCEPT

    (A) higher birth rates
    (B) higher migration to western Europe and North America
    (C) lower infant mortality rates
    (D) decreased death rates

64. The English Bill of Rights of 1689 contained all of the following provisions EXCEPT

    (A) the king could not maintain an army without Parliamentary approval
    (B) only members of the Protestant church could rule England
    (C) people had the right to petition the king to redress grievances
    (D) jury trials were guaranteed to accused criminals

65. In *The Communist Manifesto*, Karl Marx outlined how he believed a communist revolution should proceed and what results would be produced. In which of the following ways did the Russian Revolution NOT fit Marx's model?

    (A) The Russian Revolution involved less violence and took far less time than Marx had envisioned.
    (B) Russia was less industrialized than Marx believed was necessary for revolution to occur.
    (C) The Russian Revolution involved far more bourgeoisie and elite citizens than Marx had predicted.
    (D) Marx thought that women had little to contribute to the success of communism, but they were more involved in the revolution and received more benefit from it than Marx had predicted.

66. The primary goal of the Meiji Restoration was to

    (A) diminish the power of the shogun and the samurai
    (B) isolate itself from foreign influences
    (C) liberalize civil and criminal legal codes
    (D) increase agricultural and industrial productivity

GO ON TO THE NEXT PAGE.

67. Which of the following statements about Europe during the period 1450 to 1750 is the LEAST accurate?

   (A) Political stability brought economic growth that fueled advances in the arts and sciences.

   (B) While European nations were successful at exploration and exploitation in the western hemisphere, little colonization occurred elsewhere.

   (C) Europeans benefited from contact and exchange with other civilizations more than other civilizations benefited from contact with Europeans.

   (D) While more women had the opportunity to be educated, most Enlightenment ideas about freedom and equality were not applied to women.

68. The foundation of ancient Indian civilization is best described by all of the following EXCEPT

   (A) reincarnation
   (B) the Dao
   (C) caste
   (D) karma

69. "I content that we are the first race in the world and that the more of the world we inhabit the better it is for the human race . . . I content that every acre added to our territory provides for the birth of more of the English race, who otherwise would not be brought into existence."

   Source: Cecil Rhodes, *A Plague of Europeans: Westerners in Africa Since the Fifteenth Century.*

   Cecil Rhodes's statement is consistent with which of the following?

   (A) Laissez-faire economics
   (B) Manifest destiny
   (C) Liberalism
   (D) Social Darwinism

70. The civilizations of the Sumerians, the Phoenicians, and the Maya were similar in that each

   (A) developed extensive writing systems
   (B) emphasized equality in education
   (C) established monotheistic religions
   (D) encouraged democratic governments

END OF SECTION I

WORLD HISTORY
SECTION II

You will have 10 minutes to read the contents of this green insert. You are advised to spend most of the 10 minutes analyzing the documents and planning your answer for the document-based question essay in Part A. You may make notes in this green insert. At the end of the 10-minute period, you will be told to break the seal on the pink free-response booklet and to begin writing your answers on the lined pages of the booklet. Do not break the seal on the pink booklet until you are told to do so. Suggested writing time is 40 minutes for the document-based essay question in Part A and 40 minutes for each of the essay questions in Part B and Part C.

BE SURE TO MANAGE YOUR TIME CAREFULLY.

Write your answers in the <u>pink</u> booklet with a <u>pen</u>. The green insert may be used for reference and/or scratchwork as you answer the free-response questions, but no credit will be given for the work shown in the green insert.

DO NOT OPEN THIS BOOKLET UNTIL YOU ARE TOLD TO DO SO.

GO ON TO THE NEXT PAGE.

WORLD HISTORY
SECTION II
Part A
(Suggested writing time—40 minutes)
Percent of Section II score—33 1/3

Directions: The following question is based on the accompanying Documents 1-8. (The documents have been edited for the purpose of this exercise.) Write your answer on the lined pages of the Section II free-response booklet.

This question is designed to test your ability to work with and understand historical documents. Write an essay that:

- Has a relevant thesis and supports that thesis with evidence from the documents.
- Uses all of the documents.
- Analyzes the documents by grouping them in as many appropriate ways as possible. **Does not simply summarize the documents individually.**
- Takes into account both the sources of the documents and the authors' points of view.
- Explains the need for one type of additional document.

You may refer to relevant historical information not mentioned in the documents.

1. The Chinese have a saying, "You can win a kingdom from horseback, but you cannot rule from there." Throughout history, the world's leaders have had to persuade everyone else that they deserve the authority they hold.

   Using the following documents, evaluate the different rationales for the legitimacy of power. Is there one "best" way to govern? What additional documents would be useful in attempting to answer this question?

GO ON TO THE NEXT PAGE.

Document 1

Source: Procopius, author of official histories of Emperor Justinian's reign such as *On the Wars*, excerpt from Chapter VII, *Secret History*, c. 550 C.E.

As soon as Justinian came into power he turned everything upside down. Whatever had before been forbidden by law he now introduced into the government, while he revoked all established customs: as if he had been given the robes of an Emperor on the condition he would turn everything topsy-turvy. Existing offices he abolished, and invented new ones for the management of public affairs. He did the same thing to the laws and to the regulations of the army; and his reason was not any improvement of justice or any advantage, but simply that everything might be new and named after himself. And whatever was beyond his power to abolish, he renamed after himself anyway.

Of the plundering of property or the murder of men, no weariness ever overtook him. As soon as he had looted all the houses of the wealthy, he looked around for others; meanwhile throwing away the spoils of his previous robberies in subsidies to barbarians or senseless building extravagancies. And when he had ruined perhaps myriads in this mad looting, he immediately sat down to plan how he could do likewise to others in even greater numbers.

Document 2

Source: Mao Zedong, concluding remarks at the Sixth Plenum of the Central Committee, 1938.

Every community must understand this truth: Political power grows out of the barrel of a gun. Our principle is that the Party commands the gun; the gun shall never be allowed to command the Party. But it is also true that with the gun at our disposal we can really build up the party organizations; the Eighth Route Army has built up the Party organization in North China. We can also rear cadres and create schools, culture, and mass movements. Anything can grow out of the barrel of a gun. Viewed from the Marxist theory of the state, the army is the chief component of the political power of the state. Whoever wants to seize and hold on to political power must have a strong army. Experience in the class struggle of the era of imperialism teaches us that the working class and the toiling masses cannot defeat the armed bourgeois and landlord except by the power of the gun: In this sense we can even say that the whole world can be remolded only with the gun. As advocates of the abolition of war, we do not desire war; but we can only be abolished through war—in order to get rid of the gun, we must first grasp it in the hand.

Document 3

Source: Nicolo Machiavelli, excerpt from Chapter VIII, *The Prince*, (1513).

Hence it is to be remarked that, in seizing a state, the usurper ought to examine closely into all those injuries which it is necessary for him to inflict, and to do them all at one stroke so as not to have to repeat them daily; and thus by not unsettling men he will be able to reassure them, and win them to himself by benefits. He who does otherwise, either from timidity or evil advice, is always compelled to keep the knife in his hand; neither can he rely on his subjects, nor can they attach themselves to him, owing to their continued and repeated wrongs. For injuries ought to be done all at one time, so that, being tasted less, they offend less; benefits ought to be given little by little, so that the flavour of them may last longer.

GO ON TO THE NEXT PAGE.

Document 4

Source: A sourcebook in Chinese Philosophy.

What is meant by saying that peace of the world depends on the order of the state is this: When the ruler treats the elders with respect, then the people will be aroused toward filial piety. When the ruler treats the aged with respect, then the people will be aroused toward brotherly respect. When the ruler treats compassionately the young and the helpless, then the common people will not follow the opposite course. Therefore, the ruler has a principle with which, as with a measuring square, he may regulate his conduct . . .

Therefore the ruler will first be watchful over his own virtue. If he has virtue, he will have the people with him. If he has the people with him, he will have the territory. If he has the territory, he will have wealth. And if he has wealth, he will have its use. Virtue is the root, while wealth is the branch . . .

Document 5

Source: John Locke, *Two Treatises on Government*, Section 95, 1690.

Men being, as has been said, by nature, all free, equal, and independent, no one can be put out of this estate, and subjected to the political power of another, without his own consent. The only way whereby any one divests himself of his natural liberty, and puts off the bonds of civil society, is by agreeing with other men to join and unite into a community for their comfortable, safe, and peaceable living one amongst another, in a secure enjoyment of their properties, and a greater security against any, that are not of it. This any number of men may do, because it injures not the freedom of the rest; they are left as they were in the liberty of the state of nature. When any number of men have so consented to make one community or government, they are thereby presently incorporated, and make one body politic, wherein the majority have a right to act and conclude the rest.

Document 6

Source: Ashoka Maurya, the third emperor of the Maurya Dynasty, converted to Buddhism and applied Buddhist philosophy to ruling a pluralistic society, excerpt from *The Rock and Pillar Edicts of Ashoka*, 304–232 B.C.E.

Beloved-of-the-Gods speaks thus: This royal order is to be addressed to the Mahamatras at Samapa. I wish to see that everything I consider to be proper is carried out in the right way. And I consider instructing you to be the best way of accomplishing this. All men are my children. What I desire for my own children, and I desire their welfare and happiness both in this world and in the next, that I desire for all men.

The people of the unconquered territories beyond the borders might think: "What is the king's intention towards us?" My only intention is that they live without fear of me, that they may trust me and that I may give them happiness, not sorrow. Furthermore, they should understand that the king will forgive those who can be forgiven, and that he wishes to encourage them to practice Dhamma so that they may attain happiness in this world and the next. I am telling you this so that I may discharge the debts I owe, and that in instructing you, that you may know that my vow and my promise will not be broken. Therefore acting in this way, you should perform your duties and assure the people that, "The king is like a father. He feels towards us as he feels towards himself. We are to him like his own children."

GO ON TO THE NEXT PAGE.

Document 7

Source: The Imperial Catechism, 1806.

Question: What are the duties of Christians toward those who govern them, and what in particular are our duties toward Napoleon I, our emperor?

Answer: Christians owe to the princes who govern them, and we in particular owe to Napoleon I, our emperor, love, respect, obedience, fidelity, military service, and the taxes levied for the preservation and defense of the empire and of his throne. We also owe him fervent prayers for his safety and for the spiritual and temporal prosperity of the state.

Question: Why are we subject to all these duties toward our emperor?

Answer: First, because God, who has created empires and distributes them according to his will, has, by loading our emperor with gifts both in peace and in war, establishing him as our sovereign and made him the agent of his power and his image upon earth. To honor and serve our emperor is therefore to honor and serve God himself.

Document 8

Source: Soviet political cartoon, c. 1920.

Lenin, The New Brush that sweeps up.

END OF PART A

GO ON TO THE NEXT PAGE.

WORLD HISTORY
SECTION II
Part B
(Suggested planning and writing time—40 minutes)
Percent of Section II score—33 1/3

Directions: You are to answer the following question. You should spend 5 minutes organizing or outlining your essay. Write an essay that:

- Has a relevant thesis and supports that thesis with appropriate historical evidence.

- Addresses all parts of the question.

- Uses historical context to show change over time and/or continuities.

- Analyzes the process of change and/or continuity over time.

2. Evaluate the evolution of nationalism since 1750 in ONE of the regions listed below. Include a discussion of the relationship between nationalism, racism, isolationism, and imperialism. Describe the status of the region around 1750 as your starting point.

   The Middle East
   Eastern Europe
   South America
   The Far East

END OF PART B

GO ON TO THE NEXT PAGE.

Part C
(Suggested planning and writing time—40 minutes)
Percent of Section II score—33 1/3

Directions: You are to answer the following question. You should spend 5 minutes organizing or outlining your essay. Write an essay that:

- Has a relevant thesis and supports that thesis with appropriate historical evidence.
- Addresses all parts of the question.
- Makes direct, relevant comparisons.
- Analyzes relevant reasons for similarities and/or differences.

3. During the twentieth century, considerable effort was expended by Western nations to support democratic and western-friendly governments in developing nations. Select TWO of the nations below and evaluate the success of such efforts. For each nation, consider the reasons behind the interventionist policy, key national and world leaders involved, and whether the democratization programs have resulted in long-term political, social, and economic stability.

    Iran
    Vietnam
    Nicaragua
    Chile

STOP

END OF EXAM

Chapter 14
Answers and Explanations for Practice Test 2

ANSWER KEY TEST 2

1. D		36. C	
2. B		37. B	
3. B		38. C	
4. D		39. B	
5. B		40. D	
6. D		41. A	
7. B		42. B	
8. B		43. B	
9. C		44. A	
10. D		45. D	
11. D		46. C	
12. D		47. B	
13. C		48. C	
14. D		49. A	
15. A		50. B	
16. C		51. D	
17. B		52. C	
18. D		53. D	
19. C		54. D	
20. C		55. C	
21. D		56. C	
22. C		57. B	
23. B		58. D	
24. B		59. D	
25. D		60. B	
26. C		61. A	
27. D		62. D	
28. C		63. A	
29. D		64. B	
30. D		65. B	
31. A		66. D	
32. D		67. B	
33. A		68. B	
34. A		69. D	
35. B		70. A	

1. D   The primary difference between steppe tribes and other ancient civilizations was their settlement patterns. While civilizations in China, India, and the Middle East developed as sedentary societies, the steppe tribes remained nomadic well past 800 B.C.E.

        Using POE, you can eliminate (A) if you remember that the steppe tribes were nomadic, and thus unlikely to build monuments. (B) is not the correct answer because it is an untrue statement about all of the societies in question. While there were some monarchies in ancient China, India, and the Middle East, there were also times when these civilizations were under the control of military dictatorships, feudalistic systems, and even rudimentary democracies. Steppe tribes were governed by a tribal leader who came to power as a result of the respect of other tribal members. Indo-Europeans did develop social bonds, and their religion was based on polytheism, so (C) is not the correct answer.

2. B   In the late 800s, Byzantine missionaries spread into the Slavic regions in eastern Europe. One way to gain more converts was to present the Bible and other liturgy in native languages. St. Cyril, a missionary, developed the Cyrillic alphabet from Greek.

        To use POE, remember that, while Mongol invasion was an important path of cultural diffusion, the Mongols adopted and spread Islam, not Eastern Orthodoxy, so (A) is not the correct answer. And, while you might remember that the iconoclast controversy was resolved with the decision to allow icons and symbols to be used in the church, (C), this was not a *major* factor in the spread of Eastern Orthodoxy to distant lands. Moreover, Eastern Orthodoxy was not very flexible in its acceptance of other forms of observance, especially considering that many of the Slavic people engaged in polytheistic worship, so (D) is also incorrect.

3. B   Use POE to eliminate the Normans (C) because they were western European. While the main area of Viking raids was western Europe, they also moved into eastern Europe, but not in a sufficient enough number to be considered dominant, so (A) is out. Both the Slavs, (B), and the Russians, (D), were eastern European; however, the Slavs were the dominant ethnic group in eastern Europe. (B) is the correct answer.

4. D   Genocide is a term that is used to describe the widespread killing of masses of people belonging to a group, such as an ethnic, religious, or political group. While Mexico experienced widespread death tolls due to wars, government overthrows, and poverty during the twentieth century (especially in the earlier part of the century), there was no significant act of genocide recorded in the country.

        By using POE, you can eliminate any country where genocide existed in the twentieth century. In the 1970s, the Khmer Rouge under Pol Pot slaughtered as many as one million Cambodians, so eliminate (B). During the 1990s, the Serbs committed genocide against Bosnians, and in Rwanda, the Hutus committed genocide against the Tutsis (in a continuation of conflict that had stretched for decades in both countries), so eliminate (A) and (C).

5. B   As central governments weakened, the need for cooperation and protection provided the impetus for the formation of the feudal system. You can use POE on (C) and (D), feudalism had nothing to do with the conditions in cities, but the economic changes that did occur with feudalism were based more on political disunity than on new technology. Although (A) is a smart guess, it is incorrect because it only applies to European feudalism. The decline of these two empires had little impact on the political and economic organization of China.

6. D In the late 1700s and early 1800s, European nations were interested in establishing more trade with China. While China had many goods that the West wanted, China was not that interested in western goods. There was a trade imbalance and this was unacceptable (especially to England). To address this, Britain took opium grown in India and shipped it to China. Before long, the balance of trade had been reversed under an Open Door (permissive trade) agreement, and silver and tea were flowing freely out of China. The Opium Wars were attempts by the Chinese government to stop the opium trade and expel foreign influence from its shores. Answer choice (D) was the goal of China during the Opium Wars, but unfortunately, it was not the result.

   The other choices are true and therefore not the answer. The British won the first Opium War (1842), which required China to open up more port cities to foreign trade. This policy would soon be extended to other western European nations and eventually to the United States. England also took possession of Hong Kong, (A). (B) and (C) were also all impacts of the conflicts. China was forced to sign treaties that allowed more Western goods into the country. And, while China had kicked missionaries out of the country in the 1600s and 1700s, now organized religion was free to enter China. Furthermore, treaties signed in the mid-1800s actually legalized the opium trade in China.

7. B Feudalism was a political system characterized by a series of interlocking obligations between a monarch and nobles of different levels. The system was based on giving land in exchange for loyalty and military aid and resulted in a decentralized form of government. Manorialism was an economic system in which wealth was based on land. Peasants worked nobles' farms in exchange for food, shelter, and protection.

   Use POE and common sense to get rid of (A) and (C). During the medieval period, there was simply not a great deal of trade and commerce occurring. Plus, advancements in agricultural technology that increased yields or efficiencies would certainly have had a positive impact on manorialism. (D) is also incorrect because there certainly was a hierarchy within the feudal system. In both Europe and Japan, the class structure looked like a pyramid: the monarch at the top, followed by different levels of lords in the middle, and then the knights at the bottom.

8. B The clue here is small-pox. Using POE, you can get rid of (A) because the implication is that something was being put in, not taken out, and there is no mention of leeches. (C) and (D) are out because neither is a *procedure*. While Lady Montagu does write about "what vein you please to have opened," the important procedure that she witnessed—and that was later adopted by western nations—was (B), the use of live vaccines to prevent illness.

9. C In the late tenth century, the Shi'a movement developed to challenge Sunni dominance of Islam. The Sunni believed that while the caliphs were leaders, they were not religious authorities. On the other hand, the Shi'a thought that the caliphate was both a spiritual and political leader and that the position should only be held by a descendant of Mohammad.

   Using POE, you can get rid of (B) because this simply did not happen. And while there were philosophical differences between the two groups, the catalyst for the split between Shi'a and Sunni Muslims was not (A) or (D).

10. D   Who has nuclear weapons? Countries that have detonated nuclear bombs (either for testing or for real) include Russia, the United States, France, North Korea, India, Pakistan, China, and Great Britain. Not Argentina, (D).

11. D   By the early 1900s, the Ottoman Empire was referred to as the "Sick Man of Europe." Beginning in the 1700s, internal and external pressures eroded the power of the empire. European encroachment into northern Africa, nationalist rebellions in the Balkans, and the rise of the Young Turks contributed to political instability in the region.

Use POE on (A) and (C) because Africa is not "Eastern," and neither are the majority of Europe's less-than-entirely-compliant colonies, and because while China, Japan, and Korea are eastern, it should strike you that what this answer choice is more nearly describing is the Open Door policy, by which western nations exploited China. (B) is a smart guess because the Eastern Question did involve power plays between European nations, but the nations involved were England, France, Russia, and Italy. The issue questioned what would be done with the Ottoman Empire's land, so the presumption was that they would no longer be a power in world politics.

12. D   Remember to read the question carefully and eliminate answer choices that you know are true reasons for imperialism. Immigration into western European nations (especially into urban areas) provided sufficient labor resources to fuel industrial expansion. Imperialism was closely tied to industrialization, and as European nations began to dominate the world economy they searched for new sources of raw materials and new markets for manufactured goods. (A) is an accurate statement, and thus is not the answer.

(B) is also true and therefore not the answer. Industrialization also involved the need to move goods quickly and safely, so European nations used their colonies as military bases as well. The Panama Canal and the Suez Canal are examples of protectorates, which served both economic and military purposes. (C) is true (and therefore not the answer)—English philosopher Herbert Spencer applied the biological evolution described by Charles Darwin to social interactions. Social Darwinism justified imperialism because the supposed superiority of the Anglo-Saxon race gave them a moral imperative to "civilize" the rest of the world.

13. C   Prior to 1000 C.E., nearly all pre-modern civilizations, including China and India, traded slave labor. Indo-Aryans added a new caste, the *sundras*, to accommodate slaves and servants at the bottom of the caste system.

All the other answer choices are true and therefore not the answer. Slaves in Greece were most often prisoners of war or foreigners either living in Greek lands or brought back from Greek military and trade expeditions, (A). The Islamic Empire had a hierarchy of slaves that allowed those who served at the highest levels to attain high social status, and some even rose to high governmental positions, (B). (D) is particularly true of African societies, though the loss of honor is a common theme in slavery both worldwide and throughout history.

14. D   While the Aztec did have a formal system of writing, the Inca did not have a similar system and instead relied on *quipu*, a rope with different color and size knots, for record keeping.

Savvy POE will get rid of (A), (B), and (C). Both the Inca and Aztec were sedentary civilizations with a hierarchical social structure—both of which are characteristics of agrarian, not nomadic, societies. Likewise, you know that religion played a dominant role in all Mesoamerican civilizations and that architectural monument building was a feature of both the Aztec and the Inca. Finally, general knowledge about Mesoamerica includes polytheism and the supremacy of the sun god. Both the Aztecs and the Inca expanded their empires to control large territories at the height of their respective reigns. At one point, the Aztec Empire stretched from northern Mexico to Guatemala.

15. A   This question asks you to draw a broad generalization about the various revolutions in Latin American nations. What you need to do is find an equally broad answer that fits a diverse range of independence movements. In the late 1800s, independence movements occurred in Peru, Chile, Argentina, Brazil, Bolivia, Mexico, Venezuela, Columbia, and Ecuador (among other nations). The only answer that applies to the nations of Latin America is (A). The revolutions in many nations were led by the upper and middle classes who were frustrated at the lack of mobility. In other lands, lower-class workers led independence movements. Simon Bolivar, himself a member of Venezuela's upper class, proclaimed that successful revolutions depended on the participation of all groups. The results of revolution, however, were similar in this one regard: Social stratification continued to exist, clashes among different classes and races persisted, and the economic gap among groups of people grew.

Using POE, remember that there were few key industries emerging in Latin American nations, and these countries relied on significant foreign investment to build their economies. Foreign concerns ran most of the rubber, coffee, rail, and sugar industries in Latin America. These nations did not nationalize their key industries, (B). Few economic reforms were instituted because, in some nations, elites led the revolution and were opposed to long-lasting change. In other lands, reforms might have been desired, but political and social instability prevented them from occurring. (C) is incorrect as well. While some Central American countries were originally part of New Spain (Mexico), they gained their independence by the end of the nineteenth century as well. By and large, constitutional democracies failed in Latin American nations. Military dictators ruled in some nations (Mexico, Brazil) and civil wars broke out in others. (D) is not the correct choice.

16. C   The downfall of communism in the old Soviet Union occurred in large part because of economic problems associated with a huge bureaucracy that wasn't flexible enough to respond to changing global economic conditions. Communism was abandoned throughout Eastern Europe and most of the rest of the world. Even China, the largest remaining communist country, made massive economic adjustments by adopting many elements of capitalism, a change which further supports the idea that, during the 1990s, most people concluded that there are some inherent problems with too much central economic planning.

Using POE, you can get rid of any answer choice that either doesn't describe Russia or that isn't a result of changes in Russia. (B) and (D) don't describe Russia during the 1990s. Cultural and ethnic differences fueled nationalism (which, after the downfall of communism, led to independence movements and the subsequent breaking up of the Soviet Union into different republics, including Russia, the Ukraine, Latvia, and Uzbekistan). Plus, a substantial middle class didn't develop under communism, so it couldn't have brought about the political changes in the early 1990s. Modernization also lagged behind the west during the communist years; so, even though efforts to modernize increased throughout the 1990s, you can get rid of (A) because it's too early to tell whether that will lead to long-term social and political stability.

17. B To use POE, find *one* product in the choice that is not correctly matched to its geographic location. (A) and (D) are the most obvious wrong choices, but (C) is also no good. (A) is incorrect because sugarcane came first from Africa to the Caribbean—where, incidentally, it was often turned into rum—and (D) is out because slaves did not come *from* North America but rather were sent there. Coffee came from South America, so (C) is incorrect.

18. D Remember that the correct answer must contain statements that are true about both of these civilizations. The Tokugawa Shogunate worried about the influence Christian missionaries and foreign traders might have on Japan, so it created a closed society. On the other hand, the Ottomans were influenced by many of the cultures with which they had contact. The Ottomans converted to Islam, blended Byzantine and Persian art, and learned about gunpowder and Confucianism from China.

Use POE to get rid of answers you know are untrue about either the Ottoman Empire or the Tokugawa Shogunate. Although it is correct to state that the Tokugawa did ban Christianity to prevent Spanish and Portuguese colonization attempts, the Ottomans embraced Islam, not Christianity, so (A) is incorrect. One defining feature of the Tokugawa Shogunate was its success in removing power from the daimyo and establishing a strong, central government, making (B) the wrong answer. (C) is also incorrect because it misrepresents both the Ottomans and the Tokugawa. The Ottoman Empire was built and sustained on expansionism; the Tokugawa brought peace and prosperity to Japan through isolationist policies.

19. C One way to tackle this question is to eliminate answer choices that contain cities that are not in Italy. If you read the answers quickly, (D), the word Vienna looks a lot like Venice. But, Vienna is in Austria, so (D) isn't the right answer. That leaves you with (A), (B), and (C). Remember the important role played by Venice, not only in the formation of strong maritime city-states, but also in the Renaissance. Even if you are unsure about the other cities, you know that Venice needs to be part of the answer, so pick (C).

20. C If you know the dates of World War I and the dates of the independence movements in India and Africa, you'll know that France and Great Britain didn't grant independence to their colonies until after World War II, not World War I. One of the reasons World War II spread throughout much of the world was that Europe *still had* its global empire.

Using POE you can eliminate anything that you know was true in the years following World War I. You should know that both the League of Nations and the Treaty of Versailles were direct results of World War I, so eliminate (A) and (B). Even though the League was promoted by President Wilson, the U.S. Congress failed to join due to its continued isolationism from the rest of the world (recall that it reluctantly entered World War I in the first place), so eliminate (D) as well.

21. D   Remember that Confucianism is a philosophy and not a religion. The notion of salvation and how to attain it are features of many religions, but not hallmarks of philosophical systems.

Use POE to eliminate the answer choices that are characteristics of Confucianism. One of the principles of Confucian thought is that a harmonious society is built on five important interpersonal relationships, each of which springs from filial piety, or respect for parents and elders. (A) is a valid statement and, therefore, an incorrect answer choice. So is (B) because the philosophy is based on the proper conduct for each role in society. Confucianism also served as the basis for the meritocracy system and civil service examinations, which were embraced by Chinese dynasties. Benevolent rulers surrounded by well-educated scholars acted to promote the common good. Thus, Confucianism *does* address government organization, and (C) is not the answer.

22. C   Western Europe was already noncommunist. Using the map, you can eliminate (D) because China did not have any holdings in Africa during this period, (B) because you cannot tell this information from the map, and (A) because the map contradicts this information. While France, Russia, and the United States are represented in the graphic, England is not. And, while most of the fighting took place in Southeast Asia (Korea, Vietnam, Cambodia), there were wars of independence in Pakistan (Bangladesh), civil wars throughout sub-Saharan Africa (Uganda, Zaire) and Latin America (Nicaragua, Chile) where military aid from both sides was used to try to influence political outcomes.

23. B   The ability to produce a surplus of food due to better farming technology led to more permanent settlements, which grew into cities. This gave rise to more formal social systems, including the need to govern groups of people. Remember you are looking for the answer that is not true.

Use POE and your knowledge of the Bronze Age to get rid of answers that are true. You know that the Bronze Age had a significant impact on the movement of people and the interaction of cultures. Don't forget to read the question carefully, and then use POE to select the answer that is not an accurate statement. (A) is true, and therefore not the answer, because weapons made out of bronze were expensive and were reserved only for the higher classes. (C) is also not the answer for two reasons. First, with an agricultural surplus, more people were free to pursue life as artisans and craftspeople. Second, new materials were available for different types of art such as jewelry making. If you weren't sure what to do with (D), you should take your best guess between (D) and (B), but historians and archaeologists believe the Bronze Age saw the development of the first plank-built boats.

24. B   The impact of Mongol invasions on European, Asian, and north African countries is uneven. While Mongols brought peace and prosperity to China (under Yuan rule) and India (under the Sultanate of Delhi and the Mughal Dynasty), their conquest of Russia resulted in the destruction and emigration of native Russians. (This is why (D) is an incorrect answer choice!) While ruling China, Mongols integrated elements of Chinese culture and society (most notably the formation of a strong, central bureaucracy to help run government). Through subsequent invasions of other lands, cultural diffusion occurred.

Using POE, remember that the Mongols were unsuccessful in spreading Islam to China and Russia; however, many Indians converted to Islam during Mongol reign as a way to break free of the social constraints of the caste system. (A) is not the correct answer. Make sure you read all the answers carefully! Yes, the Mongol invasion was successful (for a time) in China, but the Mongols never successfully occupied Japan—though they tried numerous times during the Yuan dynasty. Korea *did* fall to the Mongols under Kublai Khan's reign. (C) is not the right answer. Akbar was a Mughal leader who modernized the military and instituted land reform programs. He is best known for his interest in other religions and building a society based on tolerance.

25. D Manorialism was the dominant medieval European economic system and was characterized by a focus on agricultural production. While there were certainly bad seasons of drought and flood, this was not really an important reason for the end of manorialism. Remember, you are looking for the answer that is *not* true.

Use POE to get rid of choices that are true. You should eliminate (B) and (C) because anything that competed with farms and farming or undermined the labor force was bad for manorialism. (A) is also out because the manorial system equated land with wealth; the development of a money economy based on the production and sale of goods was one feature that led to its downfall.

26. C Cultural synthesis means that something created in one civilization was blended with something from another civilization. The galleon was based on a Chinese design that was then modified by the Spanish to increase its utility for cross-Atlantic travel. The galleon became the dominant ship used in exploration and supply missions to the Americas (numerous galleons are sunk off the coast of Florida). Independent development or adoption of an element from another society is not synthesis, nor is a society inventing something on its own, so (B) and (D) are incorrect—cross them off. Similarly, translation of the Bible into French did not *change* the text, so (A) is out.

27. D While you might not remember the exact year, it should have occurred to you that India did not gain its freedom in the nineteenth century. Independence was won in 1947. The Sepoy Rebellion resulted in the removal of the British East India Company as the governing body in India, but did not free India from foreign rule.

Use POE to eliminate answer choices that are accurate statements about British rule in India. Compared with France and Spain, England was not the worst colonizer, and certain segments of Indian civilization did benefit from British rule. (A) is a true statement because the British did develop extensive rail lines and road systems in order to facilitate the movement of goods. The British imported various forms of Western civilization into India: for instance, education, culture, and 4:00 afternoon tea. However, the caste system persisted. In a way, a new, higher caste was added that contained the English who moved to India. (C) is accurate and therefore not the answer. So, too, is (D): cotton was grown in what is now India (and Pakistan) as early as the fifth century B.C.E., but the Indian cotton market did suffer due to the policies and practices of the British East India Company.

28. C   Even if you have no idea who Morgagni and Kepler are, you can answer this question! Use POE to eliminate those pairs you know are incorrectly matched. Copernicus studied astronomy, not chemistry, so (B) is out. Now you might be stuck. However, looking at the two remaining choices, you *know* that the little experiment with the apple and gravity means that Newton's field of study was physics, so (C) is the correct answer. You don't even need to know that Kepler also studied astronomy and physics or that Morgagni was somewhat famous for his work in medicine, especially anatomy!

29. D   It is rumored that the wealth displayed by Mansa Musa on a pilgrimage to Mecca persuaded Ibn Battuta to journey to Mali. Mansa Musa opened trade routes and brought Islam to Mali. Even if you aren't sure who Mansa Musa was, the word *Islamic* will help you eliminate some of the answer choices and take a smart guess. Ethiopia, (B), was one of the few east African nations to remain Christian. Axum, (C), was also converted to Christianity. (More importantly, note that Axum reached its height of power in the mid-500s).

Speaking of the Axum, it was the successor civilization to the Kush in northeast Africa. Another interesting point is that the Kush could not have been Muslim because their rule ended before 570 C.E. (Muhammad's date of birth). So, for a variety of reasons, (A) is an incorrect answer.

30. D   While other European nations were adopting absolutism in the fifteenth and sixteenth centuries, the Netherlands retained a localized governance structure with power held by provincial legislatures. Naturally, disagreements arose over various policies and actions, mostly those having to do with foreign affairs, so there was a federal assembly (the States General) who met in The Hague.

Use POE and common sense to eliminate answer choices you know are wrong. The Hague is in the Netherlands, so it would probably have little involvement in the activities of central European nations, such as those listed in (B), and little interest in running Scandinavian government, (A). (C) is not a bad answer choice, but it is not correct.

31. A   Think in relative terms. The British were *relatively* better imperialists than the Portuguese (and the Spanish and Belgians, for that matter). In India and Hong Kong, the English cultivated a class of native citizens to help run the government and who could rise to *relatively* high positions of power.

You can use POE to eliminate (C) and (D). The fact that Brazil is in South America makes (C) the wrong answer choice, and you are well aware of the use of slaves on sugarcane plantations throughout Latin America, so (D) cannot be the right answer either. (B) is an incorrect choice because all colonizers built their economic relationships with their colonies on mercantilism and monoculture. European nations had little concern with the long-term economic survival of their protectorates; the need for agricultural products and natural resources was more important. In Brazil, those resources were coffee and sugar.

32. D   You might associate the Holy Roman Empire with Italy because that's where Rome is located. However, the empire encompassed the parts of central Europe that eventually became Germany, Austria, and some of the Slavic nations. Remember you are looking for the choice that is *not* true.

During the Age of Absolutism, the Holy Roman Empire stood as an example of how not to form a nation-state. The empire was a loose confederation of Germans, Italians, French, Hungarians, and Slavs that was held together by religion and little else. (A) is accurate, so it's not the answer. The ruler of this large territory, for part of its history, was elected by a council (Diet) of nobles who were autonomous, regional rulers, so (C) is not the answer. The Roman Empire granted full citizenship to men in Rome automatically, but the same was not true of men in conquered territories. The empire offered citizenship to men in conquered areas to minimize resistance to its rule, but also to encourage men to enlist in the Roman armies, which needed a constant source of new recruits to maintain and expand the empire. So (B) is not the answer.

33. A   The Austria-Hungary annexation of Bosnia, Slavic desires for their own homeland, and, ultimately, the assassination of Archduke Ferdinand led to World War I. The German occupation of Austria and Czechoslovakia was one of the causes of World War II.

Use POE to eliminate answer choices you know cannot be correct. The League of Nations was created *after* World War I, so (D) cannot be the right answer, even though the weaknesses of the League contributed to the tensions leading up to the Second World War. Similarly, the huge debts accumulated by Germany occurred during World War I, so (C) is also incorrect. Remember, if it is half-wrong, it is all wrong. Secret alliances were one of the factors contributing to World War I. As a matter of fact, one of Wilson's Fourteen Points was to prohibit secret agreements between nations. Yet, secret alliances were not a real cause of World War II. (B) is out.

34. A   By the beginning of the twentieth century, Japan was an industrial power and competed with Western nations for colonies and influence. That is not to say that Europe was any less interested in gaining land in Asia. Looking at the cartoon carefully, you will see Japan "cutting off" Korea from the rest of Asia. The cartoon does not focus attention on European colonization efforts, so (B), (C), and (D) are all out.

35. B   Through all three time periods, the ratio of men to women will remain roughly consistent. Using the information on the charts, you can eliminate (A), (C), and (D) because none of those are accurate statements. The number of people reaching old age will grow slightly by 2025; in 2025 the largest age category will be 15- to 24-year-olds; and whether the infant mortality rate will rise or fall is unclear. (What is shown is that there will be fewer very young children. This could be due to a number of factors.)

36. C   The fragile ecosystem of sub-Saharan Africa could not support the population growth that came with new farming technologies developed by the Bantu. In addition, desiccation turned much of the available agricultural and grazing lands to desert.

It is theorized that the biggest Bantu migrations, from about 400 B.C.E. to 500 C.E., began in eastern Nigeria and moved south and east along the path of the Congo River. (A) and (B) are out because, while trade and religion did open up significant parts of Africa to exploration and settlement, they were not primary causes of the Bantu migration. (D) is also incorrect because, while new technologies certainly did open up more areas of Africa to development, this was not a reason for Bantu migrations.

37. B   While it is an accurate statement about Rome, (B) is not true about the Han. The Han conquered parts of Korea, southwest China, Vietnam, and central Eurasia, which not only strengthened existing trade routes and formed new ones but also exported Chinese culture to other lands.

Use POE to eliminate answer choices that are *true* for both the Han and Roman civilizations. If an answer choice is true for only one of the groups, keep it. (A) is out because it is an accurate statement about both groups. Military expansionism, the need to govern large territories, and the cost of maintaining a professional military were economic drains in both societies. (C) is also true of both groups. In the Roman Empire, provincial governors and administrators who were loyal to Rome had considerable autonomy. During the Han Dynasty, feudal land holdings were transferred back to the central governments, diminishing the political power of lords. (D) is also true, as China was eventually reunified (under the Sui), yet Rome was never again restored (despite the efforts during the Byzantine Empire).

38. C   In 1980, Polish workers organized the first nonsanctioned union in the Soviet bloc. While their demands began with better working conditions and wages, Solidarity eventually took on the communist government, calling for free elections. While initially unsuccessful, the ideas espoused by Solidarity spread to other satellite nations. Make sure you choose the answer that is not only accurate but also had the greatest impact on the collapse of the Soviet Union.

Using POE, remember that reunification, (A), was a result of the collapse of the Soviet Union, not an antecedent to it. In 1989 and 1990, the Soviet Union allowed reunification to occur, mainly because they no longer had the power to do anything about it. While Ceausescus' reign was one of terror and abuse, worldwide awareness of these atrocities was not a contributing factor to the end of the Soviet Union, so (B) is out. In 1989, there was a peaceful overthrow of the communist government in Czechoslovakia known as the Velvet Revolution, (D). While an important landmark in Eastern European politics, this was a less significant factor in the fall of the Soviet Union than (C).

39. B   The primary difference between industrialization in Japan and England was that Japan lacked natural resources. England had ample supplies of coal and had huge amounts of resources in its colonies. Japan had comparatively fewer natural resources and colonies, and therefore had to import most of the energy sources and raw materials for its factories.

Using POE, you can get rid of anything that doesn't accurately describe Japan or England. Both countries are island nations that built rail lines between their major cities (although England had more rail lines) and were entirely dependent on water transportation for contact with the outside world, so eliminate (A). Additionally, class tensions existed in both Japan and England, but working conditions improved in England as progressive policies were enacted by Parliament and as unions formed, so (C) and (D) have to be eliminated.

40. D   The stated purposes of the Congress of Vienna were to establish a lasting peace throughout Europe and maintain the balance of power among major European powers by restoring some European borders to their pre-Napoleon locations while also drawing some new ones. One of the ways that the Congress chose to maintain the balance of power was to reassert the authority of the monarchs, specifically in France and the Netherlands.

You may remember that Napoleon Bonaparte was exiled to the island of Elba. However, this was not a consequence of the Congress of Vienna; it actually occurred months before. Napoleon returned from exile in Elba in 1815, but was soon crushed at Waterloo. He was then sent into exile again, this time in St. Helena. So get rid of (A). Eastern Europe was not divided among Great Britain, Italy, and Germany, so get rid of (C). Great Britain was given no possessions in eastern Europe, and Germany didn't even exist as a country until more than 50 years after the Congress of Vienna. None of this had anything to do with the Ottoman Empire, so cross out (B).

41.   A   Japanese feudal society was organized in a hierarchy similar to that in feudal Europe. Use POE to cross off the positions you know were part of the system: samurai and shogun. If you weren't sure about (D), taikun, take the 50-50 shot between (A) and (D) and move on to something you know more about. But if you remembered that Shinto is a religion, not a social position, you should have been able to eliminate (D) and pick (A).

42.   B   First use POE to eliminate (A) because it is not a religion. Syncretism means, "the integration of different religious beliefs and practices." Akbar the Great's attempt to synthesize Hinduism, Zoroastrianism, Jainism, and Christianity is one example. Christianity, Judaism, and Islam are monotheistic religions with relatively strict doctrines, none of which encourage integration of competing religious thoughts into its belief systems, so cross off (C) and (D). The right answer is (B). Greek paganism combined different ideologies and rituals as it expanded its territory and absorbed other cultures.

43.   B   Russia and Poland opened up their borders in order to bring in more settlers. Religious intolerance in western Europe certainly played a role in the Jews' willingness to migrate. If you look at the map, you'll see that Jews migrated into eastern Europe, Russia, and Lithuania. Get rid of (C) because this might have accounted for some movement from Crimea, but not from Germany and Hungary. (A) is not the correct answer either. The Crusades (and the Reconquista in Spain and Portugal) had more of an impact on religious tolerance in western Europe, the Mediterranean, and the Middle East. It was not a major factor in the movement of Jews. However, the impact of the Crusades on the Jewish population in western Europe is a clue to the correct answer. (D), then, makes for a decent guess, but (B) will be the answer.

44.   A   While Roman civilization made significant contributions in the field of engineering, the Cyrillic alphabet was invented in the Byzantine Empire. Tricky!

       Make sure you read the question carefully to ensure that you select the answer that is not true. Use POE to eliminate the choices that you know are true. In the Islamic civilization, literature consisted of complex poetry forms and mathematical advances included the creation of algebra, so (B) is not the answer. You should remember that drama, especially tragedies, were invented by the Greeks and that the work of mathematicians such as Pythagoras and Euclid led to the field of geometry. (D) is out. And (C) is correct—and therefore not the answer, so cross it out— because the Mayans did indeed develop the concept of zero (they weren't the only ones) and a complex understanding of astronomy.

45. D   Don't forget to read the question carefully—you need to find the answer choice that is not accurate. While the Crusades did involve converting the Holy Land back to Catholicism, a Jewish state was not established in the Middle East until 1947. The Crusades were a series of military campaigns with a strong religious overtone that occurred from the late eleventh century through the thirteenth century. While the primary purpose of the Crusades was to take Jerusalem back from the Muslims, it turned into a quest to prevent the spread of Islam and to acquire more wealth and power for European leaders. As a consequence of the Crusades, feudal power diminished and commerce and cultural diffusion increased. However, they also resulted in widespread religious intolerance.

Use POE to eliminate answers that are true. During the Crusades, kings became more powerful because they were the only ones who could put together the substantial resources to mount such extensive campaigns. There was also competition among the various monarchs for the wealth and power associated with the Crusades to the Holy Land. (A) is true and therefore not the answer. Because you know that the Crusades were religious in nature, you can eliminate (B). There were many risks and few rewards facing the average Crusader, and the promise of salvation was an incentive offered by the Church to recruit soldiers. While the original idea for the Crusades was religious, returning crusaders brought back goods and tales of the thriving commercial trade network they saw in the Middle East. With the decline of feudalism, European aristocrats (and royalty) saw the Crusades as a way to expand economic power and influence, so (C) was a reason behind the Crusades (and therefore not the answer).

46. C   Before we consider what made Spain different from other European nations, use POE to eliminate answer choices you know are wrong. For instance, (A) makes no sense. Somehow, the Renaissance spread to England and France, and neither of those nations was Italian-speaking. You also know that (B) is wrong. Spain is *not* isolated. It borders France to the north, and England is geographically farther from Italy than Spain.

Knowing that (D) is the incorrect answer is the key to understanding why (C) is the correct answer. During the 700s, Spain and Portugal came under Muslim rule with the invasion of the Moors. For hundreds of decades, Spain fought to free itself of Islamic influence, and what resulted was a strong nation-state with extremely little tolerance for religious dissent. So the Catholic rulers of Spain did not warmly embrace the ideas of the Renaissance.

47. B   The various treaties signed by the United States and the Soviet Union, such as SALT I and II and the Intermediate Range Nuclear Forces Treaty did signal the success of détente and diplomacy, and they were also a sign that neither nation was in a position to continue unchecked military spending. The most important reason for the resolution of the Cold War was, simply, the economic costs.

Using POE, remember that, while tension did increase between the Soviet Union and China beginning in the 1950s, this had little impact on the end of the Cold War between the USSR and the United States, so (A) is not the correct answer. (C) is out because tensions between North and South Korea remained high, and the resolution of conflict in Vietnam and Cambodia did not play an important role in ending the Cold War. While (D) is a true statement, it is not the correct answer. While numerous nations now have the ability to create nuclear, chemical, and biological weapons, this did not lead to the end of the Cold War.

48.   C   Remember that you are looking for the answer that is not true. Urban populations swell as people migrate from rural areas hoping to build better lives.

Cross off the answers that are true. Developing nations have a difficult time becoming self-sufficient for political, social, cultural, and economic reasons. Political instability prevents foreign firms from investing in some of these nations. The inability to ensure profitable operation plus employee safety has prevented companies from investing in many countries in Africa, Southeast Asia, and Latin America. (A), (B), and (D) are not the answer. In some countries, the colonial power built infrastructure to serve its own imperialist purposes.

49.   A   As other nations in sub-Saharan Africa and Southeast Asia fell to imperialism, both Ethiopia and Thailand managed to maintain their independence. Ethiopia successfully defeated the Italians in the late 1800s. Thailand closed its ports to foreigners until the 1820s.

Using POE, you can eliminate (D) because Thailand is a predominantly Buddhist nation. Both nations were able to maintain their independence as a result of the rule of strong monarchs, so (C) is out. Because neither country came under colonial rule, (B) is incorrect.

50.   B   The Treaty of Nanking (1842) was an unequal treaty that granted significant rights to western nations who wanted to engage in trade with China. It also gave Chinese land to the British and justified English involvement in Chinese government. The Monroe Doctrine (1823) was meant to prevent further European imperialism in the western hemisphere. However, it was used to justify American intervention in Central and South America and in the Caribbean. The Roosevelt Corollary to the Monroe Doctrine was invoked when the United States interfered in the affairs of the Dominican Republic, Nicaragua, Honduras, and the Panama Canal. The Treaty of Nanking certainly benefited more nations than did the Monroe Doctrine.

The Treaty of Nanking explicitly allowed for foreign (British) intervention; the application of the Monroe Doctrine resulted in U.S. interference. (A) is not an accurate statement about the two treaties. Nor is (D) because only the Monroe Doctrine was designed to limit European influence. (C) is also incorrect because the Monroe Doctrine did not really undermine stable governments in Latin America.

51.   D   While the focus of much of the literature is on the transatlantic, European-dominated slave trade, Islamic and Asian nations also engaged in slavery. Remember to read the question carefully—the correct answer is the one that is *not* true. Use POE and eliminate the choices that you know are true about the slave trade. (A) is true. In the New World, intermarriage led to the creation of the mestizo, mulatto, and zambo classes. While the slave trade decimated Africa's population, its impact on African rulers was not always negative. Numerous kings, such as those in Ashanti and Benin, saw cooperating with the Europeans as a path to riches. Trading slaves for guns, these rulers were able to maintain strong control over their empires; therefore, (B) is not the answer. As a result of triangular trade, crops such as corn were introduced to Africa. Some of these were more tolerant to drought and some produced higher yields than native plants, so diet and health were improved. (C) is not the answer.

52.   C   The trans-Saharan trade route ran from west Africa to north Africa to Europe. East and central Africa became more prosperous with the success of this route, which was also responsible for increased European and Muslim missionary efforts in the region. While cloth, silk, and spices from Europe and Asia did comprise some of the goods transported on the Trans-Saharan Route, the question asks what *African* goods were involved. Use POE to eliminate answer choices containing Asian goods (tea, silk, and spices). But in doing so, be very careful—both rice and sugar cane were African products, even though you may associate rice with Asia and sugar cane with the Caribbean. Sugar cane came to the Caribbean as a result of the Columbian Exchange, but rice cultivation developed separately in both Africa and Asia, with each continent using different strains of rice. Africans, however, generally grew only enough rice for themselves and their families without a tradable surplus, so it would not have been part of the trans-Saharan movement of goods, products, and people.

53.   D   The term *nation* implies certain bonds among people. Early nation-states in Europe (England, France, Germany, Italy) met with varying levels of success, depending on how strong those bonds were. Don't forget that you are looking for the answer choice that is not true. Think about the successful nation-states (England, France) and use POE to eliminate the features you know were present in these two lands. In both England and France there existed a common language, (A), a distinct territory, (B), and common laws (no matter how unevenly applied), (C). Not only was feudalism, (D), not a necessary feature of nationalism, but such fragmentation actually had to be eliminated for strong nation-states to arise. One of the problems in Italy and Germany (in addition to cultural and language barriers) was the persistent power of regional nobility.

54.   D   Read the question carefully— you need to select the reason the College Board would think the Roman law code is most important in terms of World History. That happens to be because it serves as the basis of the modern codes of law in Western Europe, so (D) is the correct answer. Use POE to eliminate answer choices that aren't so significant or unique to Roman Law, such as (A) and (B). While (C) is true, it isn't necessarily the most important ramifications of the Roman law code for World History as a whole and therefore the answer must be (D).

55.   C   (A) is not correct because traditional laissez-faire economics state that economies function best with the least governmental interferences, and Mun's quote clearly calls for some policies that would interfere with the workings of laissez-faire, so (D) is out. While Mun's quote fits into the reasons for imperialism, (B) is not the correct answer. Colonialism alone did not create the economic conditions favorable to the mother country. Instead, it was the imposition of mercantilism on colonies that allowed for this favorable balance of trade to occur.

56.   C   One reason for Japan's rapid industrialization and growth as a global power was because the nation could devote all of its resources to rebuilding its economy. While the United States (and its allies) and the Soviet Union spent billions of dollars on the Cold War, Japan was free to focus on internal growth—meaning (D) can't be the answer. Use what you know about post-World War II Japan to eliminate (A) and (B).

57. B Simply put, *every* colonizing nation engaged in mercantilism with its colonies. Under mercantilism, the economic relationship between colonies and European nations was developed to create a favorable balance of trade for the mother nations. Colonies were restricted in what they could trade and with whom, and they were prevented from developing self-sufficient economies. For example, the British colonies in America were required to buy certain goods (tea) from England and were not allowed to trade certain items with France and Italy. Colonies became not only sources of raw materials, but also captive markets for goods manufactured in Europe. The correct answer to this question is the one nation who was not involved in colonization: Italy, (B).

58. D If you remember that Islamic society was pretty egalitarian in terms of social hierarchy, you can apply this to the rights of Muslim women. Also keep in mind that most civilizations granted few women any substantial rights in pre-modern times. Using POE and common sense, eliminate (A) because the Hindu caste system did not only discriminate against those in lower castes, but against women as well. (B) is out because only men could sit for the civil service exam and serve as mandarins. As in other faiths, Jewish women were not allowed to hold positions in the religious hierarchy, so (C) is also incorrect.

59. D A major theme on the AP exam is change and continuity in societies over time. Change can occur through different methods: invasion, migration, independent population growth, innovation and invention, and so on. The Song Dynasty went through a period of tremendous social, economic, and cultural growth beginning in the late 900s. Innovations in agriculture led to the growth of huge commercial cities and increased prosperity. To use POE, remember that during the period from 600 to 1450 c.e. there was a tremendous increase in the contacts among different people. Many of these exchanges occurred as a result of migration, trade, and war. The correct answer to this question will be the society that experienced tremendous change yet *not* as the result of outside influence.

    In Africa, the Great Zimbabwe changed as a result of the discovery of new trade routes and valuable natural resources. (A) is not the right answer. As you (hopefully) remember, Mongol invasions of Russia had a long-lasting (and not very positive) impact. The Tartars destroyed the Kievan city-state system and isolated Russia from European civilization. Kiev was changed through invasion, so (C) is out. Byzantium society was changed greatly as a result of invasion; not only because of Arab, Slav, and Bulgur invasions into the empire but also as a result of Byzantium expansionism. Moreover, western Catholics led an attack on Constantinople as part of the Fourth Crusade, which further weakened the empire and left it open to later Arab attack. (B) is not the correct answer.

60. B Use POE to eliminate (A) and (D) because Queen Victoria is looking at Africa on the map. Although it's not terribly clear, Queen Victoria's paintbrush is perched at the southern tip of Africa. Make sure you look at the cartoon carefully before answering the question.

61. A The Neolithic Revolution (about 8000–3000 b.c.e.) was characterized by people moving from nomadic lifestyles to agricultural lifestyles. Even if all you remember is that the Neolithic Revolution happened way in the past, near the beginning of the history covered in your AP World History class, you should be able to eliminate some answers. People began to use bronze near the end of the Neolithic Revolution, and iron didn't come until way after that, so (B) has to go. "Revolutions" usually describe a totally new way of doing things or an overthrow of leadership or government, so (C) and (D) don't make much sense.

62. D The purpose of the Truman Doctrine was to contain the spread of communism. The United States perceived a communist threat to Greece and Turkey and approved a $400 million aid package for these two nations. If you remember that the Truman Doctrine was not applied in communist nations, then you can use POE to eliminate answer choices with Czechoslovakia, (A), Poland, (B), and Yugoslavia, (C).

63. A In industrialized nations, birth rates are generally lower for a number of reasons. Children were the primary sources of labor in nations that were highly agrarian. More children died during their early years in these lands, so families had more offspring. Remember, you need to find the one trend that is not true.

     If you can remember that industrialization has positive impacts on most population demographics, then you can eliminate (C) and (D). With higher standards of living and better health care and education, fewer people in industrialized nations die young. During the time period mentioned, the industrialized nations of the world were centered primarily in western Europe and the United States. So (B) is true (and therefore not the answer) because people migrated to where the jobs were.

64. B Because you know that the American Bill of Rights was based on key provisions of the English Bill of Rights, you can guess that religious restrictions were not included. The correct answer is the provision that was *not* part of the Bill of Rights. The Test and Corporation Acts of the late seventeenth century ensured that British office-holders were Anglican.

     The Bill of Rights placed numerous limitations on the power of the English monarch. Among those restrictions was one that stated the king could not raise taxes or establish an army without Parliamentary approval. It also gave jury trials to those accused of crimes and allowed British citizens the right to appeal decisions made by the king. Furthermore, it allowed those in Parliament to speak freely and even to criticize the monarch. Finally, it prohibited excessive bail and cruel and unusual punishment. So (A), (C), and (D) were all parts of the Bill of Rights. Use POE to get rid of these choices.

65. B Marx built his argument on the need for the proletariat to rise up against the capitalist-industrialist regime. In 1917, Russia did not have a large industrial worker base, so Lenin and Trotsky adapted Marxism to include all oppressed people, including peasants. The great irony of communism is that it has been most successful in less-industrialized nations.

     Use POE and eliminate answers you know are wrong or don't make sense, like (A). Marx probably did not envision how long a revolution would take or how bloody it would be. (C) is also not an accurate statement. The 1905 (non-communist) Revolution was run by the bourgeois, and the 1917 Revolution was more radical and proletariat in nature. (D), too, is out, because Marxism appealed to women because it promised equal treatment of all people under communism, and Marx wrote extensively about the unequal burden assumed by women in industrial societies.

66. D   The key thing to remember about the Meiji Restoration is that it was a time of great modern-ization and westernization in Japan. All class distinctions were eliminated, the emperor was reinstalled as the leader of Japan, laws were modernized, and the nation rapidly industrialized. A two-house legislature (Diet) was established. Japan also set out to become an imperial power in the world. Choices (A) and (C) were outcomes of the Meiji Restoration, but not goals so you can eliminate those two choices. Japan believed the only way it could avoid entering into unequal treaties and be subjected to foreign influences (like what happened in China) was to build its own industrial and military bases. (B) is not an accurate statement about the Meiji Restoration.

67. B   Exploration took Europeans to Africa, India, and the Far East in addition to the western hemisphere. Remember to read the question carefully and choose the answer that is the least accurate statement about Europe during this time period. Use POE to eliminate answers that are true. (A) is true. A direct result of the establishment of stable, centralized political units in France, England, and Spain was the ability to spend resources on art, literature, education, and exploration, so (A) is not the answer. Eliminate (C) because you know that the benefits of exploration and colonization rarely, if ever, accrued to the native populations of North and South America, Africa, and India. (D) is true and cannot be the answer, because while there were some European women who played important roles as nuns, writers, painters, and salon hosts, the rights and roles of women were not greatly expanded during the Enlightenment, even though more women had access to education. There simply were no opportunities to become equal members in society.

68. B   If you know that Hinduism is an ancient religion that developed in India and if you understand its general components, this question is easy. That's because all of the wrong answer choices have to do with Hinduism. The correct answer choice has nothing to do with Hinduism. The Dao is defined as the "way of nature" and it is the central component of Daoism, an ancient Chinese belief system.

Reincarnation, (A), the caste system, (C), and karma, (D), are all associated with Hinduism. Karma goes hand-in-hand with another important term you should know called dharma. Dharma refers to the behaviors necessary to maintain natural order, and karma refers to the law of moral consequences (of violating those behaviors), which holds that one's status in the pres-ent life has been determined by the deeds in previous lives (reincarnation). That status is known as one's caste, and it can change as one's karma changes. After reincarnation, a higher or lower caste awaits a person whose karma improved or declined in the previous life.

69. D   Cecil Rhodes, a British adventurer who became the prime minister of the Cape Colony, was a firm believer in English imperial power. While his reasons for capturing more land for Mother England did involve power and advantage, they also centered on the idea of European supremacy and a moral imperative to convert "savages." These sentiments are most consistent with (D), Social Darwinism.

70. A   The Sumerians, Phoenicians, and the Maya all developed extensive writing systems. The Phoenicians laid the groundwork for the alphabet later used by the Greeks, the Sumerians used cuneiform, and the Maya used hieroglyphs.

Even if all that you remember is that these were ancient civilizations, you can eliminate a couple of answer choices. None of these civilizations emphasized equality in education because none of them emphasized equality at all. Equality is a fairly modern concept, so get rid of (B). The same goes for democracy. It was attempted for a while in ancient Greece and Rome, but it didn't re-emerge until the Age of Enlightenment, so get rid of (D). All of the societies were polytheistic, so even if you just remember one of them, you have to get rid of (C).

HOW TO SCORE PRACTICE TEST 2

Section I: Multiple Choice

$$\underline{\hspace{4cm}} \times 0.8571 = \underline{\hspace{4cm}}$$

Number of Correct   Weighted
(out of 70)   Section I Score
                                   (Do not round)

Section II: Free Response

(See if you can find a teacher or classmate to score your essays using the guidelines in Chapters 3 and 4.)

Question 1 $\underline{\hspace{3cm}} \times 2.2222 = \underline{\hspace{3cm}}$
                 (out of 9)   (Do not round)

Question 2 $\underline{\hspace{3cm}} \times 2.2222 = \underline{\hspace{3cm}}$
                 (out of 9)   (Do not round)

Question 3 $\underline{\hspace{3cm}} \times 2.2222 = \underline{\hspace{3cm}}$
                 (out of 9)   (Do not round)

AP Score Conversion Chart World History	
Composite Score Range	AP Score
77–120	5
64–76	4
48–63	3
34–47	2
0–33	1

Sum   = $\underline{\hspace{4cm}}$
                 Weighted Section II
                 Score (Do not round)

COMPOSITE SCORE

$$\underline{\hspace{3cm}} + \underline{\hspace{3cm}} = \underline{\hspace{3cm}}$$

Weighted   Weighted   Composite Score
Section I Score   Section II Score   (Round to nearest
                                               whole number)

ABOUT THE AUTHORS

Monty Armstrong has been teaching Advanced Placement for more than 16 years and has been an Advanced Placement Exam reader for 10 years. He is a sample selector and table leader for the AP World History Exam and is also the moderator of the Electronic Discussion Group for this test. He has been a presenter at numerous state and national meetings and AP institutes and workshops. Mr. Armstrong teaches at Cerritos High School in Southern California.

David Daniel has taught for The Princeton Review for more than 11 years. A graduate of The University of Texas at Austin and The Ohio State University College of Law, David currently makes his home in New York City, where he is Director of Guidance Services for The Princeton Review.

Alexandra Freer has been teaching students how to beat the SAT since 1987. As Executive Director of The Princeton Review in New Jersey, Alex not only helped prepare thousands of students for the SAT, LSAT, GMAT, GRE and MCAT but also worked to refine The Princeton Review's test-taking strategies. Alex's writing credits include The Girl's Guide to the SAT, Cracking the System for the SAT 2000 Edition, and Cracking the AP Psychology Exam.

Abby B. Kanarek received her doctorate in Environmental Analysis and Design from the University of California, Irvine. She has been involved in test preparation at all grade levels for more than fifteen years with particular emphasis on verbal skills and social studies.

Completely darken bubbles with a No. 2 pencil. If you make a mistake, be sure to erase mark completely. Erase all stray marks.

1.

YOUR NAME: _____
(Print) Last   First   M.I.

SIGNATURE: _____ DATE: ___/___/___

HOME ADDRESS: _____
(Print) Number and Street

_____
City   State   Zip Code

PHONE NO.: _____

IMPORTANT: Please fill in these boxes exactly as shown on the back cover of your test book.

2. TEST FORM

3. TEST CODE

4. REGISTRATION NUMBER

5. YOUR NAME

First 4 letters of last name				FIRST INIT	MID INIT

6. DATE OF BIRTH

Month	Day	Year
JAN		
FEB	0 0	0 0
MAR	1 1	1 1
APR	2 2	2 2
MAY	3 3	3 3
JUN	4 4	4 4
JUL	5 5	5 5
AUG	6 6	6 6
SEP	7 7	7 7
OCT	8 8	8 8
NOV	9 9	9 9
DEC		

7. GENDER

MALE
FEMALE

The Princeton Review

1. A B C D
2. A B C D
3. A B C D
4. A B C D
5. A B C D
6. A B C D
7. A B C D
8. A B C D
9. A B C D
10. A B C D
11. A B C D
12. A B C D
13. A B C D
14. A B C D
15. A B C D
16. A B C D
17. A B C D
18. A B C D
19. A B C D
20. A B C D
21. A B C D
22. A B C D
23. A B C D
24. A B C D
25. A B C D
26. A B C D
27. A B C D
28. A B C D
29. A B C D
30. A B C D
31. A B C D
32. A B C D
33. A B C D
34. A B C D
35. A B C D
36. A B C D
37. A B C D
38. A B C D
39. A B C D
40. A B C D
41. A B C D
42. A B C D
43. A B C D
44. A B C D
45. A B C D
46. A B C D
47. A B C D
48. A B C D
49. A B C D
50. A B C D
51. A B C D
52. A B C D
53. A B C D
54. A B C D
55. A B C D
56. A B C D
57. A B C D
58. A B C D
59. A B C D
60. A B C D
61. A B C D
62. A B C D
63. A B C D
64. A B C D
65. A B C D
66. A B C D
67. A B C D
68. A B C D
69. A B C D
70. A B C D

The Princeton Review

Completely darken bubbles with a No. 2 pencil. If you make a mistake, be sure to erase mark completely. Erase all stray marks.

1.

YOUR NAME: _____
(Print)   Last   First   M.I.

SIGNATURE: _____   DATE: ___ / ___ / ___

HOME ADDRESS: _____
(Print)   Number and Street

_____
City   State   Zip Code

PHONE NO.: _____

IMPORTANT: Please fill in these boxes exactly as shown on the back cover of your test book.

2. TEST FORM

_____

3. TEST CODE   **4. REGISTRATION NUMBER**

0	A	J	0	0	0	0	0	0	0	0
1	B	K	1	1	1	1	1	1	1	1
2	C	L	2	2	2	2	2	2	2	2
3	D	M	3	3	3	3	3	3	3	3
4	E	N	4	4	4	4	4	4	4	4
5	F	O	5	5	5	5	5	5	5	5
6	G	P	6	6	6	6	6	6	6	6
7	H	Q	7	7	7	7	7	7	7	7
8	I	R	8	8	8	8	8	8	8	8
9				9	9	9	9	9	9	9

5. YOUR NAME

First 4 letters of last name				FIRST INIT	MID INIT
A	A	A	A	A	A
B	B	B	B	B	B
C	C	C	C	C	C
D	D	D	D	D	D
E	E	E	E	E	E
F	F	F	F	F	F
G	G	G	G	G	G
H	H	H	H	H	H
I	I	I	I	I	I
J	J	J	J	J	J
K	K	K	K	K	K
L	L	L	L	L	L
M	M	M	M	M	M
N	N	N	N	N	N
O	O	O	O	O	O
P	P	P	P	P	P
Q	Q	Q	Q	Q	Q
R	R	R	R	R	R
S	S	S	S	S	S
T	T	T	T	T	T
U	U	U	U	U	U
V	V	V	V	V	V
W	W	W	W	W	W
X	X	X	X	X	X
Y	Y	Y	Y	Y	Y
Z	Z	Z	Z	Z	Z

6. DATE OF BIRTH

Month	Day		Year	
JAN				
FEB	0	0	0	0
MAR	1	1	1	1
APR	2	2	2	2
MAY	3	3	3	3
JUN		4	4	4
JUL		5	5	5
AUG		6	6	6
SEP		7	7	7
OCT		8	8	8
NOV		9	9	9
DEC				

7. GENDER
- MALE
- FEMALE

The Princeton Review

1. A B C D
2. A B C D
3. A B C D
4. A B C D
5. A B C D
6. A B C D
7. A B C D
8. A B C D
9. A B C D
10. A B C D
11. A B C D
12. A B C D
13. A B C D
14. A B C D
15. A B C D
16. A B C D
17. A B C D
18. A B C D

19. A B C D
20. A B C D
21. A B C D
22. A B C D
23. A B C D
24. A B C D
25. A B C D
26. A B C D
27. A B C D
28. A B C D
29. A B C D
30. A B C D
31. A B C D
32. A B C D
33. A B C D
34. A B C D
35. A B C D
36. A B C D

37. A B C D
38. A B C D
39. A B C D
40. A B C D
41. A B C D
42. A B C D
43. A B C D
44. A B C D
45. A B C D
46. A B C D
47. A B C D
48. A B C D
49. A B C D
50. A B C D
51. A B C D
52. A B C D
53. A B C D
54. A B C D

55. A B C D
56. A B C D
57. A B C D
58. A B C D
59. A B C D
60. A B C D
61. A B C D
62. A B C D
63. A B C D
64. A B C D
65. A B C D
66. A B C D
67. A B C D
68. A B C D
69. A B C D
70. A B C D

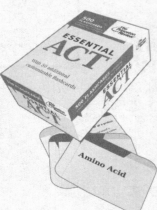

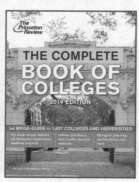

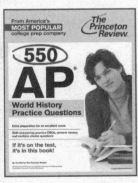